NETCENTRIC COMPUTING

Computing, Communications, and Knowledge

Hugh W. Ryan
Michael W. Alber
Stanton J. Taylor
Richard A. Chang
Yannis S. Arvanitis
Michael C. Davis
Nancy K. Mullen
Shari L. Dove
Prem N. Mehra
Craig Mindrum

ANDERSEN
CONSULTING

AUERBACH

Boca Raton   Boston   London   New York   Washington, D.C.

Acquiring Editor:	Vivian Rothschild
Project Editor:	Albert W. Starkweather, Jr.
Cover Designer:	Denise Craig

Library of Congress Cataloging-in-Publication Data

Catalog record is available from the Library of Congress.

About the authors

Hugh Ryan is a partner with Andersen Consulting and the current Managing Director for an innovative group within Technology Integration Services-Worldwide devoted to large complex systems. In his 25-year career with Andersen Consulting, he has worked on leading-edge applications of information technology, from the earliest online systems and DBMSs in the 1970s through today's emerging client/server applications built on the convergence of computing, communications, and knowledge. He has written more than 30 articles on various aspects of computing and contributes a regular column on systems development to Auerbach's *Information Systems Management* journal. He has been a featured speaker at more than 50 conferences on the impact of computing on business solutions.

Michael W. Alber is a partner in the Communications Industry group of Andersen Consulting. In his 15-year career with Andersen Consulting, he worked extensively with network and systems architectures using mainframe, client/server, and netcentric technologies. For six years, he was responsible for the Network Architecture group in Andersen Consulting's Technology Integration Services-Worldwide organization. He has worked with a broad range of companies in the telecommunications, financial services, oil & gas, pharmaceutical, retailing, and transportation industries.

Stanton J. Taylor has more than 12 years' experience working with large U.S. and European corporations in applying emerging information technology for competitive advantage. He is currently a partner with Andersen Consulting's Technology Integration Services-Worldwide organization. He has extensive experience in the planning, design, and implementation of client/server workstation-based solutions using state-of-the-market technologies and products, and he has helped more than a dozen organizations in the conceptualization and implementation of enterprisewide technology strategies. He specializes in the financial services, transportation, retailing, pharmaceutical, and oil and gas industries.

Richard A. Chang, a partner with Andersen Consulting's Technology Integration Services-Worldwide organization, is responsible for the Enterprise Architecture group, which specializes in the strategy and planning of enterprisewide information technology (IT) architectures. He has developed and is responsible for the firm's enterprise architecture planning methods, used in IT planning engagements, and he has written several articles on this topic. He has extensive project experience in the strategy, planning, design, and delivery of solutions involving distributed computing, client/server, high-volume transaction processing and data base technologies, working with clients in financial services, insurance, utilities, consumer and industrial products, and government.

Yannis S. Arvanitis is an associate partner with Andersen Consulting's Technology Integration Services-Worldwide organization. He is a member of the Architectures group, which supports Andersen's worldwide consulting organization in planning, designing, and implementing systems using new and emerging technologies. He has extensive project experience with client/server architectures and applications, GUI design and development, object-oriented development, and Internet technologies, including HTML and Java. He is also an inventor on a patent held by Andersen Consulting for client/server architecture and tools.

Michael C. Davis is an associate partner with Andersen Consulting's Technology Integration Services-Worldwide organization. A member of the Solutions Architecture group, he has responsibility for knowledge management and collaborative technologies and is a frequent presenter on these topics at seminars and industry gatherings. He is experienced in the financial services, insurance, and health care industries.

Nancy K. Mullen is an associate partner in the Technology Integration Services-Americas organization of Andersen Consulting. She leads the Information Delivery group, which supports Andersen's worldwide consulting organization in the planning, design, and implementation of data warehouses and of complex OLTP data base applications. She has extensive experience with data design methodologies, data base design and tuning, and data base performance management. She specializes in the consumer products, insurance, financial services and manufacturing industries.

Shari L. Dove is an associate partner with Andersen Consulting's Technology Integration Services-Worldwide organization. As Program Director for the Worldwide Systems Delivery Continuous Improvement program, she is responsible for planning and managing the continuous improvement of the Andersen Consulting systems building capability, including methods, tools, training, and architectures. Previously, she served as Project Manager responsible for Andersen Consulting's Reinventing Testing project, which included the development of a comprehensive client/server testing methodology, defining testing metrics and estimating guidelines, developing practice aids, and defining/developing integrated tool suites.

Prem N. Mehra is a Senior Architectural Engineer with Microsoft Corporation. His expertise is in developing technical architectures that exploit active platform technologies including relational data base, transaction and message servers, and enterprise connectivity products to provide scalable, robust, and highly available solutions. Before joining Microsoft Corp., he was an Associate Partner in the Technology Integration Services-Worldwide organization of Andersen Consulting.

Craig Mindrum teaches at DePaul University in Chicago, and has more than 15 years of experience as a consultant and writer in the areas of organizational ethics and the effects of information technology on workforce performance and purpose. He is a regular conference speaker on issues related to human performance within organizations. He previously served as primary researcher and editor for *FutureWork: Putting Knowledge to Work in the Knowledge Economy* (New York: The Free Press, 1994) and is a co-author of *Practical Guide to Client/Server Computing*, also published by Auerbach. He received his doctorate from the University of Chicago, following previous studies at Indiana University and Yale University. His current research involves a forthcoming book on the subject of dignity in organizations.

Introduction

When most people are trying to understand the revolutionary development of netcentric computing, an example from the Internet often suffices. Try this one: Using your favorite Internet search engine, type in the word *shopping*. How many hits did you get? Probably well over one million.

Success stories about doing business on the Internet soon will also number more than a million. Consider, for example, the cookie company located in Newcastle, in the United Kingdom. When the company built its Web site, it was suddenly selling cookies 5,000 miles away in Newcastle, WY, and 10,000 miles away in Newcastle, New South Wales. Profits doubled in four months. What happened to the Newcastle cookie company was not just that new technology became available, but that the technology enabled a new business capability: selling to an international market.

The real power of netcentric computing, however, cannot be captured by a mere Internet story. Consider another example: A consumer is redesigning the back sun room on his house. He goes to a nearby home supply store and works with a salesperson at a computer kiosk to design a certain configuration of windows for the new room. Another customer with similar needs decides not even to drive to the store but works instead from home on a similar window design application offered through the window company's Web site. When processed, the design and ordering application automatically triggers a chain of operations at the company's headquarters. Supplies are ordered from inventory, and order-entry and billing applications are triggered.

At some point in the process, a certain critical material needed for the window is depleted, and one of the window company's suppliers is automatically notified by E-mail of the urgent need for delivery of this material. Each order is captured in reports available in real time by the company's strategy group, as well as by the marketing and advertising groups. One of the orders placed by a customer involves a complicated custom design; the designers at company headquarters place a call to one of their freelance designers located on the other side of the continent. A groupware application allows all of them to work online simultaneously to resolve the problems involved with this customer's design. The designers at headquarters realize that this solution will affect many other designs currently in process at the company, so they notify their supervisor by E-mail of the need for an urgent meeting. The supervisor, on site with a client, is paged through her personal digital assistant, which has automatically scheduled her for a meeting based on her previous availability.

This story begins to capture both the amazing power and the amazing complexity of netcentric computing — a world in which computing, communications, and knowledge have converged into a business solution with a seemingly infinite array of possibilities. Although IT professionals have acknowledged for years that in current computing solutions, the network is everywhere, recent developments have — as the name *netcentric* implies — shifted the center of focus of computing solutions to the network itself.

THE NEXT STAGE IN EXTENDING HUMAN POWER

Computing has always been about extending human capabilities. We can still see the original extensions of human power in the name *computer.* Those first primitive business machines primarily extended the computational abilities of humans. As that computational power was transferred into the world of business, computing first focused primarily on business transactions. The advent of the personal computer broadened that sense of extension by dramatically heightening the rich world of content available to the human mind. It allowed us to create information in new ways and allowed information to be presented to us in new ways.

Beginning in the 1980s, when client/server computing models began to rise in prominence, information technology became not just about transactions and not just about content, but about *reach* as well. Computing suddenly connected people together in new ways; the distinctions between computing and communications and content, or knowledge, began to blur. Client/server computing brought with it new kinds of business solutions, new ways of organizing companies, and new ways to serve companies. Again, the technology turned out really to be about new kinds of business capabilities.

Today, we are in the midst of another generational shift in the business capabilities enabled by information technology: what we call network centric or netcentric computing. As client/server technologies broke down organizational barriers and put knowledge into the hands of knowledge workers, so the new era of ubiquitous computing and communications is putting knowledge into everyone's hands. Netcentric computing — the convergence of computing, communications, and knowledge — is the era we are now witnessing.

We are only just now beginning to understand the new business capabilities of netcentric computing. But those who understand it first will reap the most benefits. Netcentric technology has incredible potential. It makes it possible to extend reach *within* an enterprise, among its departments, business units, or its globally dispersed groups; it enables the sharing of information and allows everyone to tap into the company's brain power. Netcentric technology also reaches *outside* an enterprise, to a company's suppliers, customers, and business partners wherever they are situated on our planet, creating new business capabilities for everyone. To be here at a time of technological change such as this is truly challenging.

DEFINING NETCENTRIC COMPUTING

Consider the previously discussed example of the window company. Several features of the example are particularly important. First, it is clear that in this particular computing solution, many different people are users of the system: not just company employees, but also consumers, business partners, and suppliers. Second, multiple information sources are at work, as well as multiple ways in which to access that information. Finally, although it is not immediately apparent, the solution would not work if it were not built on a common architecture and did not employ open standards.

These features form the basis of our definition of netcentric computing:

- *A common architecture*
  - that supports *multiple electronic access channels* (e.g., personal computers [PCs], network computers [NCs], personal digital assistants [PDAs], kiosks, and telephones)
    - to *multiple sources of information* (e.g., internal data bases and external information sites)
      - by *multiple types of users* (e.g., internal users, customers, suppliers, and business partners)
        - by means of *technologies that employ open, commonly accepted standards* (i.e., standards for the universal network, universal client and components, such as Internet, TCP/IP, Web Browser, ActiveX, DCOM, CORBA, and Java).

In other words, netcentric computing is a common architecture built on open standards that supports:

- many different ways for
- many different kinds of people to collaborate and to reach
- many different information sources.

Although netcentric computing sounds new, and although some breathless analysts and vendors may want people to believe that it is new, netcentric represents, in fact, an evolution from what we already know about client/server computing. For example, we can use the Gartner Group's well-known five stages of client/server (Exhibit 1) to illustrate how netcentric computing fits into a technical model.

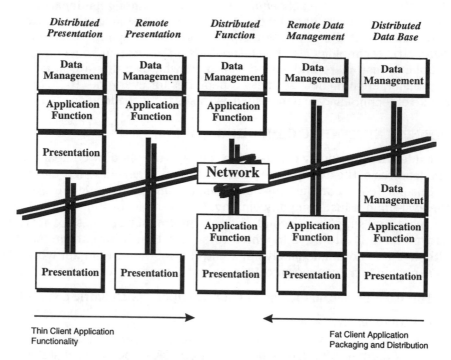

Exhibit 1. Gartner group's five stages of client/server computing.
Source: Gartner Group, *Strategic Analysis Report*, CS: R-200-108, Oct. 25, 1996.

The Gartner Group continuum plots the distribution of processing and data on either sides of a network. Gartner's own recent work on network computing models demonstrates how emerging forms of distributed applications can implement these five styles using such technologies as Web-based terminals, hypertext markup language (HTML), applets, servlets, intelligent dyamic platform adjustment mechanisms, and proxies. On the far left-hand side of the five styles diagram, there are almost no distributed processes or data, so there are very thin clients — the thinnest used to be the old dumb 3270 terminal. Everything went across from the network to the terminal. As we move to the right, we progressively get more intelligence, more processing, more function, and more data close to the end user. So at the far right-hand side of the continuum are the richest and fattest of the clients; that is where the distribution of function, data, and presentation logic is maximized.

Using the Gartner model, netcentric computing is somewhere in the middle. What netcentric does with these five stages, however, is to add a new layer, characterized by a set of open, common standards that the

Internet has legitimized. HTML, Java, and Java data base connectivity enable the coexistence of applications that will let the desktop become the universal client capable of connecting to multiple servers and the recipient of an enterprise server reaching out to touch it.

To take another viewpoint on this different world, let us think about what it is like to build netcentric infrastructures. When we were in the mainframe world, we may have had three or four major infrastructure components: the data base, the CPU, a network, and some terminals. Two or three suppliers provided all those major components, so life was relatively constrained. Because there were only six to eight combinations of all of components and vendors, the complexity was manageable.

When we went to client/server, we had five or six infrastructure components, made up of maybe three tiers of the client/server model, a data base, and a couple of networks. Each of these has five or seven possible suppliers. So instead of six to eight combinations, we are now looking at up to 40– about five times as many. The size of the problem was bigger and the nature of the problem got more complex.

With netcentric computing, if we add only 20% more components and, let us say, 30% more providers — which is probably an underestimate — we go from up to 40 combinations to up to 100. And to make things even more exciting, the components and providers change practically by the day.

It is not just the infrastructure that changes; almost every other aspect of systems delivery is different. Think what it is like to implement and test an application that runs on multiple platforms through a universal network. Think about what it means when most of the people in the world and potentially many of the computers are connected to the network. It makes user testing rather different, does it not?

INTEGRATING STRATEGY, PROCESS, TECHNOLOGY, AND PEOPLE

Advances in information technology often expose certain flaws in the way organizations operate. Client/server computing, for example, exposed as never before the silos that had developed within companies — silos that restricted the optimum flow of information. Because netcentric computing is so all-encompassing and involves such an array of players, it is likely as well to expose limitations to business that few people have yet thought about. Organizations would benefit from a model that would help them deal with these changes.

Netcentric computing cannot be considered apart from the organizational, economic, and commercial system of which it is a part. Although the system here must be understood organically, organizational theory has

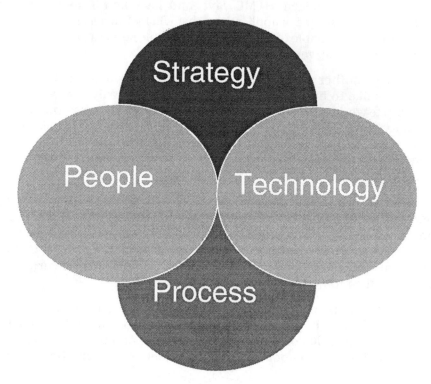

Exhibit 2. A visual depiction of the concept of business integration.

rarely stressed this organic dimension. It may speak of the interaction of various components, but the image has generally been more mechanistic than organic.

In our experience, Exhibit 2 is extremely useful in understanding what Andersen Consulting calls business integration — the proper wholeness of today's business organization.

The exhibit depicts the organization as an integrated whole, comprising its people, strategy, processes, and technology. None of these elements can be understood if isolated from any of the others. People perform processes, enabled by technology. Processes and technology arise from strategic intent, yet technology also allows new kinds of strategies. Strategy arises from people and then helps to direct them. The list of interconnections is long and complex.

Using the business integration model, we can better understand how organizations are likely to be affected as they move from a more basic client/server model of computing toward a netcentric model.

From the end-user perspective, for example, client/server provided a way to take systems with powerful front ends and link them up to back-end systems. The main impact of the technology in that case was more productive, empowered individuals. Rather than supporting individuals or single processes, however, netcentric computing connects *collections* of people, both inside and outside the enterprise. Suddenly, it is the communication and the information sharing between these people that creates the difference.

Client/server supported the reengineering of processes, because it took the technology closer to the point at which the business process was actually being executed. However, with netcentric computing, the technology allows the enterprise to reach outside itself and others to reach in. For example, when Federal Express provided the means for its customers to track their own packages on its company Web site, it saved five million dollars a year in customer service costs, simply because customers no longer had to talk with a person. Obviously, this kind of ability to change how business is conducted has profound implications for how a business even thinks about what it does, why it does it, how it does it, and how it should change its people and processes to exploit the new capabilities created by the technology.

EMERGING INITIATIVES

In such an emerging field, we should expect to see companies take a wide range of approaches to implement new solutions using the netcentric model. Three in particular appear to be emerging:

1. A basic, read-only, nonspecific service, which is essentially advertising.
2. A targeted read-only inquiry service.
3. A fully interactive service.

Read Only

With this first type, a company is basically publishing or advertising, as the Newcastle cookie maker did. But even something as simple as that — a new, free, outward flow of information such as "our cookies are delicious and here's how to order by phone or mail" — can dramatically change a business. Remember, the cookie company doubled its sales.

Targeted Read Only

The next type of solution involves inquiries and interaction, which is basically client/server on the Internet. A classic example is the utility company that offers its customers a Web site where they can inquire about their electricity use, usage pattern, and account status. These specific, inquiry-only types of transactions can be a potentially powerful marketing and client-satisfaction tool with a real business case.

Fully Interactive

The third type of solution creates a one-to-one interactive relationship with the enterprise and its employees, customers, or business partners so that they can hold virtual meetings, order things, pay bills, or customize requests. Companies can even share supply-chain information, as competitors GM, Ford, and Chrysler hope to do when they pilot a system linking the three manufacturers with their suppliers through an Internet service for a projected savings of one billion dollars a year.

A critical point for companies today is this: Even if current business solutions do not involve netcentric computing, it is vital to maintain the flexibility in technical architecture that will permit a move to netcentric computing in the future.

Case in point: Our firm has been working on a systems development project for a large automotive manufacturer. Recently we were reviewing the technical infrastructure for the system — a stand-alone dealer system to be integrated with local dealer systems. We asked the company executives this question: What if, at some point in the future — one or two years — the way in which the business is transacted changes? What if, for example, somebody walked into a dealership on a Thursday or Friday, interacted with the system (i.e., created a customized car, selected the color, looked at the finance or lease package) but then said, "I want to go away and think about this for the weekend."

Then suppose the company had a 24-hour call center. That same customer could call and, by speaking to a customer service representative about the details of the package designed at the dealership, talk through the deal on a Sunday afternoon. Right there, the customer could make some adjustments and close the transaction over the phone. Of course, being a 24-hour operation, the call center could be based anywhere in the world.

Now this would be a new way to buy cars. It may not be dramatically different, but it would have a big impact on the technology infrastructure. All of a sudden, all of the context of the transaction from the showroom conversation on Thursday or Friday would have to be made available to a call center three days later, potentially on the other side of the world.

We asked our client if this scenario was within the realm of possibility. It was. Was it being considered? No.

This brings us back to the organizational impact of netcentric computing. From the point of view of business integration, the technology has a major impact on the dealer's business process; it is a new strategy for the automotive manufacturer. It is a perfect example of business integration: blending strategy, process, people, and technology. No particular aspect of the change by itself is earth shattering. But taken together in the perspective of the business integration model, the new solution could have a major effect on the company's position in the marketplace.

This book provides an overview of the technical and business issues relating to netcentric computing. In the middle sections, we also introduce a comprehensive netcentric architecture and discuss the many factors affecting netcentric implementation. A final section of the book looks at emerging technologies and issues that are certain to affect the evolution of netcentric solutions throughout the coming years.

Contents

Contents

Section I
Overview of the Netcentric Computing Environment

Section I sets the context for the more detailed descriptions of netcentric architectures, technologies, and implementation issues presented in the rest of the book. That context involves both business and technological issues. The point of netcentric computing, ultimately, is not just the new technology, but the new business capabilities enabled by that technology.

Companies today face a problem in their ability to compete — what we call the myth of the sustainable competitive advantage. Such an advantage no longer exists, because competitors can imitate and improve faster than ever before. The answer today is to find and deliver astounding solutions. These solutions depend on the connectivity and efficiency that is only possible through netcentric computing.

Today's complex technical environment can no longer even be captured by focusing on rapid developments in computing, communications, and knowledge-creating technologies. Complicating the picture is the convergence of these three elements. Convergence is really another name for the netcentric environment. The netcentric architecture or framework that forms the heart of this book is introduced and broadly explained in this section.

1

Chapter I-1

Netcentric Computing and New Business Capabilities

One of our firm's research scientists enjoys illustrating today's amazing technological environment by telling his "water softener" story. After moving to a new condominium in the Chicago suburbs, he and his wife found that a very nice man from a water softener company kept showing up every couple of months to replace the salt supply in the softener. One day, they kidded the man that he seemed to know exactly when the softener needed refilling. In fact, the man did know. There was a chip in the softener that monitored the salt level. The condominium telephone system was rigged so that when the level of the softener fell below a certain level, a call went to the company letting them know it was time to deliver salt.

This is a great story of what we call "convergence"; it's not a computing story and it's not a communcations story. It's both, and more.

THE CONVERGENCE MODEL

The dominant forms of information technology — computing and communications — developed for years independent from one another. Today, however, these technologies are converging, producing new capabilities that are far greater than a mere sum of the parts. Today's information systems based on a client/server model, for example, cannot even really be called computing solutions, because the computer is in fact the entire communications network. The phenomenal ascent of the Internet as a market force is another expression of convergence. We will see most business solutions in the future built on a converged sense of computing and communications.

The true "convergence model," shown in Exhibit 1, contains a third component: *knowledge*. Without that component, there is no point to the computing and communications — nothing for them to do. Knowledge is the

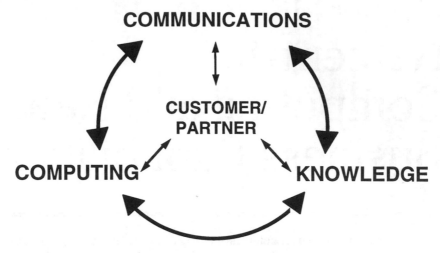

Exhibit 1.   Convergence diagram.

"blood" running through the veins of today's business. It includes both raw content, as well as the logical schemata for interpreting that content. That is, it can include traditional data as well as rules and procedures that capture people's expertise. It can include simple digitized raw video as well as complex representations that combine multiple points of view and extensive cross-indexing. It can include kinds of captured objective reality such as photographs and transactional data, as well as subjective interpretations such as opinions and problem-solving heuristics. It can be static and waiting to be used, like a photograph or a movie; or it can be dynamic, like an expert or an intelligent agent.

Finally, the convergence model shows the ultimate point of it all: the ability to focus on the customer in new ways, and the ability to partner and form alliances in new ways. The convergence model is also the most basic model of netcentric computing.

Netcentric computing is making new kinds of capabilities possible — for individuals and for businesses. For companies around the world, netcentric computing means new business solutions, new ways of organizing companies, and new ways to serve customers. As client/server technologies broke down organizational barriers and put knowledge into the hands of knowledge workers, so the new era of ubiquitous computing and communications is putting knowledge into everyone's hands. That is the promise of netcentric. But there is a threat, as well.

Banking

1980

Rank	Company	Assets (Millions)
1	Citicorp	$109,551
2	Bank America Corp.	$106,803
3	Credit Agricole Mutuel	$106,646
4	Banque Nationale de Paris	$105,584
5	Credit Lyonnais	$98,833
6	Societe Generale	$90,794
7	Barclays Group	$88,474
8	Deutsche Bank	$88,242
9	National Westminster Bank Ltd.	$82,447
10	Da-Ichi Kangyo Bank Ltd.	$79,451

1994

Rank	Company	Assets (Millions)
1	Sanwa Bank Ltd.	$588,349
2	Dai-Ichi Kangyo Bank Ltd.	$587,773
3	Fuji Bank Ltd.	$577,107
4	Sumitomo Bank Ltd.	$571,942
5	Sakura Bank Ltd.	$565,381
6	Mitsubishi Bank Ltd.	$553,515
7	Norinchukin Bank	$500,434
8	Industrial Bank Ltd.	$437,853
9	Mitsubishi Trust & Banking Corp.	$394,001
10	Long-Term Credit Bank of Japan	$375,515

Exhibit 2.   Technology's effect on bank rankings.

Discount Retailing

1980

Rank	Company	Revenues (Millions)
1	Kmart	$11,208
2	Woolco Department Stores	$1,710
3	Gamco Department Stores	$1,266
4	Zayre Corp.	$1,223
5	Gibson's Discount Stores	$1,125
6	The Fed-Mart Corp.	$975
7	Wal-Mart Stores Inc.	$961
8	Target Stores Inc.	$899
9	Two Guys	$702
10	Korvettes, Inc.	$638

1994

Rank	Company	Revenues (Millions)
1	Wal-Mart Stores Inc.	$58,000
2	Kmart	$28,632
3	Target Stores Inc.	$13,622
4	Meuer	$ 6,000
5	Fred Meyer	$ 3,128
6	Caldor	$ 2,749
7	Ames	$ 2,143
8	Venture	$ 2,017
9	Bradlees	$ 1,916
10	Hills	$ 1,872

Exhibit 3.   Technology's effect on discount retailers rankings.

THE MYTH OF THE SUSTAINABLE ADVANTAGE

The age of convergence — the age of netcentric computing — promises to restructure entire industries. That restructuring is simply an affirmation of what has been happening already in the information age. Exhibits 2 to 5 demonstrate the impact of new business and technology solutions on major players in various industries over the past 15 years.

These lists are striking because they reveal the absolute lack of permanence in industry leadership. In 1980, Dai-Ichi Kangyo Bank Ltd. brought up the rear with a full 25% fewer assets than Citicorp, the clear leader. By 1994, Dai-Ichi was running a close second, and Citicorp was not even ranked in the top 10. In discount retailing, Wal-Mart decided to compete on both price and service. It came from the back of the pack to take the lead.

Computers

1980			1994		
Rank	Company	IT Sales (Millions)	Rank	Company	IT Sales (Millions)
1	IBM	$26,213	1	IBM	$64,052
2	Honeywell	$4,925	2	Hewlett-Packard	$19,250
3	Sperry Corp.	$4,785	3	Digital Equiptment Corp.	$13,500
4	NCR	$3,322	4	AT&T	$11,264
5	Burroughs	$2,857	5	Compaq	$10,866
6	Rank Xerox	$2,840	6	EDS	$10,052
7	Control Data	$2,766	7	Apple	$ 8,549
8	Olivetti	$2,551	8	Unisys	$ 6,216
9	Digital Equipment Corp.	$2,368	9	Sun Microsystems	$ 5,348
10	ICL	$1,624	10	Microsoft	$ 4,650

Exhibit 4.   Technology's effect on computer company rankings.

Airlines

1980			1994		
Rank	Company	Revenues (Millions)	Rank	Company	Revenues (Millions)
1	United Airlines	$4,373	1	American Airlines	$12,894
2	American Airlines	$3,675	2	United Airlines	$12,529
3	Pan Am	$3,639	3	Delta	$11,326
4	Eastern	$3,453	4	Northwest	$ 7,314
5	Delta	$3,302	5	USAIR	$ 6,082
6	TWA	$3,278	6	Continental	$ 4,552
7	Northwest	$1,628	7	TWA	$ 2,571
8	Braniff	$1,444	8	Southwest	$ 1,992
9	Western	$996	9	Alaska	$ 582
10	Continental	$988	10	Hawaiian	$ 264

Exhibit 5.   Technology's effect on airline rankings.

In the early 1980s, the companies at the top of the list were respected leaders in their industry. DEC, for example, was a minicomputer vendor. Today's DEC is a provider of services and support software for other major software vendors. Southwest is succeeding in the airline industry with a business model that was all wrong, at least in theory. In a time of spokes and hubs and an industry built on elegance, Southwest followed the obsolete route model and bargain-basement prices and performed beyond all expectations.

A great deal of ink has been spilled trying to determine why these companies succeeded or failed. Deregulation had a huge impact in airlines. Technology and market segmentation made a difference for retailing. Banking was hit by consolidation related to deregulation and investments. The computing industry was tremendously affected by client/server technologies. Even though several factors can be identified, it is extremely difficult to learn many replicable lessons from either the successes or the failures, because there are so many ways to fail and so many ways to flourish. The ultimate lesson from these lists is this: Over time, there is no sustainable competitive advantage.

Whatever advantage a company gains today is fleeting. Either competitors adopt the advantage, or they find a better alternative. Certainly they do not give up. For example, every airline today is focused on reducing costs following the Southwest Airlines model. Retailers are following the Wal-Mart model, reducing money in the supply chain by shifting inventory and delivery to suppliers.

If competitors cannot improve on the company's basic process, they will invent a new process, a better way of doing things. The story of the microprocessor vs. the mainframe is one example. The winning companies did not try to make a better or cheaper mainframe; they decided to do something completely different. They came up with a processor that behaved and worked in ways a mainframe could not, at prices the mainframe could not meet. That difference totally restructured the computer industry over the last 15 years.

Finally, if no one can come up with a better or different answer and one company becomes dominant in an industry, a regulator may step in. Today, discussions about the information superhighway and the telecommunications industry often include what role the government should play in ensuring open and free competition. In a sense, however, ongoing open competition is another way of saying, "No winners." Therefore, even if a company does find a sustained competitive advantage, the regulator will find a way to make it unsustainable.

The inability to sustain competitive advantage can be seen in the story of Tom Peters's well-known book, *In Search of Excellence*. This book profiled a number of companies that had emerged as clear leaders in their industries. It implied that by following certain principles of excellence, one could not fail. A relatively short time after the book was published, most of the companies profiled were out of business or in serious difficulty. Peters himself began his next book with the admission that "there are no excellent companies." There is no such thing, Peters writes in *Thriving on Chaos*, as a "solid, or even substantial, lead over one's competitors. Excellent firms do not believe in excellence — only in constant improvement and constant change. That is, excellent firms of tomorrow will cherish impermanence — and thrive on chaos." (Tom Peters, *Thriving on Chaos: Handbook for a Management Revolution*. New York: Alfred A. Knopf, 1987, 3–4.)

Can the challenge of unsustainable competitive advantage be addressed? Perhaps it can. For example, an insurance company gains a clear edge in the marketplace by creating a customer focus that provides very high levels of service, reduces costs, and increases sales. As with information processing over the last 30 years, the next step is to drain the costs of doing the business. Often, information technology is the means to achieve those cost reductions, but cost reduction is not just an IT strategy. Over the past couple of years, numerous companies have announced extensive layoffs, even in the face of sound financial results. Although occasionally the reductions have been tied to reengineering initiatives, often the goal was simple cost reduction to stay competitive.

Many methods can achieve cost reduction. IT is one, but another, surprisingly, is the creation of bureaucracy. That word may seem anathema to those looking for competitive advantage, but bureaucracy, before it became a bad word, was simply a system for making routine decisions. Bureaucracy ensures that the least expensive person gave just the right amount of attention to the problem at hand before moving on. In this sense, it is a way to standardize a process to make it predictable and well controlled. So, the principles of bureaucracy can be applied to the problem of reducing costs.

This process of concentrating first on what people know how to do says a lot about human beings. It is entirely natural for people to prefer working with what they know rather than wanting to start all over. So, people focus on reducing costs within the processes they know how to perform. They can quantify the impact of change so that risk is reduced.

Then, there comes a point at which cost reduction is not very impressive anymore. When all the heads have rolled, there are no more costs to reduce. By illustration, 50% of 50% of 50% of anything is not much.

Next, the systems put in place to reduce costs — IT and bureaucracy — become a barrier to leaping to the next competitive advantage. They become the legacy that prohibits change. The systems cannot be changed to provide a view of the customer. The bureaucracy has measures and rewards that focus on an efficient current process, and the new process means new measures and rewards. The cost-reduction process becomes a hindrance to the development of the next astounding solution.

The Role of the "Next Astounding Solution"

Of course, the most obvious reason why the next astounding solution is so difficult to achieve is that it never stands up and introduces itself as an astounding solution. Sometimes, the solution may appear at first to be insignificant or even suspect, or it may just be something at the right place at the right time. An often-cited example is the Sabre airline system, which was devised just to facilitate the reservations process; only later did people realize that it was changing the rules of competition. Another example is the study done by IBM that concluded that the PC would never amount to much. As IBM and countless other organizations have proved, one of the functions of a bureaucracy is to stamp out anything threatening to the bureaucracy. *Fumbling the Future,* the story of Xerox's failure to capitalize on its development of the first personal computer, asks the key question: "Why do corporations find it so difficult to replicate earlier successes in new and unrelated fields?" (Douglas K. Smith and Robert C. Alexander, *Fumbling the Future.* New York: William Morrow, 1988, 19.)

The answer to this question is both obvious and difficult to accept. Companies must:

- Find and deliver an astounding solution.
- Manage the costs out of the solution until the company finds the next astounding solution.
- Obliterate all the bureaucracy, process, and procedure that the company has built to deliver the old astounding solution.

This unending cycle is called the "competition cycle." The cycle sounds exhausting, and it certainly is, but the only other alternative is to be among those three-fourths of your friends who are no longer around.

Have any companies succeeded at the competition cycle? With the obvious caveat that one can only speak about the present moment, the growth of Microsoft is one example. Microsoft has grown from a compiler company to an operating system company to a productivity company. All of these transitions, if one looks at the change in the core technology, were huge, but the company seemed to achieve them with relatively little trauma. As this is written, Microsoft is chasing several "next" solutions, including software for the enterprise, such as the NT operating system, Explorer for the Internet, and Team Metaphor. Only time will tell whether Microsoft will succeed at the next competition cycle.

Another example is Hewlett-Packard, which has consolidated many of its internal UNIX efforts. Also, it is opening up solutions past its own software base through the use of Microsoft NT. In addition, historically HP has pursued its own chip design and implementation. Looking at the market realities of chip-fabrication-plant costs, however, it has entered into agreements with Intel to build a common chip design. In addition, HP is pursuing the possibility of services as hardware goes to a commodity status in the mass market. All of these strategies represent astounding change for HP, but it is uncertain whether these changes will become the next astounding solution for HP.

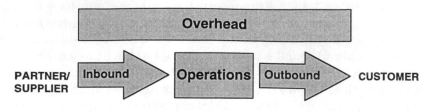

Exhibit 6. A typical enterprise's high-level value chain.

Could one begin to forecast where the source of the next astounding solutions might lie? The next section examines this question from two standpoints. One is to think of where the solutions have focused in the past. Wherever they are, the assumption is that they ceased to be astounding long ago and have become the target of cost reduction. Looking past these solutions may reveal the opportunity for the next astounding solution. The other is to look at technology today and ask what solutions the technology can enable. What comes out of this discussion is a remarkable situation in which the next business opportunity is aligned exactly with what the technology can do.

TRADITIONAL COMPETITIVENESS: INTERNAL OPERATIONS

Exhibit 6 represents, at a very high level, the value chain for a typical enterprise.

The typical enterprise must manage its inbound flows of resources and its relationships with partners and suppliers. The enterprise must provide internal operations that deliver the services and products it brings to market and then manage the outbound flow of these services to customers. In addition to all this are the typical overhead activities, such as human resources or accounting, which must be done to survive in the market. At this very high level, the diagram applies across a wide range of industries and businesses.

Over the last 30 years, most companies have devoted most of their attention to internal operations and overhead activities. For example, in insurance, many companies have set up and revised claims systems as the technology progressed from IBM 360 architecture to online to data base architectures. Many companies have gone back and addressed their internal processes as they participated in total quality management (TQM) and business process reengineering initiatives. However, in spite of these changes, many claims systems today still primarily reflect the accounting need to reserve for loss and the assignment of loss to appropriate categories for management and actuarial evaluation. This situation remains, in spite of the increasing recognition in the industry that the customers' view of the company is primarily defined by their experience with the claims process, not with the policy sales process.

In manufacturing, the focus over the years has been on material requirements planning (MRP), shop floor control, inventory management, cost accounting, and quality control. Even with order entry, which is dependent on customer contact, much of the focus is on reserving inventory and feeding MRP efforts for smooth shop floor operations. These are essentially internal focuses and fall under internal operations and overhead activities.

In banking, the focus over the years has been on "back-office" operations, including check clearing, account updating and reporting, loan processing, and statement issues. Over time, these processes and supporting automation have become increasingly efficient. For example, check clearing at a large bank is something to behold from both an automation and process standpoint. Once again, in each of these cases the work has focused on internal operations and overhead activities, with the result that the processes have become very efficient.

The point here, again, is that over the last 30 years, much of the work with design and automation of business processes has focused on the internal operations and the overhead activities. Furthermore, in our experience, much of this work has been done and re-done as industries moved from batch processing in the 1960s, to online processing in the 1970s, to data base architectures in the 1980s. Many of the processes are being reinvented because of client/server capabilities. This is not to say, however, that the work has been fruitless. Many of these systems were re-done with clear and evident bottom-line impact and were well worth the investment. With all the iterations, however, companies may be increasingly dealing with big percentages of small percentages — that 50% of 50% of 50%. It is now time to look elsewhere.

THE NEW COMPETITIVENESS: INNOVATIVE DISTRIBUTION CHANNELS

It is important as well to focus on the inbound and outbound channels. The opportunity lies outside the enterprise, at the boundaries between business partners and customers. The opportunity lies in obliterating the traditional inbound logistics channels and the outbound distribution channels, by implementing new kinds of channels — electronic or otherwise — that are in themselves astounding solutions. In this obliteration the opportunity and challenge of re-thinking the entire structure of industries starts to become manifest. The next astounding solutions lie at the boundaries of the traditional enterprise.

ATMs as an Electronic Distribution Channel

Identifying the next astounding solution may seem both obvious and highly questionable. As noted earlier, astounding solutions can be characterized in their early days by being almost invisible. One example of change in a distribution channel is banking with an ATM machine. Originally, the view was that this was a means to displace bank clerks and reduce headcount and costs. The impact has been far wider. ATMs have indeed reduced clerk headcount, but more important, they have convinced many customers that they do not need to interact directly with a banker to do business. At the same time, ATM use has allowed bankers to realize that a bank branch does not need to be a large capital investment of brick and mortar; it may only need a wire and a programmable vault. From this realization has come the growth of online, home-banking tools. In the end, it is clear that banking can and will become a virtual enterprise. The biggest impediments to this evolution are regulatory concerns rooted in brick-and-mortar banking institutions and current banking laws based on geographic boundaries. For anyone who has begun to bank through such a tool as *Quicken* or *Money*, the relevance of either concern is increasingly questionable.

Data Warehousing

Another example of reaching out to customers is seen in the increasing use of data warehousing approaches to segment and understand customer interest and behaviors. Although data warehousing is not an example of expanding direct interaction with the customer, it does reflect a step in the direction to understand the customer better by understanding what the customer is doing. Also, as the capability grows, it allows the organization to understand more clearly the impact that its actions are having on the customer. Some commentators have viewed this as trying to manipulate the customer. However, more often the sellers change their behaviors based on the actions that the customer takes. In this sense, convergence through the channels is making the seller change and adapt to meet customer needs more effectively, based on the feedback they obtain.

Antiquated Distribution Channels

Financial services and retailing are industries where obliterating distribution channels already has made a big difference. Other industries are following, among them, insurance. The traditional distribution channel for insurance is the local agent. Today, that distribution channel is in need of renewal. Agents represent challenges in terms of cost, training, and turnover. High turnover rates disrupt the connection to the customer or even sever the connection when the customer follows the agent to another company. Because agents tend to sell what they know, they often represent a hindrance when bringing new products to market.

In addition, the insurance industry is currently redefining its very identity. An insurance company today no longer considers itself simply the provider of coverage of loss against unexpected risk. Today, they are providing financial security. The products devised to provide this service are complex and difficult to sell. Many agents will not take on the demands to sell these products. This means that the typical distribution channel for insurance can, on occasion, contribute to customer distance rather than customer closeness. At the same time, because consumers appear willing to move to in-home banking, it is feasible to expect them to be able and willing to undertake some of their own product evaluation if they have the right tools and capabilities. As a result, many insurance companies are looking at alternative distribution channels to make the connection to the customer.

THE RISKS OF CHANGING DISTRIBUTION CHANNELS

The insurance example illustrates why altering distribution channels can be difficult. First, the distribution channel is the single most difficult thing to change in an organization. To illustrate: Consider the fictional example of General Motors deciding to sell something really different: spaghetti. It could readily purchase the means of production for spaghetti and begin pumping GM spaghetti into its sales channel, but there it would encounter problems. It would find a distribution channel of hundreds of thousands of sales people who would simply say, "I sell cars, not spaghetti." Over time, GM could create alternative channels, but that is not changing the channel; rather, it is creating a parallel channel. If GM grew insistent on the change, it would probably find its sales people leaving to go to companies where they could sell cars again.

The GM spaghetti example illustrates the fundamental risk of changing the sales channel, a risk this book refers to as the "Tarzan problem." Tarzan is swinging through the jungle on a vine. He reaches for a new vine so he can keep moving, but he has to be careful not to release the current vine until he has the next one firmly in his grasp. At the same time, when he has the new vine, it is equally important that he release the hold on the other one so he can continue his journey.

A company trying to change a distribution channel faces an equivalent issue. In reaching for the new distribution channel, it is vitally important that the company not relinquish the current channel too soon or it will lose the sales in the current market and any hope of profits. At the same time, once the new channel is in place, the company needs to displace the current one to reduce costs and have a focused message for the new sales channel.

Losing the Existing Channels Too Soon

Mishandling this problem can totally stop change for the unwary company. In insurance, a fairly common conclusion is that there is no way to go past the current agent network to the customer without risking having all the agents stop selling. This is clearly the case for companies that deal with independent agents, who sell from a variety of sources and can simply avoid a source that is threatening to become a competitor in the customer's home. Captive or tied agents are also a problem, as they typically have a fairly high turnover. These agents can easily anticipate that before too long, their annual sales will begin to decline as a customer goes directly to the company. The result is that companies with captive agents will suffer increased agent turnover and difficulty in attracting new agents simply because the agents' future may be limited, at least in their current roles.

Companies have attempted to deal with this problem in a number of ways. One is to encourage the agents to move to more complex products, where they can continue to add value. These products continue to need the agent's assistance in selling and provide potentially higher margins. However, the difficulty is that agents often are reluctant to learn and sell such products. Another approach to the problem is to continue to have the agents participate in the revenue stream from the customer, even if they are not directly involved with the sale. The issue in this case is that a significant portion of the cost of distribution remains in the sales channel.

Risking Competitiveness by Not Building Alternative Channels

The result of these concerns is that many insurance companies have looked at this astounding solution and said, "Not astounding enough." By doing so, however, they place themselves at risk. The competition cycle demonstrates that if the legacy insurance companies do not address the issue, other companies that do not have an established distribution channel and a bureaucracy will do so very quickly. Without the baggage of an existing distribution channel, a new company can quickly seize significant market share. For example, Microsoft seized the encyclopedia market, eventually overtaking the old and venerable *Encyclopaedia Britannica*, because it could go directly to the consumer with CD-ROM versions of *Encarta*. Banking is also beginning to move into the markets traditionally held by the insurance industry. The combination of home banking and ATMs could mean that banking could pursue this route very quickly.

This example goes beyond the insurance industry, and seems to be a characteristic of any industry with a traditional sales channel. One manufacturer, for example, wanted to sell over the Internet. It encouraged its sales people to inform customers that they could buy products over the Internet and would be able to do so at reduced costs resulting from the elimination of sales peoples' take. Not surprisingly, not many salespeople did much to encourage this new distribution channel. The Web site is now a product catalog site while the company rethinks its approach.

Ensuring Customer Appeal

A second challenge to changing the sales channel is getting customers to use it. Companies frequently make the mistake of assuming that its customers will use the new sales channel simply because it is so much easier for the company. The fact is that there must be some benefit to the consumer to use the new channel, such as faster delivery, more customized products, or less expensive products. "Cheaper and easier for the company" is not a customer benefit.

Knowledge Management. The challenge in this case is to deliver on the promise. How can the customer's willingness to work with the sales program result in quicker delivery? Can it cut the time to get the order back? Can it cut the time to assure the customer that the stock is available? Can the process by which customers work through the order make the product better suited to their needs? This can be a complex problem simply because one may need to package the knowledge of the talented sales person in a set of programs — an example of knowledge management — and then make the programs attractive to use. The distribution channel can account for as much as 60% of the cost of a product. (Robert Benjamin and Rolf Wigand, "Electronic Markets and Virtual Value Chains on the Information Superhighway," *Sloan Management Review,* Winter 1995, 62–72.) Is a company willing to share some of the savings with a customer?

Can the sales effort be made a transparent part of the business process? In insurance, companies could tie the entry of purchases into the insurance process. For example, in a package such as *Quicken*, an account is named "Automobiles," and new entries are monitored in the account. When a large new entry is made in the account, a pop-up window asks, "There seems to have been a large change in the Auto account. Should you look at your current auto insurance to see if it needs changes?" Obviously, such an approach is not foolproof, but done correctly and improved over time, it could be much better than hoping the customer remembers to call or expecting the agent to drive by the house looking for new cars in the driveway.

Facilitating Change in Distribution Channels

Converging on the customer through new sales channels is not for the faint of heart. Most companies that undertake the challenge either are desperate and have no other option or are outsiders who have no legacy of culture, regulation, or systems to hinder the change. In a few other cases, the enterprise has a visionary leadership that simply wills the change to happen and drives the process forward.

To address the sales side of the business, one needs some special mix of characteristics to succeed. At the same time, the cycle of identifying an astounding solution, draining the costs from the processes, and moving to the next astounding solution suggests that if one organization does not take on the change demands, another will. At some point, a company can be certain that it will be desperate enough to make such a change. One of the key themes of this book is how to make these changes easier to accomplish.

NEW COMPETITIVENESS: INNOVATIVE PARTNER CHANNELS

Similar issues may be seen with the business partner channel, which supplies raw materials or services so that the enterprise can operate. One well-known example of innovation on this side of the business equation is Wal-Mart. Some years ago, Wal-Mart recognized the significant costs tied up in inventory on the inbound side to stores. Further, this inventory tended to be an impediment to responding to changes in buyer patterns. If there was a shift in popularity from GI Joe to Power Rangers and one had a huge inventory of GI Joes, costs were involved in selling the inventory at discount, and time was involved in getting the Power Rangers through the distribution channel. To address this problem, Wal-Mart began working with its suppliers. It moved the inventory back to the suppliers. Further, it worked with the suppliers on predicting demand so that stores needing restocking got the products when they needed them. These types of actions significantly reduced costs for the product on the shelf. For an industry in which margins are often near zero, the effect was to bring Wal-Mart to the top of the retailing lists.

In essence, a change in partner channels can mean a great many things based on industry, product, and life cycle. In the auto industry, it has meant moving much of design and assembly to suppliers. Similarly, in the aircraft industry, it has meant moving design of major components to partners on a worldwide basis. In property and casuality insurance, it has meant contracting with repair offices, agreeing to use bids as submitted, and directing customers to preferred providers. For banking, it is beginning to mean ties with banks skilled in particular markets or products. For example, a bank skilled in commercial customers may team with a broad-based bank dealing with private customers.

In each case, these were difficult transitions. Internal groups watched "their work" go outside to other companies, some of which had been or continued to be competitors. In each case, the new ties provided benefits in terms of better time to market, less ongoing cost, or access to local markets. In addition, as the first technology connections were made, it soon became apparent that more synergy can be found by extending the reach and insight of the network. As this continues to happen, the virtual enterprise will begin to emerge. Such an enterprise is very much a network on which the events of the business are communicated and shared among the components. In this case, the network becomes the enterprise. That, in itself, is an astounding solution.

SUMMARY

In today's environment, businesses must begin to cope with the absence of a sustainable competitive advantage. In place of competitive advantage is the competition cycle: A business delivers an astounding solution, manages the costs out of the solution, and then moves to the next astounding solution.

Many opportunities for the next astounding solution reside at the boundaries of the enterprise where it meets its customers and partners — more specifically, in eliminating some of these boundaries through direct ties to the customer and to partners.

Converging on one's customers and partners opens up many opportunities but also presents many challenges and issues. This convergence is breaking down old boundaries, creating new visions of the enterprise and what it means to do business. The notion of the virtual enterprise becomes real, in this context.

Although the virtual enterprise will mean many things, it will increasingly mean that the distinction between customer, enterprise, and suppliers will become less clear. Clearly huge challenge and opportunity are part of this environment, but careful thought, planning, and determination are the ingredients to meet the challenges and maximize the opportunities. Also necessary is technology on which to base the convergence of the business. That is the focus of the next chapter.

Chapter I-2
A Technical Architecture for Netcentric Computing

The convergence, or netcentric, environment represents a true partnership of business and technology. It is also a partnership between humans and the machines that serve them.

PUTTING INTELLIGENCE AT ORGANIZATIONAL BOUNDARIES

To bring about successful change at the boundaries of the traditional enterprise, where it meets its customers and partners, an organization needs to put intelligence at the boundary. Part of this intelligence must be delivered by human beings, simply because human intelligence is necessary to handle nonroutine and variable processes. Not all the intelligence, however, can be provided by humans. Any one organization has too many partners and customers; the company cannot possibly have a staff member available to all partners and customers whenever they need help. To meet this need, part of the intelligence must be computer based, responding to and interacting with the partner or customer in a highly responsive and intelligent manner and at the same time communicating what is happening within the enterprise.

The primary client and server split, which is still inherent in netcentric solutions, gives us another view of how intelligence is managed. The client side of client/server computing corresponds to the need to put intelligence where the partner or customer is doing the work and then to manage the communications side of the work. The server side of client/server computing in the company provides a place to summarize and share the contents of events that are happening with many partners and customers. This mixture of computing and communications allows management of the process at a macro level. The company can know where the business is, based in part on what is happening at the partner and customer sites as it happens. The communications core is essential to make all this happen. And finally, the material that needs to be shared is the knowledge of what is happening in the business.

The ability to put computing where the events are happening is key to making the vision of netcentric computing a reality. Local processing allows people to sense and respond to things around them. For example, as a large airplane component moves through the assembly process, the bar-coding of individual assemblies gives one an atomic view of the process. When these various atomic views are assembled, they provide a holistic view of when the aircraft component will be available. This view is provided, however, only if it can be communicated to everyone concerned in the process. Once again, the local processing provides the intelligence to decide who needs to know what and to communicate on that basis.

In addition, the local processing such as that found in home banking really makes the process feasible. If one had to wait for each screen to go to a central site for processing, the responsiveness seen in such client-based systems would quickly vanish. The technology lets the organization apply immediate committed processing power to the question at hand. Also, the local power allows the organization to create interfaces so the person can interact naturally with the system while performing the work.

As events occur, such as a sale or an addition to inventory that a supplier needs, the data, information, and knowledge of what is happening must be shared with the right people. An example of this knowledge transfer is the online catalog that is made available to customers as they enter their own sales. Another example is the posting of a change to a design component which a supplier must have in order to build the component.

From a business point of view, as noted in the last chapter, many companies are reaching maximum efficiency in overhead and internal operations, which leads them to netcentric technologies and the opportunities at the boundaries of the enterprise, in the inbound and outbound channels. From the technological point of view, netcentric computing presents new business opportunities with customers and suppliers. In short, the business opportunities today are what the technology opportunities are letting companies do. From this point of view, convergence or netcentric is the natural, inevitable solution. The competition cycle now needs the next astounding solution, and someone will take advantage of the technology that wants to make the business solution happen.

The business/technology scene today is more crowded than ever. The public is reading about the Internet every day. Business media report on Lotus Notes and Exchange Server. Java has become a hot topic. Novell is being described as having an outstanding directory structure. Network vendors are consolidating to build the next generation of networks. Video and voice and image are assumed in the computers with which employees work. Very high transmission rates, such as those as found in ATM, are described as keys to the future. Compaq is acquiring network providers. Microsoft has conceded it missed the impact of network. IBM sees netcentric computing as its future. The subject of electronic cash comes up repeatedly in technology discussions.

These are not independent events, nor are they simply technology events. Rather, they are reflections that the business enterprise must converge on its customers and suppliers, not because of some plan or conscious effort, but because most businesses have drained much of the opportunity from the current processes and now must find new ones. The new opportunities will be found in new connections to the customer and partner.

THE CHALLENGES OF NETCENTRIC SOLUTIONS

Netcentric computing presents two key challenges, discussed in the previous chapter. The Tarzan problem concerns how to transition to new distribution channels while not destroying the current ones, which would cut off the business. There are several possible methods to avoid hitting the floor of the jungle. One is to provide incentives to the current sales channel so that the new channel is seen as a source of revenue rather than as a competitor. For example, a company could pay sales people for all sales in their region, whether they make the sale or whether it is made through the direct efforts of the customer. Another method is to track customers that have moved to alternate channels and provide compensation to sales personnel based on the moved customers and on expected sales going forward. There are certainly other methods, but all must begin with the recognition that the natural concerns of the old channel during such a transition must be addressed.

The second challenge is to make a business case, as it were, for the customer to participate in the newly defined channel. Once again, organizations must realize the obvious fact that customers will not use the channel simply to help the company out. Customers must see tangible benefits in terms of better products or sales, quicker delivery, cheaper products, or the potential to participate in broader markets.

Similarly, new partner channels must be instituted only after serious forethought about incentives for partners to participate. Here again, they will not participate just to be nice to the company; customers must see something in their own self-interest. Perhaps working with the company will ensure a shorter cycle to delivery. Possibly the value can be found in assurances that cooperation will decrease the tendency to have competitors bid on price. In any case, there must be a value to the vendor that makes the proposition attractive.

The word *coopetation* has been coined to describe this approach to business. Although the concern in working with partners may not be as great as when working with the sales channel, the fact is that forming ever tighter partnerships is often a difficult transition, particularly for internal groups. The idea of giving up on the annual bid and evaluation processes, and accepting a vendor for a period of years may just seem wrong to some people. Internal groups may see a possible loss of independence in partnerships. Having partners take over work that has been done internally is always a concern, because internal people may be displaced, giving jobs to competitors. Developing trust is also a major issue, and rightfully so. Competitors yesterday may be partners today, and then competitors again tomorrow. Partners have access to information that could be of great value if they then become competitors. Each of these issues must be confronted and addressed.

A TECHNICAL FRAMEWORK FOR NETCENTRIC SOLUTIONS

Much of the discussion to his point has dealt with the business necessity and the business impact of the convergence of computing, communications, and knowledge. Such a discussion is necessary because so many issues are dependent on the business and its leadership. If the processes and people issues are not dealt with as a part of the entire problem, the technology will fail. By answering such questions as how the customer will interact with the enterprise in a netcentric environment, one begins to define the functional requirements of the netcentric systems themselves.

This section examines the architectural impact of netcentric solutions, or their effects on the major structure and components of systems in the enterprise.

Netcentric means reaching out to customers and partners with computing and knowledge over a communications backbone. This means that one will need components in a future architecture that address the communications and computing dimensions and that allow the organization to share knowledge and processes with customers and partners.

To define such an architecture, this section begins by defining the interactions needed to support the needs of the netcentric environment (Exhibit 1). The exhibit shows three primary levels. At the top, organizations need support for their dealings with customers and business partners. The middle layer contains support for internal processes and the work of both individual knowledge workers as well as teams of workers. At the bottom of the diagram is the traditional layer of transactions, data, and knowledge.

Given these primary activities in the netcentric environment, a conceptual architecture can be mapped against them (Exhibit 2).

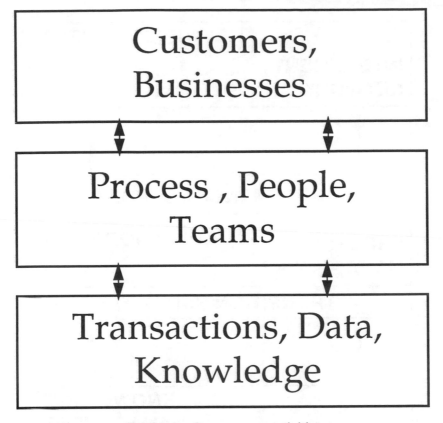

Exhibit 1. Convergence activities.

The following sections introduce the major components of the netcentric architecture. Subsequent chapters in the book will go into more detail about what these components are and how they are created and used.

KNOWLEDGE MANAGEMENT

Knowledge management applications capture, store, and make available the knowledge capital of a company. In doing this, applications can turn data and information into knowledge. In addition, they provide richer forms of information, including such media as image, voice, and video. They can provide information and knowledge in rich mixtures based on the needs and interests of the individuals working with them. To this end, the applications have indexing and accessing schemes to find knowledge, simulating the means of finding knowledge in a library. Unlike a library, however, these applications can create new forms of knowledge from underlying knowledge sources based on the specifics of the requester.

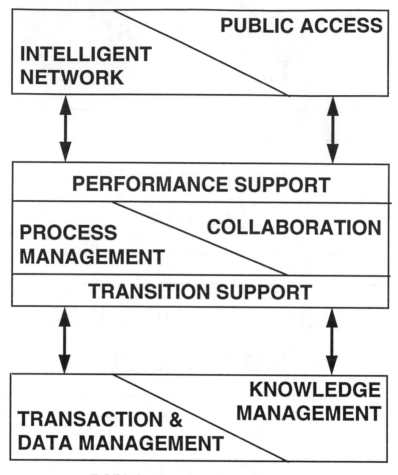

Exhibit 2. Convergence architecture.

Simple examples of these capabilities include supplying customers with a custom catalog based on their needs and concerns. Another is the ability to provide to suppliers very rich data types, such as CAD/CAM-based data, so that business partners can extend, revise, or even move designs to computer-driven manufacturing machines to control manufacturing.

At Andersen Consulting, the Knowledge Xchange™ knowledge management system, built on Lotus Notes, is becoming the backbone of the organization. Currently more than 19,000 of Andersen's consultants have access to Notes, and they are getting information from more than 2,000 so-called data bases. Very little traditional transaction data resides in those 2,000 "data bases."

Knowledge management is a burgeoning area. The types of knowledge contained in these applications will broaden, and the applications will move beyond capturing, storing, and displaying knowledge. They will begin to provide more and richer ways to organize knowledge so that even a vague request is met by a high-quality response of useful knowledge. In addition, sources of knowledge will expand far beyond the boundaries of the enterprise. In an Internet-like style, users will be able to reach into the world to find the knowledge they need. In addition, the knowledge component will have the ability to detect similarities and patterns in knowledge and provide analogues and related knowledge components based on these patterns.

The Department of Defense provides one example of the effective leveraging of knowledge. In the U.S., the DoD's logistic command has developed a system called Trans-ASK, which helps train soldiers. It puts at the user's fingertips the answers to more than 12,000 questions; the answers come from lessons learned from Desert Storm. For a distributed team like the U.S. Army, this has a huge benefit. Trans-ASK provides knowledge around the world, just in time, at the point of need. It makes the knowledge of the most experienced people available to every soldier.

Experience suggests that the components to manage and process transaction data, when compared to those to manage and process the extended data types of knowledge described in this chapter, are quite distinct. Obviously, they can and do have a high level of interaction that must be managed. To this end, the netcentric architecture contains distinct applications to manage transaction data.

TRANSACTION AND DATA MANAGEMENT

Transaction and data management — data processing — is the foundation of information technology, and transaction and data management still includes the majority of today's applications. These applications — order entry and billing, to name two — primarily deal with individual transactions and clerical tasks.

During the past decade, organizations have been moving these applications beyond transaction accounting to providing operational support. Over the last several years, these applications have been moved from the mainframe to client/server architectures.

A U.S. telecommunications company provides an example of transaction and data management within the netcentric architecture. The telecommunications company supports its customer service representatives through new, sophisticated transaction and data management. The system analyzes customer call patterns and then recommends changes to the customer's call packages to save them money. The system prompts the representative, who then makes the call.

As one would expect in the age of convergence, these applications are increasingly distributed and moving closer to the customer. For example, if customers can enter sales transactions whenever and wherever they need to, this component can capture the sale as it is made. In addition, organizations may be able to capture market data about customers, such as when they are likely to place orders, and perhaps correlate marketing activities with order placement as the customers act.

The size and complexity of these applications will continue to grow rapidly. They will contain larger and larger data bases of potentially valuable data. The recent interest in data warehousing and data mining to draw more useful information out of these data bases will grow more critical in these systems as netcentric computing provides the opportunity to know more as it happens.

TRANSITION SUPPORT

Transition support applications provide a bridge between existing systems and new systems for the integration of data and knowledge. They help leverage legacy system assets as organizations move from one set of technologies and applications to the next generation. These applications also shield the application from the tools used to access and store data and knowledge, which provides a level of flexibility and future proofing, which is always desirable.

Screen scrapers and data base interface architecture components are current examples of these applications. The data base interface components, for example, may allow one to access legacy data bases and connect together sets of physical records into a logical record that meets specific application needs.

Building interfaces between old and new systems is vital. Organizations moving to such software packages as SAP, for example, spend up to 50% of the total effort building interfaces to legacy systems. Processes and supporting tools are being developed to automate the creation of these interfaces.

A second kind of transition support application involves building new systems so they are easier to integrate with future systems. One utility company, for example, is building a new customer system using object technology. Given the size of the data base, it decided to use DB2. The company is, however, building an object layer or wrapper around the DB2 data base. This will help enable a smooth integration with future object-oriented applications and technologies.

Finally, transition support applications will increasingly support companies as they team with other enterprises. If alliances are to be successful, companies must share data and information stored in a wide variety of systems. Transition support applications will help companies connect and integrate with their external partners and customers.

PROCESS MANAGEMENT

Process management can be compared to transaction and data management applications. These latter forms deal with clerical functions and individual transactions. Process management applications, on the other hand, support knowledge workers and address entire processes. They provide front-to-back management of critical processes such as customer service or product development.

Many of the initial process management applications in this area have involved imaging, document management, and workflow management technologies. These applications can improve business process performance significantly. They improve quality, reduce elapsed time, and lower costs. The applications found in process management are those that are based on well-defined processes, which although flexible, nonetheless follow a set of well-defined and predictable steps. For example, entering an order or checking on inventory stock or setting up an insurance claim are examples of applications found in process management.

For instance, a large U.S. insurance company has been working on its customer service processes. The goal was to automate 95% of the new business and renewal processes. For these customers, new applications and renewals are not seen or worked on by employees. For the remaining 5%, a workflow automation system routes the case files to underwriters for personal attention.

In the netcentric environment, these applications are extended out to customers and partners, taking advantage of the automation that such extensions offer. For example, the business partner would be able to check on-hand stock and the volume of usage and, on this basis, automatically restock on-hand inventory. Customers will be able to complete the insurance policy application in their homes and get a quote and an indication of acceptance of the risk.

The first important trend here is not only to manage the process but to perform it as well. The ultimate goal is for the application to do everything except what requires human intelligence or physical transport.

Second, these applications make it easier to adjust processes as business conditions or strategies change. For these applications, document management and workflow technologies continue to be important. Object technology holds promise relative to tailorable business processes.

COLLABORATION

Whereas process management applications support the execution of well-defined processes, collaboration applications support less-defined processes that involve teamwork. These applications arise when the steps and sequence of doing the work are unclear. They also arise when the process is complex and requires the interaction of people to see that a job is done well.

The following cases provide contrasting examples. The application for a simple loan to cover the costs of a new piece of furniture could well be completed by a bank customer from home using a well-defined process found in process management. Conversely, settling on a home loan with complex interest arrangement and the use of stocks for collateral could well require human interaction and would be managed out of the collaboration component.

Collaboration applications are increasingly adding computing value to what has initially been primarily a communications solution. One Japanese consumer goods manufacturer, for example, is working on improving innovation and time to market. By setting up a global R&D team linked with teamware, it has flattened its R&D organization and accelerated new product development. These applications help organizations respond quickly and cohesively to changing market conditions.

Collaboration support is critical in the netcentric environment, but it is a challenge, as well. It is critical because collaboration is a way to ensure that the "human touch" is still present for the customer or partner, when needed. Also, it is central to avoiding automating things that are just too complex to automate. For example, a consumer trying to set up a home loan will need help to understand all the financial and legal implications of such a transaction.

Collaboration support is also a challenge because many people with an IT background believe that anything less than the 100% solution is not enough. IT experts tend to view the unstructured nature of collaborative systems as a failure. Another challenge is that some of the key technologies to deliver collaborative applications are not widely available and tend to be incompatible. Further, they make demands on the telecommunications component that the component is not always able to handle.

PERFORMANCE SUPPORT

Performance support applications improve the performance of knowledge workers, teams, partners, and customers. In the past, these applications have supported the unique needs of employees, especially system users. They help workers learn and use systems that have become increasingly complex. They also help workers get up to speed more quickly, and enable them to achieve higher levels of performance.

Performance support is mandatory in the applications that organizations make available to their customers and partners. These applications need to reach out and pull in customers, who are highly intolerant users and are unwilling to learn an organization's systems. For the customer, application usage revolves around performance support. Customers must find it easy to buy and to develop relationships with companies.

Several trends are important here. First, organizations are increasingly emphasizing learning, not just training. Performance support applications are becoming more self-directed, allowing knowledge workers to find what they need, instead of what managers think they need. This is clearly key in the netcentric environment, where a system user such as the customer has little interest in being trained on the organization's systems.

Most performance support applications today are standalone systems. The trend will be to build integrated applications with embedded performance support. These applications will sense, based on customer or partner activities and prior interactions, when the person needs help in doing the work. Letting customers, partners, and employees learn just in time, at the point of need, and providing them with advice and direction enable significant improvements in performance and acceptance of systems by those engaging them.

PUBLIC ACCESS

Public access applications address the needs of public users — specifically, consumers — and narrow the gap between the company, its products, and the consumer. Effective applications give customers what they want, when they want it. They will let the customer participate directly in such processes as order entry and product design. For example, Andersen Windows has a kiosk system called "Window of Knowledge." Using the kiosk, customers can enter a drawing of their floor plan and try out standard window options. But they can go beyond that and design their own custom windows. The system tells them what can be built and what cannot. When they have made a final decision, the system automatically generates parts lists, prices, and places the order.

One important trend in public access is integration with home devices. Moving these applications into the home is having a tremendous impact on business, education, and entertainment. Another trend is mobility — making an organization available wherever and whenever a customer wants it to be. Smart cards are one way mobility is achieved today. Wireless communications and PDAs will be the way this is done in the future. Mobility will extend the reach and power of the enterprise, eliminating barriers and making it closer and more direct with its customers.

INTELLIGENT NETWORK

Intelligent network applications also can be called business-to-business applications. With these applications, the enterprise establishes and maintains its links with other organizations, such as suppliers, distributors, alliance partners, and the government. The first stage of these applications has primarily been a communications link for transaction exchange. Electronic Data Interchange (EDI) is one well-known example.

The direction in this application area is to take full advantage of the convergence of computing, communications, and knowledge. These applications provide more direct links with business partners and allow them to coordinate more effectively their response to changes in customer demand.

Eventually, the intelligent network will enabled almost total supply chain integration. The window design application noted earlier is already part way there. Parts lists are generated for contractors and orders are placed. For some products, information is sent right to the shop floor, where windows are built to specification. In that case, the glass suppliers are also connected into the process.

Applications that manage and perform business-to-business processes enable the ultimate virtualization of business, bringing together strategy, people, process, and technology in a unique configuration across multiple companies to serve the customer in a more powerful way than any one company could on its own. The final convergence will be one in which barriers between companies and their customers have been removed.

SUMMARY

At an overview level, these are the components of the netcentric application framework. As the saying goes, however, the whole is greater than the sum of the parts. The whole, in this case, is an organization that is not constrained by time, place, or physical form. Its information technology is indispensable, integral, and invisible.

The netcentric framework shows how technology will be applied to enable exceptional business results. With these applications, enterprises can deliver astounding solutions.

Sections II and III set forth in detail the types of architectures, technologies, testing, and change management activities necessary to succeed in the age of networkcentric computing. Section IV discusses some significant technologies on the horizon that are ready to help companies deliver on the next competition cycle.

Section II
Netcentric Architectures and Technologies

Section II takes the reader into a more detailed discussion of the architecture for delivery of netcentric solutions. It also focuses on certain critical technologies — communications, data warehouses, parallel processing — that are primary enablers of these solutions. Because testing and knowledge management are also key issues in the netcentric environment, each of these topics is addressed here as well.

The focus of this section is primarily on the *what* rather than on the *how* — the latter issue is reserved for the implementation discussions found in Section III.

Chapter II-1
The Netcentric Execution Architecture

The netcentric execution architecture comprises run-time services and control structures coupled with an application infrastructure. This chapter looks in detail at the common services that can be used by all types of applications.

As shown in Exhibit 1, the netcentric execution architecture is best represented as an extension to a client/server execution architecture. (This architecture is discussed in detail in *A Practical Guide to Client/Server Computing*, also published by Auerbach.) The exhibit shows the logical representation of a requester and a provider, designated by the client and the server. Although the exhibit shows only one client and one server, a physical implementation of an execution architecture typically has many clients and many servers. Thus, the services described here can be located on one physical machine, but most likely will span many physical machines as shown in Exhibit 2.

The common execution architecture services can be broken down into logical areas: presentation services, information access services, communication services, communication fabric services, transaction services, environment services, web services and business logic (see logical representation figure). Although physical implementation considerations are addressed, this chapter aims to present a logical-level discussion of the execution architecture services.

At the high-level, Web browser services and Web services are new netcentric elements added to the traditional client/server execution architecture. Also, within each element (e.g., information services, environment services) additional services pertaining to netcentric computing have been added. Because of their important role in the netcentric environment, component services are also emphasized in this high-level picture.

PRESENTATION SERVICES

Presentation services (Exhibit 3) enable an application to manage the human-computer interface, including capturing user actions and generating resulting events, presenting data to the user, and assisting in the management of the

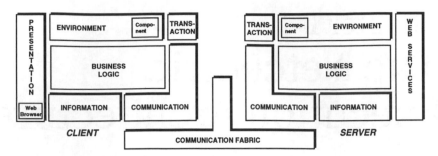

Exhibit 1.   Execution architecture: logical picture.

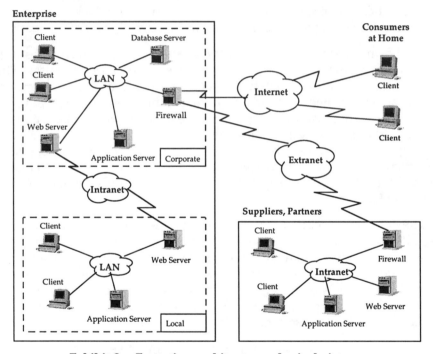

Exhibit 2.   Execution architecture: physical picture.

dialog flow of processing. Typically, presentation services are required only by client workstations.

The major presentation services are:

- Window system
- Desktop manager
- Web browser
- Input device

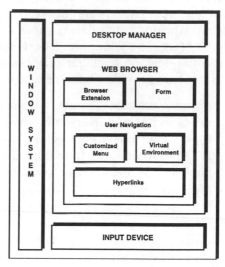

Exhibit 3. Presentation services.

Window System

Typically part of the operating systems, the window system contains the base functionality for creating and managing a graphical user interface (GUI): detecting user actions, manipulating windows on the display, and displaying information through windows and graphical controls. Examples of windowing systems include Microsoft Windows, Windows 95 and Windows NT, Macintosh OS, Presentation Manager for OS/2, and X-Windows/Motif.

Window systems expose their functionality to application programs through a set of application programming interfaces (APIs). For the Microsoft windowing platforms, this API is called Win32, a documented set of over 400 C functions that allow developers to access the functionality of the windowing system as well as various other operating system functions. Developers are able to call the Win32 API or its equivalent on other platforms directly, using a C language compiler; however, most development is done using higher-level development languages, such as Visual Basic or PowerBuilder, which make the lower level calls to the operating systems on behalf of the developer.

Desktop Manager Services

Desktop manager services provide for implementing the "desktop metaphor," a style of user interface that tries to emulate the idea of a physical desktop. It lets the user place documents on the desktop, launch applications by clicking on a graphical icon, or discard files by dragging them onto a picture of a wastebasket. Desktop manager services include facilities for launching applications and desktop utilities and managing their integration. Most windowing systems contain elementary desktop manager functionality (e.g., the Windows 95 desktop), but often more user-friendly or functional desktop manager services are required. Some representative products that provide desktop manager services include:

- *Norton Navigator.* Targeted at users who often interact with the Windows 95 desktop, Norton Navigator provides multiple virtual desktops, enhanced file management, including direct file transfer protocol (FTP) connectivity, long file-name support for some Windows 3.x applications, file unerase, and other features.
- *Microsoft Windows 95 Task Bar.* The user shell environment in Microsoft's Windows 95 interface extends the desktop metaphor by introducing graphical elements such as the launch bar, which allows users to access recently used documents, to launch applications, or to switch between active applications. The Windows 95 desktop and launch bar are programmable — allowing developers to extend and customize the desktop manager for their specific application or user. For example, the desktop can be extended with icons or Start Menu options for creating a new customer account or finding an order.
- *Xerox Tabworks.* This utility presents the user with a notebook metaphor for application and document access. It allows creation of tabbed sections that contain related files (e.g., a "Winston Account" or "New Product Launch") for easier access.
- *Starfish Software Dashboard.* This desktop utility is designed to simplify application and system management. It provides quick launch buttons, system resource gauge, drag-and-drop printing and faxing, and a calendar.

Web Browser Services

Web browser services allow users to view and interact with applications and documents made up of varying data types, such as text, graphics, and audio. Browsers typically provide support for navigation within and across documents no matter where they are located, through the use of links embedded into the document content. Much of the appeal of the Web browsers is the ability to provide a universal client that offers users a consistent and familiar user interface from which all types of applications can be executed and all types of documents can be viewed, regardless of the type of operating system or machine, as well as independent of where these applications and documents reside. Browsers employ standard protocols, such as hypertext transfer protocol (HTTP) and FTP, to provide seamless access to documents across machine and network boundaries.

Examples of products that provide browser services include:

- *Netscape Navigator.* One of the original browsers, Navigator currently has a large share of the installed browser market and strong developer support.
- *Microsoft Internet Explorer (IE).* Leveraging the market strength of Windows, Internet Explorer is tightly integrated with Windows and supports the major features of Netscape Navigator as well as Microsoft's own ActiveX technologies.

It should be noted that the distinction between the desktop and Web browser may well disappear with the release of products that integrate Web browsing into the desktop, and give a user the ability to view directories as though they were Web pages. The Web browser, as a distinct entity, may even fade away with time.

Browsers require new or at least revised development tools for working with new languages and standards such as HTML and Java. Many browser content development tools have flooded the market recently. The following are several representative products that provide browser services:

- *Netscape LiveWire and LiveWire Pro.* This visual tool suite is designed for building and managing complex, dynamic Web sites and creating live online applications.
- *Symantec Visual Café.* This is the first complete rapid application development (RAD) environment for Java. With Visual Café one can assemble complete Java applets and applications from a library of standard and third-party objects, without writing source code — for very simple applications. Visual Café also provides an extensive set of text-based development tools.
- *Microsoft FrontPage.* This product provides an integrated development environment for building Web sites, including WebBots, which provide services for implementing common features such as search engines and discussion groups.
- *Microsoft Visual J++.* A product similar to Visual C++, VJ++ allows the construction of Java applications through an integrated graphical development environment.

Web browser services can be further subdivided into:

- Browser extension services.
- Form services.
- User navigation services.

Browser Extension Services. Browser extension services provide support for executing different types of applications from within a browser.

These applications provide functionality that extend browser capabilities. The key browser extensions are:

- *Plug-in.* A term coined by Netscape, a plug-in is a software program specifically written to be executed within a browser for the purpose of providing additional functionality that is not natively supported by the browser, such as viewing and playing unique data or media types. For example, early browsers did not natively support multimedia data types like sound. Sound plug-ins were used by the browser to play back the sound component of a document. Other plug-ins allow mainframe 3270-based applications to be viewed directly or mapped into a more friendly form-style interface. Plug-ins cover everything from streaming video to interactive conferencing, and new ones are being released every week. Typically, to use a plug-in, users must download and install the plug-in on their client machine. Once the plug-in is installed it is integrated into the Web browser. The next time a browser opens a Web page that requires that plug-in to view a specific data format, the browser initiates the execution of the plug-in. Special plug-in APIs are used when developing plug-ins. Until recently plug-ins were only accessible from the Netscape browser. Now, other browsers such as Microsoft's Internet Explorer are beginning to support plug-in technology as well. However, plug-ins written for one browser will generally need to be modified to work with other browsers. Also, plug-ins are operating system dependent. Therefore, separate versions of a plug-in are required to support Windows, Macintosh, and UNIX platforms.
- *Helper application/viewer.* This software program is launched from a browser for the purpose of providing additional functionality to the browser. The key differences between a helper application (sometimes called a viewer) and a plug-in are:
  - *How the program is integrated with the Web browser.* Unlike a plug-in, a helper application is not integrated with the Web Browser, although it is launched from a Web browser. A helper application generally runs in its own window, contrary to a plug-in, which generally is integrated into a Web page.
  - *How the program is installed.* Like a plug-in, the user installs the helper application. However, because the helper application is not integrated with the browser, the user tends to do more work during installation specifying additional information needed by the browser to launch the helper application.
  - *How the program is initiated.* Usually the user initiates the launching of the helper application; with a plug-in, the browser does the initiation.
  - *How the program is executed.* The same helper application can be executed from a variety of browsers without any updates to the program, unlike a plug-in which generally needs to be updated for

specific browsers. However, helper applications are still operating system dependent.

- *Java applet.*   This applet is a program written in Java that runs within or is launched from the client's browser. This program is loaded into the client device's memory at runtime and then unloaded when the application shuts down. A Java applet can be as simple as an animated object on an HTML page or as complex as a complete windows application running within the browser.

- *ActiveX control.*   This program can be run within a browser, from an application independent of a browser, or on its own. ActiveX controls are components, developed using Microsoft's standards, that define how software components should be built. Although Microsoft is positioning ActiveX controls to be language and platform independent, today they are limited to the Intel platforms. Within the context of a browser, ActiveX controls add functionality to Web pages. These controls can be written to add new features like dynamic charts, animation, or audio. Plug-ins and ActiveX controls are functionally similar, but ActiveX controls provide more functionality, such as a self-installing capability.

- *JavaBeans.*   This is JavaSoft's (Sun's Java development and marketing unit) counterpart to ActiveX controls, based on CORBA standards. JavaBeans also can be anything from small visual controls, such as a button or a date field, to full-fledged applications, such as word processors, spreadsheets, and browsers.

Quickly changing technologies and companies make viewers and plug-ins are among of the most dynamic segments of the browser market . What was yesterday's plug-in or viewer add-on often becomes a built-in capability of the browser in its next release.

The following are examples of plug-in execution products:

- *Real Audio.*   This is a plug-in designed to play audio in real-time on the Internet without needing to download the entire audio file before the user begins listening.

- *VDOLive.*   Similar to real audio, this plug in is designed to view real-time video streams on the Internet without needing to download the entire video file before the user begins viewing.

- *Macromedia Shockwave.*   This plug-in is used to play back complex multimedia documents created using Macromedia Director or other products.

- *Internet Phone.*   This is one of several applications that allow two-way voice conversation over the Internet, similar to a telephone call.

- *Information Builder's Web3270.*   This plug-in allows mainframe 3270-based applications to be viewed across the Internet from within a browser. The Web3270 server provides translation services to transform a standard 3270 screen into an HTML-based form. Interest in Web3270 and similar plug-ins has increased with the Internet's ability to provide customers and trading partners direct access to an organization's applications and data. "Screen scraping" viewers can bring legacy applications to the Internet or intranet very quickly.

Form Services. Form services enable applications to use fields to display and collect data. A field may be a traditional 3270-style field used to display or input textual data, or it may be a graphical field, such as a check box, a list box, or an image. Form services provide support for:

- *Display.* This service supports the display of various data types (e.g., text, numeric, date) using various output formats (e.g., American/European date format, double-byte characters, and icons).
- *Input/validation.* This service enables applications to collect information from the user, edit it according to the display options, and perform basic validation, such as range or format checks.
- *Mapping support.* This eliminates the need for applications to communicate directly with the windowing system. Instead, applications retrieve or display data by automatically copying the contents of a window's fields to a copybook structure in memory. These services may also be used to automate the merging of application data with pre-defined electronic form templates.
- *Field interaction management.* This service coordinates activity across fields in a window by managing field interdependencies and invoking application logic based on the state of fields and user actions. For example, the field interaction manager may disable the "OK" button until all required input fields contain valid data. These services significantly reduce the application logic complexity inherent to an interactive windowed interface.

In traditional client/server applications, forms are windows that contain widgets (e.g., text fields and combo-boxes) and business logic. Form development tools such as Visual Basic and PowerBuilder allow the form designer to specify page layout, entry fields, business logic, and routing of forms. From a developer's perspective, these products typically expose form and control handling functionality as a set of proprietary or product specific APIs.

The HTML standard also includes support for form-based applications. The HTML standard includes tags for informing a compliant browser that the bracketed information is to be displayed as an editable field, a radio button, or other form-type control. Currently, HTML browsers support only the most rudimentary forms — basically providing the presentation and collection of data without validation or mapping support. When implementing forms with HTML, additional custom form services may be required.

The following are examples of development/execution products supporting form services:

- *JetForms' JetForm Design.* This product provides tools to design, fill, route, print and manage electronic forms, helping organizations reduce costs and increase efficiency by automating forms processing across local and wide area networks as well as the Internet. JetForms acquired Delrina software, which had a product used to perform similar E-form functions.
- *Lotus Forms.* This product is Lotus Development Corp.'s electronic forms software for designing, routing, and tracking forms to automate business processes for the workgroup or the extended enterprise. Lotus Forms is designed to run with Lotus Notes or as a standalone application. It comprises two parts: *Forms Designer*, an application-development version, and *Forms Filler*, a runtime version for users.
- *Visual Basic.* This development tool provides a comprehensive development environment for building complex applications.
- *FrontPage.* This Web site management tool supports creation of Web pages, Web site creation, page and link management, and site administration.

User Navigation Services

User navigation services provide the user with a way to access or navigate between functions within or across applications. Historically, this has been the role of the text-based menuing system, which provides a list of applications or activities for the user to choose from. The more capable workstations found in client/server environments, however, have given rise to new metaphors or ways to expose information and functionality to the user. The desktop metaphor previously described can be useful for organizing applications and overall resources, but it is not as applicable for presenting functions within an application. The document metaphor is appropriate for presenting a specific activity, such as filling in a loan application, but it is not as useful for presenting the user with a choice or list of activities. Additional navigation metaphors that may require architectural support services are described in the following two sections.

Customized Menu. A common method for allowing a user to navigate within an application is to list available functions or information by means of a menu bar with associated pull-down menus or context-sensitive pop-up menus. This method conserves screen real estate by hiding functions and options within menus, but for this very reason it can be more difficult for first time or infrequent users. This point is important when implementing electronic commerce solutions in which the target customer may use the application only once or very infrequently (e.g., pricing and purchasing auto insurance). Also, browsers themselves can be programmed to support customized menus. This capability might be more applicable for intranet environments where the browsers need to be customized for specific business applications.

Hyperlink. The Internet has popularized the use of underlined key words, icons, and pictures that act as links to additional pages. The hyperlink mechanism is not constrained to a menu but can be used anywhere within a page or document to provide the user with navigation options. It also can take a user to another location within the same document or a different document altogether, or even a different server or company for that matter. There are three types of hyperlinks: hypertext, icon, and image map.

1. *Hypertext.* This hyperlink is very similar to the concept of "context sensitive help" in Windows, where the reader can move from one topic to another by selecting a highlighted word or phrase.
2. *Icon* This is similar to the hypertext menu, but selections are represented as a series of icons. The HTML standard and popular browsers provide hyperlinking services for nontext items such as graphics.
3. *Image map.* This link also is similar to the hypertext menu, but selections are represented as a series of pictures. A further evolution of image map menu is to display an image depicting some place or thing (e.g., a picture of a bank branch with tellers and loan officers).

Client/server development tools such as Visual Basic and PowerBuilder do not provide specific services for image map navigation, but the effect can be recreated using graphical controls (such as picture controls or iconic push-buttons) programmed to launch a particular window when clicked on.

The hyperlink metaphor makes it possible for the user to jump from topic to topic instead of reading the document from beginning to end. For many types of applications, this can create a more user-friendly interface, enabling the user to find information faster.

An image map menu is useful when all users share some visual model for how business is conducted, but it also is painfully slow if a slow or even moderate speed communications connection is used. Additional image map services are required to map the location of user mouse clicks within the image to the corresponding page or window to be launched.

Virtual Environment Services. A virtual environment or virtual reality interface takes the idea of a graphical map to the next level by creating a three-dimensional environment for the user to "walk around in." Popularized by such PC games as *Doom*, the virtual environment interface can be used for business applications. The consumer can "walk" through a shopping mall and into and around virtual stores or "fly" around a 3D virtual version of a resort complex being considered for holiday.

To create sophisticated user navigation interfaces such as these requires additional architectural services and languages. The virtual reality modeling language (VRML) is one such language gaining in popularity. Additionally, many tool kits and code libraries are available to speed development. The following are representative products that provide or can be used to implement virtual environment services:

- *Silicon Graphics Open Inventor.* This object-oriented 3D toolkit is used to build interactive 3D graphics using such objects as cameras, lights, and 3D viewers and provides a simple event model and animation engines.
- *VREAM VRCreator.* This is a toolkit for building interactive virtual reality environments. It supports gravity, elasticity, and throwability of objects, textured and colored 3D objects, and construction of networked multiparticipant worlds. It provides support under Windows for DDE and ActiveX.
- *Dimension X Liquid Reality.* This set of Java class libraries comprise a VRML toolkit that can be used to build VRML viewers and tools, and is extensible using Java to create custom VR environment viewers.

Input Devices

Input devices detect user input from a variety of input technologies, such as pen based, voice recognition, touch-screen, mouse, and digital camera.

Voice response systems are used to provide prompts and responses to users through the use of phones. Voice response systems have scripted call flows that guide a caller through a series of questions. Based on the user's key pad response, the voice response system can execute simple calculations, make data base calls, call a mainframe legacy application or call out to a custom C routine. Leading voice response system vendors include VoiceTek and Periphonics.

Voice recognition systems are becoming more popular in conjunction with voice response systems. Users are able to speak to the phone in addition to using a keypad. Voice recognition can be an extremely powerful technology in cases where a key pad entry would be limiting (e.g., date/time or location). Sophisticated voice recognition systems have been built that support speaker-independence, continuous speech, and large vocabularies.

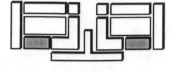

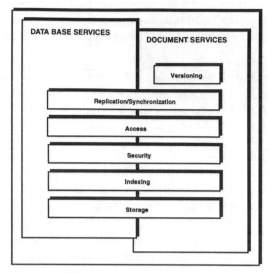

Exhibit 4. Information services.

INFORMATION SERVICES

Information services manage information assets and enable applications to access and manipulate data stored locally or remotely from documents, data bases, or external data sources. They minimize an application's dependence on physical storage and location within the network. Information services may also be used directly by the end user when ad hoc data and document access is integral to the application work task. Information Services are grouped into two primary categories:

1. Data base services
2. Document services

Exhibit 4 illustrates the schema for Information Services.

Data Base Services

Data base services are responsible for providing access to a local or remote data base, as well as maintaining integrity of the data within the data base. These services also support the ability to store data on either a single physical platform, or in some cases across multiple platforms. These services are typically provided by DBMS vendors and accessed through embedded or call-level SQL variants and supersets. Depending on the underlying storage model, non SQL access methods may be used instead.

Data is often stored as relational tables (an RDBMS) but may also be stored in object-oriented format (OODMBS) or other structures. Often, legacy applications are based on relational technology, but this is not necessarily the case. Some legacy applications may be based on IMS or VSAM, for example. Regardless of the underlying DBMS technology, legacy systems hold critical data that must be accessible by new team computing solutions. This legacy data must be accessed in its current form so as not to disrupt the legacy systems.

Many of the netcentric applications today are broadcast-type applications, used to market a company's products and publish company policies and procedures. Also, there is now a growth of netcentric applications that are transaction-type applications used to process a customer's sales order or maintenance request. Typically these types of applications require integration with a data base manager.

The core data base services of access control and storage and retrieval are provided by all major RDBMS products. Additional services, such as synchronization and replication and merging, are available only in specific products. The following representative products provide or can be used to implement data base services.

- *Oracle.* A market leader in the UNIX client/server RDBMS market, Oracle is available for a wide variety of hardware platforms including massively parallel processing (MPP) machines. Oracle's market position and breadth of platform support has made it the RDBMS of choice for a variety of application software packages in financials, accounting, human resources, and manufacturing.
- *Sybase.* Traditionally focused upon medium-sized data bases and distributed environments, Sybase provides strong architecture support for data base replication and distributed transaction processing across remote sites.
- *Informix.* With a smaller market share than Oracle or Sybase, Informix is often selected for its ability to support both large centralized data bases and distributed environments with a single RDBMS product.
- *IBM DB2.* The leader in MVS mainframe data base management, the IBM DB2 family of relational data base products are designed to offer open, industrial strength data base management for decision support, transaction processing and line of business applications. The DB2 family now spans not only IBM platforms like personal computers, AS/400 systems, RISC System/6000 hardware and IBM mainframe computers, but also non IBM machines from Hewlett-Packard and Sun Microsystems.
- *Microsoft SQL Server 6.5.* This is the latest version of a high-performance client/server relational data base management system. Building on version 6.0, SQL Server 6.5 introduces key new features such as transparent distributed transactions, simplified administration, OLE-based programming interfaces, improved support for industry standards, and Internet integration.

The following sections discuss the primary services within data base services:

- Storage services
- Indexing services
- Security services
- Access services
- Replication/synchronization services

Storage Services. Storage services manage data physical storage. These services provide a mechanism for saving information so that data will live beyond program execution. Data is often stored in relational format (an RDBMS) but may also be stored in an object-oriented format (OODBMS) or other structures such as IMS and VSAM.

Indexing Services. Indexing services provide a mechanism for speeding up data retrieval. In relational data bases, one or more fields can be used to construct the index. So when a user searches for a specific record, rather than scanning the whole table sequentially, the index is used to find the location of that record faster.

Security Services. Security services enforce control regarding which records authorized users can view and edit, and which functions they can execute. Most data base management systems provide access control at the data base, table and row levels to specific users and groups, as well as concurrency control. They also provide execution control for such things as stored procedures and data base functions.

Access Services. Access services enable an application to retrieve data from a data base as well as manipulate (insert, update, delete) data in a data base. SQL is the primary approach for accessing records in today's data base management systems.

Client/server systems often require data access from multiple data bases offered by different vendors. This is often due to integration of new systems with existing legacy systems. The key architectural concern is in building the application where the multivendor problem is transparent to the client. This provides future portability, flexibility and also makes it easier for application developers to write to a single data base access interface. One of the following methods could be used to achieve data base transparency:

- *Standards Based SQL API.* This approach uses a single, standards based set of APIs to access any data base. It includes the following technologies: open data base connectivity (ODBC), Java data base connectivity (JDBC), and object linking and embedding (OLE DB).

- *SQL Gateways.* This provides a mechanism for clients to transparently access data in a variety of data bases (e.g., Oracle, Sybase and DB2) by translating SQL calls written using the format and protocols of the gateway server or primary server to the format and protocols of the target data base. Currently there are three contending architectures for providing gateway functions:

  — *Distributed Relational Data Access (DRDA).* This is a standard promoted by IBM for distributed data access between heterogeneous data bases. In this case the conversion of the format and protocols occurs only once. It supports SQL89 standard and a subset of SQL92 standard and is built on top of APPC/APPN and TCP/IP transport stacks.

  — *IBI's EDA/SQL and the Sybase/MDI Open Server.* These architectures use SQL to access relational and nonrelational data base systems. They use API/SQL or T-SQL respectively as the standard interface language. A large number of communication protocols are supported including NetBIOS, SNA, DECnet, TCP/IP. The main engine translates the client requests into specific server calls. It handles security, authentication, statistics gathering, and some system management tasks.

One consideration to bear in mind: because all the clients go through a single gateway, gateways may create bottlenecks. When selecting a communication mechanism (i.e., middleware) for sending data and requests from one source to another, TP monitors and Object Request Brokers (ORB) should be considered, especially for medium and large-scale systems.

Replication/Synchronization Services. Replication services support an environment in which multiple copies of data bases must be maintained. For example, if ad hoc reporting queries or data warehousing applications can work with a replica of the transaction data base, these resource-intensive applications will not interfere with mission critical transaction processing. Replication can be either complete or partial. During complete replication all records are copied from one destination to another; during partial replication, on the other hand, only a subset of data is copied, as specified by the user or the program. Replication also can be done either real-time or on-demand (i.e., initiated by a user, program or a scheduler). The following might be possible if data bases are replicated on alternate server(s): better availability or recoverability of distributed applications, and better performance and reduced network cost, particularly in environments where users are widely geographically dispersed.

Synchronization services perform the transactions required to make one or more information sources that are intended to mirror each other consistently. This function is especially valuable when implementing applications for users of mobile devices, because it allows a working copy of data or documents to be available locally without a constant network attachment. The emergence of applications that allow teams to collaborate and share knowledge has heightened the need for synchronization services in the execution architecture.

The terms *replication* and *synchronization* are used interchangeably, depending on vendor, article, book, etc. For example, when Lotus Notes refers to replication, it means both the services provided by replication and synchronization as previously described. When Sybase refers to replication it only means copying data from one source to another.

Replication/synchronization services sometimes are supplied as part of commercial data bases, document management systems or groupware products such as Lotus Notes, Microsoft Exchange, and Oracle.

With Windows 95 and Windows NT 4.0, Microsoft has also introduced the concept of replication/synchronization services into the operating system. Through the *briefcase* application users can automatically synchronize files and SQL data between their Windows PC and a Windows NT server. Underlying this application is the user-extensible Win32 synchronization services API, which can be used to build custom synchronization tools.

Document Services

Document services provide similar structure and control for documents that data base management systems apply to record-oriented data. A document is defined as a collection of objects of potentially different types (e.g., structured data, unstructured text, images, multimedia) that a business user deals with. An individual document might be a table created using a spreadsheet package such as Microsoft Excel, a report created using a word processing package such as Lotus AmiPro, a Web page created using an HTML authoring tool, or a combination of these types of documents. Regardless of the software used to create and maintain the component parts, all parts together constitute the document, which is managed as a single entity.

Examples of products to support document services include the following:

- *Documentum.* Documentum Enterprise Document Management System (EDMS) automates and accelerates the creation, modification, and reuse of business-critical documents, Web pages, and other unstructured data and all of the collaborative efforts involved.
- *Saros.* Saros Discovery Suite is the next generation client/server solution that integrates Saros Document Manager, FileNet Ensemble,

and Watermark Client to provide powerful, tightly-integrated electronic document management, workflow, and document-imaging capabilities.

Specific document services discussed in the following sections are:

- Storage services
- Indexing services
- Security services
- Access services
- Replication/synchronization services
- Versioning services

Storage Services. Storage Services manage physical storage of documents. Most document management products store documents as objects that include two basic data types: attributes and content. Document attributes are key fields used to identify the document, such as author name and created date. Document content refers to the actual unstructured information stored within the document. Generally, the documents are stored in a repository using one of the following methods:

- *Proprietary data base.* Documents (i.e., attributes and content) are stored in a proprietary data base (one that the vendor has specifically developed for use with a product).
- *Industry standard data base.* Documents (i.e., attributes and content) are stored in an industry standard data base such as Oracle or Sybase. Attributes are stored within traditional data base data types (e.g., integer and character); content is stored in the data base's BLOB (binary large objects) data type.
- *Industry standard data base and file system.* Documents' attributes are stored in an industry standard data base, and documents' contents are usually stored in the file-system of the host operating system. Most document management products use this document storage method today because it provides the most flexibility in terms of data distribution and also allows for greater scalability.

Indexing Services. Locating documents and content within documents is a complex problem and involves several alternative methods. The Windows Explorer (i.e., file manager) is a simplistic implementation of a hierarchical organization of files and collection of files. If the user model of where documents should be stored and found can be represented in this way, the use of structure and naming standards can be sufficient. However, a hierarchical document filing organization is not suitable for many types of document queries (e.g., retrieving all sales order documents for over $1,000).

Therefore, most document management products provide index services that support the following methods for searching document repositories:

- *Attribute search.* This scans short lists (i.e., attributes) of important words associated with a document and returns documents that match the search criteria. For example, a user may query for documents written by a specific author or created on a particular date. Attribute search brings the capabilities of the SQL-oriented data base approach to finding documents by storing in a data base the values of specially identified fields within a document and a reference to the actual document itself. To support attribute search, an index maintains documents' attributes, which it uses to manage, find and catalog documents. This is the least complicated approach of the searching methods.

- *Full-text search.* This method searches repository content for exact words or phrases and returns documents that match the search criteria. To facilitate full-text search, full-text indexes are constructed by scanning documents once and recording in an index file which words occur in which documents. Leading document management systems have full-text services built-in, which can be integrated directly into applications.

- *Context search.* In addition to searching repository content for exact words or phrases, like full-text search, context search also searches for related words or phrases by using synonyms and word taxonomies. For example, if the user searches for car, the search engine also should look for *car, automobile*, and *motor vehicle.*

- *Boolean search.* This searches repository contents for words or phases that are joined together using boolean operators (e.g., AND, OR, NOT). The same type of indexes are used for Boolean search as for full-text search.

The following examples of execution products are used for Web and non Web documents:

- *Verity Topic.* This product delivers accurate indexing, searching, and filtering of a wide variety of information sources and formats. Verity Topic is integrated directly into several document management products, allowing systems to full-text index its unstructured information. Verity Topic also offers a variety of products to help full-text index Web sites.

- *Fulcrum.* This provides a variety of robust, multiplatform indexing and retrieval products that delivers full-function text retrieval capabilities. Fulcrum's products are typically integrated with custom data bases, Web sites, and document management systems.

The following products are mainly used for Web documents:

- *Microsoft Index Server 1.1.* This allows for search of Web documents, including Microsoft Word and Microsoft Excel. It works with Windows NT Server 4.0 and Internet Information Server 2.0 or higher to provide access to documents stored on an intranet or Internet site. It supports full-text searches and retrieves all types of information from the Web browser including HTML, text, and all Microsoft Office documents, in their original format.
- *Netscape Catalog Server 1.0.* This provides an automated search and discovery server for creating, managing, and keeping current an online catalog of documents residing on corporate intranets and the Internet. Catalog Server offers query by full text, category, or attributes such as title, author, and date. It also supports multiple file formats, including HTML, Word, Excel, PowerPoint, and PDF.

Security Services. Documents should be accessed exclusively through the document management backbone. If a document is checked-in, checked-out, routed, viewed, annotated, archived, or printed it should be done only by authorized users. Those access privileges should be controlled at the user, role, and group levels. Check-in/check-out services also can be used to limit concurrent editing of documents.

Access Services. Access services support document creation, deletion, maintenance and retrieval. These services allow users to capture knowledge or content through the creation of unstructured information, i.e., documents. Also, access services allow users to effectively retrieve documents that were created by them and documents that were created by others.

Replication/Synchronization Services. Replication services support an environment in which multiple copies of documents must be maintained. A key objective is that documents should be shareable and searchable across the entire organization. Therefore, the architecture needs to provide logically a single repository, even though the documents are physically stored in different locations. If documents are replicated on alternate server(s), it may provide better availability or recoverability of distributed documents, better performance, and reduced network cost.

Synchronization services perform the transactions required to make one or more information sources that are intended to mirror each other consistent. They support the needs of intermittently connected users or sites. Just like for data bases, these services are especially valuable for users of mobile devices who need be able to work locally without a constant network connection and then be able to synchronize with the central server at a given point in time.

Products, such as Lotus Notes and Microsoft Exchange, allow remote users to replicate documents between a client machine and a central server, so that the users can work disconnected from the network. When reattached to the network, users perform an update that automatically exchanges information on new, modified and deleted documents.

Both Lotus Notes and MS Exchange provide a limited subset of the document services described in this section. This should be carefully considered when evaluating these products to provide document management services.

Versioning Services. These services maintain a historical record of the changes to a document over time. By maintaining this record, versioning services allow for the recreation of a document as it looked at any given point in time during its evolution. Additional key versioning features record who made changes when and why they were made.

COMMUNICATION SERVICES

Communication services enable an application to interact transparently with other applications regardless of whether they reside on the same computer or on a remote computer. There are three primary communication services categories (Exhibit 5):

Exhibit 5.   Communication services.

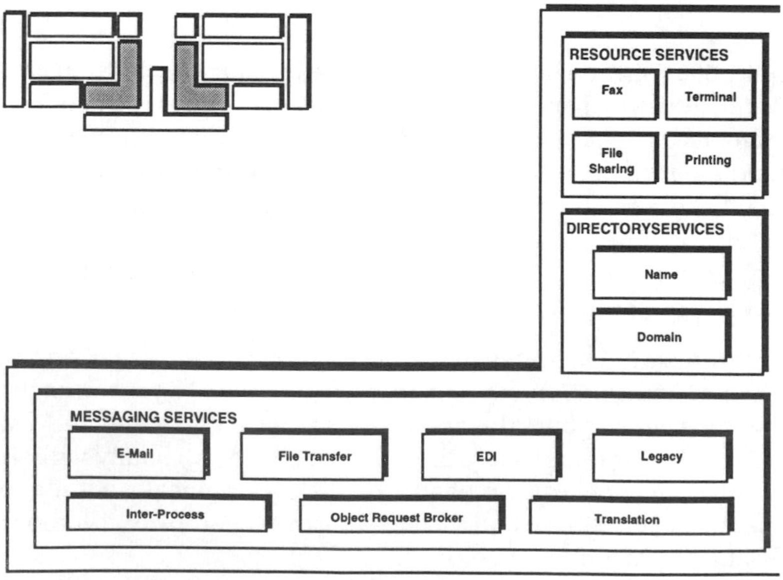

- Messaging services
- Directory services
- Resource services

Messaging Services

Broadly defined, messaging is sending information or commands between two or more recipients. Recipients may be computers, people, or processes within a computer. A protocol is a set of rules describing, in technical terms, how something should be done. Protocols facilitate transport of the message stream. For example, there is a protocol describing exactly what format should be used for sending specific types of mail messages. Most protocols typically sit "on top" of TCP/IP protocol. TCP/IP, or Transmission Control Protocol/Internet Protocol, is the principle method for transmitting data over the Internet today. This protocol is responsible for ensuring that a series of data packets sent over a network arrive at the destination and are properly sequenced.

Messaging services can be further divided into:

- Inter-process messaging services.
- Object request broker services.
- Message translation services.
- E-mail services.
- File transfer services.
- EDI services.
- Legacy services.

Inter-Process Messaging Services. There are a variety of architectural options in a client/server messaging environment. They can be divided into store and forward, synchronous, and asynchronous message services:

- *Store and forward message services.* These services provide deferred message service processing. A store and forward service may use an E-mail infrastructure upon which to build applications. Common uses would be for forms routing and E-mail.
- *Synchronous message services.* These allow an application to send a message to another application and wait for a reply before continuing. Synchronous messaging is typically used for update and general business transactions. It requires time-out processing to allow the application to re-acquire control in the event of failure.
- *Asynchronous message services.* These allow an application to send a message to another application and continue processing before a reply is received. Asynchronous messaging is typically used for larger retrieval type processing, such as retrieval of larger lists of data than can be contained in one message.

The underlying inter-process messaging services also are typically one of two messaging types:

- *Function Based.* This type uses the subroutine model of programming. The message interface is built upon the calling program passing the appropriate parameters and receiving the returned information. The most common function-based messaging system is the Remote Procedure Call (RPC) implementation. There are a variety of RPC implementations on the market.
- *Message Based.* The message-based approach uses a defined message format to exchange information between processes. While a portion of the message may be unstructured, a defined header component is normally included. A message-based approach is not limited to the call/return structure of the function-based model and can be used in a conversational manner. Products providing this type of service may build upon IBM's LU6.2 protocol.

Object Request Broker Services. Object request broker (ORB) services provide a mechanism that enables objects to transparently make requests of and receive responses from other objects located locally or remotely. In that respect it has been said that ORBs will become a kind of "ultimate middleware" for truly distributed processing. A standardized Interface Definition Language (IDL) defines the interfaces that applications must use to access the ORB Services. The two major Object Request Broker standards/implementations are:

- *COM/DCOM.* Component Object Model (COM) is a client/server object-based model, developed by Microsoft, designed to allow software components and applications to interact with each other in a uniform and standard way. The COM standard is partly a specification and partly an implementation. The specification defines mechanisms for creation of objects and communication between objects. This part of the specification is paper-based and is not dependent on any particular language or operating system. Any language can be used as long as the standard is incorporated. The implementation part is the COM library, which provides a number of services supporting a mechanism that allows applications to connect to each other as software objects. COM is not a software layer through which all communications between objects occur. Instead, COM serves as a broker and name space keeper to connect a client and an object, but once that connection is established, the client and object communicate directly without having the overhead of passing through a central piece of API code. Originally conceived of as a compound document architecture, COM has been evolved to a full object request broker including recently added features for distributed object computing. DCOM

(Distributed COM) contains features for extending the object model across the network using the DCE Remote Procedure Call (RPC) mechanism. In sum, COM defines how components should be built and how they should interact. DCOM defines how they should be distributed. Currently COM/DCOM is only supported on Windows-based machines. However, Microsoft is in the procress of porting this object model to other platforms such as Macintosh and UNIX.

- *CORBA.* Common Object Request Broker Architecture (CORBA) is a standard for distributed objects being developed by the Object Management Group (OMG). The OMG is a consortium of software vendors and end users. Many OMG member companies are then developing commercial products that support these standards and/or are developing software that use these standards. CORBA provides the mechanism by which objects transparently make requests and receive responses, as defined by OMG's Object Request Broker (ORB). The CORBA ORB is an application framework that provides interoperability between objects, built in different languages, running on different machines in heterogeneous distributed environments. The following communication protocols are based on CORBA:
  - *GIOP.* General Inter-ORB Protocol (GIOP) specifies a set of message formats and common data representations for communications between ORBs.
  - *IOP.* Internet Inter-ORB Protocol (IIOP) specifies how GIOP messages are exchanged over a TCP/IP network.

Although ORBs provide a mechanism for transparently communicating among components located locally or remotely, performance issues need to be thoroughly addressed before moving components around the network. Making requests and receiving responses among components located on different machines will take longer than having the same communication between components located on the same machine. Performance is dependent on what type of network is available (LAN, type of LAN, WAN, type of WAN, dial-up, wireless, etc.), size of messages and number of messages that go across the network.

Message Translation Services. Message translation services format application data for transport over the physical network; they provide two types of support for communications between unlike systems:

- Conversion for systems that operate with different character representations.
- Protocol conversion for systems that cannot communicate directly using lower level inter-networking devices.

A simple example of message translation would be developing a software module that would transform an SMTP based mail into an Open Mail format for use on a Hewlett-Packard system. A more complex Message Translation might take an outgoing mail message and reformat it into an EDI form that is eventually intended for an EDI-based trading partner.

E-mail Services. E-mail takes on a greater significance in the modern organization. The E-mail system, if it has sufficient integrity and stability, can function as a key channel through which work objects move within and between organizations in the form of messages and electronic forms. An E-mail server stores and forwards E-mail messages. Although some products like Lotus Notes use proprietary protocols, the following protocols used by E-mail services are based on open standards:

- *SMTP.* Simple mail transfer protocol (SMTP) is an Internet standard for sending E-mail.
- *MIM.* Multi-purpose Internet mail extensions (MIME) is a protocol that enables Internet users to exchange multimedia E-mail messages.
- *POP3.* Post office protocol (POP) is used to distribute E-mail that is typically stored on the SMTP server to the actual recipient.
- *IMAP4.* Internet Message Access Protocol, Version 4 (IMAP4) allows a client to access and manipulate electronic mail messages on a server. IMAP4 permits manipulation of remote message folders, called "mailboxes," in a way that is functionally equivalent to local mailboxes. IMAP4 also provides the capability for an off-line client to re-synchronize with the server. It even adds standards for message handling features that allow users to download message header information and then decide which E-mail message contents to download.

A number of E-mail servers from vendors including HP and Netscape are built around SMTP, and many proprietary protocol E-mail servers now provide SMTP gateways.

The multipart Internet Mail Extensions (MIME) standard is gaining acceptance as the Internet mechanism for sending E-mail containing various multimedia parts, such as images, audio files, and movies. S/MIME, or secure MIME adds encryption and enables a secure mechanism for transferring files.

Although currently POP3 is the popular Internet E-mail message handling protocol, recently the lesser known IMAP4 protocol has been gaining in adoption among mail server and mail client software providers. IMAP was designed to add features beyond POP that allow users to store and archive messages and support mobile users that need to keep messages on a central server as well as on their laptop.

Organizations are looking to use vehicles like E-mail and the Internet to enable communications with customers and trading partners. The least common denominator E-mail capability today is very rudimentary (ASCII text). But as the standards listed here as well as others become integrated into most of the popular E-mail products and gateways this will change — enabling a more flexible and useful commercial communications medium.

The following E-mail products are based on the open Internet standards defined above:

- *Netscape Mail Server.* Netscape's implementation of an open standards-based client/server messaging system that lets users exchange information within a company as well as across the Internet. It includes support for all standard protocols, and is packaged with Netscape's SuiteSpot server line.
- *Post.Office.* This is one of the leading POP3/SMTP mail servers for the Internet community as well as corporate intranets. This message transport agent is based entirely on the open standards of the Internet, ensuring maximum compatibility with other systems.
- *NTMail.* This is an open SMTP and POP3 mail server for Windows NT.

The following are major proprietary E-mail servers used in large organizations today:

- *Lotus Notes.* This is a platform-independent client/server mail system. Notes Mail can support more than 1,500 active users per server, offering Internet integration, distributed replication and synchronization. Lotus Notes also provides integrated document libraries, workflow, calendaring and scheduling, and a cc:Mail user interface.
- *Microsoft's Exchange Server.* Exchange 4.0 provides a messaging and groupware platform to support collaboration solutions on Windows machines. Microsoft Exchange 5.0 has support for all of the key Internet protocols. These include POP3 for mailbox access, SMTP for mail sending and receiving, NNTP for newsgroups and discussion forums, LDAP for directory access, HTTP and HTML for access via a Web browser, and SSL for security.

File Transfer Services. These services are specialized messaging facilities for sending and receiving files or other large data streams between two processes or physical machines. In addition to basic file transport, features for security, guaranteed delivery, sending and tracking sets of files, and error logging may be needed if a more robust file transfer architecture is required. The File Transfer Protocol (FTP) is one of the process layers of TCP/IP and is a very common method for basic file transfer particularly in the Internet community. FTP allows users to upload and download files across the network. FTP also provides a mechanism to obtain filename, directory name, attributes, and file size information.

Web servers handle client requests for HTML pages and deliver these pages via the following protocols:

- *HTTP.* Hypertext transport protocol (HTTP) is used to send hypertext data over the Internet and is currently the most popular Internet protocol. HTTP was originally developed to reduce the inefficiencies of the FTP protocol. It runs on top of the Internet communications layer (TCP/IP) and was developed specifically for the transmission of hypertext between client and server. HTTP can be thought of as a lightweight file transfer protocol optimized for transferring a small file.
- *S-HTTP.* A secure form of HTTP, mostly for financial transactions on the Web. S-HTTP is slowly gaining acceptance among merchants selling products on the Internet as a way to conduct financial transactions (using credit card numbers, passing sensitive information) without the risk of unauthorized people intercepting this information. S-HTTP incorporates various cryptographic message formats such as DSA and RSA standards into both the Web client and the Web server.

Additional options for file transfer services in a homogeneous environment could include the native operating system's copy utility, i.e., Windows NT Copy features.

EDI Services. EDI is in use today by many companies to streamline transactions within the corporate supply chain. Today, EDI is seen primarily as a system-to-system interchange standard for data and describes record layouts for such transactions as purchase orders. EDI services include facilities for transforming information into and out of the appropriate EDI formats, addressing EDI messages, sending messages and providing an audit trail.

EDI messages have traditionally been sent between companies by using a VAN (Value Added Network). VANs have been criticized for their relatively high cost in comparison to public networks like the Internet. Recently, EDI messaging vendors such as Premenos have been creating software with built-in encryption features to enable companies to send EDI transmissions securely over the Internet.

HTTP Web server developers including Microsoft, Netscape, and Open-Market are putting plans in place to add EDI transmission capabilities into their HTTP server products. OpenMarket Inc. is working with Sterling and Premenos to integrate their EDI management software with OpenMarket's OMTransact electronic commerce server software. Netscape is working with GEIS in creating Actra Business Systems to integrate EDI services with Netscape server products.

Legacy Services. Legacy services provide gateways to mainframe legacy systems. The protocol most typically used is SNA, Systems Network Architecture. SNA is a networking, connection-oriented protocol architecture developed in the 1970s by IBM. Currently, SNA and TCP/IP are two of the most widely used networking protocol architectures.

Directory Services

Directory services allow resources to address other virtual resources. Therefore, each machine that is attached to the network can view the network as a whole instead of logging onto one server at a time. The directory services accomplish this by providing a naming service and a domain service that translates a logical name to a physical name. For example, for each logical name, directory services might track the name of an actual file, the server on which the file is stored, and the address of the server port with which it interfaces (e.g., program CUSTSRV3.exe on server NYSRV04 with Ethernet address xxxxxx can be accessed as "Customer-Service"). A client searching for that file would only need to know the file name, and the directory services would provide the mapping necessary to physically retrieve the file. Directory services may be provided entirely by a specific server or be provided by a variety of interconnected severs within the network infrastructure.

One of the most popular network directory services is Novell Directory Services (NDS) used with Netware 4.x. This system allows users to access services and resources with a single login, regardless of where the user location is or where the resource location is. Another example of a directory service is the ISO X.500 standard. This method is not widely used due to its high overheads. In addition to these two protocols, Windows NT uses a similar system called Primary Domain Control. This system allows for the same type of directory mapping as NDS and X.500.

Another protocol that has emerged is the Lightweight Directory Access Protocol (LDAP), which is a slimmed-down version of the X.500 directory client and is seen as a possible replacement for X.500. LDAP is a standard protocol for accessing and updating directory information in a client/server environment; it has evolved into an emerging standard for directory replication for the Internet, and is backed by vendors such as Netscape, Novell, Microsoft, IBM and AT&T that can provide low-level compatibility among directory systems.

Another helpful feature to look out for is support for dynamic IP addressing via DHCP. This lets the router handle the process of sharing a small number of IP addresses among the members of the workgroup. Support for dynamic IP addressing is now part of Windows 95 and Macintosh System 7.6, among other operating systems.

Directory services can be further subdivided into two categories:

1. Name services
2. Domain services

Name Services. Name services are a logical component of directory services provided to create a logical "pronounceable" name in place of a binary machine number. These services could be used by other communication services such as file transfer, message services, and terminal services. The most common and widely used name service on the Internet is domain name service (DNS) which resolves a pronounceable name into an IP address and back. DNS is a service that runs on many computers within the network; it performs the actual lookup of the address associated with the name. For instance, DNS could resolve the domain name of ac.com to be 228.125.10.10. More complete proprietary directory services such as Novell NDS and NT Primary Domain Control include their own integrated name services.

Domain Services. Domain services provide a mechanism by which various nodes are recognized. These services use the domain portion of an address to transport the data to the corresponding node. Therefore, domain services are functions that track and recognize different logical organizations and then map them to physical resources as tracked by the naming services.

Resource Services

In the networked client/server environment, sharing devices such as printers, file systems, and fax machines is a common requirement. These services include:

- File-sharing services.
- Print services.
- Fax services.
- Terminal services.

File-sharing services, such as those provided by Novell, NT, and NFS provide for sharing files among users including facilities for restricting file access and locking files during update to avoid data corruption.

Print services provide printer selection and application or user routing of printing in the environment. The print server may be run either on a dedicated machine or on a machine shared with other server functions, depending on the size of the network and the amount of resources the server must manage.

Fax services provide for the management of both in-bound and out-bound fax transmissions. If fax is used as a medium for communicating with customers or remote employees, in-bound fax services may be required for centrally receiving and electronically routing faxes to the intended recipient. Out-bound fax services can be as simple as supporting the sharing on the network of a single fax machine or bank of machines for sending faxes. More sophisticated out-bound fax architecture services are required for supporting fax-back applications. Fax-back applications, when coupled with computer telephone integration (CTI) are popular for automating customer requests for product or service information to be faxed to them.

An example of a product supporting Fax Services is the Lotus® Fax Server (LFS). It provides fax services to users working on a network running NotesMail®. In addition to combining outgoing and incoming fax capabilities in a single product, the LFS provides additional features, such as automatic routing, and print-to-fax driver software that extends fax capabilities to any Windows™-based Notes client. The LFS supports a wide variety of fax modems, fax cards and fax file formats through the incorporation of device technologies from Optus Software, Inc.

Terminal Services. Terminal services allow an intelligent workstation to connect to a host via a network and to emulate the profile (the keyboard, screen characteristics, etc.) required by the host application. If connecting to a mainframe or other host master/slave configuration, the user's client workstation performs as a "dumb terminal" (e.g., IBM 3270). Terminal services receive user input and send data streams back to the host processor. If connecting from a PC to another PC, the user's client workstation might act as a remote control terminal (e.g., PCAnywhere). Examples of protocols used to support terminal emulation capabilities include:

- *Telnet.* This is a simple protocol that is part of the TCP/IP protocol suite that provides a standard text based interface from terminal to host. Telnet operates by first having the user establish a TCP connection with the remotely located login server, minicomputer or mainframe. The client's keyboard strokes are sent to the remote machine while the remote machine sends back the characters displayed on the local terminal screen.
- *rlogin.* This is a remote terminal service implemented under BSD UNIX. The concept behind rlogin is that it supports "trusted" hosts. This is accomplished by having a set of machines that share common file access rights and logins. The user controls access by authorizing remote login based on a remote host and remote user name.

COMMUNICATIONS FABRIC SERVICES

As communications networks become increasingly complicated and interconnected, the services provided by the network itself have by necessity increased as well. Clients and servers are rarely directly connected to one another but are commonly separated by a network of routers, servers, and firewalls providing an ever-increasing number of network services such as address resolution, message routing, and security screening. (Exhibit 6).

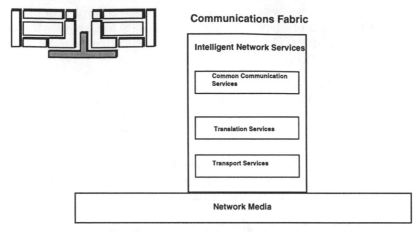

Exhibit 6. The communications fabric.

The communications fabric extends the client/server computing model by placing intelligence into the physical network, acknowledging the network as a sort of standalone system which provides intelligent shared network services. The communications fabric is discussed in detail in Chapter II-2.

ENVIRONMENT SERVICES

Environment services provide miscellaneous application and system level services that do not deal directly with managing the user-interface, communicating to other programs, or accessing data (Exhibit 7). These services are divided into the following categories:

- Operating system services
- Runtime services
- System services
- Application services
- Component framework services
- Batch scheduling services
- Report distribution services

Operating System Services

These are the underlying services such as multitasking, paging, and memory allocation that are typically provided by today's modern operating systems. When necessary, an additional layer or API may be provided to gain either operating system independence or a higher level of abstraction for application programmers.

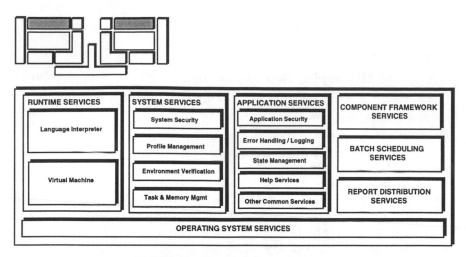

RUNTIME SERVICES	SYSTEM SERVICES	APPLICATION SERVICES	COMPONENT FRAMEWORK SERVICES
Language Interpreter	System Security	Application Security	
	Profile Management	Error Handling / Logging	BATCH SCHEDULING SERVICES
	Environment Verification	State Management	
Virtual Machine		Help Services	REPORT DISTRIBUTION SERVICES
	Task & Memory Mgmt	Other Common Services	
OPERATING SYSTEM SERVICES			

Exhibit 7. Environment services.

Runtime Services

Runtime services convert interpreted compcuter languages into machine code (i.e., executable code) during the execution of a program. Runtime services can be further subdivided into:

- Virtual machines services.
- Language interpreter services.

Virtual Machine Services. Typically, a virtual machine is implemented in software on top of an operating system, and is used to run applications. The virtual machine provides a layer of abstraction between the applications and the underlying operating system, often used to support operating system independence.

Virtual machines such as the Java virtual machine or the Smalltalk virtual machine implement their own versions of operating system services in order to provide the application with complete platform independence.

- *Java virtual machine* — software implementation of a "CPU" designed to run compiled Java code. This includes stand-alone Java applications as well as "applets" that are downloaded and run in Web browsers.
- *Smalltalk virtual machine* — runtime engine that interprets application code during execution and supports platform independence.

Language Interpreter Services. Language interpreter services decompose 4GLs and/or scripting languages into machine code at runtime. An example of a product supporting this service is the Java byte code interpeter that tanslates programs written in Java.

System Services

Services which applications can use to perform "system-level" functions. These services include:

- System security services.
- Profile management services.
- Task and memory management services.
- Environment verification services.

System Security Services. System security services allow applications to interact with the operating system's native security mechanism. The basic services include the ability to login, logoff, authenticate to the operating system, and enforce access control to system resources and executables.

Profile Management Services. Profile management services are used to access and update local or remote system, user, or application profiles. User profiles, for example, can be used to store a variety of information such as the user's language, color preferences, basic job functions, etc. This information can be used by various applications to provide the users with personalized support.

Task and Memory Management Services. Task and memory management services allow applications and/or other events to control individual computer tasks or processes, and manage memory. They provide services for scheduling, starting, stopping, and restarting both client and server tasks (e.g., software agents).

Memory management, the allocating and freeing of system resources, is one of the more error prone development activities when using 3GL development tools. Creating architecture services for memory handling functions can reduce these hard to debug errors.

Java removes, in theory, the problem of memory management, by providing a garbage collector. However, its implementation is not very efficient in current implementations of Java. Future releases of the Java VM promise a background-running garbage collector with significantly increased performance.

Environment Verification Services. Environment verification services monitor, identify and validate environment integrity prior to and during program execution (e.g., free disk space, monitor resolution, correct version, etc.) These services are invoked when an application begins processing or when a function or a program within an application is called.

Applications can use these services to verify that the correct versions of required execution architecture components and other application components are available.

In client/server applications, it may be necessary to implement environment verification services to ensure that the client and server applications are of a compatible release level.

The ActiveX framework provides services for automatic installation and upgrade of ActiveX controls when launched from within a Web browser. JavaBeans also provides a similar capability.

Application Services

Application services are common functions that can apply to one application or can be used across applications. They include:

- Application security services.
- Error handling/logging services.
- State management services.
- Help services.
- Other common services.

Application Security Services. In addition to system level security such as logging into the network, there are additional security services associated with specific applications. These include:

- *User access services.* A set of common functions that control application access to authorized users, groups and roles (e.g., employees within a company, external customers, marketing department group, managers, etc.)
- *Data access services.* A set of common functions that control access to specific data within an application by authorized users, groups and roles.
- *Function access services.* A set of common functions that control access to specific functions within an application by authorized users, groups and roles.

In the netcentric environment, application security becomes a more critical component primarily because there are more types of users (e.g., employees, customers) and additional types of transactions (e.g., e-commerce, help-desks). In traditional client/server environments most users are employees of the company. In the netcentric environments there are typically also external users (e.g., vendors, registered users) and the general public. Usually, different types of users have different application security requirements limiting what data they can see and what functions they can execute. Also, new types of transactions such as verifying credit when doing e-commerce transactions also require additional application security services.

Error Handling/Logging Services. Error handling services support the handling of fatal and nonfatal hardware and software errors for an application. These services take care of presenting the user with an understandable explanation of what has happened and coordinating with other services to ensure that transactions and data are restored to a consistent state.

Logging services support the logging of informational, error, and warning messages. These services also record application and user activities in enough detail to satisfy any audit trail requirements or to assist the systems support team in recreating the sequence of events that led to an error.

Primarily there are three types of errors: system, architecture and application. System errors occur when the application is being executed and some kind of serious system-level incompatibility is encountered, such as memory/resource depletion, data base access problems, network problems or printer related problems, because of which the application cannot proceed with its normal execution. Architecture errors are those which occur during the normal execution of the application and are generated in architecture functions that are built by a project architecture team to isolate the developers from complex coding, to re-use common services, etc. These architecture functions perform services such as data base calls, and context data management. Application errors are also those which occur during the normal execution of the application and are generally related to business logic errors such as invalid date and invalid price.

Typically an application is written using a combination of various programming languages (e.g., Visual Basic and C). Therefore, a common error handling routine should be written in a language that can be called from any other language used in the application.

Errors and audit trail records can either be logged locally on the client machine or across the network, globally on the server.

State Management Services. State management services enable information to be passed or shared among windows/Web pages and/or across programs. Suppose that several fields in an application need to be passed from one window to another. In pseudo-conversational mainframe 3270-style applications passing data from one screen to another screen was done using context management services that provided the ability to store information on a host computer (for purposes here, the term context management refers to storing state information on the server, not the client). Client/server architectures simplified or eliminated the need for context management (storing state information on the server). However, there is still a need to share information between windows and programs. Typically, in traditional client/server systems this type of state management (i.e., data sharing) is done on the client machine using hidden fields, global variables, messages, files or local data bases.

The popularity of the Internet's HTTP protocol has revived the potential need for implementing some form of context management services (storing state information on the server). The HTTP protocol is a *stateless* protocol. Every connection is negotiated from scratch, not just at the page level but for every element on the page. The server does not maintain a session connection with the client nor save any information between client exchanges (i.e., Web page submits or requests). Each HTTP exchange is a completely independent event. Therefore, information entered into one HTML form must be saved by the associated server application somewhere where it can be accessed by subsequent programs in a conversation.

Advances in netcentric products now offer additional options for implementing state management on both the client and server machines. (See Chapter III-1, "Overview of Design and Implementation Considerations."

Help Services. Help services enable an application to provide assistance to a user for a specific task. This assistance can be provided at the field, window, Web page and application levels.

Other Common Services. Catchall category for additional reusable routines useful across a set of applications (e.g., date routines, time zone conversions, field validation routines, etc.)

Component Framework Services. Component framework services provide an infrastructure for building components so that they can communicate within an application and across applications, on the same machine or on multiple machines across a network. COM/DCOM and CORBA are the two leading component industry standards. These standards define how components should be built and how they should communicate.

Object Request Broker (ORB) services, similar to CORBA and COM/DCOM, focus on how components communicate. Component framework services, also based on CORBA and COM/DCOM, focus on how components should be built. Leading component frameworks include:

- *ActiveX/OLE.* ActiveX and Object Linking and Embedding (OLE) are implementations of COM/DCOM. ActiveX is a collection of facilities forming a framework for components to work together and interact. ActiveX divides the world into two kinds of components: controls and containers. Controls are relatively independent components that present well defined interfaces or methods that containers and other components can call. Containers implement the part of the ActiveX protocol that allows for them to host and interact with components — forming a kind of back plane for controls to be plugged into. ActiveX is a scaled-down version of OLE for the Internet. OLE provides a framework to build applications from component modules and defines the way in which applications interact using data transfer, drag-and-drop and scripting. OLE is a set of common services that allow components to collaborate intelligently.

In creating ActiveX from OLE 2.0, Microsoft enhanced the framework to address some of the special needs of Web style computing. Microsoft's Web browser, Internet Explorer, is an ActiveX container. Therefore, any ActiveX control can be downloaded to, and plugged into the browser. This allows for executable components to be interleaved with HTML content and downloaded as needed by the Web browser.

- *OpenDoc.* CI Labs was formed in 1993 and created the OpenDoc architecture to provide a cross-platform alternative component framework — independent of Microsoft's OLE. The OpenDoc architecture is constructed from various technologies supplied by its founding members — IBM, Apple and Word Perfect. The technologies include: Bento (Apple's object storage model), Open Scripting Architecture (OSA — Apple's scripting architecture) and SOM/DSOM (IBM's System Object Model/Distributed SOM). IBM's SOM architecture provides analogous services to that of Microsoft's DCOM architecture.

OpenDoc provides an "open" compound document infrastructure based on CORBA. It uses CORBA as its object model for inter-component communications. OpenDoc architecture provides services analogous to those provided by OLE, and OpenDoc components also can inter-operate with OLE components. The OpenDoc equivalent of an object is termed a "part." Each type of part has its own editor and the OpenDoc architecture has responsibility for handling the communications between the distinct parts.

Supporters claim OpenDoc provides a simpler, more technically elegant solution for creating and manipulating components than does OLE. The drawback is that OpenDoc is not yet commercially proven, like OLE. Ironically, one of the more popular uses of OpenDoc tools is for creating and implementing OLE clients and servers. Because OpenDoc provides a more manageable set of APIs than OLE, it may be that OpenDoc gains initial acceptance as an enabler of OLE applications before becoming recognized as a complete component software solution itself.

- *ONE.* Open Network Environment (ONE) is an object-oriented software framework from Netscape Communications for use with Internet clients and servers, which enables the integrating of Web clients and servers with other enterprise resources and data. By supporting CORBA, ONE-enabled systems will be able to link with object software from a wide array of vendors, including IBM, Sun Microsystems, Digital Equipment, and Hewlett-Packard. Netscape is positioning ONE as an alternative to Microsoft's Distributed Common Object Model (DCOM). ONE also complies with Sun Microsystems' Java technology.

- *JavaBeans.* Sun Microsystems' proposed framework for building Java components and containers. The intent is to develop an API standard that will allow components developed in Java (or beans), to be embedded in competing container frameworks including ActiveX or OpenDoc. The JavaBeans API will make it easier to create reusable components in the Java language.

An architecture that utilizes components brings many of the benefits of object orientation to applications. Component-based or document-centric applications are composed of intelligent components, each of which contains logic, possibly data and a set of well defined interfaces or APIs to the services they provide (e.g., a customer component or an Excel chart component). The similarities to object oriented are more than just coincidental. Component software is viewed by many as a more viable object approach focusing on larger grain of modularity and reuse.

Two important issues driving the decision what should be a component will be software re-use and software packaging. Software re-use will primarily stem from defining components at a level at which they can be re-used within the same application and across many applications. Although reusable components can be at any level, more often they will probably be at an object level where they are more granular. Software packaging will be driven by defining components at a level at which they can be distributed efficiently to all users when business logic changes occur. If the application is large, perhaps it is better to package the application by breaking it up into process components such as customer maintenance, sales order maintenance, etc. So when a change to one of the processes occurs, only that component needs to be distributed to client machines, rather than the whole application. For example, a developer can create an ActiveX control that will encapsulate the "Employee Maintenance Process," which includes adding new employees, updating and deleting existing employees. This ActiveX control can be a part of an overall human resource intranet application. When the functionality within the "Employee Maintenance Process" changes, the next time the user accesses the human resource application from the Web browser, ActiveX technology will automatically download the latest version of the ActiveX control containing the most recent update of the "Employee Maintenance Process" to the client machine, if the client machine does not have the latest version.

Batch Scheduling Services. Batch scheduling services support the execution of batch application programs. Batch application programs can include business processing such as payroll and billing, and also can include report generation. This is an often overlooked area in client/server architectures. Traditional client/server solutions and netcentric solutions often require batch processing, but unlike the mainframe, the typical platforms and development environments used often do not have batch architecture facilities.

Batch scheduling services are typically supported by commercially available schedulers. Schedulers support management of jobs, job steps, interdependencies of applications and resources, and restart/recovery of batch programs. If any batch program fails during execution, the scheduler's restart/recovery services would support the restoration of context information and the repositioning of application's programs and data sets to the point prior to the failure. This saves time in data recovery and program execution. Without these services, long running batch programs may need to be completely re-run when they fail and this could jeopardize completion of the batch run within the defined batch window.

Batch scheduling services support common batch functions for all types of applications. Each company has its own business requirements and therefore needs additional application-specific batch services to support the company's overall batch requirements.

Report Distribution Services. Report distribution services are facilities for supporting the distribution of reports. These services assist in the splitting of reports into defined sections and the electronic routing of these report sections to specific targets. These targets include: users screens, E-mail, printers, and other device types.

Report distribution services support common functions for distributing various types of reports. Each company has its own business requirements and therefore needs additional application-specific report services to support the company's overall reporting requirements.

WEB SERVICES

Web services provide support for managing computing environments that use Internet and intranet technologies, which are a major subset of the netcentric technologies (Exhibit 8). Web services can be divided into the following areas:

- Web security services
- Web server services
- Push/pull services

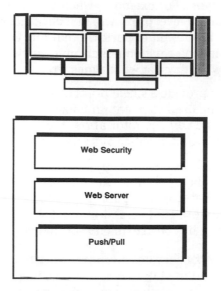

Exhibit 8.   Web services.

Web Security Services

Web security services protect an organization from unauthorized access that can occur in an Internet environment. To address these security needs, four types of protection services are employed:

- Firewall services
- Proxy services
- Authentication services
- Encryption services

Firewall Services. Firewall services protect sensitive resources and information attached to a network from unauthorized access by enforcing an access control policy. A variety of mechanisms exist for protecting private networks including:

- *Packet filter.*   This provides protocol-based services which check the address portion of data packets (i.e., IP packets) and make their decisions based on the packets' source addresses, destination addresses and port numbers. Administrators can block certain address combinations that are categorized as unauthorized or permit access to certain address combinations that are categorized as authorized.
- *Application-level proxy.*   This provides more intelligent filtering based on the actual contents of packets (i.e., application layer) rather than relying on looking at only packet header information (i.e., transport

73

and network layer). For example, when a request is received from a user, an application-level proxy will first check its internal data base to see if the user is allowed to perform that function. The internal data base can include information describing which users can use which functions, on what days, at what times, etc.

Firewalls also can provide a single point of access to the company's network, which could be used to maintain an audit trail. Some firewalls provide summaries to the administrator about the type of traffic and amount of traffic passed through it, number of break-in attempts, etc.

Most commercial firewalls are configured to reject all network traffic that has not been explicitly allowed, thus enforcing the policy, "Only allow traffic that has been categorically permitted, otherwise prohibit." This policy provides much more control and is much safer than a policy which allows traffic unless it has been explicitly prohibited.

Proxy Services. Proxy services support mediation of traffic between a protected network and the Internet by establishing a shielding or screening server address. These services are typically supported by commercial proxy servers, which are sometimes referred to as an application gateway or forwarder. Proxy servers shield outsiders from knowing the specific addresses of servers within the private network (and later targeting them). When a user places a request to access a Web site, the request first goes to that Web site's proxy server; the proxy server makes a request to the Web site, collects the requested information from the Web server and returns it to the user. Proxy servers are application specific and must be able to interpret the application protocol being used. So for example, an HTTP proxy may be configured to block certain HTTP requests and permit other HTTP requests.

Services provided by firewall software and proxy software are converging. What previously was supported by proxy servers becomes part of firewall software in the next releases, and vice versa.

Authentication Services. Authentication is proving one's identity. For secure systems, one or more authentication mechanisms can be used to validate authorized users and to verify which functions and data they have access to. Within the corporate network, authentication services are often included in directory services products like Novell's NDS. NDS requires the user to have an established account and supply a password before access is granted to resources through the directory.

Authentication for accessing resources across an Internet or intranet is a rapidly evolving area. When building e-commerce Web sites there may be a need to restrict access to areas of information and functionality to known customers or trading partners. More granular authentication is required where sensitive individual customer account information must be protected from other customers. Popular Web mechanisms for providing authentication services include:

- *Basic authentication* requires that the Web client supply a user name and password before servicing a request. Basic authentication does not encrypt the password in any way, and thus the password travels in the clear over the network where it could be detected with a network sniffer program or device. Basic authentication is not secure enough for banking applications or anywhere where there may be a financial incentive for someone to steal someone's account information. Basic authentication is however the easiest mechanism to setup and administer and requires no special software at the Web client.

- *ID/password encryption* offers a somewhat higher level of security by requiring that the user name and password be encrypted during transit. The user name and password are transmitted as a scrambled message as part of each request because there is no persistent connection open between the Web client and the Web server.

- *Digital certificates or signatures* are unique digital IDs that identify an individual to a site. They enable organizations to issue, sign and manage public-key certificates for secure, private communication over the Internet or an intranet. Digital certificate schemes like VeriSign's require that some organization issue the certificates in order to guarantee uniqueness and that the recipients are in fact who they say they are. Most digital certificate and signature approaches rely on encryption to guarantee that no tampering has occurred, but as yet no single standard has become wide spread. This may change with the release of Netscape 4.0 with built-in support for VeriSign's certificates.

Encryption Services. Encryption is the process of scrambling bits of information so that it is ideally impossible, or practically not worthwhile, to recover the original message without knowing the appropriate secret key. Encryption has two main components: the encryption algorithm, which is the series of steps performed to transform the original data; and the key, which is used by the algorithm in some way to encrypt the message. Typically, the algorithm is widely known, while the key is kept secret. There are several types of encryption used:

- *Secret key cryptography* uses one key (the secret key) both to encrypt the message on one side and to decrypt the message on the other side.

- *Public key cryptography* uses two keys, the public key and the private key. The public key and private key are mathematically related so that a message encrypted with the recipient's public key may be decrypted with the recipient's private key. Therefore, the public key can be widely published, while the private key is kept secret.

There are also varying methods of employing encryption types described above to encrypt data sent across a network:

- *Data link layer.* Data is encrypted before it is placed on the wire. Data link encryptors are generally hardware products.
- *Application layer.* Data is encrypted by the application. Netscape's Secure Sockets Layer (SSL) is one example of application-layer encryption for Web browsers. SSL uses RSA encryption to wrap security information around TCP/IP based protocols.
- *Network layer.* Data is encrypted inside the network layer header, therefore relying on the network layer protocol.

The advantage of SSL over S/HTTP (discussed earlier) is that SSL is not restricted to HTTP but also can be used for securing other TCP/IP based services such as FTP, Telnet, etc. SSL can provide session level data encryption and authentication to enable secure data communications over public networks such as the Internet.

The need for encryption services is particularly strong where electronic commerce solutions that involve exchanging sensitive or financial data are to be deployed over public networks such as the Internet. Cryptography can be used to achieve secure communications, even when the transmission media (for example, the Internet) is untrustworthy. Encryption services also can be used to encrypt data to be stored (e.g., sensitive product information on a sales person's laptop) to decrease the chance of information theft.

There are complex legal issues surrounding the use of encrypting in an international environment. The U.S. government restricts what can be exported (in terms of encryption technology), and the French government defines encryption technology as a "weapon of war" with appropriate legal and regulatory restrictions. This is a key issue in international e-commerce today.

Web Server Services

Web server services enable organizations to manage and publish information and deploy netcentric applications over the Internet and intranet environments. These services support the following:

- Managing documents in many formats such as HTML, Microsoft Word, etc.
- Handling of client requests for HTML pages. A Web browser initiates an HTTP request to the Web server either specifying the HTML document to send back to the browser or the server program (e.g., CGI and ASP) to execute. If the server program is specified, the Web server executes the program which generally returns a formatted HTML page to

the Web Server. The Web server then passes this HTML page just as it would any standard HTML document back to the Web browser.

- Processing scripts such as common gateway interface (CGI), active server pages (ASP). Server side scripting enables programs or commands to be executed on the server machine providing access to resources stored both inside and outside of the Web server environment. For example, server side scripts can be used to process requests for additional information, such as data from an RDBMS.
- Caching Web pages.   The first time a user requests a Web page, the Web server retrieves that page from the network and stores it temporarily in a cache (memory on the Web server). When another page or the same page is requested, the Web server first checks to see if the page is available in the cache. If the page is available, then the Web server retrieves it from the cache, otherwise it retrieves it from the network. Clearly, the Web server can retrieve the page from the cache more quickly than retrieving the page again from its location out on the network. The Web server typically provides an option to verify whether the page has been updated since the time it was placed in the cache, and if it has to get the latest update.

The following are relevant products for providing or implementing HTTP Web server services:

- *Netscape Enterprise Server.*   This is an enterprise-strength Web server that enables organizations to manage and publish their information and deploy netcentric applications. Netscape Enterprise Server is built on open Internet standards that enable information and applications to scale easily. Supports S-HTTP, Java, and SNMP.
- *Microsoft Internet Information Server (IIS).*   This is an add-on product for NT server that implements basic HTTP services. Future versions of NT Server (4.0 and beyond) will have HTTP features built directly into the operating system.
- *Oracle WebServer.*   This is a multithreaded HTTP server that provides integrated features for translating and dispatching client HTTP requests directly to the Oracle7 Server using PL/SQL™.

Push/Pull Services

Push/pull services allow for interest in a particular piece of information to be registered and then changes or new information to be communicated to the subscriber list. Traditional Internet users "surf" the Web by actively moving from one Web page to another, manually searching for content they want and "pulling" it back to the desktop via a graphical browser. But in the "push" model, on which subscription servers are based , content providers can broadcast their information directly to individual users' desktops. The technology uses the Internet's strengths as a two-way conduit by allowing

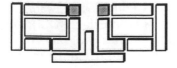

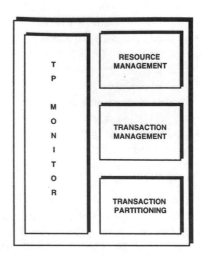

Exhibit 9.   Transaction services.

people to specify the type of content they want to receive. Content providers then seek to package the requested information for automatic distribution to the user's PC.

Depending upon requirements, synchronous or asynchronous push/pull services may be required. Synchronous push/pull services provide a mechanism for applications to be notified in real time if a subscribed item changes (e.g., a stock ticker). Asynchronous push/pull services do not require that a session-like connection be present between the subscriber and the information. Internet ListServers are a simple example. Subscribers use E-mail to register an interest in a topic and are notified via E-mail when changes occur or relevant information is available. Asynchronous push/pull services can be useful for pro-actively updating customers on changes in order status or delivering information on new products or services they have expressed an interest in.

TRANSACTION SERVICES

Transaction services provide the transaction integrity mechanism for the application (Exhibit 9). This allows all data activities within a single business event to be grouped as a single, logical unit of work. In small- to moderate-scale environments of less than 150 simultaneous users on a single server, this service may be provided by the DBMS software with its restart/recovery and integrity capabilities. For larger client/server environments, an emerging class of software, referred to as distributed online transaction managers, is starting to appear. These transaction managers provide sharing of server processes across a large community of users and can be more efficient than the DBMSs.

The following are commonly-used transaction managers:

- *BEA TUXEDO* provides a robust middleware engine for developing and deploying business-critical client/server applications. BEA TUXEDO handles not only distributed transaction processing, but also application and the full complement of services necessary to build and run enterprise-wide applications. It enables developers to create applications that span multiple hardware platforms, data bases and operating systems.
- *IBM's CICS/6000* is an application server that provides industrial-strength, online transaction processing and transaction management for mission-critical applications on both IBM and non IBM platforms. CICS manages and coordinates all the different resources needed by applications, such as RDBMSs, files and message queues to ensure completeness and integrity of data.
- *Transarc's Encina* implements the fundamental services for executing distributed transactions and managing recoverable data, and various Encina extended services, which expand upon the functionality of the toolkit to provide a comprehensive environment for developing and deploying distributed transaction processing.
- *Microsoft's Transaction Server ("Viper")* is a component-based transaction processing system for developing, deploying, and managing high performance, and scalable enterprise, Internet, and intranet server applications. Transaction Server defines an application programming model for developing distributed, component-based applications. It also provides a run-time infrastructure for deploying and managing these applications.

Key transaction services include:

- Transaction monitor services.
- Resource management services.
- Transaction management services.
- Transaction partitioning services.

Transaction Monitor Services

The transaction monitor services are the primary interface through which applications invoke transaction services and receive status and error information. Transaction monitor services, in conjunction with information access and communication services, provide for load balancing across processors or machines and location transparency for distributed transaction processing.

Resource Management Services

A resource manager provides for concurrency control and integrity for a singular data resource (e.g., a data base or a file system). Integrity is guaranteed by ensuring that an update is completed correctly and entirely or not at all. Resource management services use locking, commit, and rollback services, and are integrated with transaction management services.

Transaction Management Services

Transaction management services coordinate transactions across one or more resource managers either on a single machine or multiple machines within the network. Transaction management services ensure that all resources for a transaction are updated, or in the case of an update failure on any one resource, all updates are rolled back.

Transaction Partitioning Services

Transaction partitioning services provide support for mapping a single logical transaction in an application into the required multiple physical transactions. For example, in a package or legacy-rich environment, the single logical transaction of changing a customer address may require the partitioning and coordination of several physical transactions to multiple application systems or data bases. Transaction partitioning services provide the application with a simple single transaction view.

BUSINESS LOGIC

As depicted in Exhibit 10, business logic is the core of any application, providing the expression of business rules and procedures (e.g., the steps and rules that govern how a sales order is fulfilled). As such, the business logic includes the control structure that specifies the flow for processing business events and user requests. There are many ways in which to organize business logic, including rules-based, object-oriented, components, and structured programming.

The execution architecture services described thus far are all generalized services designed to support the application's business logic. How business logic is to be organized is not within the scope of the execution architecture and must be determined based upon the characteristics of the application system to be developed. This section is intended to serve as a reminder of the importance of consciously designing a structure for business logic which helps to isolate the impacts of change, and to point out that the underlying netcentric architecture is particularly well suited for enabling the packaging of business logic as components.

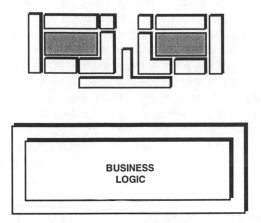

Exhibit 10. Business logic.

The developers of business logic should be shielded from the details and complexity of other architecture services (e.g., information services, component services), and other business logic for that matter.

It is important to decide whether the business logic will be separate from the presentation logic and the data base access logic. Today, separation of business logic into its own tier is often done using an application server. In this type of an environment, although some business rules such as field validation might still be tightly coupled with the presentation logic, the majority of business logic is separate, usually residing on the server. It is also important to decide whether the business logic should be packaged as components in order to maximize software re-use and to streamline software distribution.

Another factor to consider is how the business logic is distributed between the client and the server(s) — where the business logic is stored and where the business logic is located when the application is being executed. There are several ways to distribute business logic:

1. Business logic can be stored on the server(s) and executed on the server(s).
2. Business logic can be stored on the server(s) and executed on the client.
3. Business logic can be stored and executed on the client.
4. Some business logic can be stored and executed on the server(s) and some business logic can be stored and executed on the client, etc.

Having the business logic stored on the server enables developers to centrally maintain application code, thereby eliminating the need to distribute software to client machines when changes to the business logic occur. If all the business logic executes on the server, then the application on the client will make requests to the server whenever it needs to execute a business function. This could increase network traffic, which may degrade application performance. On the other hand, having the business logic execute on the client may require longer load times when the application is initially launched. However, once the application is loaded, most processing is done on the client until synchronization with the server is needed. This type of an architecture might introduce complexities into the application that deal with the sharing of and reliance on central data across many users.

If the business logic is stored and executed on the client, software distribution options must be considered. Usually the most expensive option is to have a system administrator or the user physically install new applications and update existing applications on each client machine. Another option is to use a tool that performs automatic software distribution functions. However, this option usually requires the software distribution tool to be loaded first on each client machine. Another option is to package the application into ActiveX controls, utilizing the automatic install/update capabilities available with ActiveX controls, if the application is launched from a Web browser.

Currently, Internet applications house the majority of the business processing logic on the server, supporting the thin-client model. However, as technology evolves, this balance is beginning to shift, allowing business logic code bundled into components to be either downloaded at runtime or permanently stored on the client machine. Today, client side business logic is supported through the use of Java applets, JavaBeans, Plug-ins and JavaScript from Sun/Netscape and ActiveX controls and VBScript from Microsoft.

Chapter II-2
Communications Architecture

Netcentric computing transforms the old cliché "the network is the computer" into "the network is everywhere." Certainly the topic of networking and communications is on everyone's lips today. The popular and academic journals, professional gatherings, and our firm's work with organizations all bear witness to the fact that people have now realized the scope of communications issues in developing business solutions today.

In netcentric computing, the network is no longer simply a pipe that moves data from point A to point B. Instead, networks are typically composed of a complex set of hardware and software providing a rich set of services that are increasingly more intelligent to keep pace with the requirements of convergence applications.

This chapter explores an architectural model to aid in categorizing and understanding the services that are provided by the network and explores areas in which these services are evolving. Chapter III-3, "Communications Options for Netcentric Implementation," focuses on how specific communication technologies are evolving to support netcentric applications.

WHAT IS THE NETWORK?

The evolving role of the network can be seen in the advent of such concepts as "electronic commerce" and the "virtual enterprise." A network at a hypothetical company in the year 2000 will continue to support traditional types of data traffic within an individual corporate enterprise (i.e., LANs and WANs). However, nontraditional business flows will also need to be supported, as the virtual enterprise introduces new relationships. Companies that produce the final packaged product or service will interact with their suppliers through a seamless information infrastructure. In addition, the need to support an ever-increasing base of public access from home and mobile locations further stretches and redefines the old network boundaries. As computing becomes more distributed and pervasive, the role of the network will grow to support and enable this exchange of content between any point that generates or uses information.

Thus the domain of the network may be defined as the portion of the overall enterprise technology architecture that supports the movement of knowledge in a digital, electronic format between different locations. To provide this capability, the network is composed of communications hardware, software, and services. The network does not include the computing platforms, knowledge technologies, or business logic and applications. However, all network components must provide well-defined services and interfaces to interact effectively with these other technology components.

GUIDING PRINCIPLES

How is this definition of a network any different from the way the role of the network is perceived today? At first glance, the answer may be, "Not much." However, some fundamental concepts are introduced here that are keys to how network architectures will be viewed in the foreseeable future. While the following guiding principles affect all aspects of near-term computing architectures, their specific impacts to the network domain will guide the characteristics of future network architectures.

- *Individuals.* The physical network infrastructure is shifting to support more dynamic human-to-human communications styles, instead of the traditional, precise computer-to-computer communications. Until now, application requirements were the sole driver for network designs. Now, with interaction styles mimicking more human traits, networks must incorporate multimedia, workflow, collaboration, and other qualities that better support how different individuals use the network.
- *Mobility.* As individuals drive out new requirements, an "anywhere, anytime" computing paradigm must be addressed to support new classes of personal devices. These new devices no longer follow the "bigger, better, faster" characteristics of legacy workstations and servers and hosts, but rather the "smaller, cheaper, faster" characteristics of phones, personal digital assistants (PDAs), and laptop computers. This forces the network to support more devices, more variety of devices, and the added overhead of intermittent connectivity.
- *Distributed structures.* Whereas most enterprises are still extremely hierarchical, some are learning how to flatten their reporting structures by providing more autonomy, which requires vendors to provide systems that support distributed data, applications, and infrastructure. However, as the network is the only part of the infrastructure that has a logical and physical end-to-end view of all resources, the network architecture will need to provide services to help manage processes that transcend central implementation.
- *The virtual enterprise.* As more enterprises begin to partner and cooperate, networks will need to support relationships with services that

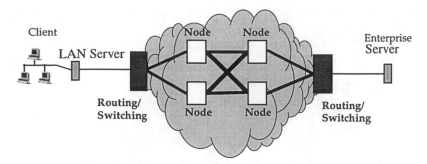

Exhibit 1.   A client/server network separated by LAN and WAN.

never had to exist before. The challenge to the network architecture is not in providing the connections, but in enabling the end-to-end processes associated with them. Many of these processes will require the network to provide independent, reliable, dynamic services that transcend organizational boundaries.

* *Open network services and interfaces.* The network architecture must support common, open network services and interfaces that are easily shared. Not only must there be well defined standards that can be shared between the client and server, but an "intelligent network" role will need to exist to help proxy capabilities, as well. This will allow more rapid expansion of enterprises as they take advantage of virtualization.

THE NETWORK ARCHITECTURE

Exhibit 1 represents a form of a client/server network with the enterprise server and the client separated by a local area network (LAN) and a wide area network (WAN). The WAN cloud could represent an intranet, the Internet, or a number of other kinds of networks that provide WAN connectivity.

In Chapter II-1, a netcentric execution architecture was presented. Exhibit 2 is the high-level view of the architecture. The components of the architecture that represent the network architecture have been colored gray.

The Communications Services component on the client and server and the communications fabric component represent a high-level view of the communications architecture. The client and server components of this architecture, represented in Exhibit 3, were discussed in Chapter II-1. The remainder of this chapter focuses on a description of the communications fabric portion of the netcentric architecture.

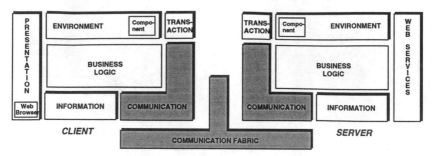

Exhibit 2.   The netcentric execution architecture.

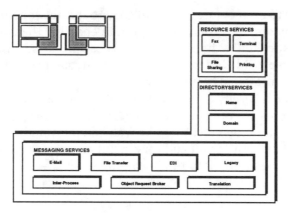

Exhibit 3.   The client and server components of the extended client/server architecture.

THE COMMUNICATIONS FABRIC

The communications fabric is the portion of the network architecture that provides common network services to platform-specific network services residing on the client and server nodes. In Exhibit 1, the communications fabric includes all the hardware, software, and services between the client and server nodes. These common network services can be used to perform network functions across the enterprise or between enterprises. Common network services provided by the communications fabric can be further divided into two main sub-architectures: intelligent network services and the physical network media layer, as shown in Exhibit 4.

Current client/server architectures are predominantly based on legacy LAN technologies, which place the burden of networking intelligence at the

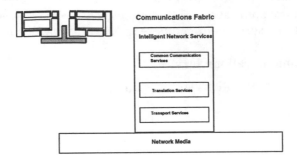

Exhibit 4.   Common network services.

client and server nodes. Today's network architecture does not typically provide intelligent network services and functionality is limited only to the physical network media.

Limiting functionality in the communications fabric avoids additional overhead, thus enabling higher theoretical bandwidth in traditional, hierarchical LAN-based client/server architectures. However, this architecture style begins to inhibit performance when it must support the communications requirements between a diverse set of devices and resources. Because the physical network media does not support intelligent networking services, a more cumbersome solution is used, in which most of the management, control, and proxy functions are shifted to the client and server nodes.

With more intelligence at the end nodes, each client and server must negotiate and maintain information about each resource available or required. The overhead to maintain information at the client and server not only slows responsiveness but also reduces the accuracy of finding the resources required.

To support the communications requirements outlined by the guiding principles described earlier in this chapter, organizations are starting to see a shift toward more intelligence residing in the network itself, acknowledging the network as, in a sense, a standalone system that provides intelligent shared network services. The evolution of these intelligent network services will entail a major shift in the design of network architectures over the next five years.

INTELLIGENT NETWORK SERVICES

As represented in Exhibit 4, intelligent network services do the following:

* Manage and control common communications services for end nodes.

87

- Provide standard and proxy translation services for end nodes.
- Provide transport services that effectively isolate any common communications services from differences in physical network media.

Common Communications Services

Common communications services has three subcategories:

- Directory
- Security
- Messaging

These categories are also found in the client and server portions of the netcentric architecture, but their focus in the communications fabric changes. This change in focus is worth exploring.

Directory. Directory services enable nodes to address other virtual resources. Directory services accomplish this by providing a naming service and domain service that maps all logical names and physical names that a resource may be known by. In addition, directory services track unique context information for each resource. This context information may include such information as the type of resource, age or version, and access rules and size, and it could be used by the requesting node to determine if a resource should even be requested.

In a fully distributed directory system, the communications fabric serves as the main manager for the resource information. While the directory system itself can be distributed, such as in the case of netware directory services (NDS), centralizing management within the communications fabric allows a more dynamic and accurate repository to exist for end nodes and users.

Most of today's organizations still are primarily hierarchical, and domain services can be controlled by the nodes. It is usually clear to which organization structure a node belongs; therefore, resources mapped to a physical and logical organization structure are either mapped 1:N or N:1. However, in more virtual environments, a node may belong to multiple entities, in which case resources are shared and access control is unclear. This is a case of an N:N mapping and requires knowledge of domains to track the different overlapping relationships. To manage this, directory services need to reside in the communications fabric, because it is the only part of the overall architecture which directly has both a physical and logical view of all system resources.

It is unclear whether directory products in use today (e.g., Novell's Netware Directory Services and Banyan's StreetTalk) can evolve to support the needs of the virtual enterprise. A class of "meta" directory service products may begin to emerge that work to provide inter-directory synchronization and resolve names across systems.

Security. Security services provide capabilities to maintain common information necessary for the communications fabric to establish a known level of trust between the different nodes and resources. Security functions will also exist within the physical network, to provide a separate layer of access protection, and they can be implemented with tools such as line encryption systems and firewalls.

One aspect of security services is authentication, which is focused on verifying that a node requesting resources is who it states it is, and that it has authorization to use the resource. Whereas this type of activity can occur at the data or application level of the architecture, the network must also provide a level of security services to prevent an un-authenticated packet from ever reaching the resource. Within the communications fabric, authentication can be provided by different mechanisms:

- *Proxy servers can act as a gateway device providing a virtual resource.* The proxy server's main purpose is to serve as a trusted client which has access to resources and provides those resources indirectly to other clients. Whereas these functions also overlap with virtual resource functionality, the key purpose of proxy implementations is to provide a centrally managed security solution from which access rights can be controlled. Examples of proxy server implementations include Internet gateways.
- *Security servers provide a single repository for all user IDs, access rights, and privileges.* A security server provides a common interface and security protocol for all technical architecture components, including the network. These other components would use this repository for authenticating access. This not only enables single sign-on capabilities, but also provides a trusted source of security information that is maintained separate from the execution environment. Examples of security servers can range from PIN-number enabled calling cards to token based devices such as Security Dynamics' SecureID product.
- *Monitoring is a passive security function that tracks and logs events in the communications fabric.* By establishing a set of event thresholds in conjunction with monitoring, the security function can alert applications and initiate a set of actions to deal with any unauthorized intrusions. By distributing monitoring between the three system roles (Client, Communications Fabric, and Server), correlated events also can be tracked to provide an even more sophisticated set of responses.

Messaging. The purpose of the messaging service is to ensure that the packet received by intelligent networking services is properly forwarded to its logical destination. Messaging services residing in the communications fabric, whether provided by a public EDI or private mail system, are not the end receiver of the message. However, the communications fabric must still understand enough about a particular message stream to help identify where or how a message needs to be routed.

The messaging service must also provide stream management to track and recover from any errors in the sending of the original massage, and reroute messages based on the addressing information used in message management. If the information is time sensitive, messages may need to be requeued. Additionally, resources may request and receive simultaneous access to multiple resources. This requires a need to prioritize across the different streams servicing each access request.

The messaging service must also monitor the messaging system. This need is very apparent considering a style of store-and-forward communications, such as the message-handling system (MHS). For example, if one person sends a mail message through Microsoft Mail to a person on cc:Mail via a MHS gateway and the gateway is down, part or all of the message might be lost. This is extremely important for client/server architectures that are time-sensitive (e.g., high-transaction reservation systems and trading systems) or that require a high degree of simultaneous exchanges between concurrent resources (e.g., agent-driven, collaborative environments).

Translation Services

The purpose of translation services is to provide a proxy interface with network services residing on the client or server (or other origination and destination nodes). These services allow each end of the communications to be unaware of the other, even if the functions or protocols implemented on the ends are different. Products that provide this capability have been generically referred to as gateways. In most cases gateways, such as Microsoft's SNA Server, will also need to provide translation at the network media layer, as well.

This section explores four subcategories of translation services:

- Directory translation.
- Security translation.
- Message translation.
- Virtual resource translation.

Directory Translation. Directory translation is not typically found today. Most architectures expect the client and server resources to use the same directory structure. This is mostly because directory services reside on an end node and are not fully distributed yet. As these services mature, more examples will exist. Some limited use of directory translation exists today to support migration within a vendor implementation (e.g., compatibility between Novell's Bindery Service and Novell's Netware Directory Service) or for unique custom architectures, such as computer telephony integration (e.g., CTI software to convert from PBX numbers to an electronic user phone list).

Security Translation. Security translation is needed when the primary security protocol utilized by the each of the end nodes is different. Today, most architectures expect the client and server resources to use the same security structure, so security translation services are not widely implemented yet. Once again, this is mostly because of security residing on an end node and not being fully distributed. An example is Security Dynamic's security server, which has multiple protocol interfaces so that it can converse with resources that may be running a client portion of their proprietary protocol, or can converse with some standard protocols, such as TACACS. Only rudimentary translation is required, as the security server can understand and process the requests of both types of devices.

Message Translation. The message translation function provides two types of support for communications between unlike systems:

- A conversion for systems that operate with different character representations.
- A protocol conversion for systems that cannot communicate directly using lower-level internetworking devices. An example of this is changing formats between E-mail and fax messages. This would allow someone to "listen" to e-mail or read voice mail.

Virtual Resource Translation. The actual virtual resources, as described in Chapter II-1, tend to be located on the end nodes to best support interaction with the resources owned by the operating system on each end node. However, when migrating from one environment to another, a virtual resource translator may be implemented in the communications fabric to isolate the client and the server or host from changes within each of those environments. This function is typically performed by a gateway.

Gateways can translate within a virtual resource type. For example, terminal translation functions are intended to allow a workstation to emulate the keyboard and screen of a remote device. Once a control session is established, the remote user is effectively on the host computer and can do anything a user actually sitting at the host computer can do. An example of this is Microsoft SNA Server. Its purpose is to translate from a sessionless, bit-oriented PC screen to a session-based, character 3270 screen. Another example could also be remote control software, such as PCAnywhere. In this instance, the remote workstation maps keyboard commands to the host device.

Gateways also can help translate between the different input/output (I/O) formats of each of the messaging services (e.g., terminal, fax, print, and file services). Each of these delivers I/O as a form of audio, text, or image format. To allow information to be shared between applications requiring these services, gateways that translate between message type are used to convert the data format. For example, fax-to-print conversions are regularly bundled with most fax servers. Another example is consolidated messaging architectures offered by communications providers that allow voice mail (phone), E-mail (terminal), and paging messages to be interchangeable and shared by different device types.

Transport Services

The function of the transport services layer is to provide a translation service between the transport services on the client(s) and on the servers or hosts. This layer of translation effectively isolates any common communications services from differences in physical network media. This is important as the network begins to transform itself from a LAN-based architecture to one that is driven by public access across point-to-point connections. This requires the communications fabric to provide services that match to the transport architecture of the end nodes. Open and published transport standards are critical for organizations moving from "transport-less" LAN architectures to switched architectures that use transport services.

In most cases, the transport services are implemented as part of the overall transport protocol architecture. Examples of these implementations in a data-oriented architecture are:

- *Sequence Packet Exchange (SPX)* SPX is a connection-based service used in Netware by Novell. It reliably delivers data and notifies the user if any errors occur during data transmission. Upon encountering a data transmission error, SPX retries a certain number of times before closing the connection and notifying the connection user. SPX also notifies the user if a disconnection indication is received from the remote connection endpoint.
- *Transmission Control Protocol (TCP)* TCP provides a connection oriented, reliable, byte stream service. TCP, not the application, decides how much data to send. TCP is connection oriented in the sense that the user must establish a connection prior to beginning communication.

Exhibit 5 breaks transport services into a number of subservices. The following section will explore each of these in order.

Connection Control. The connection control service is responsible for establishing, terminating, and maintaining the connections between processes. Traditionally, this service was performed on an end-to-end basis. That is, the connection was managed between the sender and receiver. However,

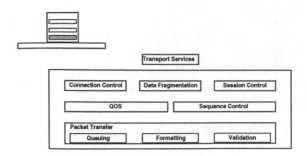

Exhibit 5. Transport services.

due to the complexity of networking today, the communications fabric is being included in this functionality. The functions performed by connection control are:

- Establishing a connection.
- Terminating a connection.
- Monitoring session control for traffic.
- Notifying participants if connection is terminated.

The connection control service within the communications fabric becomes involved when the information being transferred takes on different forms or encounters a long delay as part of the normal process. For example, if a remote user with a personal digital assistant (PDA) gains access to a LAN system via a wireless gateway, the connection control would establish a connection between the PDA and the wireless gateway while another connection would be established between the gateway and the LAN resource.

Data Fragmentation. The data fragmentation service provides a similar set of functions as the connection control service just described. Data fragmentation performed at a transport services level is an end-to-end process. The functions performed by data fragmentation include:

- Reading the content header information.
- Partitioning the data into smaller units.
- Communicating with the sequence control to accept the data stream.

The communications fabric implementation of data fragmentation is also required, because of the possibility that there will be multiple types of components that are encompassed in the communications fabric between the sender and receiver. Some of these components may have different limits on frame and packet sizes. Therefore, if the original sender does not know of all the components within the path to the receiver, the data fragmentation service is required to fragment the data packets further.

Session Control. One of the functions of session control within the communications fabric is to manage dialogue. With some systems, the order of communications must be managed. If the end processes communicate in a one-way interactive session, a mediator is required to determine who goes next in the session. This dialogue management is clearly seen in a token-based network where the session control service acts as the administrator of the token.

Another function of session control is synchronization, through which checkpoints are inserted and deleted. This function is used to recover from failures during a large transfer. If a communication transfer terminates abruptly, the session control synchronization would report the last checkpoint as the place where the transfer needed to resume.

Quality of Service. In the context of multimedia and high speed protocols, QOS-parameters like throughput and response time become an important issue. In the last decade, the functionality and transmission capability of networks has changed dramatically. As a consequence, new protocol mechanisms are required to establish the standards of communication. New protocols are being created (e.g., NETBIT) and existing protocols are being modified (e.g., IPV6) to achieve a negotiated quality of service across the network. The following table lists the functions that are typically supported by QOS.

Parameter	Description
Connection establishment delay	The time between the connection request and a confirmation received by the user
Connection establishment failure probability	The probability that the connection will not be established within the maximum establishment delay
Throughput	In bits per second (bps) of user transmitted data
Transit delay	The time from transport sender to transport receiver
Residual error rate	The fraction of total messages that can be lost or garbled in the sampling period
Transfer failure probability	The fraction of the time when the throughput, transit delay, or residual error do not meet the rates agreed upon at the start of the connection
Connection release delay	The time between the initiation of the release and the other end performing the release
Connection release failure probability	The fraction of release attempts which did not succeed
Protection	The parameter that specifies the desire to have a secure connection
Priority	Indicates the priority of the traffic over the connection
Resilience	The parameter giving the probability of the transport layer spontaneously terminating

Sequence Control. The sequence control reorganizes packets into the original order in which they were sent. This is performed by the communications fabric in the event that during the process of communication, a point is reached at which a large amount of buffering is taking place. Here, the sequence control would buffer and reorganize the transmission and retransmit the data in its original order.

Packet Transfer. The packet transfer service performs three functions:

- *Queuing.* Provides buffering for data streams when the stream is being translated into a different format.
- *Formatting.* Performs a function of reinstalling header information on a new and perhaps, fragmented packet.
- *Validation.* Performs filtering on packets not meant for a particular system or node.

An Internet firewall is a common example today of validation services. Firewall security controls are built on addressing services to filter packets entering and leaving the secure portion of the communications fabric without making Internet access prohibitively difficult for the end user. State-of-the-art firewalls offer management control over secure Internet and intranet resources.

In short, they combine access control mechanisms, detailed logging, usage and chargeback reports, intrusion detection capabilities and graphical administrative interfaces to provide secure, managed access network solutions.

Exhibit 6 illustrates a basic logical location of a firewall. As shown, any access to the corporate backbone to access resources, whether it be internal or external, must pass through a security firewall.

NETWORK MEDIA

The final piece of the communications fabric description is the physical network media. The network media includes all physical Internetworking components, as well as the physical networking components on the client and server. This discussion is framed around a discussion of on-premise and off-premise components of the physical network.

The network media can be divided into three subdomains, as seen in Exhibit 7.

The enterprise has control over the on-premise domains and can determine implementation standards and products. This has been the only consideration of legacy LAN-based architectures. Two on-premise domains are shown in the figure to reflect the domains of the originating node or client, and the receiving node or resource. Examples of on-premise domain tech-

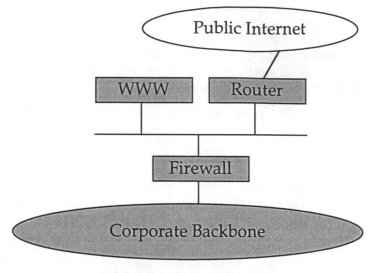

Exhibit 6.   A security firewall.

Exhibit 7.   Subdomains of the Network Media.

nologies and components include office LANs, campus fiber optics, satellite interface units and POTS service.

Off-premise domains are environments in which use is either restricted (usually by government), or standards are dictated by other entities. This is the domain of regulated technologies. Examples of off-premise domain technologies include RF use (e.g., frequency and power), access lines (CO trunks), and carrier services (IntraLATA, InterLATA).

Today's network architectures must provide an off-premise component in every architecture. The reality is that users are mobile and require more publicly available solutions for more open communications access. The key to designing around off-premise technologies is knowledge about interfaces and other restrictions for available off-premise solutions.

In addition, this network media architecture requires the network architect to develop operational and management requirements far earlier in the process. These requirements are necessary for selecting the off-premise technology, where choices may be available. Additionally, these requirements will most likely factor into the service level agreements needed to support business requirements.

On-Premise

The on-premise portion of network media provides for connectivity from the client or server to an access network. In legacy LAN architectures, this was one and the same. However, with the proliferation of devices, the on-premise network architectures on each end may be different.

An example of different on-premise architectures would be a standalone PC workstation accessing a corporate Web server. Whereas the on-premise network for the PC workstation might include serial RS-232 interfaces, SLIP protocol, and a V.42 modem, the on-premise architecture for the corporate Web server might include 10Base-T Ethernet interfaces and the TCP/IP protocol. An off-premise network is needed to transmit the signal between the locations and adapt to the different protocol types. The services of the on-premise component are:

- Physical interface management
- Physical communication interface
- Addressing services
- Flow control
- Transmission error control
- Regeneration

Physical Interface Management. The physical interface management service is responsible for establishing relationships between the data streams coming into and leaving the network media layer. This service also coordinates if multiple transport service protocols are contending for the same physical interface card.

The functions performed by the physical interface management service are:

- Performing conversions between physical and logical addresses.
- Binding physical addresses from addressing services to local port addresses.
- Coordinating with the flow control, regeneration, and transmission error control services when notified by the physical communications interface that a network interface is receiving data.

An example of product implementation for physical interface management service is the network driver interface specification (NDIS) from Microsoft as part of Windows NT.

Physical Communications Interface. As its name indicates, the physical communications interface is responsible for connecting physically with the network. The functions implemented by the physical communications interface are:

- Communicating with the addressing services to convey formatting information. This function becomes more important when multiple types of interfaces are supported by the same physical device.
- Working with physical interface management to ensure a connection control is established to higher layer services if there is an incoming transmission.
- Specifying the electrical and mechanical characteristics of the physical interface.
- Providing physical connectivity to the medium.
- Providing encryption of the physical interface as necessary.
- Specifying technical parameters of the medium being used.

The physical communications interface informs the physical interface management service of the type of physical connections that are available on a machine. Depending on the hardware vendor, the physical interfaces along with their drivers may be monitored by a performance management system that will measure how well the interface is performing against some predetermined parameters.

During the course of normal operations, the physical communications interface signals the physical interface management of an incoming transmission and the port that it is coming in on. This allows the physical interface management to set up a buffer for the incoming data and to pass along information relating to what protocol the data packets are formatted under to higher layer functions. One example that implements a physical communication interface is an Ethernet protocol. This type of interface specifies individual machine network interface cards (NIC) and their accompanying drivers. These cards have a physical address associated with them that comes from the manufacturer. The NIC card, which is the actual physical interface, communicates with a utility (driver) embedded in the operating system. By interfacing with this driver, multiple higher level protocols can be bound to a single NIC card. In addition to these functions, Ethernet specifies a means of detecting traffic through its physical interface for the reason of optimizing the use of the shared median. It also performs this function to help regulate traffic over the physical link.

Other examples of the physical communications interface are the serial communication specification EIA-232, Integrated Services Digital Network (ISDN), and the Universal Serial Bus (USB).

Addressing Services. Addressing services take the data packets from the transport services layer (packet transfer service) along with instructions from the physical interface management and assign them physical destinations and origination addresses. Because the transport services layer fragments data, the addressing service provides this service for each data packet that needs to be sent over the physical network. Many times, this will take the form of encapsulating the fragmented data stream from the transport layer into a separate and unique structure complete with addressing and sequencing information.

The most common addressing method in use today is the Internet protocol (IP). Also, a common implementation of mapping between an IP address and a physical address is performed by the address resolution protocol (ARP).

Flow Control. Flow control maps transmission speeds between devices. During network communications, a sending machine might have the ability to transmit information at a rate that is different from the receiving machine or intermediate hop.

The functions performed by the flow control service are:

- Communicating with network components to determine throughput rates.
- Interfacing with a data fragmentation service to adjust the size of the data packets as not to overdrive any networking device.
- Regulating the flow of data streams to and from the local system buffer depending upon available system resources. One reason for this to occur is that different network structures and topologies inherently operate at different speeds. This could also result from a node having too much traffic load.

Flow control allows the receiving device to tell the other to pause while it catches up. Flow control exists as either software (XON/XOFF) flow control or hardware (RTS/CTS) flow control. With software flow control, when the networking component needs to tell the other to pause, it sends a certain character, usually Control-S. When it is ready to resume, it sends a different character, such as Control-Q. This type of control is commonly deployed with modems.

Software flow control's only advantage is that it can use a serial cable with only three wires. Because software flow control regulates transmissions by sending certain characters, line noise could generate the character commanding a pause, thus hanging the transfer until the proper character (e.g., Control-Q) is sent. Also, binary files must never be sent using software flow control, as binary files can contain the control characters.

Hardware, or RTS/CTS, flow control uses wires in the modem cable or, in the case of internal modems, hardware in the modem. This is faster and much more reliable than software flow control. Microsoft Windows 95 has a separate control that allows the user to disable the internal software flow control if the user is capable of using an external hardware flow control.

In the Internetworking world, flow control is needed to help reduce congestion. This arises from slower links incorporated with high-speed links in a WAN environment or a single router or switch receiving too many transmissions simultaneously. IP uses the Internet Control Messaging Protocol (ICMP) to help slow down network traffic. ICMP works by transmitting a source quench to the transmitter that is overflowing a receivers buffer.

Transmission Error Control. The transmission error control checks for inaccuracies encountered during transmission. The functions provided by the transmission error control are:

- Reading header fields for information concerning the data packet.
- Computing a checksum.
- Reading a sequence number to track if any information might have been lost during communications.

Through the use of checksums, parity bits, and sequencing, the transmission error control service ensures that any information corrupted during transmission does not go undetected. In addition to direct error detection, this service also determines if data is lost during transmission. In the event that a quantity of data (e.g., packet, datagram, or cell) is not received at a destination, the transmission error control detects the lost information, initiates a recovery procedure, and restructures the data into the proper sequence.

Error correction is the method by which modems verify that the information sent to them has been undamaged during the transfer. Error-correcting modems break up information into small packets, called frames. The sending modem attaches a checksum to each of these frames. The receiving modem checks whether the checksum matches the information sent. If not, the entire frame is resent.

Though error correction may slow down data transfer on noisy lines, it does provide greater reliability. MNP2-4, as well as V.42, are error correction protocols. These protocols determine how the modems verify data. As with data compression protocols, for an error correction protocol to be used, it must be supported by both modems in the connection.

Regeneration. Regeneration service exists to "clean up" the incoming data stream within an individual platform. Packets that are received are retained by the local platform and digitally enhanced to ensure the information can be properly read. These types of systems are usually proprietary and can be part of the physical communications interface.

Off-Premise

The off-premise portion of the architecture may contain all or a subset of the functions described in the on-premise, depending on whether the on-premise nodes use the same or different architectures. If both on-premise nodes use the same network media architecture, the off-premise network will just need to provide regeneration and physical interfaces to support bandwidth needs.

If the on-premise nodes use different network media architectures, the off-premise network needs to mirror all the functions of the on-premise network architecture to translate between the different requirements. An example of this is the case of Internet users dialing into an Internet service provider (ISP) to access an information server. In this case, the remote PCs use a protocol, such as PPP or SLIP, to transmit data to the ISP premises. The protocol is then translated back to IP before being utilized for security and access control validation by the ISP. To complicate matters, because the ISP is actually performing higher level functions (i.e, communications services), it is actually a recursive architecture. The carrier used by the ISP to connect to the information server is itself another off-premise network.

The services of the off-premise component of network media are:

• Physical interface management
• Physical communication interface
• Addressing
• Flow control
• Transmission error control
• Regeneration

Physical Interface Management. Similar to the functions in the on-premise network, the physical interface management tracks the physical port resources available and functioning and allows physical and logical connections to be established over those ports.

The Physical Communications Interface. The off-premise physical communications interface has the same functions as those specified in the on-premise section. A difference between the two is that the off-premise physical communications interfaces will more likely be connecting to public carriers such as AT&T, Sprint, MCI, or a local loop access provider. These will be the connections that connect the remote office sites, corporate offices, and producing facilities to a data communications service provider. These kinds of connections often are much higher speed links than for the on-premise interfaces.

Addressing Services. From the off-premise perspective, addressing services:

- Interact with the on-premise addressing service to determine the best path over which to send data packets.
- Direct the data over the selected path.

In carrying the traffic, the off-premise portion of the network delivers the data stream as part of a connection oriented transmission or a connection-less oriented transmission. In a connection oriented communication session, off-premise addressing services establish a path over which data is transmitted .

In a connectionless system, addressing services communicates with the on-premise service in order to determine the best possible path to take. That is, because off-premise controls the traffic, it must balance the needs of all those who are requesting access. The best possible paths are those with the least amount of connections and having the least amount of traffic at the time of transmission.

An example of a technology that implements this is ATM. In ATM, an optimal route is determined and a virtual circuit is established prior to communications being implemented. Once this path is established, all data is transmitted over that circuit.

An example of a technology that uses a connectionless system is an IP-based routing system. Here, the originator of the transmission sends out a request for routing information. All routers within "hearing range" look up in their internal routing tables for a path. If a path is found, the physical address of that router is sent back to the requester in order to begin the communications process.

In addition to addressing the information over some path, the addressing service needs to be kept current. This results from new end nodes constantly being added and removed from the network. The Internet Gateway Management Protocol (IGMP) and Routing Information Protocol (RIP) are examples of protocols that implement this kind of function in an IP-based Network.

Flow Control. The off-premise flow control logically has two functions:

- Regulating the transmission rates of off-premise components to ensure that no component is overloaded.

- Dynamically allocating or reallocating bandwidth if the amount of traffic increases.

The first function is comparable to the flow control that is described in the on-premise section. This function accounts for communications that may transverse through components or links that operate at slower speeds. The second function exists for those services that have variable bandwidth. That is, the function supports the management of bandwidth so that higher traffic rates can be accounted for.

An example of a service that implements this kind of function would be frame relay service. Here, multiple virtual links from various locations converge on "the cloud," where bandwidth is dynamically allocated to accommodate the streams of bursty traffic. The frame relay protocol implements this using flow control to detect congestion, then requesting the transmitting station to reduce its transmission rate. In this fashion, data packets are not lost or dropped and complete transmissions can be made more efficiently.

Transmission Error Control. On-premise and off-premise transmission error control are similar in nature. One method that is used for off-premise networks is the cyclical redundancy check (CRC). This error-checking technique is required because some communications links can be noisy. This can result in breaks in transmission. CRC is a mathematical technique used to check for errors when sending data.

If the CRC fails to add up, the receiving end of a data transmission sends a NAK (i.e., a negative acknowledgment or a "say that again") signal until it does add up. CRCs are also used in tape backups and other streaming communications.

When an error is detected by transmission error control, it may become necessary to alert the sender that a data packet is corrupted. To accomplish this, this service interacts with an addressing services function to obtain the address of the sender. With this, a message is created that informs the sender that some of the data will have to be retransmitted. Internet Control Message Protocol (ICMP) is an example of how this function is executed within an IP network.

Regeneration. Regeneration services exist to "clean up" the incoming data stream. This "clean up" refers to the reconstruction of the digital stream in order to make the data more easily read by the hardware components. The component that performs this function for a digital signal is referred to as a regenerator. The regenerator's counterpart in the analog world is an amplifier.

CONCLUSION

Today's advanced networking architectures permit organizations to take full advantage of the convergence of computing, communications, and knowledge. Netcentric computing applications provide more direct links with business partners, and allow companies to respond quickly to fluctuations in customer demand. As communications architectures grow in sophistication, one should expect the intelligent network to enable almost total supply chain integration. Applications that manage and perform business-to-business processes will enable the ultimate virtualization of business: bringing together strategy, people, process, and technology in a unique configuration across multiple companies to serve the customer in a more powerful way than any one company could on its own. That will be the final convergence — one in which barriers between companies and their customers have been removed.

Chapter II-3
Transition Architecture

Although the netcentric computing environment today appears to capture everything that is most cutting edge about information technology, the sobering fact is that every astounding solution developed today immediately becomes a legacy solution. Most people think "mainframe computing" when they hear the word "legacy," but of course that isn't true. Somewhere down the road, someone will be complaining about the "dinosaur legacy" of client/server computing (and, eventually, of netcentric computing, as well).

Most information technology professionals look with displeasure on an organization's legacy computing, but from a business point of view, one must remember that those systems house much of the enterprise's critical knowledge and also represent a large investment. No one wants to throw an investment away. If the organization can build on that legacy and transition it to a new environment, the organization can leverage it and get further returns. More important, by ensuring that today's systems can transition to tomorrow's environments, the organization can be confident that its knowledge capital can continue to grow.

The challenge in taking yesterday's systems into tomorrow is, of course, that they are characterized by outdated technology, antiquated technical architecture, and unreliable documentation. Many systems are inflexible and costly to maintain. Unable to justify the cost of maintaining these environments, many businesses are using this as an opportunity to move the business to more technology-enabled netcentric solutions.

The netcentric framework (Exhibit 1) acknowledges that enterprises must be able to tap into the wealth of information and knowledge that exists in today's legacy environments. The transition support layer in the netcentric framework provides for access to all the transactional and analytical information and knowledge that has been collected over the years. Up to this time, nearly all information technology (IT) investments and business solutions relying on IT have been focused on transaction and data-management. However, in the netcentric environment, computing

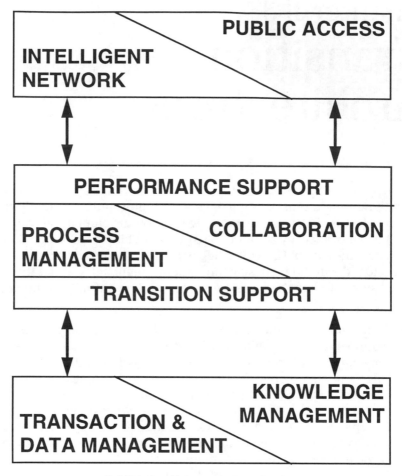

Exhibit 1. Netcentric framework.

solutions seek to obliterate organizational boundaries and provide stakeholders with more flexible, timely, and customized access to a greater array of goods and services. To do so, they must use the IT investments made to date. This transition support provides the reach into the legacy environment to continue to realize return on those investments. As today's solutions become tomorrow's legacy systems, transition support becomes embedded in the solution, making future transitions easier to implement.

Unless organizations can leverage the legacy environments through transition support, new netcentric solutions will necessarily involve reinventing the work that has occurred in the past. So although the netcentric solution from a technological point of view would be leading edge, they would lag behind older technological solutions in terms of the knowledge base represented within the solution. It might take decades to build up their respective knowledge bases to the levels of their predecessors.

This chapter takes a look at some ways of providing transition support through what is called transition architectures. These architectures enable different transition approaches to optimize the business benefits of the legacy environment, while providing a clean path to the new netcentric solution. Although the transition approach should be driven by the overall business strategy, the transition is a system-by-system decision-making process; one approach will not typically suffice for all of an organization's systems. The transition architectures implemented are dependent on the organization's unique situation, the business objectives driving the transition, the status of the legacy systems, and the expected final technology environment.

WHAT IS A TRANSITION ARCHITECTURE?

A transition architecture is made up of tools, techniques, procedures, and standards that enable the integration or interfacing between existing and target solutions through a transition period. This definition implies several things. First, target solutions have been identified. The netcentric framework offers a way of identifying the types of business solutions that will likely be built in the future. Target solutions allow an enterprise to converge on its stakeholders (e.g., customers, suppliers, and regulators), removing the boundaries that once existed between it and its stakeholders. Netcentric solutions also eliminate the boundaries between enterprises, making entire value chains tighter and closer to the stakeholders. These are solutions of the future, not the traditional transaction and data management solutions that IT has provided to date. Organizations need to refocus their IT investments on building netcentric solutions to compete in a shrinking world.

Second, the legacy environment needs to be well understood. This is often not the case. Thirty years of development and patches means that many systems are complicated, undocumented, and impossible to maintain, often because their original developers are no longer with the organization. This situation presents a challenge that needs to be addressed by the transition architecture.

Therefore, transition architectures are integral parts of the overall technology architecture rather than standalone technical architectures. They are components of the development, execution, and operations architectures of the new netcentric solutions. These architectures, therefore, must be viewed as part of the new solution rather than simply maintenance patches on the legacy.

An important factor to consider is that the transition period will likely last many years. That is, moves to netcentric solutions need to be deliberate and well-planned. This means that legacy environments, including processing logic and information, are in place for some time while the new solutions need to use the legacy's assets. Therefore, the transition architecture must be robust enough to be working throughout the transition period.

BENEFITS OF THE TRANSITION ARCHITECTURE

Transition architectures provide substantial benefits to enterprises seeking to move to new technology environments while making the most of the investment in legacy systems. A transition architecture can enable an enterprise to:

- Map the current technology environment to an organization's targeted position using well-defined, business-focused releases that are measurable and manageable.
- Assist in enabling an enterprise for technological change; the people and process aspects of the change also must be addressed through other means.
- Maximize the value of legacy systems and ensure that future systems efficiently interact or integrate with them.
- Leverage existing skills, processes, and technologies to implement change.
- Have better implementation options, because of the set of standards, procedures, and reusable components.
- Make better informed decisions about how to transition to netcentric solutions, which can translate into higher-quality systems and new solutions.

A TRANSITION FRAMEWORK

The transition architecture must encompass all issues associated with moving to new technology and netcentric solutions. The architecture must account for all the legacy system components that could be valuable to the new solution as well as methods to execute, develop, and operate the transition of the components. Just as it is useful to have a framework to assist in identifying new solutions, it is useful to have a framework for the transition strategy. This framework acts as a completeness check: It helps ensure that the transition strategy has accounted for all the issues.

Three key components make up the framework for a transition architecture, as shown in Exhibit 2.

Transition Approach. The transition approach defines the ways in which an enterprise can move from its legacy environment to the netcentric computing paradigm. The transition architecture may have to provide support

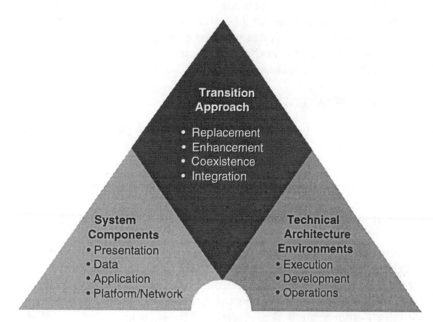

Exhibit 2.   Transition framework.

for one or more of the approaches, especially if the legacy's components can be of high value in the future. The chosen approach, or approaches, is entirely dependent on the organization's vision of the future. Without this vision, it is impossible to pick a rational transition approach.

System Components. The system components are the pieces of the legacy solution that could be leveraged by the new solutions. They include the presentation component of an application (commonly referred to as the user interface), the data, the application code itself, and the hardware platform and network on which the application runs. These components represent the primary investments made by IT over the last 30 years and are therefore pieces that may be of value to the new solution. Organizations must have a thorough understanding of the relative merits of these legacy components to have a rational transition approach and architecture.

Technical Architecture Environments. The transition framework also shows that three environments must be addressed in any transition strategy:

1. execution, or how the architecture will run in production,
2. development, which defines how to build the transition from legacy to new, and
3. operations, or what needs to be done to properly operate the transition architecture.

All three must be considered when designing and building a transition architecture. The consequences of not striking some balance could be a transition architecture that is designed to execute elegantly but cannot be reasonably developed or one that can easily be developed and executes well but is difficult to operate and maintain.

A TRANSITION STRATEGY

Based on the transition framework just discussed, the development of a transition architecture can be divided into three main steps:

- *Determining the transition approach that best fits the business's strategy.* In determining the appropriate transition approach, an enterprise must understand its legacy environment and the direction it needs to reach its vision — its business strategy, objectives, and imperatives. The direction the enterprise needs to go can be used to determine the business value of a solution — that is, an asset that could contribute to the business direction has a higher value than one that cannot. Understanding the legacy environment essentially means knowing what valuable assets of the legacy solution can have a role in the new solution environment. An analysis of these components must determine the relative functional quality (i.e., how well the legacy solution provides for supporting the business processes they were designed for) and the relative technology quality (i.e., how well positioned is the technology environment of the legacy solution relative to the new technology environment).

- *Analyzing and ranking according to priority the system components necessary for the transition from each of the three architectural perspectives: execution, development, and operations.* Next, the transition steps must be identified to implement the chosen approach. Based on the chosen transition approach, these steps define what needs to be done to build the transition architecture, what changes must occur in business and IT processes, and what people and organizational changes are necessary. The steps are then ranked according to priority so a rational plan can be established to move to the new technology environment.

- *Building the transition architecture to assist in the legacy integration with the new solutions.* Finally, as the organization and the business processes are changing, the transition architecture supporting the chosen approach is built. This architecture then allows the enterprise to focus forward toward its technology. So, first, the approach is chosen, and necessary steps are identified, prioritized, and a plan is laid out. Once this done, building the transition architecture to support the organization's move to a new business and technology environment needs to be given the same attention and stature as any comparable application development effort. The actual construction of the transition architecture should be handled as any other IT development effort.

The remainder of this chapter focuses on the transition approaches, presenting a way to determine which approach to use and giving some examples of real scenarios in which each approach was employed.

TRANSITION APPROACHES

"Cheshire-Puss," she began, rather timidly, as she did not at all know whether it would like the name: however, it only grinned a little wider. "Come, it's pleased so far," thought Alice, and she went on. "Would you tell me, please, which way I ought to go from here?"

"That depends a good deal on where you want to get to," said the Cat.

"I don't much care where —" said Alice.

"Then it doesn't matter which way you go," said the Cat.

" — so long as I get somewhere," Alice added as an explanation.

"Oh, you're sure to do that," said the Cat, "if you only walk long enough."

— from Lewis Carroll's *Alice's Adventures in Wonderland*

As enterprises create their annual budgets or map out their three-year plans, they often employ an implementation strategy just to be making progress, without clearly defining the purpose of the implementation. It is common to hear such statements as, "We will deploy all client/server technology" or "We need to move off the mainframe." However, these kinds of statements define only the path to be taken. They do not define the destination. As Cheshire Cat tells Alice, the road you take only matters if you know where you're going.

As shown In Exhibit 3, all organizations are engaged in some initiatives that, if left unaltered, will lead them to what could be called their "current future state."

Often, this end state is one of chance, simply a point reached after being in business long enough. Where an enterprise desires to be is what can be called, by contrast, the "desired future state." Unfortunately, this is infrequently articulated in any actionable way. If it were, there would likely be a vision gap between where the organization is going to end up in its wanderings compared to where it really wants to be.

To reach the desired future state, an organization should build on where it is today. Therefore, the transition approach that should be taken is based on a solid understanding of where the organization is today with respect to

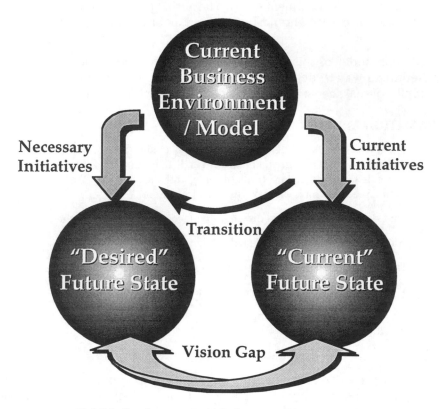

Exhibit 3.   An enterprise's "current future state."

its IT assets and where it wants to go based on solution visions, or "application blueprints," identified through the netcentric framework. An application blueprint is an articulation of a future solution that describes:

- the business functions,
- the manner in which technology (e.g., hardware, software, information and knowledge, and other equipment) might enable the functions and be used by the functions, and
- the effects of the new solution (e.g., changes in skills, organization structure, rewards, and incentives) on the people.

These application blueprints help define the future business value and provide a benchmark against which all current IT assets may be compared.

The matrix in Exhibit 4 pulls together this information to assist an enterprise in determining what transition approach to follow. The selection of an approach during the transition strategy development is a system-by-system

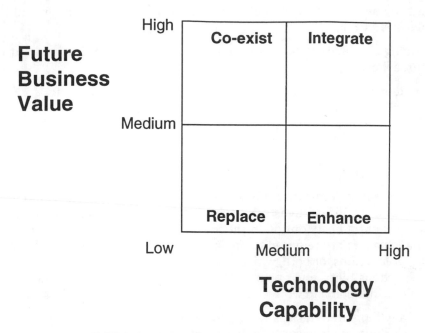

Exhibit 4. Selecting a transition approach.

decision; one approach typically does not suffice for all an organization's systems. By positioning each legacy solution in a quadrant according to a relative scoring of its future business value and its technology capability, IS managers can get an idea of the transition approach to follow to move to the new solution and technology environment.

Future Business Value. This is a determination of how well a legacy solution can contribute to the application blueprints which specify the desired future state. This determination can be based on the components of the legacy solution, such as the integrity of its information or particular functional services or routines in the legacy solution, and does not have to be based on the legacy solution as a whole. In other words, IS managers should determine whether pieces of the legacy system can be broken out and contribute to the future business value.

Technology Capability. The technology capability of a legacy solution is based on the ability of its technology components and architecture to support the new business environment as defined by the application blueprints. This assessment must evaluate user interfaces and interaction, system documentation, stability, ease of maintenance, information accessibility and integrity, extensibility or flexibility to interact with other netcentric solutions, and the ability to add new technology to extend the solutions' reach.

Using this matrix, one arrives at four different types of transition approaches:

- Replacement (low business value, low technology capability)
- Enhancement (low business value, high technology capability)
- Coexistence (low technology capability, high business value)
- Integration (high technology capability, high business value)

Replacement

A system with low future business value and technology capabilities requires a significant investment to maintain and transition, which makes replacement a likely option in this case. Major functional and technical enhancements are required to ensure that the system can reliably share data or functions, or both, with other systems. Also, a system's lack of stability, extensibility, and openness indicate that functional enhancements would be difficult and would likely act to further destabilize the system.

Is anything from the legacy solution salvageable? This is a key question to ask prior to undertaking a replacement approach. Generally, the years of data and knowledge that are stored within the legacy's data bases is of some value. There are at least two ways to maintain the value of this data:

1. convert the data to be usable and store it within the new solutions environment, or
2. use the data in parallel with the new system to compare results and assist in testing the accuracy of the new solution.

The replacement option is often favored by organizations looking for cost savings from a standard technology architecture. Organizations may also seek to use the new solution as a catalyst for other changes, such as alterations in the business processes affected by the new solution. Because this approach carries high costs and risks, significant business benefits must be identified before it is applied. If the benefits to the business are minimal, changing technology for the sake of technology alone should be avoided. Such a transitional approach may be appropriate when the application is adequate by itself but is unable to operate with other system environments. Moving to a new platform, language, or data base management system (DBMS) may also make future application changes easier to implement given better tools and skills. Exhibit 5 shows the implications of a replacement strategy for the other aspects of the transition framework: system components and technical architecture.

A development architecture will ensure an accurate and comprehensive understanding of the system components that will be replaced. The

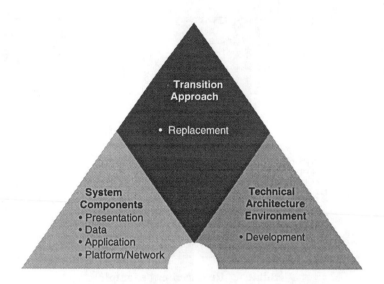

Exhibit 5.   Implications of a replacement strategy.

requirements for additional execution and operations architecture components are dictated by the target platform. The execution and operations impacts are much greater when the target environment is new to the enterprise. This is often the case when re-hosting mainframe applications to a new (e.g., UNIX) platform.

An example of an appropriate replacement approach is upsizing. The enterprise may benefit from making a single-user application available to the whole department. An example of this approach might be a PC-based dBASE-IV application that had been developed for single use but was migrated to Sybase on UNIX when others decided they wanted access to the application.

Another replacement example involved a large government agency that completely replaced an old, outdated and inflexible benefits system. A development tool was built to allow the agency to compare payments coming out of the new system with the most recent payments made by the old. This enabled the agency to quickly identify any significant differences and make manual payments if needed. This approach was needed due to the large number of payments that were processed and the importance and visibility of the system. The execution architecture components developed assisted in testing the validity of the replacement system (Exhibit 6) during the six month transition period.

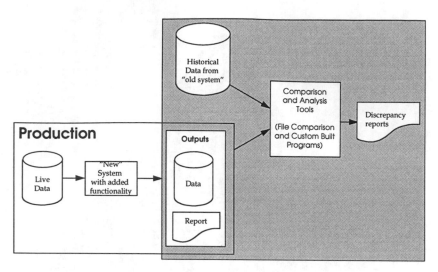

Exhibit 6. Replacement example.

Enhancement

A system with low future business value but good technology capabilities is a strong candidate for an enhancement architecture approach. Such a system is typically stable, it has been architected well, and its data integrity is acceptable. The system is often reasonably well-documented and provides a sound technical basis for the future. Functional enhancements may be the easiest way to address the future business needs specified in the application blueprints. This may be a good short-term approach while a better and possibly more strategic functional solution is being implemented. In this case, however, care should be taken to ensure that appropriate analysis is done beforehand to confirm the validity of such an approach (i.e., confirming requirements, functional fit, and its technological ability to support the vision).

With the enhancement approach, the existing application's functionality is enhanced through a new release. A fine line separates traditional maintenance and an enhancement-transition approach. Maintenance is an activity that is performed to keep the legacy running to support the way business is currently conducted. Enhancement, on the other hand, is an improvement process to allow the legacy to support the new business, as represented in the application blueprints.

Enhancing the existing application is often beneficial because it can offer a fast and cost-effective way to address the business issues identified. Such an approach is most appropriate when existing applications are well-structured

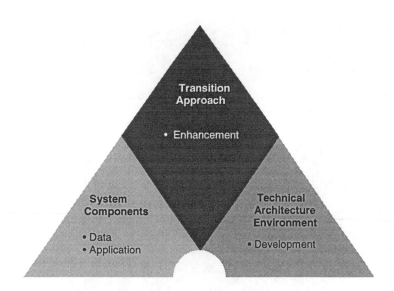

Exhibit 7. Implications of an enhancement strategy.

and relatively easy to maintain. In addition, this approach is best used when the organization's business requirements do not dictate the need for a new technology environment. Exhibit 7 shows the implications of an enhancement strategy for the other aspects of the transition framework: system components and technical architecture.

A good development architecture will ensure appropriate implementation of the application's new release, allowing a thorough understanding of the existing systems in preparation for the enhancement. Impact on the operations and execution environment is typically minimal because the technical environment (hardware, network, system software, data base management system) remains unchanged as a result of the enhancement.

An illustration of the enhancement approach can be taken from a consumer products company that sought to restructure the numbering approach used to identify its products. The company had determined that its future business was going to take it into more and different products. The application blueprints had specified the need to be able to offer these new products in very short time frames. The old product codes were inflexible and caused difficulty in introducing new products. The company restructured by consolidating product codes and including additional product information to identify each product uniquely. Because the client faced no need to move to a new technology environment, it developed an

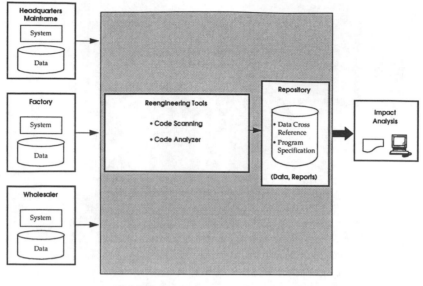

Exhibit 8. Enhancement example.

enhancement architecture that analyzed existing applications for change impacts. Again, the architecture consisted of a methodology and supporting development architecture components, such as code-scanning tools. These tools were instrumental in performing the high-volume scanning and decomposition. They also provided several reports to aid the analysts at all stages of the project (Exhibit 8).

Coexistence

If the legacy solution has high future business value but low technology capability, coexistence is an appropriate transition approach. Future value can be defined in many ways. Data bases in the legacy may contain information that will be needed in the future. Certain application functions may embody business process knowledge that could not easily be recreated or replaced.

In spite of the value in this legacy solution, however, some technology used by the solution might limit its ability to actually deliver this value in the new business environment. For example, a new application blueprint for a manufacturer envisions that customers will have direct access to the work-in-process, thus allowing them to better plan for receiving the finished product. The manufacturer's mainframe solution might contain all the information in which the customers would be interested, but the mainframe technology would limit its ability to provide direct access to the customers.

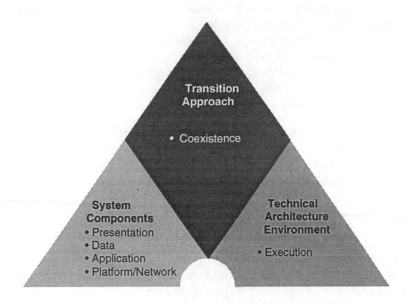

Exhibit 9. Implications of a coexistence strategy.

In this case, a coexistence approach might provide for newer, distributed presentation technology to put on the front end of the work-in-process data base, permitting the legacy to coexist in the new business environment. Exhibit 9 shows the implications of an enhancement strategy for the other aspects of the transition framework: system components and technical architecture.

The execution architecture for coexistence challenges the current notions regarding the legacy solution's presentation, data, application, and platform/network components. New technology is integrated with old in order to take advantage of new capabilities while leveraging assets from the legacy such as data or application functions. In a netcentric environment, the execution architecture's platform and network are often taxed heavily as new capabilities are driven closer to the customers, who now have access to data and application functions they never did before.

An example of the coexistence strategy involved a major credit-card processor that wanted to provide better customer service by opening a direct channel to all its customers: member banks, merchants, and end consumers. The member banks had IT departments and technology-support organizations, but few merchants and no end-consumers had such support. Because of the large and varied customer base, the solution needed to give the customers an intuitive user interface that was easily distributed to all customers. The credit-card processor had a large investment in its old mainframe CICS/DB2 solution; in addition, the information in the data base had maintained its integrity over the years and had performed well. Because the credit-card processor was eager to leapfrog its competition and get a solution out quickly, the organization created a coexistence architecture that used Internet technologies.

The biggest challenge in implementing this architecture was to integrate a set of technologies that had been used as an information publishing medium with pieces of the legacy transaction-processing application. The key to this coexistence architecture was a set of Java applets on a Web server that were able to communicate with CICS on the mainframe. A messaging middleware product was used on the mainframe to receive messages from and send messages to the Java applets on the Web server and perform the actual communication with CICS.

The Internet technologies provide a rich user interface, and minimize most of the age-old issues of application configuration management and software/hardware compatibility in a highly distributed environment. They also provide relatively easy and consistent access to the application, regardless of whether the customer is a sophisticated IT shop, such as member banks, or an individual end consumer. The solution is also fairly secure and virus-resistant for the customers (Exhibit 10).

Exhibit 10.   Coexistence example.

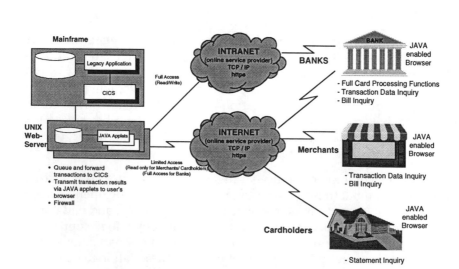

Integration

In those environments in which the future business value and technology capability is high for a legacy solution, and the legacy must work with other systems in the new environment, some form of integration is often desirable. This allows the enterprise to continue to realize a return on its investments over the years in the legacy and leverage the knowledge that has gone into its creation. There are two ways of integrating legacy with new solutions: data integration and application integration.

Integrating the legacy solution into the new solution environment is potentially the easiest transition approach. It is also potentially the most difficult. IT departments have been using a form of the data integration approach for years, as file extracts were created from a source system, transferred to the target system either electronically or mechanically by tapes or disks, and then loaded into the target's data base. This is a fairly straightforward transition approach that leverages the legacy's data by using it for purposes other than that for which it may have been originally intended. On the other end of the spectrum, however, there are now emerging requester or broker techniques using object-oriented (OO) or componentware technology. These complex architectures assist in the isolation of functions, services, or data within the legacy and the creation of application programming interfaces (APIs) with which to access them. New solutions can then utilize the functions, services, or data from the legacy by using the APIs.

Data Integration Approach. A data integration architecture approach is recommended when a system has basic data integrity. This type of system often effectively addresses the organization's business requirements and does not require immediate functional enhancements. Systems of this nature often excel in capturing and recording transactional data but do a poor job of providing analytical or decision support from this data base. Even though the system's technology capabilities may not be sufficient to enable its functions to be used by other systems, it may permit data to be exchanged in a reliable manner.

Data integration is the most flexible of all transition approaches because it enables the organization to move at the desired speed toward its vision, with the enterprise's objectives and goals as its driver. This approach, however, generates additional costs, as development and support skills are required for two environments. The IT organization may also need a support group for the data integration architecture itself.

Many organizations are also pursuing a data integration transition strategy to consolidate data from their transactional systems into a data warehouse for enhanced analysis or decision support capabilities. Data integration is also appropriate when systems covering a large functional area of a business (e.g., financials) are being consolidated into an integrated system. This scale of transition may take place over a few years requiring systems of similar function to coexist.

There are two basic types of data integration, asynchronous store-and-forward architecture and near real-time asynchronous architecture.

- *Asynchronous store-and-forward architecture.* This probably is the most straightforward of all transition approaches; it is also what IT departments have chosen for years. This is the "create extract file, transfer file, load file" scenario for sharing data from one system to another. Generally executed in batches of data, it is reacting to some particular time schedule. The asynchronous store-and-forward architecture is easy to develop and relatively easy to maintain. Maintenance is only needed when a file or data base structure changes on either end, which causes the extract file format to change. The architecture is also relatively easy to operate; if the file does not transfer properly, one simply tries again. This is a very appropriate transition approach when the new systems need the legacy data but do not need it in real-time, or when the integration architecture needs to be developed quickly.

- *Near real-time asynchronous architecture.* The second type of data integration is a much more complex architecture that requires more sophisticated automation and capabilities. Here, the transfer of information is usually triggered by a wider variety of events, such as a change in state of the legacy data or a business process event. These events trigger the architecture to extract a small piece of legacy information and send it to the target environment for processing. At the heart of this architecture is a guaranteed message and data delivery system that ensures that once information is put in the architecture, it eventually will get delivered.

As information updates occur that need to be replicated to other platforms or data bases, the updates are first performed and committed to the local data base, and then the replication architecture guarantees that the replicated target data bases will eventually be made consistent through a guaranteed message delivery system. Several middleware or messaging products offer much of this capability. This is a concept called "eventual consistency," which says that the data in both systems will eventually be consistent. This architecture delivers the data immediately, but the two systems are not synchronized in real-time. This architecture is explained in an example later.

Another approach for sharing data between two or more systems in real-time requires extremely complex two-phase commit processing and is not generally acceptable as a transition approach for data integration.

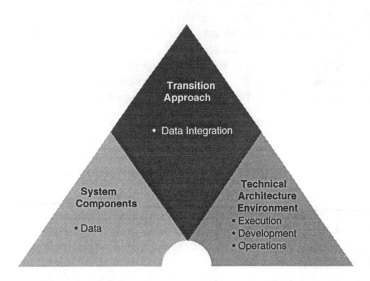

Exhibit 11.   Implications of a data integration approach.

Two-phase commit protocols exist in leading data base products but generally only work between data bases from the same vendor. Unfortunately, when transitioning from legacy systems to new technologies, the environment is usually heterogeneous from both a platform and data base product perspective. Exhibit 11 shows the implications of a data integration strategy for the other aspects of the transition framework: system components and technical architecture.

To achieve the required integrity, the synchronization among data must be defined as part of the business requirements and service levels. In some cases, overnight batch updates may be sufficient, while in other cases, immediate synchronization may be required. Each business function should be analyzed independently to define the synchronization require ments. In order to enable data synchronization in both execution and operations environments, interface components will be required. For example, application data access modules will facilitate the transparent sharing of data across applications. Some of these components may have to be custom developed since off-the-shelf products do not always satisfy all requirements.

One illustration of the data integration approach is the case of an electronics component manufacturer that wanted to move all of its enterprise or corporate systems from the IBM mainframe to UNIX servers. This decision was not made lightly, but was based on a compelling business case that is beyond this discussion. The transition to completely eliminate the manufacturer's reliance on the mainframe was determined to be a five- to 10-year program, and the first business area to move was to be inventory management. To complicate this first step, the corporation had up to 10 different inventory management systems, plus numerous other manufacturing and planning systems that needed inventory information.

A data integration transition approach was chosen that would introduce the new UNIX server computing environment to house the integrated inventory information. Thus, for the transition period, the corporation would have a three-tiered architecture for inventory management and information:

1. The mainframe systems for enterprise computing functions such as inventory planning.
2. The lower-tier transaction systems, for manufacturing and warehousing.
3. The new, mid-tier platform that all systems eventually would run on.

The data integration challenge was to be able to integrate all the inventory information on the mid-tier platform so that each application requiring this information could be moved to the new platform in a rational manner while still receiving the inventory information it needed from all the other systems. Eventually, the mainframe would not be needed for any inventory functions, and those functions could be turned off. Any new applications requiring inventory information would be built for the new processing environment.

A key design goal of the transition architecture was to minimize disruptions to the existing applications to eliminate digging into legacy code that was poorly documented and not well-understood. A data integration architecture was designed to capture all transactions that modified inventory information and replicate the results to the mid-tier platform.

Exhibit 12 depicts the data integration architecture designed for this company.

The architecture created a federated data base of inventory information composed of physical data bases at the enterprise, factory and warehouse, and mid-tier or server levels. This federated data base would function as one logical inventory data base, with all inventory-related transactions being integrated on the new server platform. A guaranteed data base synchronization component that sits on top of a guaranteed message delivery system makes the federated data base possible. This component ensures that updates performed on the enterprise DB2 or the factory and warehouse systems are reflected in the mid-tier server component and vice

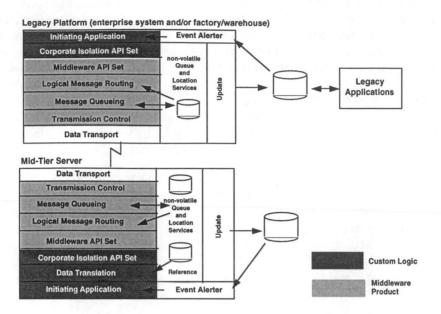

Exhibit 12. Data integration architecture.

versa. Thus, applications can trust all physical DBMSs to provide accurate, identical inventory information.

Inventory information from the manufacturing systems and the warehouses are transferred across the replication manager component, the information backbone, of the architecture. The replication manager ensures the delivery of data from the individual sites to the central, mid-tier server component. Also key to this architecture is the reference data, which provides the mapping between the multiple systems' data structures and performs syntax (e.g., the size of data fields) as well as semantic translation (i.e., the meaning of the data such as what a *sale* or *customer* actually mean between the two systems). Finally, the architecture had to be able to handle concurrent updates; updates to the same information could arrive at nearly the same time from either platform. Because of the low probability of this occurring, the simple approach was to have the architecture report to a single data base when a concurrent update had occurred and require manual intervention to resolve the conflict.

This transition architecture was developed to enable an enterprise-wide view of inventory information through asynchronous, reliable information delivery across heterogeneous platforms and to create a transition step toward the enterprises' goal of moving off the mainframe. The business benefit of this architecture is that it allowed the organization to more quickly and more accurately confirm product delivery schedules with its customers. It also ensured the data integrity, provided high availability of the data, and efficient and timely delivery of the information. Also, because the architecture was not intrusive to the legacy systems, no modifications were needed to the legacy environments. They are able to operate oblivious to the new data integration architecture. This is a good example of a transition architecture that needed to be very robust because of the expected long transition period. The legacy factory and warehouse systems will be around for a long time; they will not be replaced anytime soon.

Application Integration Approach. A system that has both high future business value and technology capabilities is a good candidate for an application integration approach. Generally, such a system has been enhanced throughout years of maintenance and includes complex business functionality. It is built on a solid architecture that allows for extension and flexion. The system is often reliable enough to allow the development of dependencies between it and the new systems; functions of this legacy system may be used by the new systems.

This approach positions legacy systems as direct participants in the new system architectures. Instead of simply exchanging key information, an application integration architecture adapts legacy systems to interact with new systems. It makes selected legacy system functions and data accessible to newly developed systems and other legacy systems; legacy components can act as service providers to new components and vice-versa. This is a reuse strategy.

An application integration approach enables the organization to add value to existing legacy functions by combining them with new systems components such as PC-based applications and networks to form more powerful solutions.

The application integration approach works best when legacy systems are well modularized. It typically takes several years to move legacy systems into new environments; often, the knowledge capital contained in these systems reflects an accumulation of efforts of many individuals. Rebuilding this type of expertise in a new system is almost impossible within a reasonable time frame. An application integration approach removes the need to rebuild this expertise. An application integration (reuse) approach eliminates the need to create multiple instances of the same functionality that can grow apart over time.

Exhibit 13 shows the implications of an application integration strategy for the other aspects of the transition framework: system components and technical architecture.

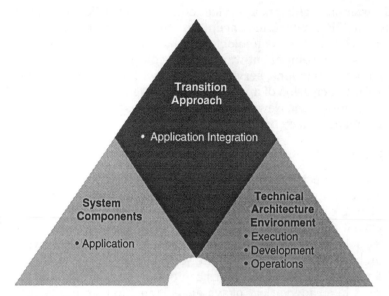

Exhibit 13. Implications of an application integration approach.

Application integration architecture components are largely required within the execution architecture to allow communication among all applications. They enable an application to communicate with legacy applications. The solution should be composed of packaged and custom components whose processing is independent of the participating applications. It supports a many-to-many interface structure.

An example of the application integration approach comes from a large overnight shipping company that was building a new client/server customer service system to include a feature enabling the quotation of shipping rates for customers. The mainframe billing application already contained the business rules for calculating the cost of a shipment and for writing the invoice. Fortunately, the relevant logic was already separated from the CICS screen presentation logic to allow invoices to be produced either in batch or on-line modes.

Using middleware messaging technology, the new customer service system supplied the package shipment information to the rating engine, and the rating engine returned the cost for the shipment. Customer service representatives are now able to quote rates to customers using the new computing environment and front-end, but through the same back-end engine that will ultimately print their bills, thus satisfying the user requirements and virtually eliminating the potential for conflicting quoted and billed amounts.

This example highlights a service request broker (SRB) transition architecture. An SRB is a generic concept driven out of emerging transition and application integration technologies such as object request broker (ORB), wrappering, and component-ware. These complex architectures assist in the isolation of functions, services, or data within the legacy solution and provide for the creation of application programming interfaces (APIs) with which to access them. New solutions can then use the functions, services, or data from the legacy by using the APIs.

CONCLUSION

Transition architectures will become increasingly important over the next decade of computing solutions. They are critical as companies leverage their existing knowledge base, embedded in their legacy systems, and also as they position their current solutions for change as those become legacies themselves. Just as important, however, is the manner in which transition architectures will support inter-organizational work. Alliances will only be successful when companies can optimally share data and information stored in a wide variety of systems. Transition support applications will help companies operate in a seamless way.

Chapter II-4
Massively Parallel Processing

In the age of netcentric computing, organizations must have a great deal more processing power to accommodate new kinds of applications, such as an information delivery facility, data mining, and electronic commerce. This need for large computing cycles may be met relatively inexpensively through massively parallel processing (MPP).

Although massively parallel processors have been around for some time, their use has been limited primarily to scientific and technical applications, and to applications in the defense industry. Today, parallel processing is moving out to organizations in other industries, which find their own data volumes growing exponentially. The growth is not only from traditional transaction systems but also from new data types, such as text, images, audio, and video. MPP is enabling companies to exploit vast amounts of data for both strategic and operational purposes.

Parallel processing technology is potentially very powerful, capable of providing a performance boost two to three orders of magnitude greater than sequential uni-processing and capable of scaling up gracefully with data base sizes. However, parallel processing is also easy to misuse. DBMS and hardware vendors offer a wide variety of products, and the technical features of parallel processing are complex. Therefore, organizations must work from a well-considered vantage point, in terms of application, information, and technical architectures.

This chapter provides a high level review of parallel processing concepts, current and potential applications, and the architectures needed to exploit parallel processing — especially MPP — in the commercial marketplace. Chapter III-4 focuses more on the implementation considerations.

A PERSPECTIVE ON PARALLEL PROCESSING

Massively parallel computing should be placed within the context of a more general arena of parallelism, which has been in use in the commercial marketplace for quite some time. Many variations and algorithms for parallelism are possible; some of the more common ones are listed here:

- *OLTP.* Concurrent execution of multiple copies of a transaction program under the management of an On-line Terminal Monitor Processing (OLTP) manager is one example. A program written to execute serially is enabled to execute in parallel by the facilities provided and managed by the OLTP manager.
- *Batch.* For many long-running batch processes, it is common to execute multiple streams in parallel against distinct key ranges of files and merge the output to reduce the total elapsed time. Operating systems (OS) or data base management system (DBMS) facilities enable the multiple streams to serialize the use of common resources to ensure data integrity.
- *Information Delivery Facility (Data Warehouse).* The use of nonblocking, asynchronous, or pre-fetch input/output (I/O) reduces the elapsed time in batch and information delivery facility environments by overlapping I/O and CPU processing. The overlap, parallelism in a loose sense, is enabled by the DBMS and OS without user program coding specifically to invoke such overlap.

Recent enhancements in DBMS technologies are now enabling user programs, still written in a sequential fashion, to exploit parallelism even further in a transparent way. The DBMS enables the user SQL requests to exploit facilities offered by the new massively parallel processors by concurrently executing components of a single SQL. This is known as "intra-SQL parallelism." Large and well-known data warehouse implementations at retail (e.g., Sears, Roebuck and Co.) and telecommunications (e.g., MCI Corp.) organizations are based on exploiting this form of parallelism. The various architectures and techniques used to enable this style of parallelism are covered in this chapter.

Facets of Parallelism

From a hardware perspective, this chapter focuses on a style of parallelism that is enabled when multiple processors are arranged in different configurations to permit parallelism for a single request. Examples of such configurations include symmetric multiprocessors (SMP), shared-disk clusters (SDC), and massively parallel processors (MPP).

From an external, high-level perspective, multiple processors in a computer are not necessary to enable parallel processing. Several other techniques can enable parallelism, or at least give the appearance of parallelism, regardless of the processor environment. These styles of parallelism have been in use for quite some time:

- *Multitasking or Programming.* This enables several OLTP or batch jobs to concurrently share a uni-processor, giving the appearance of parallelism.

- *Specialized Processing.* Such functions as I/O managers can be executed on specialized processors to permit the CPU's main processor to work in parallel on some other task.
- *Distributed Processing.* Similarly, peer-to-peer or client/server style of distributed processing permits different components of a transaction to execute in parallel on different computers, displaying yet another facet of parallelism.

Multi-processors, important as they are, are only one component in enabling commercial application program parallelism. Currently, the key component for exploiting parallelism in most commercial applications is the DBMS, whose newly introduced intra-SQL parallelism facility has propelled them to this key role. This facility permits users to exploit multi-processor hardware without explicitly coding for such configurations in their programs.

System Components

In general, from the perspective of commercial application programs, such facilities as parallelism are characteristics of the entire system, not merely of its components which include the hardware, operating system, infrastructure, and DBMS. However, each of the components plays an important role in determining the system characteristics.

Exhibit 1 shows one way to depict a system in a layered fashion. The hardware layer, which consists of a multiple processor configuration, offers the base component. Operating system (OS) and the function and I/O shipping facilities, called "infrastructure," influence the programming model that the DBMS layer uses to exhibit the system characteristics, which is exploited by the application program. encounters.

This section first discusses the hardware configurations and their characteristics, including scalability. It then discuss the DBMS architectures, namely shared-data-and-buffer, shared-data, and partitioned-data. The chapter focuses on the DBMS layer because it is generally recognized that the DBMS has become the key enabler of parallelism in the commercial marketplace. The OS and infrastructure layer will not be explicitly discussed, but their characteristics are interwoven in the hardware and the DBMS discussion.

HARDWARE CONFIGURATIONS

Processors are coupled and offered to the commercial users in multiple-processor configurations for many reasons. These have to do with a number of factors — performance, availability, technology, and competition — and their complex interaction in the marketplace.

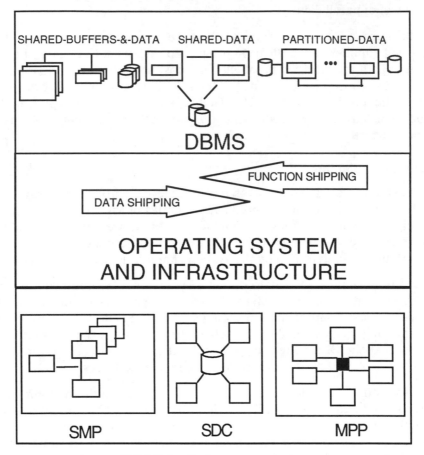

Exhibit 1. System components.

Multiprocessors provide enhanced performance and throughput because more computing resources can be brought to bear on the problem. In addition, they also provide higher data availability. Data can be accessed from another processor in the event of a processor failure. Historically, enhanced data availability has been a key motivation and driver for using multiple processors.

Multi-Processor Classification

A formal and technically precise multiprocessor classification scheme developed by Michael J. Flynn is widely used in technical journals and by research organizations. Flynn introduced a number of programming models, including the multiple instruction multiple data stream (MIMD), the single instruction multiple data stream (SIMD), the single instruction single data stream (SISD), and the multiple instruction single data stream (MISD). This taxonomy, based on the two key characteristics of processing and data, is still used. For the purposes of this chapter, however, multiprocessors can be classified into three simple types:

1. SMP (Symmetric Multi Processors)
2. SDC (Shared-Disk Clusters)
3. MPP (Massively Parallel Processors)

Sometimes this simplification can lead to misunderstandings, so it is advisable to seek clarification with these terms early in any discussion to avoid the pitfalls of oversimplification.

How are multiprocessors distinguished from uniprocessors? The basic building block for other configurations, a uniprocessor is a single processor with a high-speed cache and a bus to access main memory and external I/O. Processors are very fast and need data at high speeds to avoid wasting valuable processing cycles. On the other hand, memory, the supplier of data, is made of slow-speed, inexpensive dynamic random access memory (DRAM) chips, which cannot keep up with the demands of these processors. Cache provides a small amount of buffered data at high speeds to the processor to balance the fast data requirements of the processor and the slow speed of DRAM memory. Cache is not as fast as a processor but much faster than main memory and is made from fast but expensive static random access memory (SRAM) chips.

Even though SMPs, clusters, and MPPs are being produced to provide for additional processing power, vendors are also continuing to enhance the uniprocessor technology. Intel's 386, 486, Pentium, and Pro-Pentium processors exemplify this trend. The enhancements in the PowerPC line from the alliance among Apple, IBM, and Motorola is another example. Although research and development costs for each generation of these processors require major capital investment, the competitive pressures and technological enhancements continue to drive the vendors to develop faster uniprocessors, which are also useful in reducing the overall elapsed time for those tasks that cannot be performed in parallel. This is a very significant consideration and was highlighted by Amdahl's law.

An SMP is a manifestation of a "shared-everything" configuration (see Exhibit 2). It is characterized by having multiple processors, each with its

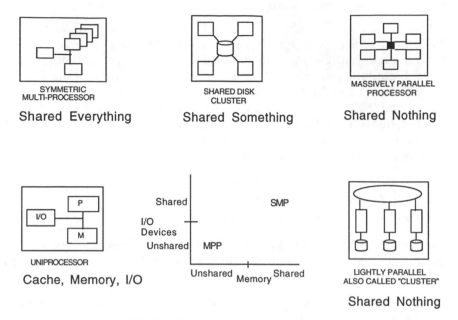

Exhibit 2. The symmetric multiprocessor.

own cache, but all sharing memory and I/O devices. Here the processors are said to be tightly coupled.

SMP configuration is very popular and has been in use for over two decades. IBM Systems/370 158MP and 168MP were so configured. Currently several vendors, including COMPAQ, DEC, HP, IBM, NCR, SEQUENT, SGI, and Sun offer SMP configurations.

A very important consideration that favors the choice of SMP is the availability of a vast amount of already written software, for example, DBMSs, that is based on the programming model that SMP supports. Other alternative platforms, such as loosely coupled multiprocessors, currently do not have as rich a collection of enabling software.

The fact that multiple processors exist is generally transparent to a user-application program. The transparency is enabled by the OS software layer, which hides the complexity introduced by the multiple processors and their caches, and permits increased horsepower exploitation relatively easily. It is also efficient, because a task running on any processor can access all the main memory, and can share data by pointer passing as opposed to messaging.

The subject of how many processors can be tightly coupled together to provide for growth (i.e., scalability) has been a topic of vast interest and research. One of the inhibitors for coupling too many processors is the contention for memory access. High-speed cache can reduce the contention, because main memory needs to be accessed less frequently; however, high-speed cache introduces another problem: cache coherence. Because each processor has its own cache, coherence among them has to be maintained to ensure that multiple processors are not working with stale copy of data from main memory.

Conventional wisdom has held that because of cache coherence and other technical considerations, the practical upper limit for the number of processors that could be tightly coupled in an SMP configuration is between 10 and 20. However, over the years, a number of new schemes, including Central Directory, Snoopy Bus, Snoopy Bus and Switch, Distributed Directories using Scalable Coherent Interconnect (SCI), and the Directory Architecture for Shared memory (DASH), have been invented and implemented by SMP vendors to overcome the challenge of maintaining cache coherence. Even now, new innovations are being rolled out, so SMPs have not necessarily reached their scalability limits. These newer techniques have made it possible to scale well beyond the conventionally accepted limit, but at an increased cost of research and development. So, economics as well as technology now become important issues in SMP scalability. The question then is not whether SMP can scale, but whether it can scale economically, compared to other alternatives, such as loosely coupled processors (e.g., clusters and MPPs).

Clusters

A cluster is a collection of interconnected whole computers that is utilized as a single computing resource. Clusters can be configured using either the shared-something or shared-nothing concept. This section discusses the shared-something clusters, and the MPP section covers the shared-nothing clusters.

Shared-something clusters may share memory or I/O devices. Shared I/O clusters are very popular; various DEC clusters and IBM sysplex are examples. Because of their wide use, people colloquially use the word *cluster* to mean a shared-disk configuration. However, sharing disks is not a requirement of a cluster; for that matter, no sharing is necessary at all for clustering.

Digital Equipment Corporation has offered VAXCluster since the early 1980s (Exhibit 3) and followed it with Open VMSCluster and, more recently, DEC TrueClusters.

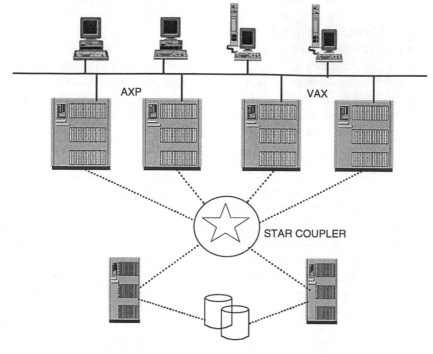

Exhibit 3. The VAX cluster configuration.

IBM Parallel Sysplex configuration uses a shared electronic storage (i.e., a coupling facility) to communicate locking and other common data structures between the cluster members. This helps in system performance (Exhibit 4).

A shared-disk cluster (SDC) presents a single system image to a user application program. OS, DBMS, and load balancing infrastructure can hide the presence and complexities of a multitude of processors. Nonetheless, a user application program can target a specific computer if it has an affinity to it for any reason, such as the need for a specialized I/O device.

Shared-disk clusters offer many benefits in the commercial marketplace, including high availability, incremental growth, and scalability. If one processor is down for either planned or unplanned outage, other processors in the complex can pick up its workload, thus increasing data availability. Additional processors can be added incrementally to the cluster to match the workload, as opposed to having to purchase a single large computer to meet the eventual workload. Also, the scalability challenge faced by the SMP is not encountered here, because the independent processors do not share common memory.

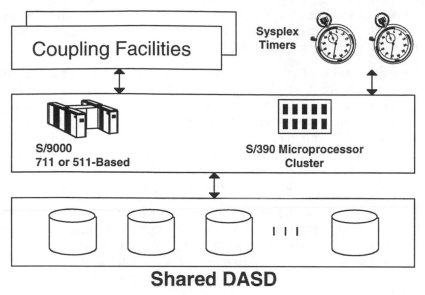

Shared DASD

Exhibit 4.   IBM Parallel Sysplex configuration.

Clusters face the challenge of additional overhead caused by inter-processor message passing, workload synchronization and balancing, and software pricing. Depending on the pricing model used by the software vendor, the sum of software license costs for equivalent computing power can be higher for a cluster as compared to an SMP, because multiple licenses are required.

The Massively Parallel Processor

In an MPP configuration, each processor has its own memory, and accesses its own external I/O. This is a shared-nothing architecture, and the processors are said to be loosely coupled. An MPP permits the coupling of thousands of relatively inexpensive off-the-shelf processors to provide billions of computing instructions. Because an MPP implies coupling a large number of processors, an interconnection mechanism(e.g., buses, rings, hypercubes, and meshes) is required to provide for the processors to communicate with each other and coordinate their work. Currently, many vendors, including IBM, ICL, and NCR offer MPP configurations.

From a simplistic I/O and memory sharing point of view, there is a distinction between MPP and SMP architectures. However, as discussed later in the chapter, operating systems (OSs) or other software layers can mask some of these differences, permitting some software written for other configurations, such as Shared-Disk, to be executed on an MPP. For example, the virtual shared disk feature of IBM's shared-nothing RS/6000 SP permits higher-level programs, for example Oracle DBMS, to use this MPP as if it were a shared disk configuration.

Before the mid 1980s, the use of MPPs was essentially limited to scientific and engineering work, which typically requires a large number of computing instructions but limited I/O. Such a task can often be split into many individual sub-tasks, each executing on a processor and performing minimal I/O. Computational fluid dynamics is an example of this. Sub-task results are then combined to prepare the final response. The decomposition of tasks and combination of results required sophisticated programming tools and skills which were found in the scientific and engineering community.

Traditional commercial work, on the other hand, requires relatively fewer computing cycles (though this is changing) but higher I/O bandwidth. In addition, typical programming tools and required skills for exploiting MPPs in commercial environments were not available. The combination of these factors resulted in minimal use of this technology in the commercial arena.

In the late 1980s, offerings introduced by NCR's DBC1012 Teradata data base machine started to permit On-line Analytical Processing (OLAP) of commercial workloads to benefit from the MPP configurations. More recently, innovations introduced by several data base vendors, such as Oracle and Informix, have further accelerated this trend.

An important point is that a key ingredient for the acceptance of MPP in the commercial market place is the ease with which parallelism can be exploited by a DBMS application programmer without the programmer needing to think in terms of parallel programs or needing to implement sophisticated and complex algorithms.

The technique used by the DBMSs to exploit parallelism is the same as mentioned above for the scientific work. A single task (i.e., an SQL request) is split into many individual sub-tasks, each executing on a processor. Sub-task results are then combined to prepare the answer set for the SQL request. In addition, the packaging of processors in an MPP configuration offers several administrative benefits. The multitude of processors can be managed from a single console, and distribution and maintenance of software is simplified because only a single copy is maintained. The system makes the same copy available to the individual nodes in the MPP. This administrative benefit is very attractive and at times used for justification of an MPP solution, even when no parallelism benefits exist.

At times, financial requests for additional hardware may also be less of an administrative concern, because the upgrade (i.e., the addition of processors and I/Os) is made to an existing installed "serial number" machine, and does not require the acquisition of a new one, which may involve more sign-offs and other administrative steps.

Currently, the DBMS vendors have focused on MPP technology to implement strategic information processing (e.g., Data Warehouse) style of applications. They have placed only a limited emphasis on operational applications. As more experience is gained and technology matures, it is likely that more operational applications, such as OLTP, may find a home on the MPP platform.

However, the current reduction in government grants to scientific and defense organizations, the slow development of the software, and fierce competition in the MPP marketplace have already started a shakedown in the industry. One analysis by the *Wall Street Journal* has suggested that by the time the commercial marketplace develops, quite a few suppliers will "sputter toward the abyss."

In addition to MPP, the shared-nothing configuration also can be implemented in a cluster of computers where the coupling is limited to a low number, as opposed to a high number, which is the case with an MPP. In general, this shared-nothing lightly (or modestly) parallel cluster exhibits characteristics similar to those of an MPP.

The distinction between MPP and a lightly parallel cluster is somewhat blurry. The following table shows a comparison of some salient features for distinguishing the two configurations. The most noticeable feature appears to be the arbitrary number of connected processors, which is large for MPP and small for a lightly parallel cluster.

Characteristic	MPP	Lightly Parallel Cluster
Number of processors	Thousands	Hundreds
Node OS	Homogeneous	Can be different, but usually homogeneous
Inter-node security	None	Generally none
Performance metric	Turnaround time	Throughput and turnaround

From a programming model perspective, given the right infrastructure, an MPP and shared-nothing cluster should be transparent to an application, such as a DBMS. As discussed in a later section, IBM's DB2 Universal Server DBMS can execute both on a shared-nothing lightly parallel cluster of RS/6000 computers and on IBM's massively parallel hardware, RS/6000 SP.

Lightly parallel shared-nothing clusters can potentially become the platform of choice in the future for several reasons, including low cost. However, software currently is not widely available to provide a single system image and tools for performance, capacity, and workload management.

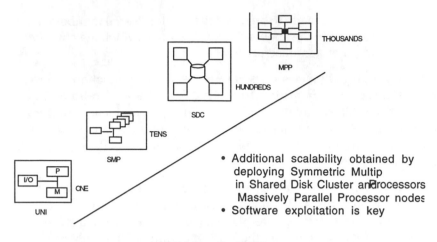

Exhibit 5. Scalability.

It is expected that Microsoft Corporation's architecture for scaling Windows NT and SQL Server to meet the enterprise-wide needs may include this style of lightly parallel shared-nothing clustering. If this comes to pass, the shared-nothing clusters will become very popular and over-shadow their "big cousin," MPP.

The various hardware configurations also offer varying levels of scalability (i.e., how much useable processing power is delivered to the users when such additional computing resources as processors, memory, and I/O are added to these configurations). This ability to scale is clearly one of the major considerations in evaluating and selecting a multiprocessor platform for use.

MULTI-PROCESSORS: SCALABILITY AND THROUGHPUT

An installation has several hardware options when requiring additional computational power. The choice is made based on many technical, administrative, and financial considerations. From a technical perspective alone, there is considerable debate as to how scalable the various hardware configurations are.

One commonly held opinion is that the uni-processors and massively parallel processors represent the two ends of the spectrum, with SMP and clusters providing the intermediate scalability design points. Exhibit 5 depicts this graphically.

As discussed in the previous section, a commonly held opinion is that an SMP can economically scale only to between 10 and 20 processors, beyond which alternative configurations, such as clusters and MPPs, become financially more attractive. Whether that is true depends on many considerations, such as hardware technology, software availability and pricing, and technical marketing and support from the vendors. Considering all the factors, one can observe that hardware technology, by itself, plays only a minor role.

SMPs currently enjoy the most software availability and perhaps a software price advantage. Shared-disk clusters, in general, suffer the penalty from higher software prices, because each machine is a separate computer requiring an additional license, although licenses are comparatively less expensive, as the individual machines are smaller than a corresponding equivalent single SMP. However, new pricing schemes based on total computing power, number of concurrent logged-on users, or other factors are slowly starting to alter the old pricing paradigm, which put clusters at a disadvantage.

Clusters and MPPs do not suffer from the cache coherence and memory contention that offer SMP design challenges in scaling beyond the 10-to-20 range. Here, each processor has its own cache, no coherence needs to be maintained, and each has its own memory, so no contention occurs. Therefore, from a hardware viewpoint, scaling is not as challenging. The challenge lies, however, in interconnecting the processors and enabling software so that the work on the separate processors can be coordinated and synchronized in an efficient and effective way.

To provide more computing resources, vendors are including SMP as individual nodes in cluster and MPP configurations. NCR's WorldMark 5100M is one example, in which individual nodes are made of SMPs. Thus, the achievement of huge processing power is a multitiered phenomenon: increasing speeds of uni-processors, combination of faster and larger number of processors in an SMP configuration and inclusion of SMPs in cluster and MPP offerings.

SOFTWARE LAYERS

All the approaches to parallelism discussed to this point have touched on multiprocessing. All the approaches manifest and support parallelism in different ways; however, one underlying theme is common to all. It may be obvious, but it needs to be emphasized. In almost all cases, with few exceptions, a commercial application program is written in a sequential fashion, and parallelism is attained by using some external mechanism. Here are some examples to illustrate the point.

During execution, an OLTP manager spawns separate threads or processes, schedules clones of the user's sequential program, and manages storage and other resources on its behalf to manifest parallelism. In batch, multiple job streams executing an application program are often organized to process different files or partitions of a table to support parallelism. In the client/server model, multiple clients execute the same sequential program in parallel; the mechanism that enables parallelism is the software distribution facility. Another way of looking at client/server parallelism is the execution of a client program in parallel with an asynchronous stored procedure on the server; the facility of remote procedure calls and stored procedures enables parallelism.

In the same way, a single SQL call from an application program can be enabled to execute in parallel by a DBMS. The application program is still written to execute sequentially, requiring neither new compilers nor programming techniques. This can be contrasted with building parallelism within a program using special constructs (e.g., *doall* and *foreach*), in which the FORTRAN compiler generates code to execute subtasks in parallel for the different elements of a vector or matrix. Such constructs, if they were to become widely available in the commercial languages, will still require significant retraining of the application programmers to think of a problem solution in terms of parallelism. Such facilities are not available. In addition, from an installations point of view, the approach of sequential program and DBMS-enabled parallelism is much easier and less expensive to implement. The required new learning can be limited to the designers and supporters of the data bases: data base and system administrators. Similarly, tools acquisition also can be focused towards the tasks performed by such personnel.

Now, SQL statements exhibit varying amounts of workload on a system. At one extreme, calls (generally associated with transaction-oriented work) that retrieve and update a few rows require little computational resource. At the other extreme, statements (generally associated with OLAP work) perform large amounts of work and require significant computational resources. Within this wide range lie the rest. By their very nature, those associated with OLAP work, performed within a data warehouse environment, can benefit most from the intra-SQL parallelism, and those are the current primary target of the parallelism.

If the user-application code parallelism is attained only through the use of other techniques listed earlier (e.g., OLTP), one may conclude that DBMS-enabled parallelism is limited to the OLAP data-warehouse-oriented SQL. This is really not valid. New enhancements to the relational data base technology include extensions that permit user-defined functions and data types to be tightly integrated with the SQL language. User-developed application code can then be executed as part of the DBMS using these facilities. In fact, Oracle7 allows execution of business logic in parallel using user-defined SQL functions.

DBMS ARCHITECTURE

As discussed earlier, from an application programming perspective, exploitation of hardware parallelism in the commercial marketplace was limited because of lack of tools and skills. It is now generally recognized that data base management system (DBMS) vendors have recently stepped up their efforts in an attempt to address both of these challenges. They are starting to become the enablers of parallelism in the commercial arena. Additionally, more and more applications are migrating to DBMS for storage and retrieval of data. Therefore, it is worthwhile to understand how the DBMS enables parallelism.

This understanding will help in choosing an appropriate DBMS and, to some extent, the hardware configuration. Also, it will help in designing applications and data bases which perform and scale well. Lack of understanding can lead to poorly performing systems and wasted resources.

In a manner similar to the three hardware configurations, DBMS architectures also can be classified into three corresponding categories:

- Shared-data-and-buffer
- Shared-data
- Partitioned-data

There is a match between these architectures and the characteristics of the respective hardware configuration (SMP, shared disk clusters, and MPP), but a DBMS does not have to execute only on its corresponding hardware counterpart. For example, a DBMS based on shared-data architecture can execute on a shared-nothing MPP hardware configuration.

When there is a match, the two build on each other's strengths and suffer from each other's weaknesses. However, the picture is much cloudier when a DBMS executes on a mismatched hardware configuration. On the one hand, in these cases, the DBMS is unable to build upon and fully exploit the power of the hardware configuration. On the other hand, it can compensate for some of the challenges associated with using the underlying hardware configuration.

Shared Data and Buffer

In this architecture, a single instance of the DBMS executes on a configuration which supports sharing of buffers and data. Multiple threads are initiated to provide an appropriate level of parallelism. As shown in Exhibit 6, all threads have complete visibility to all the data and buffers.

System administration and load balancing are comparatively easier with this architecture, because a single instance of the DBMS has full visibility to all the data. This architecture matches facilities offered by SMP configura-

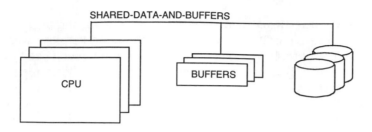

Characteristics:
- Data Partitioning not needed
- Systems management & load balancing easier
- Scalability concerns

Examples:
- Informix PDQ
- Oracle7 Parallel Query
- DB2 (MVS) CPU Parallelism

Exhibit 6.   Shared data and buffers.

tion, in which this architecture is very frequently implemented. When executed on an SMP platform, the system inherits the scalability concerns associated with the underlying hardware platform. The maximum number of processors in an SMP, the cache coherence among processors, and the contention for memory access are some of the reasons that contribute to the scalability concerns.

Informix DSA, Oracle7, and DB2 for MVS are examples of DBMSs that have implemented the shared-data-and-buffer architecture. These DBMSs and their SQL parallelizing features permit intra-SQL parallelism; that is, they can concurrently apply multiple threads and processors to process a single SQL statement.

The algorithms used for intra-SQL parallelism are based on the notion of program and data parallelism. Program parallelism allows such SQL operations as scan, sort, and join to be performed in parallel by passing data from one operation to another. Data parallelism allows these SQL operations to process different pieces of data concurrently.

Shared Data

In this architecture, multiple instances of the DBMS execute on different processors. Each instance has visibility and access to all the data, but every instance maintains its own private buffers, and updates rows within it. A two-instance shared-data architecture is shown in Exhibit 7.

Because the data is shared by multiple instances of the DBMSs, a mechanism is required to serialize the use of resources so that multiple

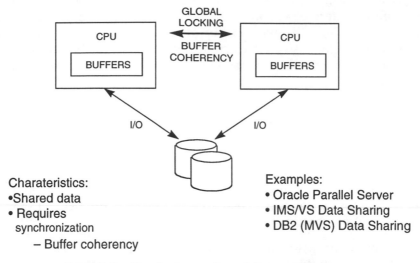

Exhibit 7. Two-instance shared-data architecture.

instances do not concurrently update a value and corrupt the modifications made by another instance. This serialization is provided by the global locking facility of the DBMS and is essential for the shared data architecture. Global locking may be considered an extension of DBMS local locking facilities, which ensures serialization of resource modification within an instance, to the multiple instances that share data.

Another requirement, buffer coherence, is also introduced, because each instance of the DBMS maintains a private buffer pool. Without buffer coherence, a resource accessed by one DBMS from disk may not reflect the modification made by another system if the second system has not yet externalized the changes to the disk. Logically, the problem is similar to "cache coherence," discussed earlier for the SMP hardware configuration.

When they are combined, global locking and buffer coherence ensure data integrity. Oracle Parallel Server (OPS), DB2 for MVS Data Sharing, and Information Management System/Virtual Storage (IMS/VS) are examples of DBMSs that implement this architecture.

It must be emphasized that intra-query parallelism is not being exploited in any of these three product feature examples. The key motivation for the implementation of this architecture is the same as those discussed for the shared-disk hardware configuration, namely: data availability, incremental growth, and scalability. However, if one additionally chooses to use other features of these DBMSs in conjunction, the benefits of intra-query parallelism also can be realized.

As can be seen, there is a match between this software architecture and the facilities offered by shared-disk clusters, where this architecture is implemented. Thus, the performance of the DBMS is dependent not only on the software but also on the facilities provided by the hardware cluster to implement the two key components, global locking and buffer coherence.

In some implementations, maintenance of buffer coherence necessitates writing of data to the disks to permit reading by another DBMS instance. This writing and reading is called "pinging." Depending on the locking schemes used, pinging may take place even if the two instances are interested in distinct resources but represented by the same lock. This is known as false pinging. Heavy pinging, false or otherwise, has a negative effect on application performance because it increases both the I/O and the lock management overhead.

System vendors use many techniques to minimize the impact of pinging. For example, IBM's DB2 for MVS on the Parallel Sysplex reduces the pinging I/O overhead by using the coupling facility, which couples all the nodes in the cluster via high- speed electronics. That is, disk I/Os are replaced by writes and reads from the coupling facility's electronic memory. In addition, hardware facilities are used to invalidate stale data buffers in another instances.

Even if the hardware and DBMS vendors have provided adequate facilities to minimize the adverse impact of pinging, it is still an Application Architect and Data base Administrator's responsibility to design application and data bases such that the need for sharing data is minimized to get the best performance. It is interesting to note that Shared- Data software architecture can be implemented on hardware platforms other than shared-disk. For example, Oracle Parallel Server, which is based on shared-data software architecture, is quite common on IBM's RS 6000 SP, an implementation based on shared-nothing hardware configuration. This is achieved by using the virtual shared disk feature of RS/6000 SP.

In this case, Oracle7's I/O request for data residing on another node is routed by RS/6000 SP device drivers to the appropriate node, an I/O is performed, if necessary, and data is returned to the requesting node. This is known as data shipping and contributes to added traffic on the node's interconnect hardware. The inter-node traffic is a consideration when architecting a solution and acquiring hardware.

In general, for the data base administrators and application architects, it is necessary to understand such features in detail because the application performance depends on the architecture of the DBMS and the OS layers.

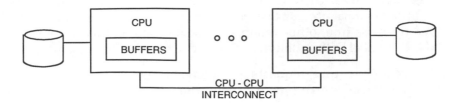

Characteristics:
* Partitioned data
* Scaleup potential: High
* Buffer Coherency: Not required
* Two-phase commit

Examples:
* NCR Teradata
* Tandem NonStop
* DB2 (AIX) Parallel Edition
* Sybase MPP
* Informix XPS

Exhibit 8.   Partitioned-data architecture.

Partitioned Data

As the name implies, the data base is partitioned among different instances of the DBMSs, as shown in Exhibit 8. In this option, each DBMS owns a portion of the data base and only that portion may be directly accessed and modified by it.

Each DBMS has its private or local buffer pool, and as there is no sharing of data, the kind of synchronization protocols discussed above for shared-data (i.e., global locking and buffer coherence) are not required. However, a transaction or SQL modifying data in different DBMS instances residing on multiple nodes will need some form of two-phase commit protocol to ensure data integrity.

Each instance controls its own I/O, performs locking, applies the local predicates, extracts the rows of interest, and transfers them to the next stage of processing, which may reside on the same or some other node.

As can be seen, there is a match between the partitioned-data option and the MPP hardware configuration. Additionally, because MPP provides a large amount of processing power, and the partitioned-data architecture does not need the synchronization protocols, some argue that this combination offers the highest scalability. Thus, it has been the focus of recent development in the DBMS community. The partitioned-data architecture requires frequent communication among the DBMS instances to communicate messages and transfer results. Therefore, low latency and high bandwidth for the interconnect are required if the system is to scale up with the increased workload.

As mentioned earlier, NCR's Teradata system was one of the earliest successful commercial products based on this architecture. Recent new UNIX DBMS offerings from other vendors are also based on this architecture. IBM DB2 Parallel Edition, Informix XPS, and Sybase MPP are examples.

In this architecture, requests for functions to be performed at other DBMS instances are shipped to them; the requesting DBMS instance receives only the results, not a block of data. This concept is called function shipping and is considered to offer better performance characteristics, compared to data shipping, because only the results are transferred to the requesting instance.

The partitioned-data architecture uses the notion of data parallelism to get the benefits of parallelism, and data partitioning algorithms play an important role in determining the performance characteristics of the systems. Various partitioning options are discussed in a later section.

The partitioned-data architecture also provides an additional flexibility in choosing the underlying hardware platform. As one can observe, partitioned-data matches well with the MPP hardware configuration. It also matches with the shared-nothing lightly parallel clusters. The distinction between these clusters and MPP is based primarily on the number of nodes, which is somewhat arbitrary.

For illustration, DB2 Parallel Edition is considered a Partitioned-Data implementation. As shown in Exhibit 9, Parallel Edition can execute both on RS/6000 SP, an MPP offering, and on a cluster of RS/6000 computers, which are connected by a LAN. However, for a number of technical and financial reasons, the RS/6000 cluster solution is not marketed actively. On the other hand, there are conjectures in the market that similar system solutions are likely to become more prevalent when Microsoft becomes more active in marketing its cluster offerings.

The Three DBMS Architectures: Summary

A great deal of debate goes on as to which of the three software models — shared buffer and data, shared data, or partitioned data — is best for the commercial marketplace. This debate is somewhat similar to the one that revolves around the choice of hardware configurations (i.e., SMP, clusters, or MPP). One might assume that making the choice of a software architecture would lead to a straightforward choice of a corresponding hardware configuration, or vice-versa; however, this is not the case.

OS and infrastructure layers permit cohabitation of a DBMS architecture with a nonmatching hardware configuration. Because of the mismatch, it is easy to observe that the mismatched components may not fully exploit the facilities of its partner. It is somewhat harder to appreciate, however, that

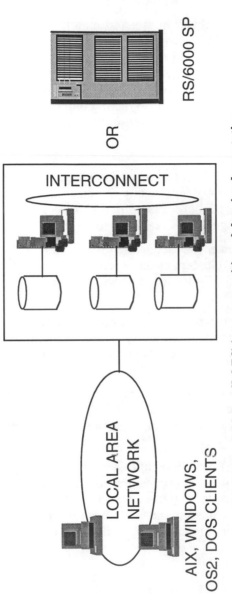

Exhibit 9. DB2 Parallel Edition as a partitioned-data implementation.

the shortcomings of one may be compensated to some extent by the strengths of another. For example, a shared-data software architecture on an MPP platform avoids the management issues associated with repartitioning of data over time as the data or work load characteristics change.

This variety and flexibility in mix-and-match implementation presents trade-offs to both the DBMS and hardware vendors and to the application system developers. Even after an installation has made the choice of a DBMS and a hardware configuration, the application architects and the data base and system administrators must still have a good understanding of the trade-offs involved with the system components to ensure scalability and good performance of the user applications.

SUMMARY

The future of MPP seems extremely promising. Making faster and faster uniprocessors is not only technically difficult but is becoming economically prohibitive. Parallel processing is the answer. In the near future, all three hardware configurations are likely to find applicability:

- SMP on desktops and as departmental servers.
- Shared-disk SMP clusters as enterprise servers.
- MPP as servers of choice for strategic information processing, and as multimedia servers.

Image and video servers, requiring large I/O capacity, seem ideal for parallel processing. This need can be satisfied by a variety of current MPP, which emphasizes scalability of I/O more than the scalability of processing power.

Lightly parallel shared-nothing clusters based on commodity hardware and ATM or Ethernet interconnect are likely to become very popular because of their low cost as soon as software for workload management becomes available.

Making long-range predictions in this business is unwise. However, one can be assured that parallel processing solutions in the commercial marketplace will be driven less by the hardware technology, and more by the software innovations, systems management offerings, pricing schemes, and most important by the marketing abilities of the vendors.

Chapter II-5

The Information Delivery Facility: Beyond Data Warehousing

Data warehousing has become a key technology in a client/server environment, and it promises to become even more important in the age of netcentric computing. Decision makers, knowledge workers, stakeholders, and customers all derive enormous benefits from a software's capability to locate meaningful knowledge about an organization. The data warehouse is still in its infancy, and early expectations have yet to become reality. The picture today is not quite, as one analyst has it, one of "managers easily gathering up valuable nuggets of business intelligence as they romp through gigabytes of suddenly understandable corporate data." The potential does exist, however, to gain competitive advantage through knowledge that is quickly located and retrievable.

The discussion in this chapter begins with basic definitions, because the term *data warehouse* has already become overused and misused. A data warehouse is not simply any system that stores data for subsequent retrieval. Data warehouses are defined more specifically as read-only, time-based collections of data that support on-line analysis. The notion of read-only helps to clarify the distinction between data warehouses and transaction processing systems.

The focus on time-based data highlights the fact that data warehouses are particularly valuable when they are used to analyze trends over time. The idea of on-line analysis highlights the fact that data warehouses are not the general solution to the general problem that users need access to data.

Successful data warehouses deliver focused solutions for specific user groups of analysts. In fact, it is probably useful to go beyond the idea of a data warehouse. Warehousing does not alter the nature of the goods being warehoused, but raw data from operational systems delivers marginal value to business users. Real value comes only if the data is transformed into content-rich information. This leads to the concept of a "data refinery," in which the product delivered to end-users has been refined from data into information and knowledge that is useful for strategic decision-making and for tactical decision-making. Accordingly, from this point forward, this chapter refers to the pool of data as the data refinery, not the data warehouse. This chapter also refers to the process that transforms data into information as the refining process.

FROM DATA REFINERY TO INFORMATION DELIVERY FACILITY

It is not enough simply to build a data refinery. A company might easily believe that, because users need access to data, it can merely build a data refinery that contains all the enterprise's data and then let the users do whatever they want with the data.

This belief is unfounded. Users are rarely knowledgeable enough about the ways of information technology to be able to take even content-rich information and manipulate it to support decision making. Furthermore, it takes too much time and distracts users from their real missions within the ongoing life of the enterprise. IT's responsibility is to deliver a data refinery, not just a data warehouse. Further, IT's responsibility is to deliver that content-rich information within a meaningful context to the user. The delivery of a meaningful context normally requires the development of an application that places the information within a user-oriented context.

IT departments need to go one step beyond the idea of a data refinery. Users need a complete Information Delivery Facility (IDF). An IDF (Exhibit 1) is an information management architecture comprised of four major components:

- End-user access applications.
- A business directory.
- A data refinery.
- A collection of refining processes.

The IDF delivers a complete architecture. The most important component of architecture is the delivery of high-value information to end users. The IDF is supported by specific data designs and robust processes for the extraction and transformation of source data. IDF solutions are custom systems. Vendors offer many products, each of which claims to be the ultimate data refinery solution. No product, however, can deliver more than a piece of the puzzle. The real value comes with the understanding of the specific business benefits to be delivered and the ability to develop unique ways to deliver those benefits. This chapter describes each component, as well as a framework that is useful for planning the development of such an

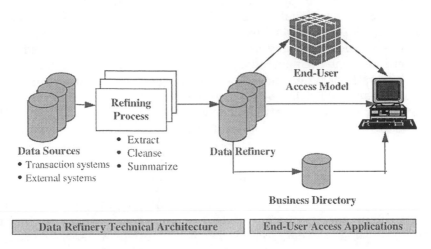

Exhibit 1.   The IDF architecture.

information delivery facility. Specific implementation guidelines are found in the implementation section of the book.

WHY BUILD AN INFORMATION DELIVERY FACILITY?

The IDF is most appropriate as support for making major business decisions, which must be supported by bringing together both internal and external data from multiple source systems and then transforming that data into accessible and usable knowledge. IDFs are the way to do this, but they are multimillion-dollar solutions, best applied to multimillion-dollar problems.

The primary industries to benefit from IDFs are products, consumer products (especially such areas as pharmaceuticals), retail, telecommunications, insurance, and health care. Almost every industry, however, appears to be interested in IDFs.

What are the applications that are justifying these investments? Product companies are using the IDF to help monitor expensive manufacturing processes, by monitoring the trends in resource consumption through the process. An IDC study published in 1996 found an average 400% ROI across 59 companies. The stars of the study raising that average, however, were major heavy metal companies. They reported extremely high ROIs, including one that reached 16,000%. These applications can be categorized as asset management processes.

Consumer products provides a powerful example of the convergence of computing, communications, and knowledge on the customer. These opportunities lie more in the category of opportunity discovery than in asset management. Manufacturers have long purchased external data from providers, who survey samples of consumers to estimate buying patterns for types of products. Today, manufacturers would like more detailed information about who their customers are and what they are buying. However, their own sales data does not answer those questions, because most manufacturers sell to distributors and wholesalers, not consumers. Manufacturers that can work out partnerships with their distributors to acquire the sales data of the distributors are much closer to understanding consumer buying patterns. Distributor sales to retail outlets can be analyzed for neighborhood demographics, producing a much richer analysis than can be obtained from the manufacturer's sales data.

Alternatively, convergence may lead manufacturers to go beyond the notion of purchasing consumer data from such companies as AC Nielsen and downloading the data to their own IDF. Future providers of consumer information may become the marketing department for manufacturers. Manufacturing personnel may reach through cyberspace to access the IDF of the provider of consumer information; conversely, the provider may reach through cyberspace to access the IDF of the manufacturer, as increasing convergence blurs the lines of corporate entities.

In an entirely different vein, manufacturers and retailers merge warranty or sales data with weather information from cyberspace to analyze the effects of weather on warranty claims or sales results.

Retailers have been the leading lights of the information delivery facility trend. Their direct access to consumer sales data allows them to conduct detailed analyses of buying patterns over time and location. Such analyses allow them to improve discounting approaches during holiday seasons to maximize profits while minimizing leftover inventory at the close of the holiday season. Such analyses also allow them to maintain much smaller in-stock inventory levels and to replenish them in patterns that match consumer demand.

Utilities use IDFs to determine resource consumption patterns, as an input to decisions about future plant construction or retirement. Northern Illinois Gas, for example, now provides annual consumption trends in its monthly consumer invoices. Might an IDF allow consumers the option to monitor consumption online? Insurance companies use IDFs to identify long-term expense patterns and trends. Credit-card processors use IDFs to search for fraud. Health providers use IDFs to search for both fraud and trends in diagnoses and treatments that may suggest a need for action by health providers or regulatory agencies. Universities use IDFs to detect trends in enrollment to project faculty staffing requirements, construction requirements, and course development requirements. In addition, most enterprises that have IDFs use them to standardize reporting. This addresses the age-old problem of reports from different departments that do not use a common base of information for enterprise reporting.

The most compelling reason to build an IDF harks back to the point made at the beginning of this book: that there is no longer a sustainable competitive advantage available to companies. Astounding solutions require divergent thinking. They require the ability to look at the marketplace and to turn the world upside down. An IDF can deliver a view into an enterprise's marketplace that is not available to any of its competitors. An IDF may result in a new offering in the market that has not even been dreamed of by the competition.

IDFs also support today's demands for analysis and strategic decision-making. Strategic decision-making requires information that goes well beyond that typically found in operational systems. These requirements include:

- A mix of consistently-defined corporate data and external data.
- Data that spans more time periods than typical operational systems retain.
- Integration of data from many sources, both within the company and without.
- Transformation of the data from those various sources to a common semantic understanding, called information.

WHO USES AN IDF?

Because everyone within the typical enterprise needs information, one prevalent misconception is that the IDF should be built to be accessible by everyone for any information need. In fact, it is not practical to develop such a resource. As mentioned earlier, IDFs are expensive solutions and need to be solving expensive problems. There is little justification for providing expensive solutions for people who would only use the information occasionally and who would find little measurable benefit from having it available. This is not to say that such user communities should be restricted from accessing an existing IDF, but their need alone is typically not enough to justify the original cost of construction.

The more sensible approach is to identify groups of individuals who would experience great benefit from access to an IDF, then tailor the IDF to their needs and deliver it to them. Such individuals are typically knowledge workers responsible for analyzing information in support of strategic or tactical decision-making.

How does the organization begin to determine which groups may or may not need an IDF? Most salespeople, for example, need to be spending their time visiting with prospects, not surfing the data refinery. They may need additional systems support, but those systems are more likely to be customer information systems or automated sales force systems than IDFs. Customer information systems and automated sales force systems are much more like operational transaction processing systems, supporting both data entry and data retrieval. A salesperson is likely to use it briefly for simple queries, such as, "What product has the customer ordered recently?" and "What items in the product line have they never ordered?" An exception to this general rule would be the salespeople who deal in very high-value items and have very long sales cycles. Under such circumstances, extra information about the customer or the competition may provide the added margin of victory in making the sale.

The knowledge workers who benefit from IDFs are people who have a primary responsibility to massage data. Such individuals tend to have little customer contact and little contact with operational systems. Instead, they are individuals who provide the analyses that form the basis for strategic and tactical decisions, such as product design and marketing, buying, fraud or abuse detection, rate-making, and usage analysis. They spend too much time gathering data and transforming it into something useful. Access to an IDF that performs those tasks automatically frees these knowledge workers to concentrate on analyzing results instead of preparing for the analysis. This is one of the promises of today's technology: knowledge workers will spend more time analyzing information than they spend gathering information. An IDF supports that kind of work.

With the convergence of computing and communications on customers, organizations can look forward to a day when online access for customers enables similar facilities. Such customers are likely to be corporate customers, such as financial analysts in companies that use service bureaus, health care specialists in customers of group insurance companies, and other linkages between information providers and their customers.

SUCCESS FACTORS FOR THE DEVELOPMENT OF THE IDF

Many approaches exist for building an IDF. One is the "build it and they will come" approach. This approach replicates most of the data in operational systems and stores it on parallel processors for use by anyone who needs it. Some enterprises have used this approach successfully, but it has not worked for most that have tried it.

One might compare this approach to the idea of General Motors opening their parts warehouses to customers, and telling them that they can build any kind of car they want. This raises a number of concerns. First, most people do not know how to build a car and do not want to learn. Second, there is no reason to think that the warehouse is stocked with the parts one particular consumer would want, if none of the company's production car models provide what that person wants. What the customer really wants from General Motors is for the company to accept the responsibility for determining what the customer wants and to provide the facility to tailor the product, not to build the whole product from scratch.

In a similar vein, IDF users want information and knowledge, not data. They want it presented in a format that is easy to acquire, easy to tailor and easy to use, so they can concentrate their energies on their jobs, not on doing IT's job. The data from most operational systems is too fragmented for users to be able to transform it into accurate and meaningful information. The data from operational systems is also incomplete and needs to be supplemented with data from external sources or from nonintegrated sources like manual files or PC systems.

THE KEYS TO SUCCESS WITH AN IDF

Seven factors are particularly key to a successful IDF:

1. A focused audience of users who have a critical need for personal access to information that describes business trends over time.
2. A committed executive sponsor.
3. A specific delivery vehicle that provides information needed by those users in a format they need and understand.
4. Extraordinary ease-of-use.
5. Transformation of source data to a data structure and level of data quality necessary for users.
6. A strong support organization that maintains and extends the refinery and provides direct support to users.
7. A business directory that allows business users to identify the contents of the refinery, its sources and transformations, and its currency.

A Focused Audience of Users

Early notions of data warehousing assumed that the warehouse should contain all corporate data, which different end users would transform for their own purposes. But most workers in an enterprise have plenty of work to keep them busy; transforming data into useful information is very time-consuming. Learning how to use an IDF, even a well-designed one, takes time that interferes with each worker's primary task. If the old task successfully gets done the old way, then there is little incentive to take the time to learn a new way of working. It is easier and safer to ignore the new system and to keep working the old way. This has been the downfall of many IT projects dealing both with transaction processing and query. Instead, successful IDFs focus on the information needs of specific user communities and provide all the transformations. Furthermore, the user community feels an urgency for the information because the business value is so great; this urgency overcomes the natural impediment of the learning or uptake curve.

Committed Executive Sponsor

A committed executive sponsor can overcome many potential difficulties. For example, the IDF runs the risk of being viewed as just another source for conflicting data. In enterprises that successfully install data refineries, a senior executive declares that the refinery is the official book of record. If other sources generate reports with conflicting results, then those other sources are, by definition, wrong. This clear directive from senior management is a key ingredient in the success of data refineries.

Specific Delivery Vehicles

The delivery vehicle refers to the application that is placed on users' desktops and allows them to view the information in the refinery. Many refineries start with a simple ad hoc query tool on the desktop, which allows users to compose their own queries. Such a solution, however, limits the value of the refinery to the sophistication of the user, because such tools expose the user to the raw data structures. Such tools are necessary but too cumbersome for everyday use. They are analogous to having to use jumper cables to start your car instead of the ignition switch.

Extraordinary Ease of Use

Extraordinary ease of use is absolutely necessary if users are to accept the IDF as a natural part of their work environment. A number of hurdles traditionally stand in the way of ease of use. The Structured Query Language (SQL) is one example. Clumsy data structures (from the users' viewpoint) and especially normalized data structures are a second. Inconsistent data is a third. As a general rule of thumb, users tolerate two or three such hurdles; by the fourth, however, they quit trying and revert to older, known techniques for getting their work done. Thus, the data structures and the tools that deliver information to the desktop must reflect the users' view of information, not IT's view.

Transformation of Source Data

The transformation of data is a major function within the IDF. Two major classes of transformations are syntactic and semantic. Syntactic transformations include such items as transforming data to conform to IDF encoding standards. Semantic transformations are those that adjust data from different sources that were defined differently in the various source systems to a standard definition in the IDF.

For example, in auto insurance, one source system may define a "claim" as an incident, such as a car accident; another source system may define a claim not as the incident but as the administrative step when someone files an injury claim from the incident. These are quite different views of a claim, and the differences must be reconciled before the data can be stored in the IDF. Without reconciliation of the differences, users will perceive the IDF as containing poor information and will refuse to trust any report based on its contents.

Strong Support Organization

Like most production systems, an IDF requires a support organization. Two key aspects of such an organization are user support and systems support. User support requires personnel who understand the contents of the IDF and also understand the tools available to users. They are the ones who can answer the questions about where information can be found in the refinery, and how to use the tools to get it. Systems support includes all the usual aspects of supporting a production system: DBA support, technical tool support, and production support. Systems support personnel are the ones, for example, who ensure that night-time batch processes to populate the IDF execute to completion and are rerun when needed.

Business Directory

A business directory tells users what information is available, where it came from, and how it was transformed. An active directory may also define the currency of the information, that is, how recently it was updated. However, most effective directories are not active. The publication of paper-based definitions is often the most effective way to get the directory into the hands of any user who wishes to examine its contents and seems to be a popular solution, given the current state of technology and users' comfort with it.

ARCHITECTURAL COMPONENTS OF AN IDF

The IDF architecture is made up of four major components:

- The data refinery.
- The refining process that populates the refinery.
- The end-user applications.
- A business directory.

Data Refinery

The data refinery itself is usually a relational data base containing information extracted from other systems and transformed under the syntactic and semantic transformations mentioned earlier. A great deal of discussion has taken place in recent years about whether the data refinery needs to be a separate data base with extracted data. Why not make it a virtual data base, physically supported by pointers back into the source systems, so extraction and duplication is avoided? Practical experience to date has shown that there are two significant problems with the virtual data base approach.

First, most operational systems operate under significant load. The additional load imposed by online queries typically cannot be tolerated by the operational system. The prospect of creating additional load, which slows down the machine response to operational processing, is usually unacceptable. It may be, however, that the advent of massively parallel processors (MPP) will allow queries to complete so quickly and to provide so much processing power that concerns about operational systems become obsolete.

However, this leads to a second problem. Operational data is typically highly fragmented under the rules of normalization. Normalization of data allows data to be highly fragmented, which then allows application programs to be modified in significant ways as the business changes, without mandating a corresponding change in the data structures. This works very well for operational programming, which permits multiple levels of testing of the data reconstruction before the program is put back into production. However, for IDF queries, there is limited opportunity for testing. This imposes a requirement that the data structures be much simpler than those used for operational systems. Furthermore, pointers back into the source systems ignore the transformation needs discussed earlier. Thus, effective IDF systems extract data from source systems, transform it to be more usable by business personnel, and store it in a data refinery.

To address the issues of usability, the data in the data refinery is not stored according to the rules of normalization. Instead, it is stored under the rules of dimensional modeling. The dimensional model is often called a star schema. Techniques for developing the star schema are described below. Dimensional modeling is used heavily with multidimensional tools which use their own proprietary data stores. But it was originally developed for use with relational DBMSs, and it is highly recommended for use with RDBMSs in decision support systems.

Data redundancy is often a concern when data is extracted from operational systems and stored in the data refinery. In fact, there is little data redundancy between the data refinery and operational systems. This is because operational systems and the data refinery have different perspectives on content and time. Operational systems contain a great deal of data which is necessary for the operational system to operate, but has little to do with the business from a tactical or strategic decision-making standpoint. This system data is not extracted and copied to the refinery.

Furthermore, most operational systems impose strict limitations on the duration of data held in the operational system, because data volumes can place a serious drag on the performance of the operational system. Operational systems usually have much higher performance demands than do data refineries. So data that must be kept for several years is placed on the data refinery, and the refinery becomes the book of record for historical information. Furthermore, the data refinery is often enriched by the inclusion of external data, purchased from external providers or downloaded from cyberspace.

Data refineries are often very large data bases. Much of the value of today's IDF was delivered in the last decade through decision support systems built on multidimensional data bases. But today's requirements have exceeded the capacity of those systems. Thus, today it is more common to build the data refinery on a relational data base system (RDBMS) on a parallel processor which is capable of supporting very large systems. It is this requirement for very large data bases that has driven the IT community to view the data refinery as a separate component from the user tools that deliver value to the business community.

Refining Process

The refining process populates the data refinery. This is the component that requires the most effort from those who would build an IDF. If this component is not well done, the IDF will fail to deliver the value it promises. The combined refining process is a major contributor to the ability of the IDF to support decision-making in ways that have not been possible under the techniques used in the past.

The refining process contains several major functions:

- Extraction
- Cleansing
- Transformation
- Summarization
- Load

Each of these functions offers significant challenges which, combined, makes the refining process the most difficult component of the IDF architecture.

Extraction. Extraction addresses the question of how to source the data. Mapping data requirements against existing systems is a major challenge with most systems in business. Few systems are well documented. Original naming standards may have changed over time to ad hoc definitions that are poorly understood. Multiple source systems offer multiple opportunities to source data, and deciding between different options may prove difficult. Trying to bring data together from multiple sources may encounter incompatible cutoff dates, which means that the data from one system does not integrate with data from another over time. The data refinery may need transaction data that passes through operational systems but is not explicitly saved as a transaction. System loads on operational systems may mean that there is no spare capacity for running extract programs. The difficulties and resultant opportunities are numerous.

Cleansing. Cleansing is also a significant challenge. The data refinery often requires data that is captured in operational systems but is considered anecdotal only. As anecdotal data, it often is not structured or validated. Data that was not validated is almost guaranteed to have data quality problems: Data values will have an extraordinarily high error rate, and data items will have inconsistent structures. What should be done? If the data refinery is to have integrity, the data needs to be cleaned up before it goes into the data refinery, and the source system itself should do the cleaning. The refining process needs to perform well-documented transformations but should not be otherwise altering data passed to it from source systems. It becomes too difficult to trace information back to its source.

Cleansing data in source systems that do not presently validate it, however, requires programming changes to those systems. Because the source system has never found it necessary to validate the data before, support personnel are unlikely to give such changes much priority. This issue restates the importance of an executive sponsor who has the authority to prioritize such system enhancements. The difficulties of achieving consensus in this area makes it one of the major challenges of building a data refinery. Difficulties aside, there is a right answer for the majority of data refineries, and that right answer is that the source systems need to validate any data which is needed in the data refinery.

Transformation. Transformation is the third major function of the refining process. This has already been discussed, and is discussed in more detail in Section III of this book.

Summarization. The fourth function is summarization, the creation of summary data. Most refineries do not store base transactions. Instead, they store lightly-summarized transaction data. For example, a retailer may store the summarized transaction by hour by SKU by store. This lightly summarized data is likely to create very large volumes by itself. The large volume is the reason that most refineries do not store actual transactions. If higher summaries can be avoided, there are substantial benefits to be derived. Higher summaries make assumptions about the product hierarchy or store hierarchy, which are highly subject to change. Changes in the hierarchies mean that the summaries have to be re-calculated. The flip side of the problem is that summaries may be required to allow queries to complete in reasonable amounts of time. This is the area in which MPP can provide enormous benefit. If MPP can place enough processing power at the disposal of the queries, higher summaries may be avoidable. As yet, however, MPP is considered too expensive and risky by most companies. So higher-level summaries are the reality today.

Load. The fifth and last function of the refining process is the load process. Load is the process of getting data into the data refinery after the refinery has completed transformation and summarization. Traditionally, the RDBMS vendors have not invested heavily in their load programs. Load programs are used offline. Operational systems load data rather infrequently, so the efficiency of the load program was not considered to be of great importance. Data refineries deal with such large volumes of data, however, that the load process has become more important. RDBMS vendors have been improving their load programs to compete with specialist vendors; the specialists have offered competitive solutions for data refineries with far superior loading capabilities.

There are three ways to add to existing data refineries. Some tables in the refinery are reloaded completely every time an update is required. Others use a load-append approach, which just adds more data to the end of the data that already exists. Yet a third set of tables are updated by inserting new rows. Most organizations find that they need to use all three techniques, depending on the volumes and volatility of the data being added to the refinery. Later sections discuss this in more detail.

End-User Applications

End-user applications provide the delivery vehicles to astound the business community with the effectiveness of an IDF. The application that sits between the user and the data refinery is what delivers value. Successful IDFs have demonstrated the importance of knowing what analyses need to be performed, and then delivering applications that provide those analyses. General-purpose solutions that allow business personnel to compose their own queries offer only marginal value compared to the value derived from sophisticated applications supporting known analysis needs. Such applications can be built rather easily by IT professionals using advanced multidimensional tools.

Multidimensional tools are pricey, however. There is a common notion that a safer approach is to build the data refinery, give end users ad hoc query tools that generate SQL, and then wait for a period of time to see if the data refinery is useful for ad hoc query before investing in expensive tools. Such an approach is a self-defeating strategy, however, because it does not deliver enough value for the data refinery to be viewed as a success.

Business Directory

The business directory is the medium for apprising end users of the contents of the IDF. At a minimum, it describes the data contents in business terms, and the transformations that have changed that data from the way the end users may be used to seeing it in the operational systems.

If the business directory can serve more than the minimum requirements, then it also provides information on the currency of the data presently in the IDF (i.e., when the last update was run). For example, knowing that the data is supposed to be updated every weekend is not the same as being able to confirm on Monday morning that the update actually ran successfully.

Ideally, the business directory will be electronic. In fact, the best technique is to use the enterprise data dictionary for this function. This strategy is actually the exception rather than the rule. Data dictionary products are not designed for use by end users, and lack the usability characteristics needed. Furthermore, the licensing of the number of copies needed for all end users to have access is often prohibitive.

A more common solution is to build a simple, minimalist business directory. Occasional success stories are found from users of such products as Information Builders' Focus, or Lotus Notes. The most common success stories describe paper directories, published as pocket guides to the IDF. Despite its inherent update problems, paper continues to be ubiquitous and readily duplicable for new users, who need it the most. Furthermore, for most companies, the business directory is a reference that supports their use of the IDF, but is not used continuously. So many users find it more convenient to use the real estate of the PC screen for doing the main work of data slicing and analysis, and keep the directory off to the side of their work space.

TECHNOLOGY ISSUES WITH IDFS

Building an IDF requires more than competent client/server development skills. There are a number of additional, unique issues that arise which need special attention:

- Dimensional modeling.
- Data definitions.
- Metadata delivery.
- Operational data store.

Dimensional Modeling

Refinery data takes a dramatically different approach to organizing data. Instead of the normalized data advocated for the last two decades, with its focus on items of interest to the enterprise, dimensional modeling focuses on capturing events. Instead of concentrating on fragmenting data into small components that can be reassembled by programs regardless of how the business process changes, dimensional modeling focuses on organizing it to match the way business users perceive it.

In the 1960s, electronic systems gained popularity as a device for automation. In those early years, there were few guidelines for the design of systems. The 1970s began to offer guidance for the structuring of programs and data. A decade of system construction had demonstrated that all systems required modification as the business changes. Natural and intuitive ways for combining data and program logic were proving to be rigid and inflexible. The search was on for a better way to build systems.

IBM, among others, began to promote the idea that data should be stored according to its own nature. This contrasted with the tendency to store it the way the application programs wanted to process it. Experience was demonstrating that certain data characteristics were very volatile. For example, it was natural and intuitive to define data buckets for 10 order lines if the company's standard order form had space for 10 order lines. It was a lot easier, however, to change the printed form than to change the computer system when customers wanted 12 order lines on the form. IBM showed how to design the data so that the number of order lines was completely flexible, and not pre-defined to the application.

More complex rules followed, as the industry developed more experience with the ways that business requirements could change. After a decade of work, it became clear that it was better to fragment data into many different files (now called tables, with the advent of relational DBMSs). Programs then had great flexibility to re-assemble the data according to the current business requirements. When requirements changed, application programs had to be changed, but it turned out that they were much easier to change than the data. In fact, re-assembling the data is difficult. Application programs require multiple levels of testing to ensure that the assembly of the data and its subsequent processing actually meet the new business requirements.

Ad Hoc Query. So began the era of ad hoc query. Advances in technology, especially the development of SQL, opened the possibility that business personnel could now meet their own data information needs without waiting for the IT organization to do it for them.

The hope exceeded the reality. So long as the data was structured according to the rules popularized by IBM's work, the data was too fragmented to allow users to re-assemble it accurately. Most organizations who believe their users generate their own SQL successfully also admit that it is common for users to call IT requesting that a long-running query be canceled. An examination of the query shows that it was improperly constructed. Had it been allowed to complete, it would have delivered the wrong information. This leads to the more frightening question of how many short-running queries also deliver the wrong information because they were improperly constructed.

A second problem exists with highly-fragmented data: the process of reconstruction may take too long. Queries often require the processing of large amounts of data. Inefficiencies in the processing are magnified because of the amount of data involved. It is not uncommon for queries to run for hours.

Dimensional modeling can be viewed as an alternative to rules of normalization of data. Dimensional modeling also can be viewed as a return to earlier days of designing data in natural and intuitive ways. It is not the free-for-all that data design was in the 1960s. Rather, it is much more oriented to the way people think, instead of being fragmented according to innate properties of the data. The consequence of returning to older ways of designing data is that the data designs are less likely to have the flexibility to meet changing business requirements that one finds with normalized data. There is no silver bullet for any problem. However, the downside of dimensional modeling is outweighed by its usability and speed of response to queries.

Star Schema. Dimensional modeling produces a data design which is often called a star schema. The name derives from the nature of the design, which creates a large central table supported by multiple dimension tables which logically form the points of the star (Exhibit 2).

The star effect is a central table with multiple reference tables that surround it. Trend analysis tends to have three standard dimensions in addition to the obvious dimension of time: location, product, and customer. The three standard dimensions gave rise to the term *data cube*. Some stars have more than the classic three plus time. The example shown in Exhibit 2 supplements the usual four dimension tables with a fifth one representing retail promotions.

This data design is intuitive to most business personnel who deal with the analysis of retail sales. Sales are typically analyzed by the dimensions of customer, location, product, promotion, and time. Results are easily

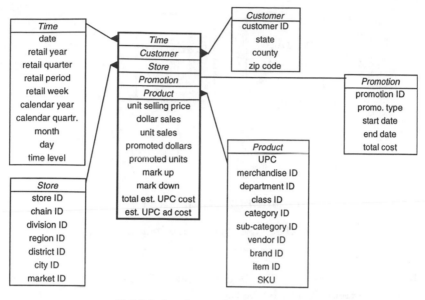

Exhibit 2. A sample star schema.

summed to analyze product across groups of customers, groups of locations, classes of products, and types of promotions in any combination.

Dimensional modeling is a necessary design technique for the successful IDF. The 1996 IDC study mentioned earlier found several instances of negative ROI on IDFs. The primary cause of negative ROI seemed to be the use of traditional normalization techniques for designing the data, instead of dimensional modeling techniques.

Data Definitions

Business users frequently complain that the data in operational systems is wrong. Sometimes it is, but many times it is correct to the people who use it the most. Other users perceive it as wrong because they use different definitions. Unfortunately, the items where most dispute exists are those items that represent the most important corporate concepts: What is a customer? What is a sale? What is a claim? Unless the semantic discrepancies can be resolved, diverse users will not believe the analyses derived from the data.

Although it is not necessary, or even possible, to get all users to agree on single definitions, they can typically be brought to consensus on a small number of different definitions for the same concept which need to be captured and differentiated. Focus groups are an excellent medium for deriving

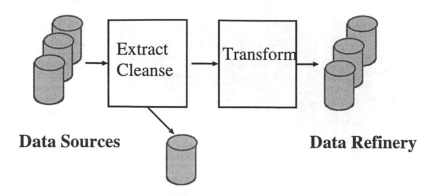

Operational Data Store

Exhibit 3. The Operational Data Store.

such consensus. The objective is not necessarily agreement that the definitions are perfect, but rather agreement that all the parties can live with the definitions as developed.

Metadata Delivery

After consensus is reached on definitions, the definitions need to be delivered to the end users in some ubiquitous medium. The paper catalog, though much reviled, is the most accepted and successful medium. It allows users to reference it while retaining and examining refinery applications on their terminals. It requires little training, and is easily available to new users. Organizations need to be very cautious about electronic delivery of metadata; metadata products are very confusing to most business users, and reflect a severe IT bias.

Operational Data Store

There is a growing desire to move operational reporting from operational systems to the IDF, but this is not easy to do. The reporting needs to occur before the data has been transformed, so reports on operational output can be directly tied to operational inputs. Therefore, a new concept called the Operational Data Store (ODS) has been developed to complement the data refinery. The ODS should be viewed as a temporary staging area within the refining process, after the data has been extracted and cleansed, but before it has been transformed, as shown in Exhibit 3.

The ODS may contain more detailed data than the data refinery itself but retains the data for only a short period, such as one day or one week. If the reporting is primarily batch reporting, then the data is likely to be normalized. If the reporting is more ad hoc, then it is likely to be dimensional instead, using the star schema.

The success of an IDF is dependent on the specific implementation techniques employed for delivering end user access, and for the refining process that converts data from source systems into warehouse data.

SUMMARY

Successful IDFs focus on specific business problems that require analysis and then deliver a high-value application to a focused group of users to help them solve that problem. Additional applications can then be added to support other user groups based on the value received by the first group.

An IDF is most useful when it is used by personnel whose job descriptions require that they spend much of their time analyzing information as a basis for tactical or strategic decision making. Retail buyers use the information for determining what and how much to buy; insurance underwriters develop risk management strategies; utilities study repair trends to determine capital investments. If the purpose of the IDF is to allow users access to data, but there is no understanding of the kinds of access needed or the use that will be made of the data retrieved, then it is unlikely that the IDF will be successful.

Chapter II-6
Knowledge Management

There is a good deal of interest these days in the topic of knowledge management. The valuation of intangible, intellectual assets is becoming an accepted part of business today. Thus, it makes sense that managing those assets effectively is now looked at as a vital aspect of maintaining competitiveness. This chapter looks at the following issues:

- What is knowledge?
- What is knowledge management?
- Why implement a knowledge management capability?
- What are the essential elements of an effective knowledge management capability?
- What is the required technology framework?

DEFINITIONS: KNOWLEDGE AND KNOWLEDGE MANAGEMENT

Providing a definition of knowledge on which everyone can agree may be impossible. There is a wide spectrum of definitions, ranging from the inclusive to the exclusive. Some hold that knowledge is simply the content provided by organizations within the convergence framework discussed in this book. Others hold a more precise sense that knowledge must attain a quality far beyond traditional data and information.

For the purposes of this chapter, knowledge is "complex content." That is, the fact that IS staff even use the word *knowledge* means that the content in aggregate has attained a level of complexity beyond that of traditional transactional data. Knowledge is captured not only in figures and text, but also in voice, images, video, and other mediums. To prevent the discussion from becoming too metaphysical, it is best to remember that content cannot be called knowledge unless it can be captured in some way, stored, and then delivered.

Since Alvin Toffler and Peter Drucker first began to talk about the "third wave" and the "knowledge economy," even academic economists have begun to accept and write about knowledge as the new form of capital in the post-industrial economy. Economist Paul Romer, for example, writes,

"Instead of just capital and labor and raw materials producing output, it is the ideas themselves and the economic incentives that lead to their creation and diffusion that are the fundamental determinants of economic well-being."

If knowledge is a form of capital, however, it must be able to move from one person to another, and it must be able to grow. "Knowledge management" is the group of activities that performs these functions. Given the criticality of knowledge in today's economy, attention must be paid to the effective management of knowledge: identifying, capturing, and making knowledge easily accessible at the point of need. Although this seems simple and obvious, in practice it is quite difficult and presents several new concepts to master.

Perhaps the clearest way to understand the potential impact of knowledge management is to illustrate how one company is pursuing initiatives to improve its knowledge management capability in the field of insurance.

An insurance brokerage places risks in the insurance marketplace on behalf of its clients. The reason that a company uses the services of an insurance brokerage in the first place, rather than going directly to the insurance marketplace itself, is the brokerage has superior knowledge about the insurance marketplace and is able to leverage that knowledge to provide its clients with more efficient service and more cost-effective coverage. In other words, the brokerage adds value through knowledge. Its only competitive advantage lies in its ability to apply knowledge effectively to provide client service during the actual risk placement process, a process that is highly complex and can take up to 12 months to complete.

One global insurance brokerage realized that it needed to decrease the elapsed time required to place risks and also to reduce the number of errors and omissions that typically occurred during the placement process. This company realized that, although knowledge and valuable experience were being created with each risk-placement deal, this knowledge was not being captured during the placement process and thus could not be leveraged effectively on subsequent risk placements, either by the same or different brokers. The only recorded information happened at the very end of the placement process, when the basic structured data elements that defined the placement transaction (e.g., client name, risk coverage amount, and premium amount) were recorded to feed the traditional back-office data processing systems, such as billing and accounts receivable. None of the real essence of broking a deal (i.e., the nuances, the negotiating techniques, or the creative approaches to handling unusual client needs) were being captured electronically. Thus, information technology was being used only for record keeping, probably the least important part of the company's value proposition to its clients.

Another important issue is that, from the perspective of the insurance brokerage, the placement process calls for constant interaction and collaboration among people from other companies: the client company and the multiple insurance carriers that might be participating in the deal. Thus, the knowledge that is created during the placement process cannot, by definition, be confined to inside the walls of the brokerage and among the brokers only.

This particular insurance company embarked upon a significant set of initiatives to try to attack the real opportunity: the entire life cycle of the broking process. Included in the entire life cycle is how knowledge could be identified, captured, and made available during the process to increase the speed and quality of client service. These initiatives are addressing not only the technology challenges, but also the process improvements (i.e., the flow of information and responsibility) and the resulting organizational changes (i.e., the measurements and rewards) required, including the cross-company aspects so important to the broking process. This chapter focuses on all of these critical aspects of knowledge management.

ESSENTIAL ELEMENTS OF KNOWLEDGE MANAGEMENT

As the above example demonstrates, effective knowledge management is a complex proposition that involves a multitude of competencies to execute. This section examines each of the primary competencies required for knowledge management: strategy, process, people, and technology, paying particular attention to the technology aspects.

Strategy

A company strategy should set an overall framework for knowledge management. In many ways, knowledge is content that has the potential to affect behavior. This is very powerful, but it also can be very dangerous if the behavior change is not in accordance with a company's overall strategic vision and mission.

One of the key management issues associated with knowledge management is that a commitment to an effective knowledge management capability is indeed a strategic commitment. Knowledge management pertains to opportunity enhancement rather than cost control; its goal is to make a quantum leap forward rather than incremental adjustments. Many companies embark upon knowledge management initiatives without any type of formal, quantitative cost-benefit analysis because it is simply the appropriate action to take.

This does not mean that a knowledge management initiative should be undertaken without the proper thought and planning. It does mean that, to most companies, knowledge management is and should be considered a strategic imperative that must be addressed in some manner. There is no formula that "proves" whether knowledge management is worthwhile to an organization.

Process

Knowledge management is a means rather than an end; it enhances a company's ability to execute its core processes in a manner that gives it a competitive advantage. The linchpins are the actual core business processes themselves, for they provide the context for both the original creation of knowledge and its effective application.

The insurance brokerage mentioned in the previous section highlights the importance of process to knowledge creation and application. This example also demonstrates the criticality of the inter-department and inter-enterprise element to the overall process. A chain is only as strong as its weakest link. Likewise, a process is only as strong as its individual participants, regardless of which department or company for which the individual participants happen to work.

Numerous companies have implemented knowledge sharing systems out of context, or at least out of synch, with underlying core business processes. Such knowledge-sharing solutions that treat knowledge management as a separate and distinct process are typically easier to implement and can definitely add value, but in a sub-optimal fashion. The most notable problem is that of knowledge capture: Capture simply does not happen consistently and with high quality if it requires significant additional effort above and beyond a worker's normal processes. Without effective knowledge capture, all other aspects of knowledge management are moot.

It might seem that the typical worker does not have the time to capture knowledge while completing business processes, and that, as a result, a separate process and a separate group of people should be responsible for knowledge capture. In fact, this section discusses some special roles and responsibilities that can greatly assist and support the knowledge management efforts, but those outside of the process cannot, by themselves, constitute effective knowledge management. The key is how to provide appropriate knowledge management support mechanisms together with the actual knowledge workers in the process, so knowledge can be captured and used with the greatest ease and efficiency.

A complete life cycle for knowledge management must address the following:

- Capture of knowledge from external or internal sources.
- Classification of knowledge.
- Valuation of the knowledge.

- Access to the knowledge.
- Use of the knowledge.
- Improvement of the knowledge.
- Retirement of the knowledge when it has outlived its usefulness.

The field of library science makes clear that there is an essential role for the librarian. This role is responsible for managing the process of classification and providing assistance to people when the "least effort" access models to the knowledge do not work. This role manages the content created in the actual work process and helps to provide access to wider sets of knowledge that may not otherwise be known to the average worker.

The librarian cannot act alone, however. A librarian is primarily concerned with the acquisition, classification, and accessing of knowledge. This role does not address the initial valuation as well as improvement and retiring of knowledge. Put another way, although librarians like to purchase books, they do not like people inserting improved ideas into existing books, nor do they like people tearing pages out of them. The initial valuation and continual enrichment of knowledge is a key aspect of knowledge management, but it can only be performed by those with the knowledge and the context of how this knowledge relates to the business processes. This synthesis role is the role of a knowledge manager. The knowledge manager represents the actual knowledge workers conducting the core business processes and has an obvious symbiotic support relationship with librarian. The following section examines the knowledge manager role in more detail.

Definition of a Controlled Vocabulary

Effective knowledge management requires a classification scheme by which to find knowledge components. Such an approach is achieved in the field of library science through the use of a controlled vocabulary. This vocabulary would be a basis for accessing the knowledge components found in a knowledge repository. The controlled vocabulary is a key step to organizing knowledge and making it available to people. If we are to provide one-stop shopping for knowledge components, the controlled vocabulary is the point where the knowledge shopping begins.

Creating a controlled vocabulary requires one to go through long lists of terms, adding, deleting, and modifying each controlled list. The field of library science suggests that such lists consist of the following:

- The primary term itself
- Related terms that might be used in place of the primary term
- Broader terms that encompass the primary term
- Narrower terms that refine the primary term
- Context terms that describe in what different contexts the primary term is typically used

The following table is an example of one such controlled vocabulary list for a technology knowledge repository:

Primary Term	Related Terms	Broader Terms	Narrower Terms	Context Terms
Asset Management	Configuration management Inventory management	Distributed systems management Managing change	Hardware management Software management	Requirements Benefits Design Architecture Implementation Tools Products Experiences Best Practices Futures Economics Contacts

The term *controlled vocabulary* does not mean that there are no changes to the vocabulary. Rather, it means that changes occur under controlled conditions. A controlled vocabulary is likely to need reassessing on a regular basis (e.g., semi-annually).

Many sources of changes are possible. One is to monitor the use of search engines and then to report those cases when the controlled vocabulary does not meet needs but when the searches found hits for requested terms. Change requests from knowledge managers would be another source of change. In addition, monitoring of usage is necessary, to watch for cases when certain terms are no longer in use. These terms can be marked for possible removal from the list because of lack of use. All of these potential changes will need to be fed into the twice-yearly update of the controlled vocabulary.

Accessing, Using, and Creating Knowledge Components

Once a controlled vocabulary list is defined, how can it be used for one-stop shopping for knowledge components? The essential idea that of a knowledge directory, which users search using the terms in the controlled vocabulary. This directory identifies, for a given term or combination of terms, the knowledge components that have been identified for the terms. The directory also includes a knowledge descriptor for each component. The knowledge descriptor is typically sufficient to determine if the component is of value to a given user in a given situation. The descriptor thus prevents the user from having to actually access the entire knowledge component before determining its relevance.

As an example, the following are questions that one would be able to ask with a controlled vocabulary. The words in italics are controlled vocabulary terms.

> Find all knowledge components on *Architectures* for *Client/Server*.

Because of the capability of the underlying relational data base technology required for an effective knowledge directory, one could also ask more complex things, such as:

> Find all knowledge components on *Designs* of *Architectures* for *Agents* on the *Internet*.

What would come back would be a list of all such knowledge components with sufficient networking and resource information to make it feasible to get them. It should not matter whether the components were stored in Lotus Notes (i.e., .NSF files), in Word (.DOC files), or some place on a corporate intranet or the Internet. This is the point of one-stop shopping. The ability to do this would free workers from having to learn about the physical storage and format of the individual knowledge components.

The Point of Knowledge-Component Creation

To enable such a usage scenario, an understanding of how knowledge components get created in the first place is required. At what point is a knowledge component created? What is the creation process?

As discussed earlier, the integration of knowledge management with core business processes is very important, because the processes themselves provide context for both the use and creation of knowledge. The business processes produce results (e.g., a design, a spec, or a document) that are all candidates to become knowledge components. A knowledge manager is responsible for determining which particular process results should become knowledge components. The knowledge manager must identify the appropriate terms from the controlled vocabulary that properly describe the knowledge component. He or she must also develop a descriptor of the component. The descriptor gives an overview of the knowledge component in sufficient detail so one could determine the value of the knowledge component without having to actually access it. The knowledge manager also places a valuation on the component (i.e., is the content based on someone's opinion or has it gone through levels of official authorization?). Finally, the component must be made available to the appropriate personnel, both inside and outside of the enterprise. To enable this, the knowledge manager must provide a link to the actual physical technical storage location of the component (e.g., a Web page URL or a Lotus Notes data base.) and ensure that the proper security mechanisms are in place for the component.

Content-Based Index Searches

In addition to the search-and-classification capabilities that the controlled vocabulary and directory provide, powerful content-based search engines also can be helpful for situations in which the provided controlled vocabulary framework does not provide the appropriate retrieval framework for the end user. Such search engines construct a content-based index based on all the words actually contained within the knowledge components themselves. The end user can specify a word or combination of words in which he or she is interested, and the search engine retrieves all components that contain the desired word or combination of words. Several examples of this technique can be found today on the World Wide Web, such as AltaVista, Excite! and Lycos.

This approach has both advantages and disadvantages. One advantage is that the search does not depend upon the creation and maintenance of either a controlled vocabulary or knowledge directory, as these were defined above. With content-based searches, the user merely enters words or word combinations he or she is interested in and receives a list of all components that contain the desired word. Because the creation of content-based indexes is fully automated, they can be kept very current and are rarely out of date. This is different from a controlled vocabulary-based directory that probably cannot be updated for new terms or term usage more frequently than semi-annually.

The primary disadvantage to the content-based index approach today is that the typical user is often inundated with an excessively large number of items that meet his or her search criteria, most of which are not necessarily in context of the original search request and are therefore useless. This problem should improve as search agents become more sophisticated, but today such an approach should not be considered as the only knowledge access technique.

An example of these two access techniques is to compare the popular Yahoo! catalog on the World Wide Web (www.yahoo.com) with the various search engines mentioned above. The Yahoo! catalog classifies hundreds of thousands of Web sites based on a taxonomy (i.e., the controlled vocabulary) consisting of more than 25,000 different categories. The user starts with the Yahoo! top-level category list and continues to drill down through various levels of subcategories until the desired information is found. This approach has been so accurate and easy to use that more than one million people per day use the Yahoo! site. However, the user must understand key aspects of the taxonomy hierarchy. For example, Yahoo! considers *Movies* to be under Entertainment rather than under Art. In essence, this categorization decision represents a particular point of view (i.e., that of the people at Yahoo! who control the taxonomy) that must be understood by the user.

If this is understood, the user can drill down and find knowledge that is likely to be highly relevant to his interest. On the other hand, the user of a search engine such as Excite! is not constrained by having to understand whether movies are considered art or entertainment; he or she can merely search for a particular movie by entering "movies AND Godfather" and receive pointers to all Web documents that contain both words. However, this user is likely to receive thousands of references, many of which may be nothing more than peoples' personal home pages stating that the Godfather was one of their favorite movies, not exactly what the user had in mind.

The point is not that one technique is necessarily more effective than the other, but that both techniques have their strengths and weaknesses, and both should be considered for usage. In fact Yahoo! now combines both capabilities together in that it provides content-based searches within a particular classification category. If a content-based search can be narrowed using a controlled vocabulary and classification scheme, then the number of useless hits can be kept to a minimum.

PEOPLE

Effective knowledge management requires a fundamental change in the way most companies do business, and people are at the heart of any effective change. Significant changes to measurements and rewards are typically required to support knowledge management. This section examines the issues for four distinct sets of people:

- Knowledge users.
- The line knowledge manager.
- The competency knowledge manager.
- The chief knowledge officer.

Knowledge Users

Several important considerations for the average knowledge user center around effective contribution and reuse of knowledge. Although the roles of the various knowledge managers are important ones, an effective knowledge management capability is heavily dependent on the users, for the users themselves are actually involved in the day-to-day core business processes that provide the primary context for knowledge capture and reuse.

This, of course, presents a natural conflict: Taking the time to capture knowledge and best practices about a given core business process typically does not contribute immediately to the successful completion of that process. Through an effective knowledge management capability, such captured knowledge is likely to contribute significantly to subsequent activities performed by other users, but because this knowledge capture does not provide immediate payback to the original contributor, it is a significant challenge to encourage knowledge capture behaviors as the norm. Managing this challenge is the responsibility of the line knowledge manager and the competency knowledge manager.

Knowledge users:

- Are trained in the controlled vocabulary so that it can be used intuitively.
- Provide feedback on the vocabulary usage for its evolution.
- Use automated tools to find and access knowledge, including tools based on the controlled vocabulary and search engines.
- Work with both the line knowledge managers and competency knowledge managers to ensure that the users are contributing effectively to the objectives of both line and competency knowledge development.

The Line Knowledge Manager

A line knowledge manager has responsibility for the management of everyday line activities within his or her area of responsibility. As it pertains to knowledge management, the line knowledge manager is also a knowledge user, but he or she also must:

- Identify the results of normal, everyday line activities in his or her responsibility area that are candidates for classification as knowledge components.
- Identify the correct controlled vocabulary terms to apply to the candidate knowledge components and develop a descriptor for each.
- Provide feedback on the controlled vocabulary for its evolution.
- Define the initial valuation of new knowledge components.
- Implement the measurements and rewards system developed by the competency knowledge managers.

The Competency Knowledge Manager

Every organization has key competencies, or skills and capabilities, that it must excel in to succeed. These competencies typically transcend individual situations or projects but ideally are enhanced as a natural part of carrying out daily work activities. For example, in the insurance broking example, some competencies are fundamental to the broking business (e.g., managing client relationships, financial services trends, industry acumen, and risk strategies). Ideally, these competencies are established in the broking professionals before they begin a specific risk placement, even though the broker can learn a lot from the knowledge that gets created during each and every placement. The role of the competency knowledge manager is to manage the knowledge for a given competency area, independent of the individual instances where those competencies are used in carrying out work activities. Competency knowledge managers:

- Define and develop a measurements and rewards structure that encourages contribution of knowledge capital from daily line activities.
- Define and maintain the controlled vocabulary framework.
- Identify an overall executive sponsor for each broad yet clearly defined competency scope.
- Determine the new knowledge components, or changes to existing ones, required to support the competency scope.
- Identify the correct controlled vocabulary terms to apply to the candidate knowledge components and develop a descriptor for each.
- Provide feedback on the controlled vocabulary for its evolution.
- Define the initial valuation of new knowledge components.
- Set security and ownership specifications for content and provide guidance on the content accessibility as a function of the value of intellectual property.
- Perform any needed analysis or synthesis of a particular subset of knowledge.
- Approve the modification of knowledge base content within area of responsibility.
- Monitor any electronic discussions related to area of responsibility.

The Chief Knowledge Officer

The chief knowledge officer (CKO) is responsible for the overall knowledge assets of a company. The CKO is responsible for defining the areas in which the knowledge capabilities of the organization should evolve, based on its ongoing mission and vision. The CKO has the ultimate enterprise-wide responsibility for the controlled vocabulary and knowledge directory and tackles the difficult issues associated with cross-department or cross-enterprise processes that have unique knowledge sharing requirements. The CKO also is responsible for ensuring that an appropriate technology infrastructure is in place for effective knowledge management. This responsibility is largely a coordination role, as the technology infrastructure needed for knowledge management is likely to be managed outside of the CKO's jurisdiction. This is because the required technology infrastructure should be used for more than knowledge management alone, as will be discussed in subsequent sections.

TECHNOLOGY

Knowledge management represents some new challenges from the technology perspective. There are new application characteristics that are typical of knowledge management solutions. In addition, some new technology architecture components are required to support these new characteristics. The remainder of this chapter will be devoted to these technology issues. (Exhibit 1) illustrates some of the newer technology components that must be considered and brought into overall technology architectures for knowledge management.)

Knowledge Management Key Characteristics

Knowledge management solutions have the following characteristics that are typically not found in traditional client/server solutions:

- *They manage rich information objects.* Teams work with a wide variety of information, far beyond the simple fixed-length data elements managed in relational DBMS products. Image, voice, video, and large amounts of unstructured text are what teams share, in addition to more structured, quantitative data.
- *They are externally aware.* Today's virtual teams focus on end-to-end business processes that span individual functional departments, and often even extend outside the enterprise. As described above, these inter-department and inter-enterprise processes must focus on external sources and destinations of information, rather than assuming that all information can be housed within internal proprietary data bases.
- *They transcend time and place.* Today's virtual team members are often mobile and must be able to participate in team processes regardless of time and place. This requires the ability to work off-line with a store-and-forward, "deferred update" scheme.
- *They are satisfying to the end user.* IT professionals have always worked to achieve a high degree of usability in their applications, but they have traditionally been creating single-function applications for more clerical, single-function users. Today's professional users demand more from application usability, and they will shun the automated solution if this demand isn't met.

Some relatively new infrastructure components are required to support the above application characteristics. These components break down into two types: lower-level infrastructure services and infrastructure applications that use the lower-level infrastructure services (Exhibit 1).

Key Infrastructure Components

Core infrastructure services are the underlying technology components required to enable the knowledge management characteristics referred to in the previous section. They also provide support for the infrastructure applications covered in the next section.

The User Shell. The user shell is a user's cross-application operating environment; it is the user interface (UI) that the user sees and interacts with. Ideally, the user shell should provide consistency across all of a

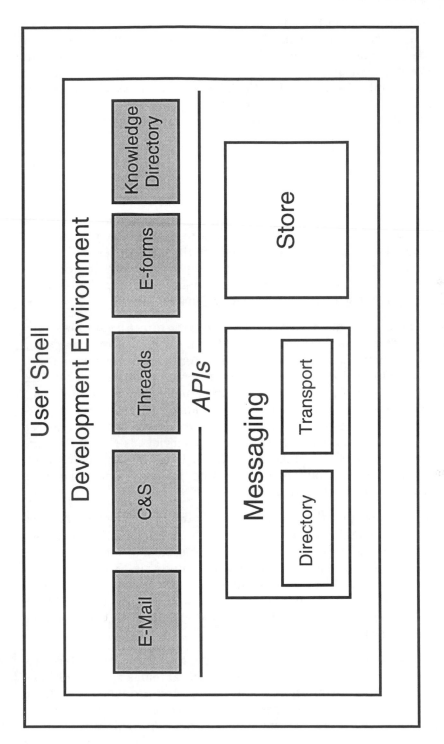

Exhibit 1.   Knowledge management framework.

user's activities, rather than having unique user interface characteristics for each specific application used. An example of a user shell is the Lotus Notes desktop: tabbed folders, data base icons, views, and forms. This shell provides a consistent set of user constructs for all Notes applications. Another example of a user shell is the Microsoft Windows 95 desktop and Explorer UI. HTML-based Web browsers are beginning to emerge as a separate user shell with a certain level of consistency between all Web pages.

The Messaging Architecture. A necessary function for a team is communication. This typically requires a messaging architecture to serve as the infrastructure for communication and sharing of information among the team members. Because of the mobility characteristic identified above, a store-and-forward capability is paramount to supporting work flows or collaborative activities. A messaging architecture is the primary technology beneath any E-mail product, but a robust offering also serves as the infrastructure for additional functionality such as group scheduling, work flow, bulletin boards and other collaborative functions, and also provides application programming interfaces (APIs) for all functions.

At the core of any messaging architecture is the directory services component. Directory services are the foundation for distributed computing systems, as they essentially define the network and its resources (both people and information objects). Today's generation of directory services typically provide only application specific administrative support (e.g., Lotus Notes Name & Address Book only provides basic resource and security services to Notes itself). In addition to the Notes Name & Address Book, another example of today's directory services is Novell NetWare Directory Services (NDS) and the Microsoft Exchange Server directory service. Directory services offer APIs to facilitate the development of custom solutions that use directory information.

Another important aspect of messaging is transport services. A transport service enables information to get from point A to point B. It provides queuing, store-and-forward communication, intermediate storage, routing, and generalized procedural and management interfaces. Examples of message transport would be the proprietary native Lotus Notes transport protocol, the X.400 protocol, and the Simple Mail Transfer Protocol (SMTP). Microsoft's Messaging API (MAPI) is a good example of a programming interface to messaging transport services.

A messaging architecture is a key strategic resource of the enterprise. This is becoming more and more true as virtual teams span traditional departmental and organizational boundaries. Any products that utilize messaging and directory services must be considered in the context of enterprise strategy, rather than individual workgroup needs alone.

Store. A generalized information store provides a server-based repository for storing unstructured and semi-structured information created by users, such as E-mail, attachments, electronic forms, images, and voice messages. Ideally, information stores allow for granular security, the establishment of storage limits and age limits, advanced information retrieval capabilities, and replication capabilities to manage distributed copies of information. Lotus Notes data bases and Microsoft Exchange folders are good examples of a general-purpose object store. HTML/HTTP Web servers are examples of simpler, file system-like information stores. Information stores should provide programming interfaces for all information management functions.

More traditional information stores (e.g., relational DBMSs, image management products, etc.) are still required for many information management needs. These products should not be ignored just because they do not come prepackaged along with the other infrastructure services in a single product.

The Development Environment. An integrated development environment is required to support the development of end-user solutions based on the above component services. For example, Lotus Notes provides integrated development capabilities that produce Notes data base applications that use the Notes user shell "look and feel," leverage the Notes Name & Address Book directory, store information in Notes data base stores, and use the Notes transport protocols to route information.

In addition, because of the APIs provided for each individual component service, more customized solutions can be developed that use alternative or additional services. For example, a developer could write a Visual Basic or Visual C++ application for a more Windows 95-like user experience that stores information in Notes data bases but uses Microsoft's MAPI as the transport mechanism. This "mix and match" approach is much more complex but does allow for more customized solutions than the "standard" development environment.

These are the component building blocks from which vendor shrink-wrapped solutions are built and on top of which custom knowledge management solutions can be built. Up until now, vendors have tended to offer vertical application solutions using only their own proprietary component services, and they have encouraged their customers to do the same. Although this is the higher productivity approach, it is also the lower capability approach, and the Internet-oriented, open style of computing is already beginning to render this vertical approach obsolete.

Infrastructure Applications

Several generic infrastructure applications typically make up part of an effective knowledge management technology environment. Although some of these applications are theoretically ready to use "out of the box," they typically require the development of significant policies and procedures and training before they can be used effectively. In addition, custom functional solutions can be built on top of or around these generic applications, and on top of the underlying infrastructure services.

E-mail. E-mail is nothing more than a correspondence application written by a vendor that typically uses that vendor's messaging, directory, transport, and store. Often, the vendor provides additional value-added features such as administration tools and end-user agents. Examples include Lotus Notes mail data bases and the Microsoft Exchange in-box application.

Group Calendaring and Scheduling. Group calendaring and scheduling provides group activity and task management capabilities to the team-based activities associated with knowledge management. This application uses a directory and information store to manage resources and schedules, transport to route meeting and task requests, the E-mail application to present request information to users, and a calendaring interface to present scheduling information. Example products include Lotus Organizer and Microsoft Schedule+.

Threaded Discussions. Threaded discussion or news reader applications enable the creation of what are commonly known as electronic bulletin boards or discussions. They enable a user to follow the history of discussion on a subject (e.g., the original item, responses to the original item, responses to responses) and to build up increasingly robust knowledge about a topic. Threaded discussion applications typically use directory services for user information, store services to manage the discussion items, and present a hierarchical drill-down user metaphor that is in concert with the overall user shell. Examples include Internet Usenet newsgroups, Lotus Notes discussion data bases, and Microsoft Exchange folder posts.

E-forms and Workflow Applications. E-forms and workflow applications enable end-users to develop simple forms-based (with or without basic routing) solutions without programming that adhere to the overall user shell metaphor. This is typically achieved through both e-forms generators and sample applications (e.g., templates). Ideally, the end-user solutions created with the e-forms generator are extensible with professional developer tools such as Visual Basic or Visual C++. These solutions typically use the information store for forms management, and directory and transport for forms routing. Examples here include Lotus Notes data base templates, and Microsoft Exchange Forms Designer and sample applications.

The Knowledge Directory. As discussed above, the knowledge directory is a key component of an effective knowledge management capability, as it contains critical information on and pointers to the individual knowledge components, regardless of where these components might be physically located. Based on a controlled vocabulary, the knowledge directory provides a needed framework for knowledge usage.

The document management model is probably the best model to consider when describing the underlying technical architecture required for an effective knowledge directory. Document management products, such as Documentum or Saros Mezzanine, provide for a control record for each document or object being managed by the product; each control record contains key data attributes about that object, as well as a pointer to the actual object itself. The data attributes are used for subsequent attribute-based searches. Check-in and check-out security as well as version control capabilities are built around the control record.

The knowledge directory is an excellent infrastructure application for a document management engine. Each knowledge component has an entry in the knowledge directory. Among the attributes stored for each knowledge component are the knowledge descriptor and the categorization terms, based upon the controlled vocabulary.

CONCLUSION

Knowledge management will continue to grow in importance in coming years. One key to watch is the extent to which knowledge assets and other intangibles become an accepted part of most companies' financial reports. Many companies already report these intangibles.

As for the knowledge management applications themselves, the types of knowledge contained will broaden, and the applications will move beyond capturing, storing, and displaying knowledge. They will begin to provide more sophisticated ways to organize knowledge, and will incorporate agent technology so that users can find a wide range of useful knowledge. The knowledge component will have the ability to detect similarities and patterns in knowledge and provide analogues and related knowledge components based on these patterns.

Chapter II-7
Reinventing Testing in an Age of Netcentric Computing

Testing is an often-overlooked and underestimated facet of systems development. In a client/server environment, testing can make up 50% to 80% of a development effort. The age of netcentric computing adds untold complexities to systems development; convergence applications integrate customers and suppliers, cross multiple technologies, and involve multiple user groups, each with varying expectations, requirements, and level of knowledge. Therefore, the importance of testing rises significantly. This chapter provides a detailed look at a structured approach to testing using a model well-suited to managing the risks of the convergence environment.

The structured approach to testing advocated in this chapter has been successfully applied to save organizations time and money while increasing software quality and delivery reliability. The savings are realized through the implementation of the V-model of testing, metrics, and automation to dramatically improve the productivity and effectiveness of the software delivery processes. This chapter discusses a framework for testing that has been successfully applied to custom development, package installation, and maintenance, in traditional development environments as well as in iterative, rapid development, and object-oriented environments.

WHY REINVENT TESTING?

Testing costs organizations significant amounts of money. Currently, too much effort goes into testing, and many testing approaches waste both time and money. The value derived from today's testing processes does not match the effort expended. For typical systems projects in which 50% to 80% of the budget goes into testing-related activities, including test execution, impact analysis, and error resolution, a mere 10% reduction in the overall testing effort can translate into significant annual savings for the average IS department. Typical testing approaches exercise only 40% of application code, leaving an average of 3.79 defects per thousand lines of code (KLOC) and as many as five defects per KLOC.

There is cause for concern, then, that testing approaches that are ineffective in the current computing environment will only worsen as the computing environment becomes more complex. The risk to the average company today is significant. Customer expectations are escalating; the average business person is now familiar with computer technology and is less tolerant of imperfect solutions. Also, IS departments are losing control of their user community, as users are now customers and cannot be trained to make up for poorly tested solutions.

Testing approaches were left behind in the client/server revolution. Design, development, code, and architecture were all significantly changed by the client/server revolution, but testing was not, and testing today looks very much like it did 10 years ago, even though the applications are very different. In addition, software testing has not kept pace with the technology revolution; automation in the testing process has been vastly underused. Tools to automate test planning, test preparation, and execution are now available in the marketplace, as are tools for test data management and configuration management. These are all highly integrated, labor-intensive tasks that can benefit from the use of tools not only to increase speed and productivity but also to reduce the occurrence of human error. However, in spite of the availability of more mature tools in the marketplace, the use of automation in the testing processes remains limited, partially because the tools available have only recently matured to the point where it makes sense to invest in them. Many organizations are either unaware that tools exist to automate testing activities, or they looked at testing tools years ago when the tools market was immature and do not realize the advances made since. Another common reason for a lack of testing automation is that IS departments begin considering the automation requirements of the testing process too late in the project, when there is not enough time to evaluate, select, and implement tools.

Today's testing processes do not address the complexities of client/server computing, much less those of convergence. Multilayered architectures, graphical user interfaces (GUIs), user-driven or decision-support systems, and the need to interface heterogeneous systems and architectures all present new risks and challenges for information technologists. A proliferation of users and user types in netcentric applications all provide and demand information from an enterprise system. This situation presents massively complex design challenges, as well as security and error-avoidance requirements. All of these complexities must be recognized, designed for, and built into a set of applications. Then, just as important, they must be tested to ensure that they perform as expected.

As development in the client/server world matures, and as the industry becomes more comfortable with client/server development, IS departments' attention increasingly turns to testing. Recent recognition of testing as an important facet of successful systems delivery can be seen in the significant increase in the number of seminars and conferences dedicated to testing and software quality. Likewise, there has been a trend toward increased emphasis on testing indicated by the identification of dedicated testing or software quality managers or entire departments within large IS organizations.

All of the factors just mentioned — increased complexity, higher level of effort spent on testing, increased risk, and minimal revision in testing approach — are leading to the inevitable: Software developers must reinvent the way they test systems. Reinventing testing is part of the current movement toward quality in systems development, making use of concepts introduced in manufacturing, such as quality management (QM) and just in time (JIT), which are modified to apply to software development. Applying these manufacturing concepts to systems development requires IS development managers to adopt new or modified models of the development process and project organization. The key components of the V-Model testing approach presented in this chapter are:

- Well-defined development processes, each with suppliers and customers, in which an overall quality product is achieved only when quality is delivered at every point in the chain.
- Structured, repeatable testing.
- Definition of metrics to be used for continuous process improvement.
- Use of automation to improve speed and reduce errors.
- New management approaches to organization and communication.

By applying a V-Model testing approach, many organizations have realized improved quality, reliability, efficiency, and delivery time. They have also achieved better risk management and cost avoidance. For example, an internal software development organization within Andersen Consulting was able to achieve an 80% reduction in the software defects delivered to customers while improving testing productivity and delivery speed. Another example is a large drugstore chain in the U.S., which realized a 100% improvement in testing productivity while achieving nearly fivefold improvements in software quality.

A MODEL FOR NETCENTRIC TESTING

This section presents a quick review of the V-Model approach, a framework for structured, repeatable testing, serving as a basis for the V-Model testing approach needed to successfully manage netcentric systems development.

The V-Model provides a structured testing framework throughout the development process, emphasizing quality from the initial requirements stage through the final testing stage. All solution components, including application programs, conversion programs, and technical architecture programs, are required to proceed through the V-Model development process.

The V-Model charts a path from verification and validation to testing. After each process in the development life cycle has been defined, each major deliverable in the development process must be verified and validated, and then the implementation of each specification must be tested.

Verification is a process of checking that a deliverable is correctly derived from the inputs of the corresponding stage, and that the deliverable is complete and correct. In addition, verification checks that the process to derive the deliverable was followed and that the output conforms to the standards set in the project's quality plan. One form of verification, for example, is desk checking, or inspection of a design specification to ensure the process was followed, the standards were met, and the deliverable is complete.

Validation checks that the deliverables satisfy requirements specified in the previous stage or in an earlier stage, and that the business case continues to be met. In other words, the work product contributes to the intended benefits and does not have undesired side effects. Given the top-down nature of systems specification, validation is critical to ensuring that the decisions made at each successive level of specification continue on track to meet the initial business needs. For example, using validation techniques, developers seek to avoid the experience of one major reservation call center, which implemented the ability to view recent print ads in the reservation systems when the overriding business case for the system was to improve the speed of the reservation agents. There was no real business need for the reservation agents to view print ads, and a great deal of time was spent designing functionality that, if implemented, would have actually slowed the reservation process rather than speed it up.

Testing is designed to ensure that the specification is properly implemented and integrated. Ideally, testing activities are not in place to ensure the solution was properly specified, that activity being done via verification and validation. Rather, testing activities associated with each level of the specification ensure that the specifications were properly translated into the final solution.

The V-model is depicted in Exhibit 1. This figure shows the work flow in the development process, with a series of design activities and systems specifications on the left side (i.e., top-down), and a series of corresponding testing activities on the right side (i.e., bottom-up).

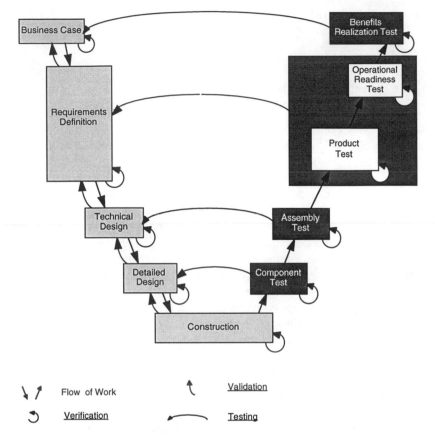

Exhibit 1. V-Model of verification, validation, and testing.

In concept, the core process stages of requirements analysis, design, and construction consist of creating a series of increasingly detailed specifications. The exhibit specifies the systems from the top down, making decisions and adding detail at each stage. Work flows between stages in the V-Model when a work packet or deliverable has met the exit criteria, that is, all the verification and validation requirements for that stage. Testing is designed to ensure that the components of the application are properly constructed, put together correctly, and that they deliver the functional, technical, and quality requirements.

The specification stages are:

- The business case.
- The requirements definition.
- The technical design.
- The detailed design.

The test stages are:

- The component test.
- The assembly test.
- The product test.
- The operational readiness test.
- The benefits realization test.

An underlying concept of the V-Model is that the boxes in the exhibit represent distinct development and testing stages. It is essential that the stages of the V-Model, and the processes to complete each stage, are well defined, structured, and standardized. Defined, standard processes are repeatable and measurable. Processes that are not repeatable or measurable therefore do not easily lend themselves to improvement. Testers cannot collect meaningful data about *ad hoc* processes because there is no clear understanding of what the steps and outcomes are meant to be. Developers cannot learn from their experiences if they take a completely different approach each time they set out to develop software. Also, there is significant margin for error in undefined processes. Too often, the designers have different expectations of what that process is to produce than do the construction and testing teams. This leads to gaps and overlaps between the processes which are at best inefficient and, at worst, error prone.

ENTRY AND EXIT CRITERIA

Of special importance is the verification and validation performed at hand-off points between work cells or teams or from the project team to the users. Each inspection, performed at hand-off points or other important checkpoints during the development process, must satisfy a set of specific entry and exit criteria. As processes are defined, it must be clearly stated what each process is responsible for, and where it begins and ends. Entry and exit criteria are a mechanism for articulating what is required from previous processes to support a given stage (i.e., entry criteria) and what is required of a given process to determine completeness (i.e., exit criteria). Entry and exit criteria are defined for each stage to ensure quality deliverables from one stage to the next. If a deliverable fails to meet these set criteria, it is demoted to the previous stage or to the stage determined to have caused the nonconformity.

One stage's exit criteria are largely the next stage's entry criteria. Some exit criteria, however, may satisfy the entry criteria of a stage other than the one next in line. Relative to testing, there are three types of entry and exit criteria:

1. Those that must be met in one test stage in order to proceed with the next test stage.
2. Those that must be met in the specification stage to facilitate test preparation.

3. Those that are required for repetition of the current stage, in maintenance or enhancement activities.

All three types of entry and exit criteria should be defined and communicated as part of the standard process definition. Entry criteria may also be inspected throughout the development process, as opposed to right before the test stage requiring the criteria to be met is about to start. Inspection helps to build quality into the process and thus the solution, rather than retrofitting the solution to work correctly, and inspection saves the cost of rework, which only gets more expensive as the life cycle progresses. Although inspections cost time and effort on the front end, experience shows that the cost of formalized inspections is more than gained back in future stages of the life cycle.

There are three key success factors for inspection of entry and exit criteria:

1. Ensure the entry and exit criteria are understood.
2. Validate and verify content as well as format.
3. Conduct inspections throughout the process.

Developers should not wait until the end of the stage to start inspecting deliverables. People are less willing to go back and rework something from a previous stage if the next stage is well underway. This reduces any rework in the next stage or in the related test stage and ensures that nonconformity to the entry and exit criteria can be communicated to the rest of the work cell or team to prevent replicating nonconformity throughout the remaining deliverables for that stage. Sample key exit criteria for each stage are shown in Exhibit 2.

VERIFICATION AND VALIDATION

Verification and validation are a means to test specifications and other deliverables. Approaches to verification and validation include walk-through or peer reviews, formal inspections, and prototypes. Other approaches are paper system testing, desk checks, and stakeholder reviews.

Verification

Verification is most commonly accomplished through an inspection. Inspections involve a number of reviewers, each with specific responsibilities for verifying aspects of the specification package, such as functional completeness, adherence to standards and correct use of the technical architecture. According to Tom Gilb, software quality expert and author of *Software Inspection*, inspection, done before an application is finished, can remove 95% of all defects before the first tests.

Stage	Sample Exit Criteria
All Stages	- Deliverables must conform to standards.
Requirements	- Requirements specification must be reviewed with user. - Test cases must be generated.
Design	- Design must be traceable to the requirements specification through cross-references.
Construction	- Code must be analyzed for adherence to standards and complexity guidelines, and analysis results must fall within defined thresholds. - Code must be traceable to the design through cross-references.
Component Test	- Component test data must be traceable to the design through cross-references. - There can be no abends in component test results. - Component test results must be repeatable.
Assembly Test	- All paths within the application flow must be executed. - Assembly test results must be repeatable.
Product Test	- The product test model must be traceable to the requirements specification (both functional requirements and quality attributes) through cross-references. - Product test results must conform to predicted results. - Product test results must be repeatable.

Exhibit 2.   Sample exit criteria.

Validation

Validation is most commonly accomplished through management checkpoints or stakeholder reviews. Two effective techniques of validation are repository validation and the completion and review of traceability matrices. Repository validation can be used when a design repository such as development workbenches, CASE tools, or even very strict naming conventions, are used and cross-checks can be executed against the repository to ensure integrity of dependencies between deliverables. Such a cross-check is designed to confirm that each deliverable is derived from a higher order deliverable, and that each higher order deliverable breaks down into one or more implementation level deliverables. A traceability matrix is a technique used in defense contracting when a matrix is developed of all requirements cross referenced to the designs, code, tests and deployment deliverables that implement the requirement. In either case, what is accomplished is a cross-check that all business-case criteria are directly linked to one or more specifications, and at each level of specification, there is a direct link back up to a business case criteria. The objective of validation in this way is the direct relation of the specifications to the requirements and business case items that they implement, facilitating the identification of missing requirements and specifications not contributing to the business case.

How validation is performed depends on the nature of the requirement in the specification document. Certain requirements can be traced directly from the specification to the implementation; they bear the same name, and there is a one-to-one correspondence between the requirement and some component in the implementation. For example, a business objective to support a new operational process may be directly tied to portions of the application under development.

In other cases, the specification concerns a quality factor or an emerging property of the implementation. Therefore, a direct comparison is not possible. In this case, validation can be done by analyzing a model of the implementation, for example, analyzing the workflow to ensure that headcount does not increase and that cost is reduced. It also can be done by creating and testing a prototype or by a peer or expert review, as in validating the design for maintainability criteria.

STRUCTURED, LAYERED TESTING

The V-Model specifies that testing in one stage must be completed before the solution moves on to the next stage of testing. Before moving major deliverables to the next stage, testers must determine that the exit criteria defined for that stage are met. A part of the exit criteria for each stage is that the test has been successfully executed. This ensures that the test objectives, or primary focus of the test, are accomplished before moving on to the next stage. This layered approach to testing is vital to successful implementation of the V-Model. Done properly, testers can now avoid the frustrations of spending hours, if not days, in the product test stage pouring over an issue, only to realize that the problem could have been identified during assembly test.

Additionally, when the objectives of one test stage are met, there is no need to repeat the same testing at the next higher stage. This is the key concept of the V-Model that proves difficult to accept and use in practice. Better-defined testing stages and objectives allow developers to understand and verify the testing done at one level so as not to repeat it at the next higher level. Additionally, definition of the testing stages allows developers to understand and communicate the objectives of each testing stage to identify potential gaps in the testing approach. In other words, when properly followed, the V-model minimizes gaps and overlaps between the testing stages while ensuring quality of delivery.

Even so, two stages of testing may be executed together, using the same scripts, but both sets of test conditions must be identified and tested (i.e., both sets of objectives must be met). While each stage of testing is distinct, it is sometimes possible to test multiple stages with very similar scripts. In such cases, it may make sense to combine the scripts into one set; however, all test conditions for each stage must be identified and tested in the resulting combined scripts. For example, a thorough assembly test cannot make up for inadequate component testing, because the objectives of each test stage are different. They are looking for different problems.

MAKING THE MODEL WORK

The objectives of the V-Model testing approach for today's applications are simple. They include:

- Stage containment of defects.
- Effective testing.
- Efficient testing.
- Risk management.

Stage Containment of Defects

Stage containment is a mechanism designed to ensure that as many problems as possible are detected during the system development stage in which they occur and are not passed along to the next stage. It is a means to build quality into the system, and the goal of containment is to decrease both the cost of fixing problems and the number of residual problems in the finished system.

Traditionally, most of the problems in the system are caused very early in the development process but are not captured and corrected until very late, that is, during testing or production (Exhibit 3).

By the time the cycle is in testing or production, the IS department has not only lost the faith of its users but also has potentially assumed a business risk of poorly performing software, downtime, or excessive costs to correct defects. Industry studies show that defects are orders of magnitude more costly to correct in the product testing or production stages than had they been contained to the stage in which they were caused. Fixing problems found at the point of introduction is generally accepted to be one-fourth to one-twentieth the cost of fixing them at the test stage, with the cost skyrocketing once the system has been deployed. Defective software is often deployed globally throughout an organization, only to be redeployed months later because of quality problems, necessitating a full repeat of the packaging, roll-out, distribution, installation and training effort for hundreds of sites.

Stage containment, for early detection of problems, coupled with process improvement to prevent problems, saves tremendous amounts of time and effort (Exhibit 4).

Stage containment is achieved through the development processes as follows. Any aspect of a deliverable that does not meet its exit criteria (i.e., that does not conform to specifications and standards) is an error. If an error is handed off to the next stage, it becomes a defect. A defect that is

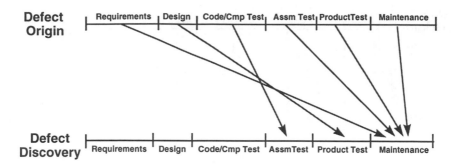

Exhibit 3. Stage containment: current.

passed along to the end customer is a fault. Stage containment aims to minimize the number of defects and faults being passed along from one stage to the next, by finding and fixing errors in the stage in which they were committed. If a team finds a problem that was caused by some error in a previous stage, this problem is classified as a defect or a fault and is passed back to be fixed by the team that created the defect (see Exhibit 5). The process of determining the stage that was the origin of the defect is called root cause analysis.

Thus, design specification errors discovered and fixed in a design walkthrough would be examples of errors. Problems in the coding of a program discovered during product testing are examples of defects. Problems in production that should have been discovered during product test or earlier are faults.

The longer a defect remains undiscovered, the more difficult and expensive it becomes to correct. Because each stage relies on the decisions made during the creation of the specification in the previous stage, detecting an error in a stage after it was made may invalidate some or all of the work done between the time the error was created and the time it was discovered. Experience has shown that as the verification and validation procedures improve, stage containment of defects also improves, saving both time and money.

Stage containment can be accomplished only by strict adherence to entry and exit criteria. Testers can measure stage containment by measuring the ratio of errors to faults, essentially what percentage of the problems are being caught and fixed as opposed to being passed along to the customer. Stage containment for any given stage is defined in the following ratio:

$$Errors/(Errors + Defects)$$

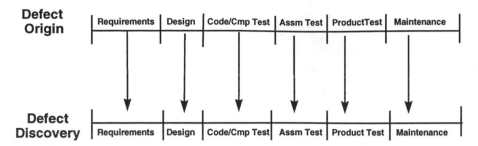

Exhibit 4. Coupling of stage containment and process improvment.

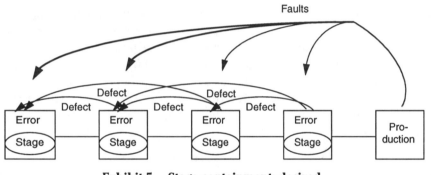

Exhibit 5. Stage containment: desired.

Stage containment for a released product is defined in the following ratio:

(Errors + Defects)/(Errors + Defects + Faults)

A level of 100% stage containment means that all errors are discovered and corrected before the software is promoted to the next stage. Whereas 100% stage containment may be unrealistic or even undesirable given the effort required to achieve it, stage containment levels of 95% to 98% have been consistently achieved by organizations applying the V-Model concepts.

Effective Testing

Effective testing improves the quality of the solutions delivered to the customer and ultimately the success of the business change. The V-Model testing approach improves the effectiveness of testing by providing a means to properly scope testing activities based on risk to the business. In a test strategy, the exact testing stages are defined, with the scope and objectives of each stage clearly documented. In determining the scope of each testing stage, consideration must be given to what can and will be tested, as well as what cannot or will not be tested. Then the risk of the untested areas of the application can be identified, documented, and managed. This approach to defining the scope of testing to be performed, combined with an approach to trace the tests back to the components of the scope, allows staff to focus testing efforts on the critical aspects of the solution, improving the coverage of testing, and quality of results.

One of the most commonly asked questions about testing applications is, "How does the staff determine when they have tested enough?" The techniques discussed in this chapter help to identify what needs to be tested (i.e., the risks), plan a test for each identified risk, and ensure coverage of those high-risk areas of the solution. The method is to trace the actual test results to the test conditions they were derived to test and the requirements and risks that gave rise to those test conditions. Testing is complete when all planned tests have successfully been executed. Structured testing is therefore not only repeatable but also more effective.

Efficient Testing

The V-Model testing approach is efficient. The approach to determining testing conditions and designing test scripts allows for increased testing density and more test conditions covered by fewer scripts. The standardized approach to test planning provides for repeatable processes and repeatable tests. Tests can be reused within a release for regression of fixes and across releases as enhancements are made, ensuring a consistent level of testing with a minimal level of effort. The traceability provided by the structured testing approach provides an efficient means to perform complete impact analysis of changes and reuse of the test model.

One organization experienced the inefficiencies of unstructured testing over and over again. The test team developed and maintained a huge test bed, with thousands of scripts. The test team had binders lined up across the back of the room. They had absolutely no idea what the test bed tested. For all they knew, it tested the same activity a thousand times. Every time they had an application change or fix, they had to add a new piece to the test model because they had no way of determining the impact on the test bed, nor could they find a piece of the test model that would test the change.

Another organization learned the same lessons. Several developers spent a considerable amount of time writing test scenarios, only to scrap their test plans and start over every time the project underwent a scope change, which happened 3 times in 18 months. Because they did not tie their test model to their specifications, they could not perform an impact analysis on the affected test components to determine where or how to update the test to reflect the scope changes.

Another common testing inefficiency is redundant testing. In the past, product tests have included testing the business functions and have itemized and executed test conditions at the component and assembly levels. If properly educated on the V-Model, the test cell or team should feel comfortable testing the appropriate levels of conditions in the appropriate test stage. In addition, formal inspections ensure that adequate testing has occurred at each level.

Another example of redundant testing is "monkey" testing. Some analysts believe that planned test models for either this test stage or the next test stage do not catch all errors and continue to examine the system. If problems are found during these efforts, the problems may be difficult or impossible to recreate in order to fix. The lesson here is that if a risk area exists within the system, it should be covered in the structured test. If it needs to be tested, it should be put it in the test plans.

Finally, automation can be introduced to the repeatable testing processes to improve productivity and reduce human error. As testing environments get increasingly more complex, automation has been successfully implemented to alleviate labor-intensive tasks, such as test data generation and test script execution. Automation also helps to increase the control over the testing environments by managing the configurations of test data, test models, and the applications being tested. Exhibit 6 is a schematic of an integrated testing environment, outlining the environment components required to support the V-Model testing process.

When planning for automation of the testing process, consideration must be given to the investment for the tools and the learning curve to be incurred, and the impact on the process vs. the anticipated benefits. Different factors have a varying degree of influence on the decision to automate testing and should be reviewed in light of the characteristics of the development approach, the application, the testing team, and the testing tools themselves. For example, the cost to automate the scripting process for a new application is likely to be warranted if enhancements to the application are anticipated requiring regression testing or if the critical nature of the application requires a high-quality level. Automation has been implemented, along with repeatable testing processes, to achieve up to 80% reduction in the effort required to fully regression test a complex suite of applications. Automation facilitates the reuse of existing test models. Reuse can occur by reuse of a test model to test future enhancements, regression tests of the same application, or across applications (e.g., an order-entry product test designed for system A may be useful in testing the order entry for business application B).

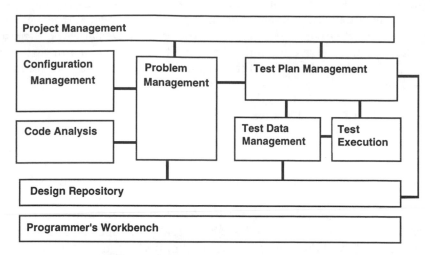

Exhibit 6. Integrated testing environment.

The decision to automate, however, affects the way tests are designed and planned, so these are decisions to be made early in the development life cycle. Automated results comparison requires the creation of expected results in an electronic format recognized by the tool.

Managing Risk through Metrics

Measurement is a crucial tool for managing progress and quality. A metric is a combination of measurements that tell something about a process or product. Without effective metrics, IS managers have no way of truly knowing their productivity levels. However, with well-defined development and testing processes and a few consistently applied metrics, software development becomes predictable, which in turn allows for more reliable delivery. Metrics also support, even drive, process improvement by identifying areas that may require attention and determining if corrective actions were successful. It is not worthwhile to measure any activity if some actions for improvement will not result. It is not only a waste of time to collect metrics that are not used for decision making or action, but it may also be detrimental to team morale, because managers will have eliminated the excuse of not knowing a problem exists.

Metrics should be used to track some significant goal or objective; if the achievement is at variance with the goal, some change must be made to increase the chances of meeting the goal, for example, improving the standard process and exit criteria. Goals are continually examined, and as improvements are made, stricter goals can be set. Tying metrics to organizational goals is important because the mere act of measuring a process causes a behavior change. For example, if a manager were to visibly measure the time of day each person on the team arrives at work, the staff would all begin to arrive on time. They might be arriving at work without having finished breakfast, but they would have begun to arrive on time, nonetheless.

The Need for Balanced Metrics. However, if the manager's goal were to improve productivity during the morning hours rather than to have everyone arrive by 8:30 a.m., that same manger may have caused a behavior change at odds with his or her goal, because the entire department now goes for snacks at 9:30 a.m. The fact that measurement causes behavior change leads to the discussion of the need for a balanced set of metrics. The manager in the example would want to measure not only the time of arrival but also whether people have had breakfast. A more realistic example would be that if the manager measured only the speed of the developers, developers would soon become very fast at completing coding work units. The quality of these work units would suffer greatly. The answer therefore, is to measure both speed and product quality.

Finally, as with all metrics, it is important to understand that these metrics should not be used to measure individual performance. The purpose is to measure the process. The assumptions are that people are following the process and a quality process results in a quality solution; therefore, if there is a problem, the process should be updated or training conducted. If metrics are perceived as measuring individuals rather than process, the behavior changes can be drastic and not only invalidate the metrics, but also potentially worsen the process.

Applied metrics during the testing process provide the capability to improve management, productivity, and quality by providing both data points and trend information required to manage with facts, focus on the problem, not the symptom, facilitate predictability, and facilitate continuous improvement.

If an organization can collect only a small set of metrics, strong consideration should be given to closely tracking defect rates and collecting a testing variation of the stage containment metric. Tracking defect rates means collecting information on incoming error and defect levels. Simple trend analysis can then provide information to support or question the management assumptions made about planning the tests, staffing levels for defect correction, and determination of readiness for production. Exhibit 7 depicts the defects detected over time by the assembly and product test stages mapped against the planned incoming rate for defects. With the graph, management easily can see if the defects levels are expected. If

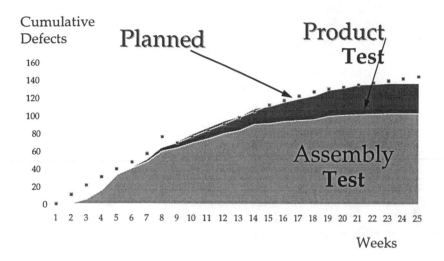

Exhibit 7.   Defects detected over time.

defect levels are higher than planned, investigation can be done to determine if:

- The application is less stable than anticipated, indicating that the entry criteria may not have been met and the code should be demoted to a previous stage.
- The tests are more robust than planned, indicating that the investment in testing and product quality may be more than required.
- The sequence of test execution is exercising a particularly difficult section of the application, and it is anticipated that the defect levels will recede as testing progresses.

In any case, the information on the graph derived from measurement allows management to manage by facts, rather than going on blind faith that staff can somehow make up the time.

A second set of measurements, the testing variation of the stage containment metrics defined earlier in the chapter, can be defined as tracking all problems found during the testing stages, with recognition of where they should have been found. This metric provides information on the quality levels of each testing process by quantifying what percentage of the problems that each testing stage is designed to catch are being captured, as opposed to being passed along to a subsequent stage.

This information can be used to identify the holes in the testing process, which continuous improvement techniques can address, and to make management decisions for the remainder of the project. For example, if the testing stage containment metrics indicate that a significant level of defects being found in the product test should have been found by the assembly test process, management can analyze the assembly testing process to plug the hole so these problems do not continue to slip through. Management could also analyze the actual problems to address the specification or construction process which caused them in the first place or use the information to determine the level of regression testing to be completed by the product test stage. If metrics indicate that the deliverables from the assembly testing process of work cell A are at a 95% to 100% stage containment level, decisions can be made to relax the regression testing requirements for that work cell's deliverables, or it may be feasible to accept code from that cell in the middle of a cycle execution, because data indicates that it is relatively safe. However, if metrics indicate that the deliverables from work cell B have a much lower level of stage containment, the decision may be made to require full regression testing of all code completed by cell B, and to only migrate code from that cell before the start of a new product test cycle.

NEW MANAGEMENT CHALLENGES

Managing the test process is a continuous task, beginning with completion of the test strategy and continuing until the release is in production. Testing is where all work cells or teams and the user communities come together to ensure the solution works as specified. Testing is also characterized by numerous complex issues and risks, requests for changes, aggressive schedules, budget overruns, and low morale. Effective management of these factors is critical to ensure delivery of a quality solution within the expected time frame and budget constraints. New management challenges are facilitating communication and managing resources and monitoring scope and schedule, to increase the overall effectiveness of the test process.

Coordination and Communication

The testing process requires more communication and coordination among work cells or teams than any other process. The activities of the architecture, development, training, user, and technical support work cells or teams are very much interdependent, and communication and coordination are critical to success. For example, requirements for testing the solution's ability to perform in a production setting often necessitate large, complex, and expensive environments, yet management may still tell the technical support team on Friday that a full test system for product test is needed on Monday. Effective coordination of activities and schedules means that management, at the beginning of the project, determines responsibilities, and ensures all activities are on the appropriate work schedules. This planning also allows for optimizing the use of these environments, sharing test configurations to minimize both acquisition and setup costs.

Too often, test teams plan to run the conversion programs first to build data for the product test, and conversion routines are the last thing the development team plans to code.

Changes should not be accepted, approved, and implemented by architecture and development cells or teams without communication to the test cell. Although it is not intentional, at the peak of development, additional client requests or changes are communicated to development and implemented so quickly that communication to testing is overlooked. To minimize these types of changes, managers ensure the test cell is required to sign-off on changes as an indication that they have been notified of the change request.

Scope Control

Testing stages are a breeding ground for scope creep. Many of the defects identified in testing stages are really enhancement requests, leading to additional effort and missed deadlines. There are both planned and unplanned changes in scope during testing. Unplanned scope changes resulting from process problems can be mitigated with process improvements including validation and verification, education on the V-Model approach, and a formalized issue control process.

In contrast to scope changes caused by process problems, scope changes may also result from changing user or technical requirements becauseof external business conditions, forces, or regulations. The traceability embedded in the test model allows us to determine the effort required to react to these changes, information that should be considered when deciding whether to address the requested changes.

THE IMPACT OF THE V-MODEL TESTING APPROACH ON DEVELOPMENT

The V-Model approach to testing forces developers to consider testing challenges from the start of the development effort. This allows them to design and build the system to be testable, including the introduction of probes and diagnostics to facilitate error detection, handshaking between applications to ensure configuration management integrity, and even having the application take the date from a table rather than the system to ease month-end and year-end testing.

Additionally, testing exit criteria from requirements analysis and design, and early planning of test conditions may increase the effort on the left side of the V, with anticipated payback in quality and productivity during the test execution stages, maintenance, and future release projects.

Although this may result in a better product, all of these have impact on the activities completed before what is traditionally considered the testing stages. World-class testing requires an update of the entire development approach.

THE IMPACT OF THE V-MODEL TESTING APPROACH ON THE ORGANIZATION

The increasing need for professional testers demands people with the skills to develop complex systems, which are not necessarily the skills required to test complex systems. As mentioned earlier in the chapter, many organizations are establishing testing directors and even entire testing or software quality organizations. Experience has proven this to be effective. Dedicated testing teams provide for testing experts, people who know the difference between assembly and product test conditions. Also, a dedicated testing team provides for ownership of the test model, ensuring that the test model is maintained and reused. Finally, a dedicated test team means developers can schedule the development of the test concurrent with the development of the solution, thus compressing the delivery time frame.

Given a dedicated test team, the test manager should be at a peer level with the development manager, if not higher. This gives him or her the authority to enforce entry criteria and creates the professional friction required to ensure a balance between schedule and quality.

CONCLUSION

The V-Model approach to software development and testing positions an organization to face the challenges of today and tomorrow through improved quality, improved productivity, and improved predictability. Defined processes, verification that those processes are followed, and the use of metrics as a monitoring and process improvement vehicle allow executive management and IS directors to be sure the issues of developing and testing applications in the age of convergence are addressed. The logical train of thought through the benefits of the new testing approaches shows that:

- Software development stage containment can be better.
- Better testing and stage containment saves time and money.
- Better testing and stage containment supports continuous process improvement.
- Continuous process improvement saves time and money and improves software quality and reliability.

Viewed as opportunity, the V-Model approach to testing positions an organization to move into advanced technology and business challenges.

Section III
Netcentric Implementation Issues

Many of the systems design principles used for client/server applications today are also applicable for netcentric applications. Netcentric computing, therefore, does not introduce a revolution in how systems are designed and implemented, but rather an evolution. This concept of evolution is not meant, however, to understate the need to realize new business opportunities and to learn new technologies offered by netcentric computing nor the effort it will take to incorporate these new technologies into the organization's computing environment. Nonetheless, many client/server design concepts and considerations are equally applicable to netcentric computing. Readers would therefore benefit from the book *Practical Guide to Client/Server Computing*, also published by Auerbach Publications.

Section III looks in particular at some of the critical and unique implementation issues in the netcentric environment. Specifically, readers will find an overview of netcentric design issues and considerations, and then more detailed discussions of implementation issues for:

- Testing.
- Communications.
- Parallel processing.
- Data warehouses.

Chapter III-1
Overview of Design and Implementation Considerations

Netcentric computing has brought new technologies to the forefront, especially in the area of external presence and access, ease of distribution, and media capabilities. This has resulted in the following key benefits:

- Browsers provide a "universal client."
- Direct supplier-to-customer relationships.
- Richer documents.
- Application version checking and dynamic update.

Provision of a Universal Client

The browser-centric application style offers a new option in distributing functionality to both internal and external users. In the traditional client/server environment, distributing an application internally or externally for an enterprise requires that the application be recompiled and tested for all specific workstation operating systems. It also usually requires loading the application on each client machine. The browser-centric application style offers an alternative to this traditional problem. Today the Web browser provides a "universal client" that offers users a consistent and familiar user interface. Using a browser, a user can launch many types of applications and view many types of documents. This can be accomplished on different operating systems/platforms and is independent of where the applications or documents reside. The browser technology is also changing the traditional desktop as companies such as Netscape and Microsoft, leading Web browser vendors, continue to evolve their products (such as Internet Explorer and Netscape Communicator), and redefine the structure and style of the traditional desktop.

Direct Supplier-to-Customer Relationships

The external presence and access enabled by connecting a node to the Internet has opened up a series of opportunities to reach an audience outside a company's traditional internal users. Consequently, the Internet is becoming another vehicle for companies to conduct business with their customers through broadcasting of product and service descriptions, exchanging interactive information and conducting actual business transactions.

Richer Documents

The ability to digitize, organize, and deliver textual, graphical and other information in addition to traditional data to a broader audience, enables new methods for people and enterprises to work together. Netcentric technologies (e.g., HTML documents, plug-ins, Java, etc.) and standardization of media information formats enable support for these types of complex documents, applications and even nondiscrete data types such as audio and video. Network bandwidth remains a performance issue; however, advances in network technologies and compression continue to make richer media-enabled applications more feasible on the Web.

Application Version Checking and Dynamic Update

Configuration management of traditional client/server applications, which tend to be stored on both the client hard disk and on the server, is a major issue for many corporations. The distribution and update problems of such applications, which are packaged as one large or a combination of a few large executables, make minor updates difficult for even a small scale user population, because every time an update is made, a process must be initiated to distribute new code to all client machines.

The advances in netcentric technologies are allowing applications to be packaged differently. For instance, ActiveX technology (from Microsoft), has introduced version checking and dynamic install and update. The need for this has long been recognized; however, it was typically at best a custom effort, often bypassed due to its difficulty and cost. The introduction of this capability into core system software changes its implementation cost and makes it a more feasible option to implement.

This chapter looks at some of the issues to be considered when designing and implementing netcentric architectures and applications. It is not an exhaustive listing, but rather a starting point for generating design discussions. The topics include:

- when a netcentric solution should be considered.
- design considerations.
- programming considerations.

WHEN TO CONSIDER A NETCENTRIC SOLUTION

When designing new applications, the prospect of utilizing netcentric models and technologies (e.g., components, Internet, etc.) should always be considered. First, it is important to evaluate whether the application would benefit from a netcentric style implementation. Second, even if a traditional approach (e.g., Visual Basic, PowerBuilder) is decided upon, the use of netcentric concepts to produce significant reductions in software packaging and distribution costs should be considered.

When deciding whether to employ a netcentric solution, such as incorporating Web-based user interfaces and Internet application styles, keep in mind that these technologies are not a panacea and should be used only when there is a solid business reason.

NETCENTRIC APPLICATION STYLE CONSIDERATIONS

The following list can help architects determine whether a netcentric application style may be applicable for the application they are designing.

- Is it likely that the company would want to expose the application or the data it accesses to an external audience (such as customers, business partners, trading partners, and regulators) now or at some point in the future?
- Does the application have a requirement to provide access to both structured and unstructured data types (text, images, sound, video, and so forth)?
- Does the application have a potentially large and/or diverse internal audience?
- Are the majority of the users nondedicated or occasional users?
- Is the user base widely dispersed geographically?
- Is there a need for the execution environment to support multilingual presentation of information?
- Is there a requirement to support multiple hardware configurations for client machines?
- Is there a requirement to support multiple operating systems for client machines?
- Is there a requirement now or at some point in the future to run the application on a device other than a PC?

Providing "Yes" answers to *most* of these questions, either now or in the future, may indicate that the application could be well suited for design using netcentric technologies.

A number of more general business considerations must be addressed, however, before the technological ones are considered. These include such issues as whether the organization can reach new customers and markets, and whether it can provide new services and products to its customers.

Traditional Client/Server Application Style Considerations

The following list can help architects determine whether a traditional client/server application style may be more applicable for the application they are designing. This list is also presented from a technical perspective.

- Is the application dependent upon short (second or sub-second) response times?
- Will the application be required to support high-volume transaction processing?
- Does the company have a large investment in existing applications in one of the 4GLs (VB/PB)?

Providing "Yes" answers to *most* of these questions may indicate that the application would be better served through development using traditional client/server tools such as Visual Basic and PowerBuilder. However, because the tools and capabilities change so rapidly, at the time of design this issue must be re-evaluated to see if a netcentric solution might be more applicable.

NETCENTRIC DESIGN CONSIDERATIONS

Many of the traditional client/server design concepts and considerations also can be used in a netcentric computing environment. Nevertheless, new technologies enable new capabilities requiring additional design guidelines. The objective of this section is to address these changes and provide an architect with a high-level description of key design considerations to think about when designing a netcentric application. The following topics are discussed:

- Fat and thin client concepts
- 2-tier to 3-tier to n-tier transition
- Component technology and application
- Multiple electronic access channels
- Information ownership
- Security
- User interface
- Content management
- Network connection
- Media streaming
- Push technology considerations
- Transaction Monitors vs. ORBs
- Internet Service Provider (ISP) considerations
- Platform independent euphoria

Fat and Thin Client Concepts:

A fat client application typically has all of the presentation logic and most of the business logic resident on the client machine. In contrast, at the opposite end of the spectrum, a thin client application has very little application logic on the client; it primarily supports the display of information stored and managed on the server. Most of the initial Internet and intranet applications followed the thin client model where a Web browser is used to display static HTML documents served by a centralized server. The Web server is responsible for executing all application logic, performing any required data access and formatting the presentation of HTML documents; the browser is used for display purposes only.

However, recent upgrades in both browser and component technologies are extending the reach and capability of netcentric solutions. Sun, and Netscape, through JavaBeans and JavaScript and Microsoft, through ActiveX controls and VBScript, are enabling a shift of application logic back to the client, thus widening the spectrum of solutions available through a browser-based interface to include more traditionally "fat-client" processing. In addition, because of an increase in mobile users, there is also a shift toward "very fat-client" applications where all of the application logic must be resident on the client machine so that the users can work without being connected to a network.

Two-Tier to Three-Tier to N-Tier Transition

According to The Gartner Group, two-tier and three-tier architectures have the following characteristics:

- *Two-tier (fat client)* — those that have all the application logic (presentation, business and data access logic) on the desktop and use the server simply to run the data base management system (DBMS).
- *Two-tier (plump client)* — those that have some of the application logic (usually presentation and business logic) on the desktop and the rest of the application logic (usually data access logic and some business logic) on the server in the form of DBMS stored procedures.
- *Three-tier* — those that have some application logic (usually presentation logic and some business logic) on the desktop and the rest of the application logic (most business and/or data access logic) running on the server in a tier that is separate from the DBMS.

Today, netcentric applications put most business rules and data access logic on the server rather than on the client, thus supporting a three-tier architecture. Although some application logic will move to the client in the form of JavaBeans and ActiveX controls, future netcentric applications will continue to exploit more of these three-tier (i.e., distributed) architectures.

The main difference between using a two-tier and a three-tier architecture is deciding how presentation logic, business logic and data access logic are separated, and which part of the application logic resides on the client and which part resides on the server(s):

- *Logical software tiers* — how presentation, business, and data access logic are separated from each other.
- *Physical software tiers* — where presentation, business, and data access logic are physically stored.

The Two-Tier Architecture. The main advantage of a two-tier architecture is its simplicity. Because most of the application logic is located in one place, developers do not have to decide how to partition the application; everything goes on the client. Additionally, tools such as Visual Basic and PowerBuilder facilitate an environment that makes it easier to build applications that use a two-tier architecture. A developer can simply paint a window containing several fields, then put business logic behind each field for various events (push-button click, field tab, and so forth) using one development tool. Because of this, when developing simpler applications, using a two-tier architecture is generally easier than a three-tier architecture, and takes less time. However, since the business logic is tightly coupled with the presentation and data access logic, two-tier application code is less reusable, portable and scaleable. Changing the presentation layer generally requires re-coding most of the business logic. Also, it becomes more difficult to re-use common business logic within the same application and across applications.

The Three-Tier Architecture. Applications using a three-tier architecture have most of their business logic located on the server, often using the concept of an application server. Typically in such an application a window places a request such as "Get customer information" to the application server, where the request gets processed and the result is sent back to the window. Three-tier applications tend to be more efficient than two-tier applications, because they send fewer and smaller messages between the client and the server.

The application logic on the server preprocesses all the data and often sends more condensed messages containing the results back to the client. Because the presentation logic, business logic and data access logic are separated into their own tiers, three-tier architectures are more flexible and scaleable. It is easier to re-use the code across applications and to port parts of the application to newer platforms. So for example, if the presentation logic needs to be ported from C++ to Java for platform independence, business logic and data access logic would largely be unaffected.

The N-Tier Architecture. Furthermore, an application can be implemented in an n-tier architecture where the application logic is distributed across many host machines. So rather than having one application server, there may be several application servers. This is often done to improve the overall performance, achieve greater reliability and reduce network costs for geographically dispersed users. As more processing gets moved toward the server, the distribution of application logic across more than one machine will become more critical, thereby increasing the need for n-tier architectures. For such applications it may be necessary to support the integration of multiple back-end services into a single transaction or user activity. This can be especially challenging if these back-end services are distributed across enterprises.

Currently-available Internet/intranet technologies and development tools lend themselves to building primarily three-tier applications and to some degree n-tier applications. A developer creates Web pages (presentation logic) using an authoring tool such as FrontPage. Then the developer builds scripts such as CGI and ASP, which reside on the server, that contain commands that process business logic and/or execute requests in a data base. Upon an event in the page such as pushing a "Products" icon, a request is sent to the server where a script containing the business logic to get the "Product" list is executed. The page containing the results is sent back to the browser.

Also, many of the packaged applications such as SAP and PeopleSoft are already three-tier or in the process of porting their environment to a three-tier architecture. Vendors are putting more emphasis on multitier development and middleware tools, and are expanding their offerings in these areas.

However, vendors are also beginning to offer Internet/intranet development tools that facilitate an environment for developing two-tier applications. Some of these tools already offer capabilities for an application to connect to a data base directly from a page, bypassing the Web server via a scripting language. Similar to Visual Basic, the developer can use one development tool to code presentation, business and data access logic in one place.

Developers must consider the nature of each application and choose between two-tier, three-tier and n-tier architectures on a case-by-case basis. For small, routine applications, a two-tier approach can be faster, simpler and less expensive to implement. For complex and/or large applications, a three-tier or an n-tier architecture may cost less to develop, maintain and administer.

COMPONENT REVOLUTION AND TECHNOLOGY CONSIDERATIONS

Because the capabilities enabled by new technologies are changing at an incredible pace, employees of corporations are demanding faster development of new applications from their IT departments, and customers are demanding faster turnaround of new products and services from companies. All of this results in corporations seeking ways to re-use existing software to streamline the development process for new applications and upgrades to existing applications, in order to reduce the overall development time. This is where components come in.

A component is a reusable chunk of logic with a well-defined interface. Components can be assembled together by less experienced developers to rapidly build robust applications. The following sections address component application and technology considerations; further discussion of the topic is found in Section IV.

Component Benefits. Use of components in the netcentric development environment carries with it the following key benefits:

- *Software distribution.* By packaging code into distribution units, code can be more effectively distributed when software is updated. Packaging an application into components for software distribution is the simplest application of components; it may be a way for a company to introduce their architects and developers to the component technologies.
- *Software re-use.* By packaging code into cross-application units, business software becomes a collection of reusable assets. Through reuse a single development effort can be leveraged across applications, functional areas within a corporation, or even across corporations. Complex business logic or technical features can be developed once and shared across applications, ensuring a uniform application of business rules in the enterprise. Effective component re-use requires adequate design time and cooperation among resources responsible for identifying an enterprise's business requirements.
- *Multiple personalities.* Ability to make applications accessible via multiple electronic devices such as PCs, kiosks, telephones, and network computers.
- *Risk management.* Because most code changes can be performed behind public component interfaces, they are much less likely to affect other parts of the system.
- *Legacy integration.* Legacy systems can be "wrapped" as one or more components and composed together with new commodity or custom components.
- *Scalability.* Freedom to distribute and reconfigure application components; therefore support all five styles of client/server computing as defined by the Gartner Group.

Component Characteristics. Components can be further described by the key characteristics they exhibit:

- *Well-defined.* Packaged so that they are predictable, well-defined and perform one or more specific functions which do not significantly overlap those of another component in the same domain.
- *Portable.* Can be used across address spaces, network boundaries, and can be hosted in a variety of operating systems and on multiple hardware platforms. Components can be built on a platform that best suits their developers, and then deployed on a different platform.
- *Plug-and-play.* Packaged so that an alternate implementation of a component can be substituted into a system without affecting other code. For components to thrive, they must be built so that they can snap in and out like Legos.

In addition to these characteristics, components are also defined by their granularity, or the relative size of components when compared to the application as a whole. Granularity can be broken down into the following categories:

- *Object level.* This type of a component encapsulates an object; it can be a text field (such as customer last name) or a combination of widgets (such as customer object) or a Web page (such as customer list page).
- *Process level.* This type of a component encapsulates a business process; it can be a combination of Web pages (such as customer maintenance process).
- *Application level.* This type of a component can be a complete application (such as a customer service application).

Component Application within Traditional Client/Server Environments.
Many developers have been introduced to components in traditional client/server environments in the form of controls (e.g., VBXs, OCXs) such as spreadsheet-style grids and multicolumn list-boxes. Often on projects where tools such as Visual Basic, Delphi, and PowerBuilder were used, these controls have been purchased to build sophisticated user interfaces. So rather than building their own multicolumn list-boxes, developers purchased these types of controls from third-party vendors and then plugged them into their own applications. These controls often reduced development costs, while providing additional functionality to develop more complex and user-friendly interfaces.

Many vendors built controls using third-generation languages (3GLS) such as C and C++. Because these languages are more complex than 4GLs, most vendors focused primarily on building "technical" or "construction" components that were used to perform specific technical functions and could be used by many different companies (thereby increasing potential market size). Few vendors have built "business" components designed to perform specific business functions such as customer maintenance or invoice creation. Because business requirements tend to be very specific to a company, it is difficult for vendors to create "business" components that could be used across many corporations. Companies themselves also tended to stay away from building re-usable components within their own organizations because of the high initial investment that was required due to complexities associated with developing such components. Consequently very few projects had successful implementations of business components.

Component Application within Netcentric Environments. However, netcentric technologies are reducing many of the complexities and limitations associated with building business as well as technical components, further raising the stakes for companies to start using components to stay competitive. These technologies include:

- *Open, commonly accepted standards.* By building this infrastructure into widely distributed products, vendors such as Microsoft and Sun have significantly reduced the amount of work required to build a component-based solution.
- *Development tools.* As the infrastructure becomes more stable, vendors are building development tools that take advantage of these open, commonly-accepted component standards. These tools provide for rapid application building and deploying of components. For example, Microsoft's Visual Basic Component Creation Environment tool can be used to quickly develop an ActiveX control (i.e., component) in a similar way a developer creates a Visual Basic application.

With the infrastructure and development tools in place, the component market is growing at a rapid pace. There is much more incentive for vendors to create business as well as technical components. The same incentives apply for organizations who are now putting more emphasis on creating business components internally so that they can be used across many applications within their organizations to support business requirements.

In summary, to gain the most from components, they need to be designed with re-use, risk management, and software distribution in mind. They need to use open, commonly accepted standards; they must be well defined, and must reduce complexity for developers. Netcentric technologies have introduced tools that considerably reduce development time for creating components. However, developing components that incorporate the characteristics described above still requires significant design time up front. So building components requires less effort, but building components that will streamline the company's computing environment still requires a large initial investment. With the rapid change of technology, companies are compelled to bring new products and services to market within much shorter time intervals. Effective use of components can provide a critical head start for building information technology solutions.

See the Chapter IV-1, "Componentware," for more detailed information.

Multiple Electronic Access Channels

The marketplace is putting pressure on vendors to use open, commonly accepted standards (e.g., universal network, component, etc.) when developing new technologies and tools for building applications. Having this infrastructure in place makes it more feasible for vendors to create additional physical devices from which electronic information can be accessed, previously limited primarily to PCs and telephones. For example, Web televisions are gaining momentum to the point where users can access the Internet from a television set, with some additional hardware. Network Computers, "thin-client" devices that download and run applications from a centrally-maintained server are generating a lot of interest. Also, users want to have access to the same information from multiple physical devices. So for example, a user might want to have access to his/her telephone billing information from a phone, from Web TV, and a PC.

Having these multiple electronic access channels is putting more pressure on companies to use components so that business logic can be re-used rather than customized and re-built for each physical device. Also, from an architecture perspective, tying all of these physical devices into a common computing environment requires a lot more design time up front, as well as support for all these devices once an approach is determined.

Information Ownership

Most Internet and intranet applications today have links to other sites. It is important for companies who are owners of these applications to continuously monitor the sites they reference in order to build credibility with their users. For such applications, key information is owned by the company itself and the reference sites are used to provide supporting or advertising information. However, applications that rely on integrating information from various Web sites they do not own will become more prevalent. So, how does a company maintain an application which relies on information that the company does not own? There will be more emphasis on getting agreements among business partners up front, upon whom the application is dependent, as well as continuously monitoring the application and the sites it relies on once the application is in production.

Security

Internet and intranet security has been on the front pages of most technical magazines for some time now. Loop holes found within both ActiveX and Java have been publicly and passionately debated. Clearly, using new technologies and allowing access to external users introduces security risks with which most organizations have not previously had to deal. As organizations gain experience with netcentric environments and the new security risks they introduce, proper protection mechanisms will be implemented and the anxieties will calm down. However, until then, considerable precautions need to be taken to protect an organization's valuable digital assets, such as customer information, purchase orders, and pricing data. This section addresses basic security issues as well as present means available to address these issues.

Security Holes in Netcentric Technologies. Because anyone can gain access to the Internet, an organization must consider the public nature of the Internet when connecting to its resources. The risks involved must be assessed through a careful examination of the company's digital assets, security policies, plans and procedures, and security infrastructure.

Today, many of the basic netcentric technologies present security risks that may be exploited by malicious hackers. Some of the risk areas include the following:

- *UNIX.* The UNIX operating system was designed under the assumption that all users are friendly and should have access to all information. As such, there may be security weaknesses in an uncustomized UNIX system that must be evaluated. Nevertheless, there are methods to securely configure UNIX. Even though all security flaws cannot be found, it is possible to "harden" the system by installing the appropriate patches, securing the appropriate files, and closing the appropriate services. Also, because the source code for UNIX has been available for a long time, many of the bugs have been discovered and patches for them have been created. These same risks exist both in traditional client/server as well as netcentric environments. However, in traditional client/server environments the UNIX servers are accessible primarily by internal users, which in itself minimizes the risks. On the other hand, in netcentric environments, the UNIX servers can be setup to be accessible by external users, which increases these risks and makes their assessment much more critical.
- *Windows NT.* The Windows NT operating system also may have security bugs. Unlike UNIX, Windows NT's source has not been available, so it has not been under the same scrutiny. Also, in a UNIX environment, the system administrator has to explicitly give access rights to

persons or groups. In the Windows NT environment, access rights typically are first given to all and are then taken away.

- *CGI.* This can leak information about the host system on which it runs, therefore providing information that could aid in a malicious attack. Also, poorly-implemented CGI scripts can be tricked into executing malicious commands, further compromising system security.
- *Client Security.* Technologies such as ActiveX controls, JavaBeans, plug-ins and other browser features can be exploited in such a way that can compromise client security, because these technologies permit access to personal files, as well as execution of programs on users' machines. Bugs have already been encountered in technologies such as Internet Explorer, Java, and JavaScript that have proven that security leaks can be introduced.

The risks mentioned above focus on malicious outsiders that attempt to break into an organization's computer systems. However, most security problems arise from internal employees, particularly those who do not protect their passwords and those who are disgruntled. In netcentric environments these security risks can be much more damaging. In a traditional computing environment, if disgruntled employees wanted to steal information, they had to use a disk or make hard-copies of the documents or programs. In the netcentric environment, that same disgruntled employee can just send the information via E-mail or give an external user access to internal systems. Therefore, to maintain a highly secure system, audit trails, policies on changing passwords, security training, etc. are critical.

Security Solutions. A number of options are available to address or at least mitigate some of the security risks in a netcentric environment.

Centralized security. Often when designing an architecture, an architect is faced with supporting many types of security: LAN, Application, Data base, E-mail, and now the Web. Centralizing security so that users do not have to remember ten passwords is usually a requirement for most applications. If having centralized security is important to an organization, supporting Web security has added another component to an already long list of other resources that must be secured. Vendors are making progress at centralizing security. For example, Microsoft has moved toward integrating user maintenance between Windows NT and Internet Information Server (i.e., Web server) in one place. However, often there are still no easy solutions that can be purchased. Often architects have to spend a considerable amount of time on designing and implementing centralized security within their computing environment.

Firewalls. Firewalls are necessary to protect sensitive resources or information attached to a network from unauthorized access. A variety of firewall implementations may be required at various levels within the network model. Different types of mechanisms exist for protecting private networks including packet filters, proxy servers, and application level firewalls.

- *Packet filters* are protocol-based services that check the address portion of data packets to determine the desired destination and intent. Administrators can block certain combinations that are categorized as unauthorized.
- Proxy server firewalls establish a shielding or screening server address which is typically placed between the router and the private network server to be protected. Proxy servers shield outsiders from knowing the specific addresses of servers within the private network (and later targeting them).
- Application proxies provide more intelligent filtering based on the actual contents of packets rather than relying on looking at only packet header information.

Another issue to consider is that many firewalls support only specific protocols like Hypertext Transfer Protocol (HTTP) or File Transfer Protocol (FTP). Object request brokers, on the other hand, use Internet Inter-ORB Protocol (IIOP), which is CORBA's Internet protocol standard, to send information across a network. So a firewall that just supports HTTP or FTP protocols would not allow IIOP messages to go through. Visigenic provides HTTP wrappers for its IIOP messages so that firewalls do not reject data sent using its ORB software. These type of protocol limitations must be considered when selecting firewalls.

Digital certificates. Once an ActiveX control or a JavaBean is downloaded to a client machine, they can do anything to the computer that a traditional software application can, such as accessing personal files or executing operating system functions. Because of this, ActiveX controls and JavaBeans are based on a trust model. Digital certificates have been established to give organizations more peace-of-mind about preserving security within the organization, while still permitting their users to download ActiveX controls and JavaBeans to their PCs.

A certificate is a specially-coded object that uniquely identifies a site. It contains the site's public key for encryption and the site's identification information such as organization's name, expiration date, and a digital signature of the issuer. These certificates are attached to the ActiveX control or a JavaBean and are used by the settings within browsers and firewalls to either permit or restrict users from downloading these components to their machines.

To obtain a certificate, a developer creates a certificate request file which contains the organization's identification and public key. This request file is sent to a Certificate Authority, which verifies the organization's identity and generates the digital signature which is sent back to the organization. The developer can than bind the digital signature to the ActiveX control or the JavaBean, as proof of the organization's legitimacy. Certificate Authorities have an initial charge for each certificate, as well as an annual maintenance charge.

In summary, a company that creates ActiveX controls and JavaBeans for the purpose of having them downloaded by their users (particularly external users), must apply for these certificates early in order to insure proper time is allotted for the Certificate Authority to validate the organization and generate the digital signature. Also, architects need to clearly understand the options that are offered by browsers and firewalls to either permit or restrict the downloading of ActiveX controls and JavaBeans to their users' machines.

User Interface

There is no doubt that the introduction of the Web has introduced significant changes to user interface design, particularly in the areas of how the user navigates through information and the display and make-up (the combination of such things as text, graphics, sound, video, and rotating advertisements) of published information. This is primarily due to the introduction of new technologies such as HTML and Web Browsers, which enable the creation and publication of complex documents on the Internet, from where they can be accessed by anyone. Because most organizations that publish their information on the Internet want to attract new customers, as well as retain existing customers, the user interface design needs to be attractive and very easy to navigate through. Also, the user interface may need to be continuously updated in order to get customers to come back, just like displays are continuously updated in stores.

However, intranet applications will tend to use more of the traditional client/server user interface design principles, particularly for transaction-type applications. The attractiveness of the interface, although also important, is not as critical for internal users who are familiar with the company's business. Nevertheless, there will still be changes to user interface design for intranet applications, particularly for published information.

When designing a user interface for a Web-based application it is important to consider the performance implications of what is included on a Web site. A number of information types — complex image maps, video, sound, advertisements, and so forth — may slow responsiveness. As with any application, if it is too slow, no matter how attractive it is, many people will not use it if they have a choice to go elsewhere.

Also, it is important to note that although the Internet has introduced new approaches for presenting information to users, basic user interface design principles such as consistency, forgiveness, error management and feedback still apply.

Content Management

The process of content management includes not only content development and the publishing of content to an internal or external Web server, but also the ongoing maintenance of content as the Web site is updated over time. In many ways, content development and management in a netcentric environment is similar to development in a more traditional programming environment: there is still a requirement for code versioning, content staging, and approval. However, managing the content associated with netcentric development and, in particular, Internet and intranet development, requires some additional considerations. The purpose of this section is to discuss those considerations.

The key point to bear in mind while designing a content management process for a netcentric environment is that content developers for Internet/intranet may be end users and graphic artists, who have different skill sets than traditional programmers. When considering architecture components to support content developers, the following items should be addressed:

- Managing centralization/decentralization of publishers and developers
- Integrating multiple content types
- Maintaining content staging
- Keeping content up-to-date
- Migrating existing content into HTML format
- Preparing a capacity plan

Managing Centralization/Decentralization of Publishers and Developers. In most development environments, the coding and testing of application code is performed in a centralized department by a group of trained application programmers using technical architecture components. Some projects have been done in a distributed development environment; however, even in those cases, the use of standardized development tools including compilers and coding standards are typically employed.

Now consider the netcentric environment, where the ease of setup and the access to a multitude of tools make centralized control very difficult. For example, many different tools can be used to create HTML documents, such as Front Page and HotDog. This is different from traditional client/server environments where typically only one tool such as Visual Basic could be used to create Visual Basic applications. Also, many of these HTML authoring tools tend to be either free or very cheap, and easy to download from the Internet. Once developers get used to these tools, it becomes more difficult to get them to switch to other tools, especially for people who are nonprogrammers.

Organizations often force their developers to standardize on a set of tools. However, in a netcentric environment, because of the tool availability, this becomes much more difficult to accomplish without creating antagonism among developers responsible for creating Web content. Sometimes alternatives will need to be found. One development project, for example, standardized on the types of HTML tags that could be used when creating content and allowed content developers to use their preferred tool as long as they only used the specified HTML tags.

Integrating Multiple Content Types. Where typical programming environments usually support only programmatic code, netcentric environments must also support the development and management of other several different content types, such as static HTML pages, pages that are generated "on-the-fly" from information stored in a data base or other repository, and multimedia components.

Maintaining Content Staging. The netcentric environment also requires a content staging process similar to more traditional programming environments. However, several considerations should be addressed:

- The approval process may be more complex, requiring sign-offs across several different internal departments including marketing, legal, and technical. The approval process may vary based on such factors as the type of content being submitted, the audience to which the content may be applicable, and the security level.
- Procedures for document management version control and code version control must be considered. Typically, requirements for each are different. For example, the make-up of static and dynamic content may not require the traditional, robust version control process which stores each additional change as a delta to a source file.

Keeping Content Up-to-Date. One of the more difficult tasks is keeping the content on a Web site current, particularly if content development is decentralized. A process should be established by which content publishers are notified as to when their content should be updated. The timeframes will vary based on the relevancy and the type of content (e.g., a 401K policy may be updated only once or twice a year whereas a departmental newsletter may be updated on a monthly basis.) Additionally, policy should be established to define when "dead" content can be removed from a site.

In addition, there is as yet no satisfactory single, integrated toolset that accommodates all the phases of content development and management mentioned above. As for content migration, there are now a number of tools available for migrating existing documents into HTML format. To date, some are better than others, but all seem to require manual tweaking to get the format desired.

Preparing a Capacity Plan. Capacity planning should be considered during the content design phase. Capacity can be affected in several ways, but the most well-known happens when a site puts up a new piece of content and is overwhelmed by an unexpected response. Another capacity planning issue to consider can occur when bandwidth intensive content is loaded.

Network Connection

When designing a netcentric application, it is critical to consider the type of network connection the users will have to the application. The users can be connected in many ways — a dial-up connection, wireless connection, LAN (as well as different types of LAN), WAN, and so forth. Each type of connection has different bandwidth and security requirements that will significantly affect the application design.

For example, when designing an Internet application it can be assumed that most users will connect to the Web via a modem. For such applications it may be best to design for the lowest common denominator, maximizing performance for machines that have small resolution screens and low memory. Another approach is to design and build two versions of the same application: one very graphical and one textual. The users then have the option to select the version that performs best on their machines given the type of network connection they have. However, today this often requires maintaining two versions of the same application.

Media Streaming

Streaming technology allows multimedia data to be delivered in such a way that it can be read or played back nearly real time or as soon as it is received, while the rest of the file is downloaded and buffered in the background. This eliminates the annoying download delays associated with prior multimedia download implementations. Today this technology is primarily used to support the listening and viewing of audio and video files.

Media (such as audio or video) intended for streaming can be served directly from the Web server or a separate media server that offers features needed to support many concurrent users. A plug-in is also typically needed on a user's machine to support playback of the audio or video stream. However, some browsers are beginning to include these types of plug-ins in their core software. It is important to note that having to support many concurrent users having access to streaming media may significantly increase the development and operations costs due to having to maintain a separate media server and plug-ins on client machines. Also, many such servers have limitations as to how many concurrent users they can handle, and therefore using more than one media server for some applications should be considered.

Media streaming on the Internet does not offer smooth, high quality audio and video, because of today's limitations of Internet protocols. Also, most streaming products today use proprietary methods for data compression, synchronization, and bandwidth management, requiring users to download a different plug-in or player for each media type. However, companies are currently working to come up with standard communication protocols to deliver real-time multimedia information over the Internet. The acceptance and implementation of such standards can significantly improve performance of delivering streaming information over the Internet, as well as drive vendors toward incorporating these commonly accepted standards in their products.

Streaming technology may be better suited for an intranet environment where network connection is under control of a centralized IS department. Nevertheless, business opportunities for incorporating media streaming into any application, Internet or intranet, need to be clearly defined.

Push/Pull Technology Considerations

In only a few years, people became swamped by the amount of information available on the Web. The availability of HTML editors and the ease of page creation have led to over 10 million Web pages thus far, and this number is continuously growing. Searching for information on the Internet has become a time-consuming task, forcing many companies to re-evaluate the benefits of employee access to the Internet. There cannot be a better time for the arrival of push technology, which redefines how we get the most out of too much information. Push technology reverses the paradigm: instead of the user searching cyberspace for information, the user can customize the type of information desired, and have it delivered directly to the desktop from a variety of sources.

However, many of today's push technologies are really pull — that is, software on the client initiates the transaction even though the server delivers the information or programs to the desktop. Because of this, there is a potential for these updates to stack up at the Internet gateway. Many push vendors are suggesting to use separate caching servers to support the delivery of pushed information to minimize such traffic risks. In general, network traffic resulting from the push delivery mechanism needs to be closely monitored. Having the technology that provides capability to deliver information to thousands of users at one time does not mean that the network can handle it.

Push technology allows companies to deliver crucial information to their employees and customers on as-needed basis. It also can make transparent to the user the process of keeping software up-to-date, simplifying software maintenance functions. For example, a user can subscribe to an Internet site to receive updates given a specific criteria. Then when that information becomes available the user is notified and the information is automatically downloaded to the user's machine. The user no longer has to keep going back to the site and checking for the availability of the information. This technology is particularly useful for intranet environments, where departments such as human resources or marketing can notify users of critical business-related information right away.

In summary, when designing a netcentric architecture, the opportunities for using push technologies for delivering critical information and software updates should be considered.

Transaction Processing Monitors vs. ORBs

An important issue in the netcentric environment is deciding when to use a transaction processing (TP) monitor and when to use an object request broker (ORB). TP monitors today are much more advanced in terms of providing an integrated environment that supports such things as security, system management, load balancing, and fail over capability. TP monitors such as Tuxedo and Encina are also extremely stable and proven in the marketplace. Today, none of this can be said of object request brokers, CORBA and DCOM. Perhaps a few years from now this may be different. Also, many TP monitors are moving towards providing Internet access through Java, and becoming CORBA compliant as well.

An application built today that requires high performance, heavy transaction processing and strong reliability, may benefit more from using a TP monitor such as Tuxedo or Encina. The drawbacks of using TP monitors are their proprietary nature, complexity and lack of direct object-orientation support.

ORBs can be an effective integration mechanism, especially for corporations where there is a requirement to provide support for an infrastructure that needs to integrate heterogeneous, distributed applications. This technology is object oriented, open, and accessible from many languages and environments. It is also relatively easy to program. The drawbacks are a lack of such things as good security, system management, and load balancing — all fundamental things needed in a systems operation center.

Internet Service Provider Considerations

Internet Service Providers (ISP) are third-party providers of dial up connectivity. For a basic fee depending on the service level required, these services provide connections to the Internet via analog or ISDN modems for customers. Businesses may also use ISPs to outsource their Web site maintenance. The choice of provider is usually dependent upon the level of service required by the application. Service Level Agreements typically cover guaranteed reliability, bandwidth, POPs (Points of Presence), and security.

Platform-Independent Euphoria

There is a lot of hype in the marketplace about platform independence, especially since technologies like Java are making this capability more of a reality. From a purely technical point of view, a developer may be able to create a platform-independent application. The question is, does this always make sense from a development and operations point of view? Also, there is some disagreement about what "platform independent" really means. Let's say the developer creates an application in Java, which is a platform independent language. However, in order for the application to be executed on a specific operating system, someone has to write a Virtual Machine to be able to translate Java instructions to the operating system's specific instructions. Therefore, there is still a dependency on a company that develops the Virtual Machine, and developers do make mistakes. This is evident by various bugs that have been found in Virtual Machines. As Java upgrades occur, again there is a dependency on companies who develop Virtual Machines to implement those changes as well.

Anytime a decision is made to support many platforms, applications need to be tested on those platforms to make sure they operate effectively. This usually means additional development and operations costs due to increased development/testing time and hardware/software support. Technologies that provide a certain level of platform independence (such as Java) are not always foolproof, because they are still dependent on some sort of platform-dependent software. Therefore, for critical applications, developers must ensure that they work on all supported platforms.

NETCENTRIC PROGRAMMING CONSIDERATIONS

Many new development tools and computer languages have been introduced to support the development of netcentric applications. Therefore, new approaches and techniques for implementing application logic within an application must be considered. The following topics will be discussed in this section:

- Java overview
- Business logic

- State management
- Data base access

Java Overview

Java, the Language. Java is a full-featured object-oriented language, created by Sun Microsystems, and as such has applicability in places where other languages — C, C++, Smalltalk — have been used. Fully object oriented, it has displaced C++ and Smalltalk as the industry's preferred object-oriented language. Its predominant use today is on the client machine when an application requires robust business logic or presentation services. However, it also can be used for processing application logic on the server. A unique feature of Java is its ability to be downloaded and executed on a machine at runtime from a browser in the form of Java applets (i.e., programs). This application distribution mechanism has led to its popularity. Furthermore, programs written in Java also can be executed outside of a browser — similar to C++ programs. Java has gained unparalleled support because of its engineering merits as a better computer language relative to C, C++, and Smalltalk. It is viewed as being able to significantly reduce application development time. Java's primary drawback is its maturity and stability, particularly in the area of performance/scalability and the lack of an integrated, robust development environment, though advances on both of these issues are made every day.

Java, the Platform. The Java platform includes the Java computer language and the virtual machine (VM). At runtime, the VM translates Java byte code into machine-specific instructions; separate VMs are written and optimized for each operating system. Together, the Java computer language and the VM (i.e., "Java platform") are intended to support the development of applications that can be run across multiple hardware and operating system implementations. Because of this, the "Java platform" has gained a great deal of momentum due to its potential for giving developers the tools to build cross-platform solutions.

Java, the Component. JavaBeans is the component architecture for Java; it is a spec for a set of software APIs that will let developers create reusable software components. JavaBeans will enable components developed in Java to run and communicate across heterogeneous environments.

Java, the Operating System. JavaSoft (i.e., Sun's Java development and marketing unit) has developed the JavaOS, which is a specialized operating system optimized for executing Java applications. It is primarily used to run Java on devices (e.g., network computers, kiosks, etc.) that do not have an operating system. Today, this operating system is very new and supports limited functionality; therefore, its future is yet unknown.

Java, the Future Hardware Integration. Today, as well as in the near future, there are plans to extend Java to hardware. This entails creating specialized computer chips optimized to execute Java in native mode. This capability would then be extended to specialized devices, such as cellular phones and pagers. Sun is currently developing Java computer chips. Also, existing computer chips can be modified to execute Java more efficiently. Intel is now optimizing its computer chips to run Java.

Business Logic

In traditional client/server environments, architects must define the development tools and computer languages developers will use to implement business logic. The same must be done for netcentric environments. During this selection, issues such as programming language learning curve, performance, scalability, complexity, capability, and development tools are evaluated. Some of the most common programming languages used for custom traditional client/server applications are 3GLs such as C, C++ and 4GLs such as Visual Basic and PowerBuilder.

Architects determine when the use of each computer language is appropriate and often employ a hybrid solution. Typically one of the 4GL languages (Visual Basic or PowerBuilder) is selected and one of the 3GL languages (C or C++) is selected. For the majority of business logic on the client a 4GL (like VB) is used; a 3GL (like C++) is used for more complex business logic on the server and more complex architecture functions such as error handling, security, and data base access. Once a computer language is selected it is nearly impossible to port code to another computer language without significant re-coding. These same issues must be considered when deciding which computer languages to use for development of netcentric applications. Some additional issues such as platform independence, component integration and vendor's adherence to open, commonly accepted standards must also be considered, more so than in traditional client/server environments.

Initially, Web documents were created using HTML. HTML is not a programming language; therefore, in and of itself, HTML cannot be used alone to perform any form of application logic, including even simple functions such as field level validation. Before the advent of client-side scripting languages, all requests for application logic had to be processed centrally by a Web server.

There have been many recent advances to enable the execution of basic business logic within the browser via scripting languages such as JavaScript and VBScript, which tie events on a Web page to functions that can handle those events such as mouse clicks or focus changes. They allow one component to pass instructions to another. In a component-based architecture, scripts contain the portion of the business logic that is not packaged within the components themselves. Scripts in a sense orchestrate or direct the components. The choice of a scripting language or mechanism is therefore an important decision when deciding upon a component architecture. Although there are many scripting languages (LotusScript, Oracle BASIC, Tabriz, and so forth), the two leading scripting languages are:

- *JavaScript* — a cross-platform Web scripting language developed by Netscape Communications, which allows the construction of interactive applications via scripting of events, objects, and actions, as well as access to events such as user mouse clicks. The JavaScript language is a platform-independent language and can be used for creating sophisticated applications or for just sprucing up static HTML pages. Although JavaScript is similar to Java and is often described as a simplified form of Java, it is not actually derived from Java. Some even say that the word "Java" is the only thing they have in common.

  JavaScript is marketed as being platform independent; however, there have been problems porting code from one platform to another. Some browsers do not support JavaScript or provide limited support for JavaScript, and there are limited development tools available. Microsoft has agreed to support JavaScript through its own implementation called JScript. However, some features are broken or missing and many existing JavaScript scripts do not run under Explorer 3.0.

- *VBScript* — a special version of Microsoft's Visual Basic programming language which has been tuned for the Internet. VBScript provides many of the same features as JavaScript, but is restricted to running on Intel platforms supported by Microsoft. The advantage of VBScript is its familiarity for developers already skilled in VisualBasic.

There is also server side scripting (SSS) which enables programs or commands to be executed on the server machine, providing access to resources stored both inside and outside of the Web server environment. SSS is most commonly performed through the following methods:

- *Common Gateway Interface (CGI) script.* The most common scripting method, CGI provides an interface that can be accessed through scripts authored in a number of popular languages including Perl and C. CGI provides an excellent method for performing simple tasks on a Web site, including providing simple operational capabilities (such as hit counters and clocks) and application logic, simple data base queries and HTML form/data merging. However, each time a CGI script is requested, the native operating system must create or spawn a new process. This is both time and resource intensive, and under higher volumes may place excess stress on the Web server. Many Web sites start off using CGI for simple Web sites, with plans to migrate to a more sophisticated processing model, such as vendor-specified APIs (e.g.,

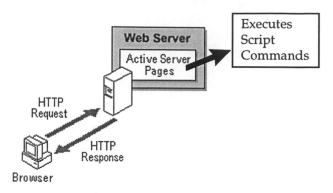

Exhibit 1. Processing ASP scripts.

NSAPI from Netscape or ISAPI from Microsoft), or third-party middleware as the site becomes more popular.

- *Active Server Pages (ASP) script.* Microsoft's server-side scripting environment that developers can use to create and run dynamic, interactive, high-performance Web server applications — similar in concept to CGI scripts (Exhibit 1). When an ASP page is called, ASP script commands are first processed by the Active Server Pages on the Web server, and then the results of the commands are returned in the form of an HTML page to the Web browser. Unlike CGI scripts, ASP allows the mixing of HTML markup language with scripting languages such as VBScript and JScript (Microsoft's version of JavaScript) in the same file, while allowing access to reusable ActiveX server components. As a result, one of the strengths of Active Server Pages is its ability to access and manipulate data base data and return the results to either an ActiveX control or an HTML form in one place. Also, unlike CGI scripts, ASP scripts do not spin off a process each time they are called. However, currently ASP scripts are limited to Intel platforms.

- *Server-side JavaScript.* Netscape has extended JavaScript to support server-side scripting, provided as part of Netscape's LiveWire tools. Today, C++ objects within the Web server can be directly called from server-side JavaScript.

The choice architects will typically make first is deciding which middleware (e.g., Visigenic ORB, Tuxedo, etc.) and which server-side scripting method (e.g., ASP, CGI, Server-side JavaScript, etc.) to use. This decision should be based on the following application requirements:

- Platform support — present and future
- Developers' learning curve and previous experience
- Number of developers

- Availability and stability of development tools now and in the future
- Future scalability
- Performance expectations
- Number of concurrent users
- Component integration
- Expected delivery date of the application
- Complexity of the application

The next step will be deciding whether to use a client-side scripting language. Usually the type of client-side scripting language will be dependent on the middleware and/or server-side scripting selected. So if ASP scripts are selected, VBScript would typically be used, though not required. If client-side scripting is used, then it is important to decide which part of the business logic to code using VBScript vs. another programming language such as C, C++, and Java. Again, this is similar to traditional client/server environments where developers have to choose which portion of the business logic makes sense to code in Visual Basic vs. C or C++. However, today client-side scripting languages support very limited functionality unlike 4GLs such as VB, PB, etc. They are very new and their future capabilities and vendor support are yet to be fully defined.

In summary, a lot of the same programming considerations such as performance, complexity, skills, and development tools still apply in netcentric environments. However, many development languages and tools have changed so the benefits of each must be thoroughly understood and evaluated. This is even more important than in traditional client/server environments because many of the technologies in the netcentric environment are immature and are constantly evolving. There is a lot more emphasis on component integration, platform independence and adherence to open, commonly accepted standards so that business logic can be scaleable across various types of computing environments.

State Management

State management is needed to pass or share information among windows/Web pages and/or across programs (Exhibit 2). In typical client/server applications, the various windows that make up a business transaction or conversation are implemented as a single executable program installed on the workstation. Because the program has a single address space, data entered on one window, whether currently visible to the user or not, is addressable by application logic associated with any window in the conversation. Therefore, in traditional client/server applications, data is typically shared between windows and programs on a client machine via global variables, shared memory, local data bases, etc. — eliminating the need for Context Data Management (in this text, Context Data Management refers to storing state information on the server, not the client).

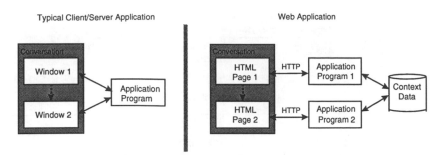

Exhibit 2. State management — traditional C/S vs. Web application.

However, this is different for Web-based applications. The HTTP protocol is a *stateless* protocol. Every connection is negotiated from scratch, not just at the page level but for every element on the page. The server does not maintain a session connection with the client nor does it save any information between client exchanges (i.e., Web page submits or requests). Each HTTP exchange is a completely independent event. Therefore, information entered into one HTML page must be saved by the associated server application somewhere where it can be accessed by a subsequent HTML page in a conversation. A Web application that requires multiple pages or exchanges with the user is structured more like a mainframe application. Each screen exchange (now HTML page) results in a specific program being invoked to process the data on the page, store any data needed by later screens or processing for future reference, and send the user the next page in the conversation. The role of context data management services is to store or otherwise make available data to future program invocations within a business transaction.

A variety of mechanisms for implementing state management services for Web applications are in use or emerging:

- Hidden fields
- Cookies
- Client-side scripting
- Transaction servers

Hidden Fields. A simplistic approach used by some Web applications is to pass context information back and forth attached to the page but not visible to the user. This is a relatively simple approach to implement but is useful only if the application's "state" requirements can be met by a few data fields and if securing context information from tampering is not a concern.

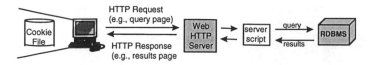

Exhibit 3. Using a cookie.

Cookies. Created by Netscape but supported by leading browser vendors, a "cookie" is a client-side mechanism for allowing Web servers to store information onto the client's PC. A cookie is a file stored in a designated directory on the user's PC that the Web server can read or write data to whenever a connection is made. For example, if a user visits a CD shopping site, the site may create a cookie on the user's hard drive to track items to be purchased while the customer is jumping from page to page. On the order summary screen, the server can read the products previously selected for purchase from the cookie file. Cookies used for spanning a transaction are designated as temporary and expire after a preset period of time. Permanent cookies, those with a future expiration date (i.e., 1/1/2070) can be useful for maintaining user profile or preferences over time (Exhibit 3).

The native cookie mechanism provides a limited and insecure way of maintaining transaction context on the client workstation. When implementing typical business transaction processing applications it is more useful and secure to hold the context data on the server machine where it is available for successive steps in the transaction. A more robust context data management approach can be implemented on the server side using the cookie mechanism only as a way to store the context record keys. The server can then determine which context record belongs to a given client workstation by extracting the key from the client's cookie file. This provides for even larger amounts of context data to be securely stored in a server-side data base and eliminates the need to pass the information back and forth repeatedly.

This approach only works for an HTML-based front end and is dependent on the type of browser/Web server combination. If alternative user interfaces are used (e.g., Java applets or voice response), this approach forces each of these user interfaces to maintain state information as well.

Client-Side Scripting. Some scripting languages, such as JavaScript and VBScript, promise to include features that will allow developers to implement more typical "stateful" client/server applications across the Internet or an intranet. These languages and their client-side libraries, for example JDBC or ODBC, will contain facilities for establishing a connection with a server hosted data base directly from the client workstation rather than

Exhibit 4. Accessing data via HTTP.

Exhibit 5. Accessing data via client-side scripting.

through an HTTP Web server. This approach in effect bypasses HTTP and its limitations. The scripting language approach does require that at least some executable application code be transferred to and run on the client workstation (e.g., the SQL statements and logic for processing and displaying results) (Exhibits 4 and 5).

The more the scripting approach is used the more the application begins to be structured much more like a traditional client/server program, that uses a two-tier architecture, where the application logic runs on the workstation and sends SQL statements, stored procedure requests or messages to a server running a shared data base management system. With JavaScript or VBScript, HTTP exchanges that open and close communications sessions are no longer required in order to send and receive information. A persistent communications and data base connection can be established and maintained across a series of calls, while multiple windows and entry fields are displayed and processed. However, if this type of a transaction occurs over the Internet, the client query will not go through most corporate firewalls nor will it securely transmit over the Internet. Therefore, this may be a more appropriate solution for simple systems running over an intranet.

Transaction Servers. Transaction Servers from various vendors (e.g., Microsoft, Sybase, etc.) are also offering capabilities for implementing state management. For example, Microsoft's Transaction Server has a Shared Property Manager that provides a mechanism to share and access global information among server processes.

Data Base Access

Access to data stored on a Web server, company's data bases, or legacy systems may be provided in several ways.

Server Side Scripting. Common Gateway Interface (CGI) scripts also can be used to pass along SQL commands to external data bases. Once information is returned from a data base call, a second CGI script is typically used to merge a pre-formatted HTML template with data returned from the call. While CGI offers a viable method for providing access to information, the overhead required to support a CGI call makes it a poor choice for all but the simplest of data base accesses.

Similar to CGI scripts, ASP scripts also can be used to access a data base. However, there are differences between the two scripting environments. The ASP environment allows a developer to combine data base access requests, HTML code, scripts (e.g., VBScript), and ActiveX controls into one ASP file making it easier for developers to process data base requests and immediately populate the resulting Web page. However, because data base logic and business logic is tightly coupled, scalability and reusability are diminished. Also, ASP supports Active Data base Object (ADO) which provides easy access to any ODBC compatible data source. ADO data base commands are similar to JET commands used in traditional Visual Basic applications. Because of this, developers with previous Visual Basic experience can quickly learn this new environment.

Vendor API. Several vendors of Web servers and data bases, including Netscape, Microsoft and Oracle, provide access to data through proprietary, vendor defined Application Programming Interfaces (APIs). These products eliminate the need for using CGI scripts for moving data between HTML format and a data base. The implementations impose far less overhead than the rudimentary CGI approach by providing multithreaded access to a reusable data base connection rather than creating a new data base connection for each query. Also, another important advantage of all API applications is their ability to maintain state. Because an API program remains resident in memory from one call to the next, information about the client can be stored and used the next time the client connects. The following are relevant products for providing or implementing Data Access Services.

- *ISAPI (Microsoft Internet Server API)* — a high-performance Web server application development interface that serves as a gateway between Microsoft's Open Data base Connectivity (ODBC) data sources and the Microsoft Internet Information Server (i.e., Web server). An ISAPI-based program is a Dynamic Link Library (DLL), not a separate program.
- *Netscape's NSAPI (Netscape Server API)* — provides lower-level services appropriate for implementing Data/Document Merging Services without resorting to CGI scripting.
- *Oracle* — provides native data base functionality through a feature called the Web Request Broker (WRB). The WRB can work in conjunction with either NSAPI or ISAPI to provide high performance, multithreaded

application access to data stored on an Oracle 7 data base. Access to internal WRB functions is provided through the Oracle's Web SDK, a lower level programming interface.

Because these are proprietary approaches that facilitate an environment for tight coupling of business and data base access logic and are bound to their respective Web servers, they are good for providing quick data base access for small scale applications that are not planned to be scaleable and portable. Development costs associated with using these APIs may also be higher than using CGI scripts or ASP scripts. For example, NSAPI is very complex to write and use. It is C++ code which must be successfully executed within the threaded environment of the Web server.

Third Party Middleware. Outside of vendor specific APIs, there are a growing number of third party middleware providers that provide tools used to manage data base connections. The level of functionality varies among products. The first two products mentioned below support two-tier architecture development for implementing the simplest, and often fastest Web-data base connectivity solution; however, these products may encounter performance problems as request volume increases. The second two products mentioned are capable of scaling to support larger, more robust Web-data base solutions, but require more setup time and are more expensive both to purchase and implement.

The following are products that support data base connectivity for two-tier architectures:

- *Cold Fusion* — a Web application development tool for building dynamic applications and interactive Web sites. It uses a proprietary markup language in a fashion similar to a 4GL, enabling the designer to build Web applications that are integrated with data base data, without having to learn CGI or Server APIs. As expected, Cold Fusion is very easy to learn and implement, but is limited by the possibility of lowered performance due to the additional processing layer.
- *dbWeb* — Microsoft's Web application development tool. It provides a bridge between Microsoft's Internet Server and ODBC, which in turn provides Web-based access to a variety of data bases. dbWeb provides a simple higher level interface for processing data base requests, formatting and displaying results.

Both of these products provide a quick, productive way to expose relational data through a Web interface. Designers should take care to understand any performance and scalability limitations these products may have before recommending them to support a particular application.

The following are products that support data base connectivity for three-tier architectures:

- *NetDynamics* — a next-generation Web application development tool built entirely in Java which can be used to create enterprise-scale Internet business applications. NetDynamics frees developers from having to code many of the technical architecture components (including functions like user session management, context data management, and security) required to support enterprise style Web applications from scratch. It also provides a robust application server that can be used to manage reentrant data base connections and dynamic application content creation.
- *WebObjects* — provides functionality similar to that contained in Net-Dynamics; however WebObjects is not Java-based. WebObjects can be used to build Web-based applications that run on multiple platforms, accessing many third-party data bases and Web servers to provide dynamic content generation and support for enterprise style Web applications.

Chapter III-2

Implementation of the V-model Testing Approach

It is somewhat unusual to place a chapter on testing in the netcentric environment so early in an implementation discussion, but this placement makes an important point: The biggest difference found with the V-model approach to testing is that it is pervasive throughout the life cycle of successful projects. Testing is not done last, as an afterthought to development. Testing must be carefully planned, designed, prepared, and executed. The requirements and the design are tested, as well as the many layers of code. Testing requires quantifiable specifications, complex testing environments, architectures and tools, trained testers, and explicit exit criteria. Systems are designed to be testable; this ensures not only quality, but also reliable delivery and maintainability. Testing is a complex activity that involves not only testing teams, but also users, technical support, development, training, documentation, roll-out, and program management teams.

This chapter builds on the V-model testing concepts discussed in Chapter II-7. As noted earlier, the V-model is a testing framework that has been successfully applied to various types of business applications, using many different development approaches. Once the fundamentals of the V-model are understood, the model can be adapted easily to a situation to identify risks, as well as to identify an effective and efficient approach to mitigate those risks.

Successful delivery of a systems solution in the netcentric environment requires that the testing at each stage of the life cycle be well-structured, clearly documented, and independently repeatable. Clearly, this is much easier when combined with integrated testing processes, tools, and techniques in order to achieve the goals of efficient, effective testing and on-time, quality delivery.

THE TEST STRATEGY

The first brick to lay in building a solid testing framework is the test strategy. The test strategy outlines a comprehensive testing approach for the entire solution. The test strategy is developed to determine and communicate precisely how the end product, complete with new hardware, software, work flows and procedures, will be tested. When developing the test strategy, developers must be sure to apply the V-model concepts not only to the applications under development, but also to the technical and application architectures, the training and documentation, and the organization and work processes.

Traditional test strategies focused only on testing the application code and basically ignored the architecture, treating it as if it were developed through black magic. In today's world, the architecture components are too complex and too integral to the success of the solutions; thus the same structure and rigor must be applied to developing architectures as to developing applications. Also, the comprehensive test strategy helps identify those forgotten, but important, components of the solution that nobody ever plans to test, such as the JCL, data conversion routines, and backup procedures.

Defining the Scope of Testing

The test strategy defines the scope of testing: what will be tested and, just as important, what will not be tested. In the V-model , applications are specified top down along the left side of the "V," with each level of specification incorporating decisions and adding increased detail. Ideally, each level of decision would be tested, every added detail with an associated testing stage on the right side of the "V." However, with the increasing complexity of netcentric application solutions, it is very often not possible, or at least not feasible, to test absolutely everything. Careful thought should be given to exactly what will be tested, what cannot or will not be tested, and how associated risks will be managed.

For example, in developing a financial services application to run distributed at 200 remote sites with several hardware and software configurations, it may be acceptable to test the application software only on the three most common configurations. The risks presented by deploying the application system to the untested configurations may be acceptable according to previous experience, or there may be plans put in place to monitor the first several weeks of operation on those platforms to identify problems. On the other hand, if the application system under development is critical to the operation of the enterprise, or if software errors would prove very costly, it may be necessary to test each and every configuration.

Another example might be the introduction of a new set of application systems and business processes into an existing business environment. Decisions may be made to test only a subset of interfaces and to use a pilot environment or a set of representative users to test the work processes. The assumption here is that the risks presented by not testing all interfaces are acceptable or that the cost to test each interface was not justified by the problems that might arise if they were to not perform. The point is to identify and communicate exactly what will and will not be tested, preferably based on the cost to test and risks to the business of not testing. Once complete, the definition of what is to be tested is often very useful in managing the expectations of the users and determining enhancements or expansions to scope.

The primary objective of the test strategy is to minimize gaps and overlaps in the testing of the end product. The test strategy should define what stages of testing will take place and what the scope and objectives of each testing stage are. Based on the development approach and the risks associated with the development project, testing stages will be defined to confirm proper implementation of each level of specification and each major risk area.

Identifying the Stages of Testing

The V-model , as presented in this book, defines the main testing stages as: component test, assembly test, product test, operational readiness test, and benefits realization test. A given project or set of projects may have more or fewer testing stages; the important thing is that the stages are identified and communicated early in the effort to ensure proper results.

Traditionally, if one were to ask the members of the typical IT organization what stages of testing were standard for solution delivery, the answers from the managers as well as the developers would most likely be inconsistent or vague. One cannot hope to achieve efficiency and effectiveness in testing processes if the people responsible for those processes do not have a consistent understanding of what the processes are. By outlining exactly what the testing stages are, where each one starts and stops, and who has responsibility for each, gaps and overlaps in testing activities can be eliminated.

Too often, redundant effort is spent in the later stages of testing, confirming things that were covered in an earlier stage. One of the most common causes of overruns in product testing stems from repeating the component testing of the application because there was not a concise understanding of exactly what was covered during the component test. Because a development team does not understand, and therefore cannot assume, what has already been tested in earlier stages, they find themselves retesting very basic conditions during product test.

Another factor here is that it is generally easier for a software developer to prepare and execute a component level test than to plan and execute a true product test. Product testing is largely a test of the requirements and business functions. It is much less tangible than testing if's and move's. Therefore, developers tend to focus on component testing at the expense of product testing. By articulating what each test is designed to accomplish — the scope and objective of each test stage, along with how conformance will be verified and validated — both the redundant testing and the omitted testing can be identified and addressed.

Another benefit of a comprehensive test strategy outlining the scope and objectives of each testing stage is that there is now a means to determine when testing is finished. One of the most common questions asked is, "How does one know testing is complete?" The answer here is that knowing when one is done depends on beginning with an established scope and approach to what will be tested and how. Only that initial agreement allows the team to know that the test, when successfully executed, has really achieved its objectives.

The test strategy should be completed as part of initial project plans. A common problem in systems development is setting in stone the project plans, budget, schedule, and due date and then telling the testing manager how many days are allocated for testing. This clearly compromises the testing, because it sets testing scope based on days available, rather than number of days required to deliver an acceptable level of quality and risk. The only way to avoid this common problem is to develop the test strategy early. To allow for the proper testing of the system and new business processes, it is crucial to consider the testing requirements up front, and to make decisions on the scope and investment for testing early, thereby allocating the proper resources in the project plans.

Defining Test Cycles

In addition to outlining the testing stages, the test strategy should include initial test cycle definitions. Preliminary definition of test cycles not only facilitates estimating the effort required to plan and execute the test, but also allows the development teams to sequence the delivery of components in alignment with the needs for test execution. The project delivery window can be shortened through tight coordination of the sequence of delivery from development to testing stages, allowing for the overlap of project activities. This is a big plus for projects facing an externally imposed due date such as a regulatory change. The test strategy allows the team to avoid the situation where the test teams plan to run the conversion programs first to build data for the product test, and conversion routines are the last thing the development team plans to deliver.

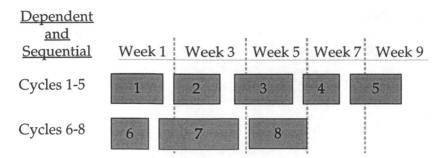

Exhibit 1. Dependent and sequential test cycles.

Definition of test cycles requires addressing the issue of overall test design. Test design considerations to be applied when outlining cycles include the balance between sequential and parallel cycle definition, and the inclusion of test cycles to cover ancillary tests.

Sequential Test Cycles. Purely sequential or horizontal test cycles most closely reflect true business processing. However, sequential cycles tend to imply single-thread executions that can lengthen the elapsed time needed to complete. Also, the built-in data dependencies leaves a team at risk that a defect in early cycles can halt execution of the entire test. Data dependencies also make the test model more likely to incur significant rework if changes to the data model occur in early test cycles. A positive consideration for sequential test models is the ability to bundle all test conditions of a particular type into a single cycle, thus reducing the number of cycles to be regression tested when a particular area changes. For example, sequential test models typically have all data creation functionality (e.g., add customer and add account) grouped into the early cycles, therefore if the add process is changed, developers need only to regression test these early cycles (Exhibit 1).

Parallel Test Cycles. Parallel or vertical test cycles are designed by establishing a small amount of base data, followed by multiple, concurrent test cycles breaking off and testing groups of test conditions. Parallel test cycles reduce the risk that one error stops all test execution in its tracks. The parallel cycles exercise independent data; therefore, the inability to progress along one path will not necessarily halt others. However, there are some inevitable tradeoffs:

- Parallel tests tend to be less representative of true business applications. Care must be taken to implement true product test level conditions as opposed to re-assembly testing.

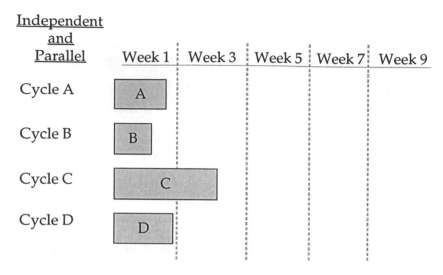

Exhibit 2. Independent and parallel test cycles.

- Test conditions around a particular requirement tend to be spread across cycles, necessitating modification and reexecution of multiple cycles for a single requirements change (Exhibit 2).

The answer here is to strike a balance in cycle design. The cycles must be dependent and sequential enough to provide a flow of data and events through the application (because this supports the testing of true business processes) and also parallel enough so that there are multiple executors active at a time, reducing risk and elapsed time for execution (Exhibit 3).

Additionally, ancillary test cycles might be designed to cover groups of test conditions such as conversion routines, security, performance, or regression of a previous version. It is often advantageous to separate these tests into independent cycles due to the technical nature of the test conditions, thus requiring more complex test environments, tools (e.g., performance monitors), and personnel (Exhibit 4).

DEVELOPING THE TEST APPROACH FOR EACH STAGE

Building on the test strategy, the next step is to develop the test approach for each testing stage. The test approach is developed as part of the specification to be tested. For example, the product test approach is developed as part of the requirements specification, and the assembly test approach is developed as part of the technical design specification. This facilitates early identification of test requirements, thus providing the time to address action items.

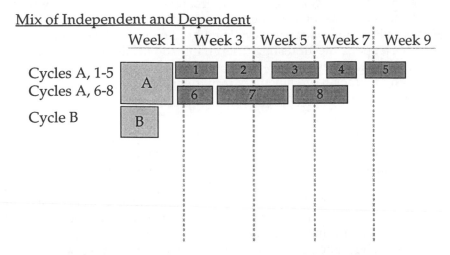

Exhibit 3. Mix of independent and dependent test cycles.

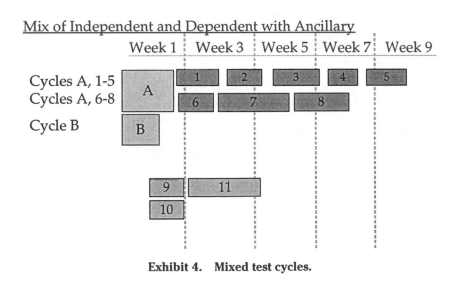

Exhibit 4. Mixed test cycles.

Whereas the test strategy stated what will be tested, the test approach for each stage defines how things will be tested. The test approach further details the process, entry and exit criteria, and roles and responsibilities. The test approach also includes the work plan, schedule, and resource requirements for that test stage.

The concept of developing a test approach document is not new. However, historically the focus of the test approach was integration or system testing, and the approach was developed by and for the development team members responsible for testing. This chapter advocates developing a test approach for each test stage, and the reach of the activities defined in the approach includes team members from development, testing, technical support, users, training, and others.

Regression Testing

In addition to the test process itself (i.e., the how), the test approach should outline the steps to be taken to regression test changes, both fixes and scope changes, made when a solution component is demoted from a testing stage. Regression testing of changes can include anything from simply testing the actual change made to testing the change and all identified affected areas and fully re-testing the entire solution. Again, these decisions should be made largely on the risk associated with the changes made and the effort required to perform various levels of regression testing.

Once the required level of regression testing is determined, several options exist for actually performing the regression tests. The most obvious approach is to have the developer and testers for the changed components perform the required regression testing as the changes are made and the component is migrated through the stages of the V-model . This implies individually regression testing each change, which can become quite costly. Other options are:

- Bundling changes and reexecuting appropriate tests (the tests are repeatable) when a threshold number of changes has occurred, for example, every 50 changes.
- Reexecuting the tests periodically; for example, every Friday afternoon, each work cell kicks off all regression test scripts to test changes made that week.

Resource Requirements

Included in the test approach are final resource requirements for the test stage. Testing convergence applications suggests the need for many varied skills. Convergence applications bring together many facets of business, and many technology components. Gone are the days when there was a single person in the technical support department who was capable of resolving any technical problem. Today, applications and the corresponding issues require a wide variety of skills to fully understand and support a solution. There may be unique requirements for business skills, organizational skills, and technical skills for the front-end, the legacy applications, the communications layers, and so forth. In addition, there are the pieces of applications developed on different platforms using different languages.

It is more than likely now that a team of technical and business experts is required to verify a system and to analyze and resolve problems. It is important to identify and schedule the proper levels of participation from all members of the team, especially developers.

When specifying the resources required for the testing effort, the level of external participation required should be defined. Applications involving major change to the business can be successful only if there is significant involvement of the user and customer communities.

PLANNING THE TEST

Test planning is made up primarily of the development of test conditions and expected results. The important difference in test planning in a netcentric environment as opposed to traditional test planning is the emphasis on when and how to derive test conditions.

When? The earlier, the better. Test conditions are now developed as part of the specification to be tested — on the left side of the "V." The completion of the test conditions for the associated test stage should be an exit criteria for delivery of the specification. Identification of test conditions as part of the specification provides two major benefits:

1. Early test planning results in more quantifiable, testable specifications. As the requirements analyst is documenting the application requirements, the tester needs to be asking, "How am I going to test that?" In this way, a team gets better requirements. If the analyst cannot answer the question of how a requirement is to be tested, it is too vague, and thus there is a significant chance that the designer and developer will not understand how to implement the requirement. Thinking through how to test something eliminates many of the ambiguities and incorrect assumptions. The result is clear, understandable specifications.
2. The second benefit is that planning tests early allows test preparation to begin early and to happen concurrent with construction. Given the test conditions with the specification, the test team is able to begin test preparation concurrent with construction of the solution. Now, as the development activities begin to wind down, the team does not have to wait for resources from development teams to transition to the test team to start thinking about testing. The team is ready to start executing the test. This can save a considerable amount of elapsed time in the delivery of a solution, typically squeezing at least two to three months out of the delivery window.

Finally, for each test condition identified, the expected result should be identified. For example, a test condition for selection of an audio explanation from an entry screen would have the expected result that the correct audio clip plays and returns control to the entry screen. It is this definition of how the condition will be satisfied that forces the designers to quantify requirements and thus reduce ambiguities in the design or devise ways to make the system more testable. Definition of expected results also makes it possible to verify the test plans against the requirements to be tested.

How are test conditions derived? Directly from the specification. It is essential to tie test conditions to the specification they test. Tying test conditions to specifications provides the traceability discussed in Section II. It also provides a means to determine and demonstrate what is and is not tested. Without a cross-reference from specification to test conditions, it is impossible to demonstrate that the test will cover all risk areas of the specification. Too often on projects, analysts sit down with a blank sheet of paper to begin documenting test conditions. The rationale for this is that the analyst is the expert, and thus best positioned to identify what and how to test. However, it is quite likely that the analyst will apply the same oversights/misconceptions to the test plan that existed during analysis.

An added risk is that it is almost certain that the analyst will be the only person who understands what is being tested and why — thus inhibiting the ability to effectively leverage the test plan for execution or reuse. In the case of drawing up test conditions from a blank sheet of paper, there is no means of identifying what each test condition, and ultimately test case, is designed to test. It is important for the test executors, and eventually those maintaining the test, to understand the objective of the test cases in order to effectively judge results and to identify the impact of changes. Likewise, if test conditions are not cross-referenced to specifications, there is no way to identify where in the test model specific requirements are tested. Therefore, we do not have the ability to judge test coverage or perform an impact analysis to effectively maintain the test model. Ideally, test conditions are generated from, and tied to, the specification they are designed to test (Exhibit 5).

Component test-level test conditions are drawn directly from the detail design specification. For example, each item on the Control-Action-Response (CAR) diagram or each video launch would have one or more associated test conditions designed to prove the item was properly implemented in the code.

Test conditions for the assembly test may be generated from application flow diagram detail or data access and window navigation specifications. Test cases can then be generated to exercise each primary or default path in the system dialogs and the passing of data from assembly to assembly to demonstrate correctness.

Likewise, each functional requirement, and each quality requirement, should have one or more associated product test conditions to demonstrate that the solution satisfies the requirement. Generating true product test-level

Specification driven testing

Specification	Objectives of Test Stage ⬅	Test Stage
Business Case	business benefits achieved	Benefits Realization Testing
Roll-out, Operations Procedures and SLA	availability reliability performance	Operational Readiness Testing
Application Requirements Specification	completion of business functions business results on screens and reports processing times	Product Testing
Application Architecture Design	screen navigation, module calls interface use context data handling	Assembly Testing
Automated Process Design	logic validation reads / writes displays error handling	Component Testing

Exhibit 5. Specification-driven testing.

test conditions may be difficult at first, particularly if previous testing experience focused on testing technical execution of code rather than systems functionality or business processes. One way of viewing product test is to take the perspective of the business user of the end solution. Assuming that the component test checked that the actual code works, and the assembly test checked that the individual modules or components can pass control and data as designed, the product test can be viewed from a largely nontechnical perspective.

Envision the users of an online banking application attempting to use the system via home telephone to transfer funds. The users know that they must provide a customer identification number and checking account number as well as the amount to be transferred. Most users neither know nor care how the system processes the data; they care only that the right transactions occur so the transfer can be completed. With this scenario, we can see that the individual component tests must check that the required data is obtained, that the customer identification number is verified, and so forth. The assembly test checks that the telephony equipment passes the right data to the system, which in turn accesses customer account information, sending data to activate the appropriate response message to the user. Product test then confirms that the funds transfer is reflected in the customer checking and savings accounts, and that the activity is recorded in the system which tracks the use of the online service for billing.

PREPARING THE TEST

For each test stage, after completion of the test approach and the test plan, one is ready for test preparation. Test preparation is defined as development of test scripts, test data, and execution steps.

The test design principles to be applied during preparation center around the desire for the test to be repeatable, modular, and expandable. It is desirable for tests to be repeatable to support audit and reuse. Generally, tests are repeatable if they are well structured and well documented. Modular tests can be executed piece by piece as need and resources dictate, thus improving productivity. Modular, well-structured, and documented tests are expandable, meaning that new or changed test conditions can be incorporated into existing test models easily. Expanding an existing test model allows for efficient testing of both new and existing risk areas.

Differences from traditional test preparation approaches arise from the increased level of structure and rigor applied to documenting tests, the high degree of reuse of scripts within and across tests, and the use of tools to automate execution and results verification.

A key consideration during test preparation is the level of detail to which input data and expected results should be defined. In general, time invested on definition of test data and detailed expected results is gained back in more efficient test execution and increased repeatability/reusability of tests.

Test Data

Done properly, the use of common test data increases productivity. All too often, however, common test data is poorly designed and inadequately maintained and controlled, which renders it useless. Ideally, common test data is created and maintained to support the testers, thus eliminating the need for testers to design, develop, and maintain their own test data. Test data should be designed to be representative of the conditions to be tested, and should be dense, such that a minimum number of transactions can be executed to exercise all test conditions. Common mistakes to be avoided when creating test data include:

- inadequate control over master data to prevent corruption,
- inadequate documentation of test data to support users,
- inadequate resources committed to maintain data as requirements and data models change, resulting in obsolete data,
- unrealistic test data, which may confuse users and/or render false results.

Another major data decision to be made is how the test model will use converted vs. created vs. system generated data. Converted data allows one to exercise the solution against real converted data, thus identifying problems with the data and/or conversion routines. This is important because many painful production problems are often due to data. However, converted data can be unwieldy and can often cause problems in the test that have nothing to do with the actual test conditions one is trying to test. Consider the ease with which a manageable subset of production data can be identified and sliced, while retaining data integrity across elements. Also, data conversion routines are typically developed very late in the project. Finally, be sure to address confidentiality issues with using production data for testing.

Created data means using the system to add the data needed to test — for example, using the customer entry application to add test customers. When using created data, start the test with essentially empty data bases (with the exception of administration and reference data) and use the actual solution (system, processes, etc.) to create all of the test data needed by subsequent cycles. This approach ensures that the solution can create data and then process that data. Conversion routines — and thus converted data — would be tested separately.

The third option is to generate data using a utility. With this option, it is often difficult, if not impossible, to get the data integrity correct due to complex dependencies among data elements. However, this may be the only option if data not created by the system is needed for testing, but is not available — for example, data to be provided by an as yet incomplete system or unsigned business partner.

In general, the best approach is usually to use a combination of two or three sources of data, designed to best address the risks being tested.

One final trick to consider when scripting and designing test data is to develop scripts in the reverse order of execution: from the last cycle to the first. This way, one can identify all of the data needed for each cycle, and feed that information to the scripting of the previous cycles so that the data can be created and/or passed. This eliminates the common dilemma of attempting to script cycle five, and discovering that one needs two additional customer types which must now be created and passed along from the very first cycle — which then results in script changes for cycles one through four.

Expected Results

As with test data, the level at which one intends to document expected results must also be defined. Typically, expected results are very detailed: field by field for all effected data bases, interfaces, and reports. Detailed expected results allow for detailed results verification, which supports maximum identification of discrepancies. Detailed expected results are also required to make the tests repeatable. Given the test script and expected results, someone other than the original test designer should be able to reexecute a test and verify results easily.

It may be difficult to predict expected results for some portions of the application, usually because of complex dependencies. In these cases, one must document input, output, and high-level expected results with a comprehensive, detailed, expert review of the actual results. Once the actual results have been reviewed and approved, these results can serve as detailed expected results for future executions.

An effective test preparation design technique is the use of multiple levels of scripts or test cases. This technique is often applied to product testing as a means to identify as many issues as early in the testing process as possible. Usually three levels of scripts are defined:

1. Level one is a set of high level scripts designed to execute all major system functionality. These scripts are designed to execute very quickly, covering the most basic processing. This allows one to identify any significant problem areas within the solution as early as possible. Because they are high level and cover all major functionality, the level one scripts are also an excellent foundation for regression tests and other testing, such as platform migration, training, and systems software upgrades. Typically, these scripts are developed by scripting the "story lines" to be executed, and checking off the test conditions that are covered by the scripts. The level one scripts usually account for 25 percent to 30 percent of the product test conditions.
2. Level two scripts are the main body of the test. The level two scripts test the detailed test conditions. These are scripted more traditionally, by grouping test conditions and writing scripts for each group until all test conditions are covered.
3. Level three scripts are sometimes used to cover independent and quirky test conditions, such as exception processing or hardware failure test conditions. These scripts are isolated from the level two scripts primarily because they require extensive set up or unique combination of data to test, and would complicate the main test. By isolating the level three conditions into separate test scripts, you can execute them as time permits, often filling down time in the main execution.

Establishing the Test Environment

Most product tests lose at least the first 2 weeks of execution because of environment problems: missing common modules, incorrect configurations, communications malfunctions, incomplete data or source libraries, and so forth. Teams should bear in mind the need to start a few weeks earlier to establish and test the test environment.

This activity will most likely start early in the project, with the selection and implementation of tools and required hardware and software, followed by the establishment of the test configurations to be tested and the loading of test data. Several factors make establishing the test environment a critical line item on the project plans:

- *Complexity/expense* — Testing a complex solution will probably require creating a "model office" — an environment that simulates a production environment. These environments, particularly in netcentric computing, are extremely complex and often very expensive. Plan ahead to allow lead time for implementation of the environment and to take advantage of the potential of sharing environments with other teams (for example, across testing stages or between testing and training).
- *Support* — To allow test execution to proceed smoothly, it is crucial to have proper technical support for the test environment. Environment support includes establishment and maintenance of test configurations, test data management, migration control, and problem solving. Migration of code and data for product testing can easily become a full time job. Repeatable tests imply backup data, and this in turn implies maintenance. If resources are not allocated to apply data structure changes to saved test data, the test model quickly becomes obsolete.
- *Control* — Strict control over the test environment — particularly the source code and data configurations — is essential to testing. Code and data changes must not be introduced directly into the test environment; instead they should be implemented in the development environment and pulled forward into the test environment. As the saying goes, "Test what you deliver, and deliver what you test." Improper configuration management too often leads to incomplete solution configurations or inadvertent changes. Be sure to have environment control policies defined, complete with change approval processes and audit capability.

Test Automation

The diagram of the Integrated Testing Environment (ITE) (Exhibit 6) was introduced in Section II. The components of the ITE fall into two categories:

1. Components not specifically dedicated to the testing phase, used during most of the phases of a project development life cycle, including:
   - Project management
   - Programmer's workbench
   - Design repository

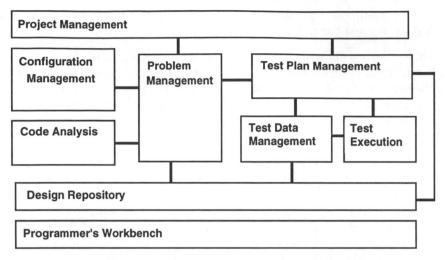

Exhibit 6.   The integrated testing environment (ITE).

2. Components that are mainly needed during the testing phase of the project and after, including:
   - Test plan management
   - Test execution
   - Test data management
   - Configuration management
   - Problem management
   - Code analysis

Project Management. Project management is not specific to the testing environment, because it obviously covers the entire project life cycle. It focuses on project planning, schedule, cost, and statistical reports. Project management tools are prevalent in the market. An example is Project Workbench for Windows (PWB) from ABT Corp., a Windows-based project planning and control system. Andersen Consulting offers its own proprietary tools, such as MANAGE/1.

Programmers Workbench. The Programmers Workbench represents the specific tools that support the coding and maintenance of the application software:

- Source code debugger.
- Source code comparator, which enables identification of changes between different versions of a program.
- Documentor, which enables recording of information about a program, data store or system, completely and systematically.

- Auditor, which enables the verification of source code conformance to pre-established rules and standards.

Programmers workbench tools are selected before the construction of the application and are not specific to the testing environment. It is important, however, that the test execution, test planning, and defect tracking system are integrated in the same environment so that the programmer can easily switch from one tool to another during the fixing activity.

Design Repository. The design repository represents the basis of the application development, providing impact analysis and application generation features. Typically, the design repository is used to centralize the application definition data. The design repository is mainly involved during the construction phase of the application.

In a testing environment, the design repository is a safe means of analyzing the impact of a problem on the whole application. Having two separated systems, one for problem management and one for application design, duplicates the information and introduces errors. Therefore, the interaction between the design repository and the defect management, test planning, and configuration management components would significantly increase productivity and reduce the risk of errors

Test Plan Management

Test plan management allows structured design and maintenance of test cases. During test planning, the business functions are broken down into test conditions. The test cycles, test data, and expected results are defined and prepared to be ready for execution. A test planning system helps the developer to find existing test cases, cycles, and scripts that may be appropriate for reuse. In addition, test planning helps keep track of test cycle execution scheduling and execution results.

All the test design data can be stored in a repository, which ideally would reference problem management information associated to a test cycle. Some of the functions that may be supported are:

- Test model definition and repository support
- Test cycle definition
- Test schedule and test execution tracking
- Test conditions generation

Test Execution

The test execution component of the integrated testing environment includes:

- Scripting and playback tools, which automate the execution of tests by simulating the end user operations.
- Emulation tools for component and assembly test, mainly:
  — Stub modules.
  — Server back-end emulation.
  — Client emulator or injector to test servers.
- Test results comparison (actual result data compared to expected results).
- Test coverage measurement comparison (during program execution, this provides comprehensive information about how many times each logic path within the program is executed in any number of runs).

Test Data Management

Test data management can be seen as a link between test planning and test execution. During test planning, data is identified in terms of need; in test data management, the data is actually created and manipulated for test cycles preparation.

Test data management assists the developer in the creation of the test data and expected results in a medium such that it can be automatically used by test execution tools or loaded to the test environment. Test data management assists in switching between cycles, by refreshing the input data before running or re-running a cycle. Test data management is composed of:

- Test data manipulator (editing).
- Test data generator.
- Extract and load facility.
- Archive facility.

Configuration Management

The main function of configuration management is to monitor and control the changes throughout the software development and maintenance process, including testing. It provides the following functionality:

- Version control of the software.
- Version control of test model elements (test scripts, test data).
- Migration of sources from one development stage to the following one. (i.e., from coding to assembly test and from product test to production).
- Migration of test model elements.

Problem Management

Problem management logs issues and problems detected during the test process, to classify problems and to generate error reports. Problem management is essential for the capture of metrics information.

The major functions are:

- SIR source and metrics information.
- SIR resolution information.
- Planning support for the SIR fixing and migration preparation.
- Impact analysis capabilities, including:
  - Interface with the application design repository to get a precise impact analysis on a defect.
  - Interface with the test plan management to keep track of the cycle where the problem occurred, the test condition and therefore the business function affected by the problem.

Code Analysis

Source Code Analysis tools contribute to software quality assurance for the project. The reports generated by these types of tools can be used by management to determine if the project's source code meets the entry criteria for their respective development or test stage. These reports also can be used to determine if the project's source code meets the exit criteria from the previous development stage.

Note that source code analysis tools measure the quality of the project's source code only; they do not measure whether or not the source code for a module matches the design for the module. This analysis must still be done manually through code reviews.

Executing the Test

Test execution is the step to execute the scripts, verify results, document and resolve discrepancies, and regression test changes. Differences from traditional test execution arise from the complexity of the environments and configurations being tested and the use of automation.

Traditionally, test execution involved the repeated execution of cycle one (until clean), followed by the repeated execution of cycle two and so forth, until all cycles are complete. Using this approach, it is very difficult to assess progress during the execution stage. The time it took to achieve a clean run of cycle one may not be any indication of the issues which will be encountered in future cycles because they are testing different areas of the solution. Also, there is a risk that major issues are lurking in the later cycles, only to be discovered very late in the execution process.

More efficient test execution may be achieved through the technique of using multiple execution passes. In this approach, multiple passes of test cycle execution are planned. For example, the first pass would attempt to execute all cycles complete as possible, and identify all major defects. Data changes and detours may be used to complete a set of scripts — for example, a "best effort" execution pass. Then, after the defect fixes from the first

Three-Pass Execution Model: Work Plan

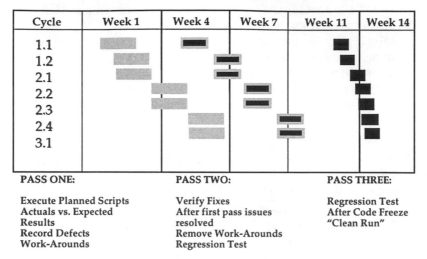

Cycle	Week 1	Week 4	Week 7	Week 11	Week 14
1.1					
1.2					
2.1					
2.2					
2.3					
2.4					
3.1					

PASS ONE:

Execute Planned Scripts
Actuals vs. Expected
Results
Record Defects
Work-Arounds

PASS TWO:

Verify Fixes
After first pass issues
resolved
Remove Work-Arounds
Regression Test

PASS THREE:

Regression Test
After Code Freeze
"Clean Run"

Exhibit 7. The three-pass execution plan.

pass are complete, the same scripts are executed a second time. In this pass, the purpose is to verify that the fixes were made correctly, to test that the fixes did not corrupt anything else, and to test those portions of the application that were not tested in the first pass due to defects or detours. Finally, a third and final execution pass is run to ensure all scripts execute successfully (Exhibit 7).

The three-pass approach to test execution allows one to identify problems with the solution as early as possible and helps give an indication of what the effort to complete the test will be. At the completion of the first pass, there is an understanding of the stability and quality of the application. The team can then make decisions for activities going forward.

For example, if the first pass uncovered a number of defects much larger than planned — defects that should have been uncovered by the component test — one might consider demoting portions of the application to be re-component-tested until the required level of stability is achieved. On the other hand, if the testing in the first pass reveals a number of defects aligned with the plans, the team can feel comfortable that the remainder of the schedule is reasonable.

For a typical product test, one should plan five execution passes. If the test is largely a regression test, or if the testing process is mature (e.g., high stage containment levels) then a three pass test may be planned.

Finally, during test execution, the goal should be to get ahead of schedule early to build schedule flexibility. No matter how well the test is planned and prepared, problems may arise. Then the team runs the risk of being at the end of the development project with no room to absorb delays.

NEW MANAGEMENT CHALLENGES

Sponsorship

Management must demonstrate a commitment to the application of the testing principles outlined in this chapter. The structure and rigor required to apply the V-model testing approach require visible sponsorship from management for successful implementation.

Estimating

It is not safe to assume that the old estimating approaches for testing will still work. Most traditional approaches estimate testing activities as a percentage of development effort. When using the V-model approach, consideration must be given to the early test planning, verification and validation activities, reusable test models and automation. Testing effort is not necessarily correlated to development effort. A more appropriate estimating model takes into account:

- What will be tested in each stage.
- The testing complexity of the units to be tested.
- Whether an existing test model will be used.

Determining what is to be tested in each stage is defined in the test strategy. Testing complexity of the units to be tested refers to the degree of difficulty involved in planning and executing a test; this is not necessarily the same as the complexity of the unit itself. An added piece of functionality may be very difficult to develop, but easy to test. On the other hand, a very simple code change may be a nightmare to test due to the dependencies required to execute the required test conditions. A current example of this is the application changes required to accommodate the year 2000. Very often, the actual code changes are isolated to a very small number of application units, but all calculation and printing applications must be tested, as well as processing that spans the millennium change.

The use of an existing test model can significantly reduce the time required to plan and prepare a test. Time should be allocated to review and update the existing test model, but this will be significantly less than building the entire test from scratch. Also, tests and regression tests built on an existing (i.e., previously executed) test model usually encounter significantly fewer execution problems and therefore actually execute faster or in fewer execution passes.

Estimates for test stages therefore view the development and execution of the test model almost as a project unto itself. The estimates should look at the units to be tested, the process to complete the test, including the approach, plan, prepare and execute steps discussed earlier, and the assumptions for time required to complete each step. Estimates of work effort then need to take into account resource constraints and dependencies to be translated into the actual work plan, thus giving the schedule.

Problem Management

Effective problem management is essential to facilitate test execution and to manage scope and progress. Problems should be identified as errors, defects or change requests, or rejected. Problems should then be resolved in accordance with defined procedures.

The first set of activities is problem identification, classification, and analysis. As each problem is identified through a review or test, it should be logged and classified as an error, defect or change request. It is essential to collect data on the numbers and types of problems for problem resolution and continuous process improvement.

Developers should monitor problem data throughout the test to identify opportunities for improvements. For example, there may be an inordinate amount of defects of a particular type which would lead to improvement in standards or training for the development teams.

Once the problem is documented and classified, it should be analyzed to determine the severity, priority, impact, and potential resolution. At this point the problem can then be approved, rejected, or deferred. The approval process should tightly control what changes are being made to the system. It is not necessarily optimal to fix all defects. Approved problems, and only approved problems, can then be addressed by the development teams responsible for fixes. Once the problem has been further analyzed, and the fix has been designed, implemented and regression tested, the problem is closed.

In addition to problem management procedures, it is important to identify escalation procedures: how will conflicts be resolved? Define who has the authority to approve design changes, change requests, migration of updates, and so forth. It is essential to have tight version control on the source code, data and test models, and this control becomes more restricted during the final stages of testing. Clearly identify what type of decisions should be escalated, and what the process is for doing so. For example, teams can document issues to management in weekly status reports, or conduct daily issues meetings with management.

Quality Management

Management is responsible for tracking and monitoring metrics (e.g., stage containment, and rework metrics) and ensuring that action is taken when the metrics data is at variance from plans.

Ideally, the original project plans established quality goals and the number of unresolved problems by type and severity that are allowed to be open at completion/conversion. These goals should then drive decisions made within the testing stage as to which defects are to be fixes rather than deferred, and when testing can be considered complete.

It is recommended that a complete analysis of problem data is executed following each project to identify major process changes. This is often referred to as "postmortem" analysis of the project, identifying both what went well and where there are opportunities for improvement. These sessions can be extremely successful if conducted in a timely and objective manner.

Organizational Challenges

The V-model testing approach will likely result in new roles and responsibilities within the organization. Specific roles now exist for test designers (i.e., planning and preparation), test execution, and test management. In addition, testing related activities such as definition of test conditions and communication of changes may change the roles and responsibilities of analysts, architects, fixers, technical support, and users. It is important to review the testing objectives and the approach outlined for the organization and identify the roles and responsibilities each person has.

An example of a typical pyramid for testing organization would include:

- An overall test director.
- A test manager for each major testing effort.
- Several (three to five) senior test architects for the test; one for each major piece of functionality being testing.
- Several (three to six) test developers per senior test architect for test planning.

For test execution, management should either add test executors to the test developer pool or have the application developers execute the test scripts as prepared, monitored by the senior test architects.

A general rule of thumb is that the test execution effort is roughly on par with the fix effort. For example, if there are nine test executors, there should be nine fixers for the duration of the test. Keep in mind that the test teams are the organization's test experts. Training on the V-model approach will be required, as will training on the tools and the testing process.

THE NEXT LEVEL

Measure for Success

Effective metrics are essential to managing and improving the testing process. Applied metrics during the testing process provides the capability to improve management, productivity, and quality. Managers should:

- *Manage with facts.* Metrics provide objective data upon which decisions can be made, actions taken, and goals achieved. When a team can know, for example, the average time it takes to fix a problem (Problem Fix Rate), they can track the number of problems found during inspection, and can calculate the fix time savings realized. This helps reinforce the importance of completing timely and thorough inspections.
- *Focus on the problem, not the symptom.* Metrics lead to greater understanding of the underlying problem. For example, one company repeatedly experienced very high defect levels during the later testing stages, in spite of numerous adjustments to their development process. It was not until they began to measure and analyze their processes that they realized that the vast majority of the defects encountered were being caused by the fix process — not the development process. They were trying to solve the wrong problem.
- *Facilitate predictability.* If appropriate metrics are used and collected accurately and consistently, one can predict the quality and productivity of the remaining work, next stage, next release, and so forth. Process metrics and product quality metrics allow a team to reduce the number of unknowns in the development and testing process, thereby reducing the risk associated with successful completion.
- *Facilitate continuous improvement.* Throughout the process, one can review and analyze the metrics, identify discrepancies from plans, determine the reasons for the discrepancies, and improve the process or the estimating guidelines. This should be a continuous process. An organization can learn from previous mistakes and benefit by eliminating the recurrence of those difficulties. Improvement can occur from stage to stage, release to release, and project to project.

As discussed in Section II, metrics are most effective when used to manage a process, and they are only worthwhile if specific actions will be taken based on measurements in question. The metrics discussed here were developed to support the following three goals:

1. Improve management of the test process.
2. Improve the quality of the test process.
3. Further refine and improve the quality of the process and the product.

Goal 1: Improve Management of the Test Process

To manage the entire test process more efficiently, organizations must start with a set of fundamental metrics: measurements of the process, which allow the team to understand and control that process.

These metrics are:

- Test planning rate: Hours per test condition.
- Test preparation rate: Hours per test cycle scripted.
- Test execution rate: Hours per test cycle executed.
- Incoming problem rate: Problems detected per hour of execution
- Problem fix rate: Problems fixed per elapsed hour.

These metrics provide a means for determining the earned testing progress and value, the amount of testing remaining, and when testing will be complete. In addition, they can justify the purchase of tools and the implementation of process improvements. Finally, these fundamental metrics also include actual productivity rates, which should be used to revise estimating guidelines. They will help management make decisions on scheduling issues, and help the estimation and scheduling for subsequent releases.

Goal 2: Improve the Quality of the Test Process

Another set of metrics allows greater understanding of a process and provides a basis for improvement of the process. The metrics associated with the second goal must provide information about the development and testing process at a level of detail to allow appropriate action to be taken. Specifically, these metrics are:

- Stage containment by stage: Errors or errors plus defects.
- Defect repair effectiveness: Percentage of defects fixed correctly the first time.

Industry studies indicate that defect repair processes are successful only 50 percent of the time, and many repair efforts simply caused additional errors. This means that every time a development team submits a defect for correction, there is as much chance of not fixing the defect or introducing another defect as there is of actually fixing the reported defect. This 50 percent failure rate is an often overlooked opportunity for process improvement.

When an organization discovers high defect rates in software, it often assumes that the problems were caused during the development process. Further investigation often reveals, however, that a significant portion of the defects are actually caused by the fix processes themselves. For example, upon analysis of the defects uncovered by the first pass of product test, one organization realized that although they had detected nearly 200 defects, over 150 of the problems were caused by the fix process. As problems were submitted for analysis and fix, they were often returned incomplete or the fixes caused other defects. Improvements to the fix process resulted in significant time and cost savings in the future development and testing stages.

Goal 3: Further Refine or Improve the Process and Product Quality

Finally, the last goal focuses on metrics that can be used to fine tune the process. They will help determine why problems are occurring by calling attention to error-prone or complex modules. These metrics are:

- Inspection effectiveness: Problems found per hour of inspection.
- Problems per module: Errors and defects and faults per module.

In addition, several industry standard metrics exist to measure the complexity and, thus, the testability and maintainability of designs and code. These are:

- Zage design metric: (Modules Called * Calls of Module) + (Data In * Data Out)
- McCabe Cyclomatic Complexity: Edges — Nodes + 2

By identifying portions of the solution that are highly complex, these metrics can be used to support a decision to allocate additional resources, or to redesign those areas. Either way, a risk area has been identified and addressed in the project plans.

Design for Testability

The V-model concepts can be extrapolated to improve not only the testing of the solution, but the design and the product itself, making the product more maintainable and thus more flexible. Several key drivers for testability include fault tolerance, controls, error handling, multiple operating modes, and self testing applications.

- *Fault tolerance.*   Developers design the systems such that errors can be recovered from, or at least logged without interrupting processing. For example, they should not allow the system to crash upon encountering corrupt data; instead, they should correct or log the data and move on. This not only makes it easier to test, but allows the system to perform better in production. In addition, people certainly would prefer not getting a call in the middle of the night because the production run abended, but instead getting an error report first thing in the morning.
- *Controls.*   Developers should put design counts and cross checks into the systems to identify problems and inconsistencies early.

- *Error handling.* Developers should implement functionality for the systems to identify errors, and upon identification of an error, log all relevant data and attempt to correct the error, such as by searching for a similar error and its associated corrective action. At a minimum, they should open a problem record and notify the appropriate parties, perhaps by E-mail or paging.
- *Test vs. production mode.* Developers should design the system so it contains a test and production mode. In test mode, control data may be logged, dates may be taken from a file rather than from the processor (to enable aging or year-end process testing), generated fields may be altered, and so forth. All this facilitates testing.
- *Self-testing applications.* Developers should embed validation of entry criteria and/or test conditions into the system at the application or object level. This allows the application or object to verify inputs before attempting to process, and to report inconsistencies in expected inputs vs. actual.

SUMMARY

Implementation of the V-model approach to testing not only produces significant improvements in the typical testing process and results, but also positions an organization to continuously improve its testing capability. Repeated, measured processes can easily be analyzed to identify opportunities for improvement, thus initiating a never-ending cycle of plan-do-measure-improve.

The testing process detailed in this chapter has been used by Information Systems organizations over the last several years to achieve significant benefits. The V-model framework is now being applied in a netcentric environment. Teams have realized as much as a 50 percent reduction in the effort required to test new applications, up to an 80 percent reduction in the effort required to regression test applications for changes and enhancements, and a 50 percent reduction in rework due to poor verification, validation, and testing in the first place. Organizations now use information gathered during the testing activities to analyze and improve the systems development processes which, in turn, can lead to further improvements in productivity and quality.

Chapter III-3
Communications Options for Netcentric Implementation

Chapter II-2 discussed an architectural model of communication services in a netcentric environment. This chapter focuses on the specific communications technologies to be considered during implementation.

To be positioned for netcentric solutions, an organization's communications infrastructure must provide support for:

- Client/server computing.
- Rich data types including multimedia.
- User mobility.
- An extended reach to the customer and to other business partners.

CLIENT/SERVER COMPUTING

Over the last several years, transaction and data management applications have continued to move off the mainframe to client/server architectures, becoming increasingly distributed and moving closer to the customer. The new architectures challenge the legacy network infrastructure in a number of ways, including the demand for more bandwidth and the need for multiple protocols to coexist.

Client/server computing requires faster networks (i.e., more bandwidth) for a number of reasons:

- There is much more dialog between clients and servers than among machines in traditional host-to-terminal architectures.
- The distributed processes and distributed data inherent within client/server computing can result in large messages and data sets passed over the network.

- The physical layout of the distributed network can slow traffic as it passes from bridge to router to gateway.
- Security checking between the client and server can slow transaction time and increase traffic.
- Failed paths in a distributed network can cause the network to be flooded with updates when the path comes back up.
- Backup and recovery can cause large bursts of data to hit the network.

Many of the new client/server systems are developed to be run over a network using the TCP/IP protocol (this is the protocol that forms the common transport basis for the Internet). Many of the legacy systems were developed under IBM's host-based SNA protocol. These protocols are fundamentally different and a fair amount of work goes into getting them to cohabitate on the same network.

RICH DATA TYPES

Significant changes are occurring in applications as they evolve to support the knowledge worker. The types of knowledge contained in these applications will broaden beyond data text and graphics to include audio, image, and video. Also, interpretation applications will allow for visualization of data and information.

These changes present some interesting challenges to the network. Moving the new rich data types across the enterprise requires a tremendous amount of bandwidth, beyond the capacity of today's local area networks (LANs) and wide area networks (WANs). Traditional text and voice may range from approximately .02 to .07 MB, requiring a transmission rate of about .08Mbps. (For static digital media, the peak communication rate is determined by the minimum acceptable delay times for transmission of a page.) By contrast, a color photograph that is transmitted in 0.25 seconds requires a transmission rate equivalent to 22Mbps. It is generally accepted that 0.25 seconds is an effective instantaneous response rate for browsing. Even with full JPEG compression, the color photograph would require 4Mbps.

From a bandwidth perspective, multimedia, or document management applications would quickly overload a typical Token Ring or Ethernet LAN as the number of users grows. The limitations of the typical WAN for an organization are even greater.

Bandwidth is not the only limitation when dealing with rich data types. Most of today's computer networks are optimized for small-packet, asynchronous data communications. Real-time media, such as full-motion video and audio, require isochronous (i.e., time-sensitive) network services with acceptable levels of network latency or transmission delay. Real-time media are highly sensitive to variations in latency, while small variations are of no consequence to data traffic. Attempting to transmit real-time media over a network that is optimized for data traffic will result in unacceptable video and/or audio quality.

USER MOBILITY

Client/server applications have the potential to greatly enhance the capabilities of the end user. Typically, though, the end users who have benefited under client/server computing are confined to the physical boundaries of the enterprise. In the netcentric environment, applications are moving outside the physical boundaries of the enterprise and into the hands of new classes of end users: the field sales or service representative, the road-warrior executive, and the customer.

The trend now is to add mobility as a standard application design feature, to make the organization available wherever and whenever a business user or customer wants it to be. Adding mobility presents a number of design challenges across all aspects of the systems architecture. From a communications perspective, the greatest challenges arise when the organization enters the domain of wireless data, a domain that enables real-time, untethered access to corporate applications.

The allure of wireless data networking can be great. The field service worker is enabled with real-time access to customer histories, in-house experts, and work-order management. The customer sales representative has real-time access to account information, credit histories, price lists, inventory status and order entry. The truck driver can send and receive real-time shipment and route status. And the executive can send and receive E-mails and access groupware applications during the course of a day that includes time in the train, taxi, airplane and client location.

Although the benefits of using wireless data can be high, there are significant network challenges to consider. Wireless networks are low capacity, low throughput, and intermittently available. There are a number of wireless data service offerings from which to choose. The coverage of each service offering can be an issue as well as the integration available between service offerings. The wireless mobile components are not standardized or prepackaged. Specialized messaging capabilities need to exist between mobile and stationary components.

EXTENDED REACH TO THE CUSTOMER AND BUSINESS PARTNERS

Under convergence, public access applications address the needs of the public and specifically consumers. These applications narrow the gap between the company, its products, and the consumer. Effective applications will give customers what they want, when they want it.

There are a number of ways to reach the end consumer. One approach is through the use of kiosk systems. Another method is to integrate with home devices. One version of this is to allow the consumer to access the system through the touch-tone telephone. Another access point is the home PC for those users who have a PC and a modem. Most users today who are connected via the home PC use the public switched telephone network at speeds of 14.4 to 33.6Kbps. This works well for small amounts of data but bogs down under the stress of images and graphics.

An access point that is getting a lot of attention these days is the television, although little has been delivered. The cable network today is, for the most part, a one-way network. The potential of a two-way interactive cable network is vast, although a number of technical and financial issues must still be overcome.

"Intelligent Network" is Andersen Consulting's name for business-to-business applications, with which the enterprise establishes and maintains its links with other organizations, such as suppliers, distributors, alliance partners, and the government. Intelligent Network applications lead toward the true virtual organization, where enterprise boundaries are no longer rigid.

For the Intelligent Network, technologies will need to support large volumes of data and to be scaleable and highly secure. Connections will need to be fluid and interface standards less rigid and inflexible than the EDI standards of today.

COMMUNICATIONS TECHNOLOGY ENABLERS

To address the communications needs just discussed, many advancements are occurring in the following communications areas, which will help enterprises address these challenges:

- LAN architectures.
- Public network offerings for WANs.
- Connectivity to the customer.
- Wireless support for the mobile user.

The remainder of this chapter is devoted to a discussion of these four areas, which form the basis for the communications fabric of the future.

LAN ARCHITECTURES

One of the key building blocks of most enterprise networks is the LAN. This section examines three areas of advancement in LAN technology: high-speed access methods, switching architectures, and ATM (Asynchronous Transfer Mode) technology.

High-Speed Access Methods

Traditional local area networks are shared media networks, which carry the traffic of multiple users over the same media. As a result, network access methods are required to regulate the usage of the shared media. Network access methods (i.e., Ethernet, Token-Ring, FDDI) are therefore responsible for determining the key network characteristics including bandwidth, latency, and throughput. The access methods with the largest installed base are Ethernet (10Mbps) and Token-Ring (4 or 16Mbps). Both of these standards are well documented and products are available from a wide variety of vendors.

Recognizing the need for increased bandwidth, vendors have pushed to develop high-speed access methods (i.e., greater than 100Mbps). The two most notable of these are Fiber Distributed Data Interface (FDDI) and Fast Ethernet. Irrespective of the particular technology, the goal of the vendors is simple: develop new cost-effective options to allow organizations the capability to upgrade their networks.

FDDI. FDDI is the most mature of the high-speed access methods, with a wide variety of products currently available and commonly implemented. Although FDDI has several beneficial characteristics, it is primarily touted for its significant bandwidth capacity: 100Mbps. In addition to the substantial increase in bandwidth, other noted capabilities of FDDI include its deterministic access and its inherent fault tolerance.

Unlike Ethernet, FDDI is a deterministic access method. Deterministic access methods regulate users' access to the network, enabling all users equal access to the network. Therefore, the performance degradation's experienced in Ethernet networks (i.e., collisions) are not replicated in FDDI networks. FDDI networks regulate the access of all users on the network ensuring that no two users are simultaneously trying to transmit. As a result, FDDI networks are able to achieve higher degrees of efficiency than traditional Ethernet networks.

Additionally, FDDI has the ability to recover automatically from link failures. Referred to as a self-healing ring, an FDDI network has the capability to wrap around the failed link and still maintain the integrity of the ring. Because of this feature, FDDI is an attractive networking topology for environments requiring high degrees of fault tolerance.

Fast Ethernet. In response to the need for more network bandwidth, a substantial number of Internetworking hardware vendors formed the Fast Ethernet Alliance. The purpose of this alliance was to develop a high-speed networking topology leveraging existing Ethernet technology. This goal was achieved by using portions of the Ethernet standards and combining them with the physical signaling standards used by FDDI. In July 1995, the

Institute of Electrical and Electronics Engineers (IEEE) approved the 100Mbps standard developed by the alliance members.

This recently approved standard, IEEE 802.3u, commonly referred to as 100Base-T, creates a new shared media networking technology: 100Mbps Ethernet. Essentially, 100Base-T is the same technology as 10Base-T operating at 10 times the speed. As a result, network managers find 100Base-T to be a relatively easy technology to understand. Although collectively referred to as 100Base-T or Fast Ethernet, this technology is also referenced by a number of other names including:

- 100Base-T: Media independent name for the 100Mbps Ethernet technology.
- 100Base-TX: Standard for 100Base-T over 2-pair, Category 5 UTP.
- 100Base-T4: Standard for 100Base-T over 4-pair, Category 3/4 UTP.
- 100Base-FX: Standard for 100Base-T over 1-pair, fiber optic cable.

Although this technology provides for a substantially increased bandwidth, many of the limitations of current Ethernet technologies, such as collisions, still remain. Additionally, 100Base-T still lacks any deterministic access method or priority queuing capabilities. As a result, 100Base-T is not suited to support large quantities of delay sensitive data such as voice or video. Due to its increased speed, 100Base-T has some distance limitations, cabling requirements, and repeater configurations which are more stringent than 10Base-T. However, despite the limitations, 100Base-T is designed to run over most existing cabling plants and vendors have announced products with prices significantly lower that other alternatives such as FDDI or ATM.

From a positioning perspective, 100Base-T is viewed as a work group technology for use with servers and high-bandwidth users. In many cases, 100Base-T and Ethernet switching will be viewed as competing solutions (see the next section for a discussion of Ethernet switching). However, many vendors are positioning 100Base-T as a complementary technology to Ethernet switching.

Switching Architectures

Migrating toward higher-speed access methods requires organizations to upgrade both the network hardware and the network interface cards located at the workstations. In an effort to allow enterprises to improve their LAN network performance without having to upgrade all of the network interface cards, vendors began to develop switching capabilities. Two forms of switching are dominant: port and frame switching.

Port Switching. Port level switches are devices that contain multiple network backplanes (i.e., network segments). Ports are then connected to the various backplanes on an individual basis. This dynamic allocation of ports between backplanes enables network managers to control the distribution of traffic between network segments, thus improving the overall performance of the network segments. In order to simplify the process of reconfiguring ports, most vendors have developed software solutions which enable network managers to manipulate port mapping from a central location.

Port switching capabilities offer the ability to balance network traffic loads among multiple user network segments. If a network manager determines that a particular network is too congested, the network manager can reallocate users to other networks through a GUI. This enables the network manager to improve the overall network performance without requiring the network manager to actively rewire end-user devices. In addition to enabling network managers to better manage network traffic loads, port level switching also enables network managers to accommodate user changes. If a user changes a business function, port-level switching enables network managers to move the user to the appropriate business network without requiring manual intervention.

However, port switching does not universally solve all network performance issues. First, port level switching does not provide location independence for LAN users (often referred to as a virtual LAN, its goal is to group users logically from a network perspective, regardless of physical location. Current LAN network technologies group users based on physical location). In a port switching solution, manual intervention is required to move users between segments. With true virtual LAN capabilities, users are automatically moved between virtual LANs as required. Additionally, users are still connected to shared media LANs. Although users can be switched between network segments, the total bandwidth available to all users connected to the same LAN is still constant. To balance network traffic effectively, network managers must use advanced network management tools to determine network traffic profiles and analyze the potential impact of user movements. In addition, moving users between segments can quickly raise issues with regard to network addressing, depending upon the overall network configuration. Therefore, although port level switching does provide some benefits, its benefits are limited.

Frame Switching. As highlighted in the previous discussion of port switching, vendors have tried to develop technologies that will enable organizations to leverage their installed base of technology. Port switching addresses some of these concerns but is not considered a robust enterprise solution. As a result, vendors have developed frame switching solutions.

Although port switching and frame switching may both be referred to as "switched" solutions, they are significantly different. With port switching, shared media access methods (i.e., Ethernet and Token-ring) are still used.

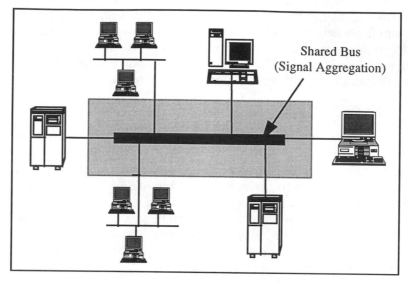

Exhibit 1. Shared media backplane.

In a shared media environment, the total aggregate bandwidth of the network is shared among all of the connected network nodes. However, with frame switching, the total aggregate bandwidth is determined by the number of switch ports.

Frame switching essentially changes the concept of shared media networks. With frame switching technology, users or LAN segments utilizing traditional shared media access methods are connected into a switch matrix. In traditional shared media networks, these users and LAN segments would be connected to a backplane which would aggregate the signals (Exhibit 1).

It was this aggregation, or sharing of the media, that limited the total bandwidth of the network and led to network congestion and network collisions. However, in a frame switch environment, the traffic is not combined. Rather, the switching matrix creates multiple simultaneous connections through the matrix, connecting only the appropriate switch ports together (Exhibit 2).

As a result of the switched nature of these networks, users are able to realize greater throughput and total aggregate bandwidth than would be possible using a traditional shared media LAN. For example, Ethernet LANs limit the total amount of traffic between network devices to no more that 10Mbps. However, when multiple users are connected to an Ethernet switch, the total traffic between network ports can easily be 20Mbps or

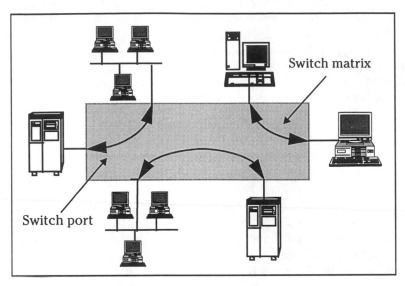

Exhibit 2. Frame switching technology.

more, depending on the traffic patterns on the network. Additionally, frame switching provides a fair amount of flexibility allowing network managers to connect either individual users or groups of users (i.e., LAN segments) to dedicated switch ports.

As of this writing, vendors have announced plans for or have begun shipping frame switches for Ethernet, Token-Ring, FDDI, and 100Base-T. From a positioning perspective, frame switching enables network managers to quickly address performance issues in congested networks. Frame switches essentially replace the existing network hubs and utilize existing network interface cards and cabling. As a result, the use of frame switching can represent an attractive alternative to upgrading to a new technology.

Asynchronous Transfer Mode Technology

Many of the LAN changes discussed are evolutionary. A revolutionary change that is receiving a tremendous amount of attention is Asynchronous Transfer Mode, or ATM. ATM is a technology with the promise of delivering video, voice, and data traffic over a single, high-speed integrated network. The rush of both telecommunications providers and data networking companies to support ATM makes it poised to revolutionize both industries and blur the distinction between local and wide area networking. ATM's unprecedented popularity stems from its many technological advantages, its open definition, and its ability to solve problems that the industry has been dealing with for years. By adopting existing standards for physical media transmission, ATM may finally make high-speed network links as common as LANs are today. By paying careful attention to the needs of all types of data (video, voice, and data), ATM designers have provided a single infrastructure capable of supporting multiple data types. ATM holds the promise of allowing enterprises to deploy video, voice and data applications using common technology.

ATM is still, however, a relatively infant technology that represents a significant departure from traditional networking. First, ATM is a connection-based technology. When devices wish to communicate over the network, virtual connections are extablished. These are paths between two nodes in an ATM network; depending on the quality of service of the path, bandwidth may or may not be reserved. Given the nature of these virtual connections, ATM allows multiple users to share the network resources simultaneously. In addition, depending on the quality of service requested for a virtual link, ATM can guarantee end-to-end timing and a relatively low variation in network access time.

Despite being a new technology, ATM and traditional networks are still able to interoperate. ATMs can host most older technologies, such as current network protocols, by emulating fixed capacity point-to-point links. In addition, ATM can reuse the physical links now in place such as twisted pair cabling and fiber-optics in both the local and wide area environments.

ATM provides many advantages for networking. ATM transports information by setting up multiple virtual connections across a shared physical media. This allows multiple devices to use the network simultaneously but at a rate that is a subset of the total capacity of the link. An ATM network does not distinguish between local area and wide area networking, because all network links are assumed to be relatively high capacity. Other characteristics unique to ATM are the ability to provide feedback to network devices about congestion and the ability to use physical connection rates of 155Mbps and higher. All of these advantages allow ATM networks to reduce congestion and intelligently manage network traffic at high speeds.

ATM has received unprecedented attention and praise despite the fact that its standards are in the infant state and still evolving. ATM has been touted as the solution of all networking problems, and numerous products are being rushed to market by the vendor community. Typically, these products can be classified into three distinct groupings: work-group solutions (i.e., small switches), premise solutions (i.e., large, local switches) and central office (CO) solutions (i.e., those used by carriers to provide public network services). From an enterprise networking perspective, the vendors developing premise and work group solutions are the key players to watch.

PUBLIC NETWORK OFFERINGS FOR WIDE AREA NETWORKS

In the past, many companies used dedicated or leased lines to provide data connectivity from their distributed locations back to corporate headquarters. These company-managed networks were typically constrained to a fixed bandwidth and rather difficult to grow and evolve. On the positive side, though, a company had control over management of the network and could more easily establish and live up to service levels.

More companies are now relying on public network offerings to connect multiple locations. These network offerings provide more flexible bandwidth management and move some of the network management burden from the purchaser of the service to the service provider. Recently, a number of new options have begun to emerge that are coming closer to meeting the challenges of convergence applications over the wide area. The service offerings discussed in this section are:

- Frame relay.
- Integrated services digital network (ISDN).
- Switched multimegabit data service (SMDS).
- ATM.

Frame Relay

Frame relay is a packet switching technology that has been adopted especially for the needs of data communications. Rather than providing a user with a dedicated circuit (i.e., circuit switching), frame relay provides many users access to the same circuit, switching each user's individual packets of information over the same connection (i.e., packet switching). As a result, frame relay services provide much more efficient bandwidth usage than with circuit switching.

Most of the time, users have little or no data to send. However, when users do send information, they typically have a large number of packets which they send over a short period of time, causing a burst in the network traffic. Because frame relay switches packets, not circuits, users may use anywhere from none of the available bandwidth to all of the available bandwidth. Thus, from a user's perspective, frame relay provides bandwidth on demand. As a result, frame relay services have become a very popular option for providing enterprise wide network connections. Frame relay services provide network managers with more flexibility regarding bandwidth allocation. In frame relay networks, users subscribe to a committed information rate (CIR), such as 256Kbps. This CIR represents the average loading of the particular link. If the amount of data that needs to be transmitted exceeds the CIR (i.e., 512Kbps) during a particular interval, the network makes a best-effort attempt to deliver all the information while guaranteeing the delivery of at least the CIR.

Essentially, frame relay networks represent an evolution from X.25 networks. X.25 networks incorporated a significant amount of overhead relative to fixed packet sizes, extensive error correction, re-transmission facilities, and fixed bandwidth links. Frame relay standards leverage the X.25 packet forwarding architectures while improving overall performance by eliminating some of the error correction and re-transmission capabilities inherent in the network equipment.

These components could be eliminated, because today's physical networks are much more reliable than those in place when X.25 was initially developed. With frame relay, error correction and retransmission is handled at the end nodes by higher-layer networking protocols, such as TCP/IP. Additionally, frame relay includes the ability to support varying packet sizes. This eliminates the inefficiencies associated with transmitting short bursty communications over the same network as larger file transfers.

From a market perspective, frame relay has demonstrated tremendous growth over the last several years, as both a wide area networking option allowing companies to link distributed facilities and as a business-to-business option linking multiple companies in a common enterprise. Frame relay presents companies with a cost-effective LAN-to-LAN connectivity option, providing bandwidth availability in the range of 56Kbps to 1.54Mbps. Bandwidth in this range helps to address some of the wide area bandwidth issues of convergence applications, although frame relay does not address the requirements of time sensitive applications. Frame relay has also proven to be an effective network option for supporting multiple protocols (i.e., the SNA and TCP/IP issue from earlier in the chapter).

ISDN

Integrated Services Digital Network (ISDN) is a public network service offering, based on digital circuit switched technology which provides the ability to integrate voice, video, and data. Due to the digital nature of the service, ISDN provides highly reliable transmissions. Additionally, ISDN is a scaleable service (up to 1.544Mbps in the U.S. and 2.048Mbps in Europe) which is normally offered in either a basic rate interface (BRI) or primary rate interface (PRI) configuration. Commonly referred to as 2B+D, the Basic Rate Interface (BRI) provides 144Kbps of throughput consisting of two bearer (B) data channels of 64Kbps and one D control channel of 16Kbps. The Primary Rate Interface (PRI) is a DS-1 speed interface (1.544Mbps in the U.S. or 2.048Mbps in Europe) and is often referred to as 23 B+D (30B+D in Europe).

ISDN services have been extremely popular in Europe and Australia. Recently, ISDN services in the Untied States have become more popular.

Much of ISDN's recent success in the U.S. has been due to its ability to provide large amounts of bandwidth on demand. Thus, ISDN has become an attractive service offering to provide dial-up, remote access. Additionally, ISDN capabilities have also been incorporated into networking equipment to provide dial-up, backup links to improve reliability. Finally, due to its switched nature, ISDN has also enjoyed significant success as a transport to support video conferencing.

Switched Multimegabit Data Service (SDMS)

SMDS is a connectionless, cell-relay (i.e., a technology based on a fixed-length cell that uses a switched architecture to provide connectivity between multiple end-nodes) service that was developed to support bandwidth-intensive applications such as LAN interconnection services. SMDS uses fixed sized cells (53 bytes) to deliver information and provides bandwidths scaleable from 1.544 to 45Mbps. The cell based nature of SMDS is similar to that of ATM; however, SMDS is optimized for connectionless data services, whereas ATM is optimized for connection oriented services.

Because SMDS is a connectionless technology, it requires minimal connection setup time at the expense of potentially increased latency. Specifically, depending on the network configuration and the current network traffic levels, it may take longer for the data to traverse a connectionless network rather than a connection-oriented network. As a result, SMDS networks cannot guarantee the timing of data arrivals, making it less suitable for delay-sensitive applications, such as those with voice, audio and video. Although SMDS is useful for high bandwidth applications, it is extremely inefficient for low bandwidths and has minimal burst capability. The underlying reason for this deficiency is the large overhead (374K bps for 1.544M bps) included in the SMDS protocol. Therefore, analysts agree that SMDS cannot carry SNA traffic efficiently.

SMDS is available only in limited geographic areas and is used typically only for niche applications. Although SMDS promises to provide high-speed LAN interconnections, many carriers are opting to provide such services using ATM technologies. SMDS's inability to support delay sensitive material such as voice and video also hinder its widespread acceptance. However, prior to the full-scale deployment of ATM services, SMDS services offer an attractive alternative when high-speed interconnection services are required.

ATM

As a technology, ATM can be integrated into an enterprise Internetwork in a number of ways. In the previous section on LAN architecture, much of the focus was on the integration of ATM into the user segments and campus backbones. This section focuses on the development of ATM public service offerings by communications providers.

As mentioned previously, ATM holds the promise of unifying communications infrastructures to support all data types, including voice, video, and data. ATM is a connection-oriented service based on fixed sized cells (53 bytes). The use of fixed sized cells and its connection-oriented nature allow ATM to provide predictable delays and provides quality of service features to support delay sensitive information. In addition, ATM is extremely scaleable, supporting data speeds from DS-1 (1.544Mbps) rates to in excess of OC-48 (2.4Gbps) rates.

The most prominent element of ATM service offerings is its quality of service capabilities. These features provide ATM service offerings the flexibility needed to support a wide range of applications. Specifically, ATM is capable of supporting constant bit rate (CBR), variable bit rate (VBR) and available bit rate (ABR) traffic. CBR traffic is primarily associated with delay-sensitive material, such as voice and video. In these cases, ATM services guarantee applications a predictable delay for a prespecified data rate. VBR traffic is commonly associated with bursty data traffic similar to that of a LAN. With VBR traffic, ATM guarantees a specific amount of throughput and then makes a best-effort attempt to deliver any data that exceeds the guaranteed rate. Finally, ATM also provides ABR services, which allow users to use as much bandwidth as is currently available at any given time. However, with ABR services, users are not guaranteed any data rates.

Although ATM encompasses many of the features provided by other service offerings, it is far more complex and expensive. Additionally, most organizations do not yet possess applications which require the sophisticated capabilities of ATM. Therefore, most organizations are still relying on frame relay and SMDS services to support their data traffic and leased lines to support their voice and video traffic. However, as ATM service offerings continue to become more ubiquitous and prices decline, ATM will become a very attractive service offering for many organizations.

CONNECTIVITY TO THE CUSTOMER

Within the convergence framework, public-access applications facilitate business-to-customer connectivity. Some of these applications may use kiosk-based delivery, when the customer comes to the kiosk, but clearly access into the customer's home is the final and most desirable frontier.

Some low bandwidth examples of commerce to the home are already in existence. One much-publicized example is home-based electronic commerce via the Internet. A typical setup would include a PC loaded with an Internet browser and a 14.4 or 28.8/33.6Kbps modem. The home shopper connects to an Internet service provider via a standard dial-up line and accesses the appropriate World Wide Web (WWW) site. There are definite constraints with this approach. Anyone who has accessed the Web on a regular basis knows the limitations of even a 33.6Kbps modem.

So clearly more bandwidth is needed to the home. Again, with the Web as a benchmark, interactions with the user are increasingly involving rich data types, which will make this problem worse under the current bandwidth constraints. The cable companies and the phone companies are racing to see who can deliver the most cost effective solution that will support applications for which customers are willing to pay. The results, however, will not become apparent for a number of years.

The alternatives positioned by the phone companies are as follows. The phone companies began upgrading their network backbones to fiber in 1977. The trend was started to allow interexchange carriers to place huge volumes of calls on backbone trunks. Current commercial implementations of fiber trunks can carry 30,000 concurrent telephone conversations on a single strand of fiber.

The expanded capacity that fiber optic cable provides over copper cable is undeniable. A problem for many of these communications companies is the large amount of deployed copper cable, which in many cases needs to be amortized before it can be replaced with fiber. One source estimates that there is more than 65 million tons of deployed copper cable in the U.S. alone. Much of this copper is in the local loop to the home (or what is sometimes referred to as the "last mile") in the form of copper-based twisted pair wiring.

The phone companies are attempting to provide broadband capabilities by making hardware and software enhancements to certain parts of their network but continuing to use the copper to the home. This allows them to ease into fiber technology and spend less money in the near term, money that would not be offset by higher revenues. Under this approach, two alternatives being positioned are ISDN and Asymmetrical Digital Subscriber Line (ADSL).

ISDN. ISDN was previously discussed in the section on public network offerings. The primary focus in that section was on enterprise and enterprise-to-enterprise communications. However, ISDN has made some inroads in the consumer marketplace. The service is typically available at a Basic Rate Interface, which supplies approximately 128Kbps to users.

ISDN can be used to integrate voice, video, and data, which makes it ideal for delivery of netcentric applications to users. ISDN take-up in the marketplace has been slowed by lack of widespread availability, incompatible standards, high installation and monthly costs, and difficulty in installation. Most phone companies have not addressed the primary needs of the consumer marketplace, which include a reasonably priced service that is simple to install. In the meantime, other options are becoming available that just may hit the mark.

ADSL. Asymmetrical Digital Subscriber Line (ADSL) is a technology that allows broadband services to be carried over existing copper twisted-pair infrastructure along with traditional telephone service. ADSL first was developed in the late 1980s as a mechanism for sending video signals at relatively low bandwidths. ADSL may be implemented as an enhancement to current telephone company service offerings such as basic rate ISDN and POTS (plain old telephone service). Some cable companies may also have an interest in ADSL technology as a way of providing telephone services on twisted pair copper loop they overlay on top of the coaxial cable in their networks. ADSL allows a greater degree of interactivity than current cable services and provides more functionality than traditional phone service.

ADSL may be viewed as an interim solution to an all-fiber network or as a component of a partial-fiber network. Projections for the completion of fully-fiber networks which promise switched digital video services range from 10 to 20 years into the future. The major factor affecting the take-up of ADSL is the cost of implementation, including the cost of ADSL modems that have to be placed on both ends of the twisted pair.

Cable Modems

The cable company alternative is the cable modem. Many of the cable companies are in the process of upgrading their network to a hybrid solution involving fiber in the backbone and coax cable to the home (i.e., hybrid fiber/coax, or HFC). Many implementers of HFC networks will look into using cable modems to enable subscribers to tap into high-speed data transmissions.

Cable modems can be used to connect personal computers (PCs) to HFC networks, using an Ethernet card to connect the PC to the cable modem. This will allow the PCs access to interactive games, interactive shopping, the Internet, and bulletin board.

Cable modem technology will be used by cable companies and others as a way to offer services to compete with such technologies as ISDN and ASDL. Cable modem standards are still evolving as the technology matures. Therefore, early cable modem systems will be proprietary, and implementors will buy the modems from vendors and lease them to subscribers.

Cable modems offer speeds that are orders of magnitude higher than traditional telephone modems used for dial-up data access: 10 to 40Mbps to the home and 1Mbps from the home. The modems make use of the existing coaxial cable infrastructure to provide high-speed data access with a moderate level of interactivity. Implementors have been drawn to cable modem technology because it can be easy to implement and cost-effective, as compared with ADSL. Cable modems have also become popular because of the increasing demand for faster information access. From the subscriber's perspective, cable modems are an attractive alternative to modems over twisted pairs, ISDN, and ADSL because of low costs (no large up-front costs or usage costs), easy installation, and high speeds.

On the negative side, cable modem technology is subject to limitations on the amount of bandwidth to the home possible over coaxial cable. There are several interference issues that must be resolved to expand the bandwidth available for upstream data access. This is due in part to the fact that cable modems share bandwidth in both directions with other services such as ham radios and television broadcasts.

Currently, most implementations of cable modems are proprietary solutions that may pose some interoperability problems. There have been informal agreements between various vendors to comply with a set of specifications to ensure equipment interoperability. Efforts by groups such as the ATM Forum and IEEE will result in formal standards within the next few years.

WIRELESS SUPPORT FOR THE MOBILE USER

Mobile applications, such as the officeless desktop, one- and two-way messaging, long-distance file uploads, and the ubiquitous E-mail, are allowing workers — and eventually customers — connectivity to anyone, anywhere, anytime. In recent years, rapid advances in technology have given wireless communication new possibilities and a growing presence in the communications market. Wireless technologies are still in a state of flux, and clear winners have yet to emerge. This section addresses the following wireless technologies that will play a large role in empowering the mobile user:

- Circuit-switched cellular.
- Cellular digital packet data.
- Personal communications services.

Circuit-Switched Cellular (CSC)

Circuit-switched cellular provides wireless connectivity to the public switched telephone network over a network of radio transceivers. The technology is circuit-switched in that a user establishes a virtual connection with the destination at the beginning of the call and maintains the connection for the duration of the call. The technology is cellular because the transceivers provide coverage in adjacent circular regions, allowing users to roam between coverage areas and still maintain their connections.

A circuit-switched cellular data session is similar to a traditional landline modem session. Several factors inherent to circuit-switched cellular, however, require the use of a special cellular modem. Factors include increased signal distortion due to inherent noise of a wireless connection, and transmission interruptions due to channel switching and cell switching.

Current efforts in the cellular industry are, in part, focused on upgrading the existing analog cellular network to digital technologies. The major cellular carriers, however, disagree on which digital access technology to implement. Differences in implementations could lead to equipment incompatibilities and limited roaming capabilities for users between different coverage areas. In addition, backward compatibility issues will require the use of dual-mode cellular phones.

The types of digital cellular methods under consideration are:

- *Time Division Multiple Access (TDMA).* TDMA technology can route multiple calls simultaneously over a single channel. TDMA allocates time slots on a frequency, then assigns a user to each time slot. Through this technique, TDMA offers a capacity increase of three times the current analog cellular systems. Many successful field tests have been completed and dual mode (i.e., analog/digital) TDMA cellular phones have been released.
- *Code Division Multiple Access (CDMA).* CDMA is a technique that uses spread spectrum technology for digital transmissions. With CDMA, information is broadcast in encoded packets over a wide range of frequencies. Cellular phones using CDMA listen to the encoded transmissions and are able to interpret the codes and pick the properly addressed packets out of the air. By allowing the sharing of frequency by multiple encoded conversations, CDMA promises increased capacity of at least 10 times that of the current analog cellular systems.
- *Global System for Mobile Communications (GSM).* GSM is the pan-European digital cellular standard based on the TDMA access method. The network offers many advanced digital features through its use of Signaling System Number 7 (SS7) and operates within the 900M Hz frequency band.

What does the future hold for Circuit-Switched Cellular? As cellular technology becomes more widespread and costs decrease, the large rise in number of users that occurred during the late 1980s and early 1990s will continue. By 1998, the expected voice and data use of cellular networks will reach 90 million users, 40 million of whom will be from North America. As digital cellular is deployed and data speeds and transmission reliability increase, the feasibility of circuit-switched cellular data as a mobile solution will increase.

Cellular Digital Packet Data (CDPD)

Cellular digital packet data (CDPD) is a method of moving data over the existing cellular communications network. The driving principle behind CDPD is that data traffic can be transmitted over the cellular network either through the empty spaces between voice calls or through a dedicated data channel. Standard cellular sites must be upgraded to accommodate CDPD and its high data transmission rate of 19,200 bps.

CDPD is based on the Internet Protocol (IP) and has potential interoperability with the IP Internetworking standard. In addition, its IP origins make CDPD "connectionless." Rather than using a dedicated channel for a transmission, each packet is a connectionless transmission that moves toward its destination independent of the movement of other packets. The movement is controlled by intermediate nodes along the path.

A mobile user who wishes to send data using CDPD must subscribe to a cellular carrier that offers CDPD and has upgraded its cell sites for CDPD in the area. The CDPD upgrade hardware allows each site to:

- Transmit CDPD packetized data over standard voice channels or dedicated data channels.
- Monitor which voice channels are available for CDPD data.
- Direct data to available voice channels.
- Switch the channel if a voice call interrupts the CDPD transmission.
- Bill CDPD services per packet sent rather than the customary cellular billing per minute.

Another component that must be used to send data via CDPD is a CDPD modem. Some CDPD modems are capable of transmitting in three modes:

- *Packet-switched.* This transmission makes data into packets, addresses it, and transmits it using CDPD to and from the cell site. When in this mode, the modem does not address data with a phone number. Rather, it designates the IP address of the data destination.
- *Circuit-switched cellular.* This transmission operates in the same manner as a CSC modem.
- *Traditional wired configuration.* This method connects the data source to a land-based phone line for data transmission.

One drawback to CDPD is that in areas of heavy voice traffic or high noise, a cell cite must reserve a voice channel for dedicated data. In this case, all CDPD transmissions are directed to this dedicated channel, and voice channels are left untouched by data traffic. Without this data-dedicated channel, a cell site gives priority to voice transmissions over data packets. Consequently, CDPD cannot operate if all channels in a cell's capacity are being used for voice communication.

Another drawback to CDPD is its lack of store-and-forward functionality. In a network with store-and-forward service, messages addressed to an unconnected mobile unit are stored until the unit reconnects to the network, at which point the messages are received. In a CDPD network, messages sent while the mobile unit is disconnected cannot be received.

As a wireless data service, CDPD is positioned in direct competition with the dedicated wireless data providers and with digital cellular data technologies such as GSM. PCS and digital cellular are also emerging as competitors. CDPD's ability to succeed in light of this competition lies in the willingness of multiple vendors and carriers to endorse CDPD and commit to implementing it.

Personal Communication Services (PCS)

Personal communication services (PCS) are a combination of services and technologies that aim to provide anytime, anywhere connectivity to information services. PCS networks are expected to rely heavily on microcell technology, a cellular concept that uses smaller coverage areas to improve in-building coverage and to lower power consumption of mobile units. Although microcells initially support voice communication in limited areas, they will eventually support multiple information services on a widespread basis and will interoperate with a variety of other networks.

Central to PCS is the concept that communications address numbers (e.g., phone numbers and fax numbers) should be assigned directly to people rather than locations. This provides users with constant connectivity to required services regardless of their location. Upcoming PCS networks will complement today's services by offering better urban and indoor coverage than existing cellular networks and supporting higher call capacities and seamless roaming.

The smaller cell sizes of PCNs offer two main advantages over existing cellular networks. The smaller cell size provides better in-building coverage because of closer proximity of mobile units to network access points, and smaller transmission range means mobile units require less power. This translates into smaller, lighter mobile units and longer battery life.

Smaller cell sizes require a larger number of base stations to be deployed to provide the same level of coverage as conventional cellular base stations. Because of limited location availability, local zoning restrictions, and public opposition to tower construction, PCS rollout schedules could be consequently delayed.

Although many of today's cellular networks use analog technology, PCS networks are envisioned to have totally digital infrastructures using one or more of the following digital communication techniques:

- Spread spectrum.
- Code division multiple access (CDMA).
- Time division multiple access (TDMA).

These techniques help to reduce power requirements and increase call volume capacity as well as allow the already-crowded radio spectrum to be shared by increasing numbers of wireless users.

PCS will most likely initially grab a small percentage of the wireless voice marketplace in the U.S. Over the next five years, though, some estimates have this number growing to 25 percent. For PCS wireless data to take off, a host of issues involving interoperability, roaming, and common air interfaces must be resolved.

The early years of PCS will see fragmentation and confusion in the wireless marketplace as carriers jockey for position. Key differentiators during this period will be quality, equipment, ease of use, and meeting consumers needs. Ultimately, all carriers will be providing high quality, seamless wireless service through low cost, small handsets. Distinctions between cellular and PCS will fade. Consumers will sign up for a wireless service, not needing to distinguish between PCS, cellular, and others.

CONCLUSION

Netcentric applications require a diverse assortment of powerful communications enablers. An organization's communications infrastructure, in addition to supporting client/server computing, must also support extended connectivity to customers and business partners, must deal with richer data types including multimedia, and must support the needs of a highly mobile user community. This chapter looked at four categories of communications enablers:

- New developments in LAN architectures help organizations meet these needs. High-speed access methods such as FDDI and Fast Ethernet are providing increased bandwidth for users. New switching architectures, particularly port switching and frame switching, now permit organizations to improve their LAN network performance without the need to upgrade all their network interface cards. ATM technology developments represent a potentially revolutionary change to traditional LAN networking.
- In the area of public network offerings for WANs, new options are appearing: frame relay, ISDN, SMDS, and ATM. They provide more flexible bandwidth management and move network management over to the service provider, rather than the service purchaser.
- Connectivity to the customer is being accomplished in a number of ways. Telephone companies are using ISDN and ADSL to enhance parts of their network, while maintaining traditional copper connections to

the home. Cable companies are offering cable modems to connect personal computers to HFC networks.

- Mobile connectivity is supported through a number of wireless technologies: circuit switched cellular, cellular digital packet data, and personal communication services.

Chapter III-4
Parallel Processing: Implementation Considerations

The earlier discussion of parallel processing in Section 2 provided an overview of the need for exploiting parallel processing and discussed the various hardware configurations and the DBMS architectures that are currently enabling most commercial parallel processing usage. This chapter discusses key implementation considerations in deploying MPP, which is important because of its newness in the parallel processing arena. The chapter identifies only the considerations and issues that are new or have become more important with this technology. The prior cumulative best design practices and other system implementation considerations continue to apply and are not included here.

Exhibit 1 is a high-level framework, used to organize the discussion.

APPLICATION SUITABILITY

Assuming that a new application has been identified and justified, one of the first considerations is to assess if there is a match with the MPP technology. Most vendors of MPP hardware and open data bases have positioned this technology to information delivery facility (i.e., data warehousing) applications only. DBMSs and MPP enable intra-SQL parallelism, which benefits complex and long-running queries associated with OLAP. A simple and quick OLTP SQL query is not likely to benefit from intra-SQL parallelism.

Because the vendors' focus has been on IDF applications, they have not concentrated on OLTP applications, which are generally destined for SMPs. However, it is possible that things may change over the next few years, as new technology components appear.

For example, one indication of this emerging change is the use of IBM RS/6000 SP MPP nodes as SAP R/3 application servers. As noted earlier, the motivation for this use is to minimize system administration cost and not

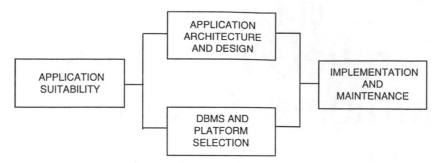

Exhibit 1. Implementation considerations in deploying massively parallel processing.

to exploit parallelism. Similarly, print and file server consolidation offers another usage scenario. Another emerging use for RS/6000 SP nodes is to host Oracle parallel server instances to provide added capacity to handle the data base requests issued by the SAP R/3 application servers. Again, the motivation is to get more capacity from additional nodes, as opposed to exploitation of intra-SQL parallelism.

However, with these exceptions, MPP use is currently limited to OLAP IDF processing.

DBMS AND PLATFORM SELECTION

The choice of a DBMS and hardware platform for a new application should be made based on many considerations, not just on parallelism. In fact, parallelism is merely one aspect of technology, whereas technology itself is just one of many considerations. This section examines the bigger picture of selection considerations and then focuses on parallel processing technology, as if the decision is to be based solely on such features.

DBMS Selection

With all the discussion about parallelism, it might be tempting to select a DBMS based on its software architecture and technical functions and features. However, DBMS is only a piece and must fit within the whole enterprise information architecture. In addition, vendors constantly leap-frog each other to offer exclusive features, which then become available sooner or later on other DBMSs, as well.

The selection process should be based on an organization's guiding principles for information technology, guiding principles which reflect the corporate values and culture. They include such factors as:

- The role technology plays in the corporate competitive positioning.
- The desire and ability to deploy leading-edge, but unproved, technology.
- The purchase of technology from a market leader vs. one from a supplier who might not be a leader but can provide innovation.

Thoughtful analysis in decision making is beneficial; however, it should not lead to the analysis/paralysis syndrome, which may negate a competitive marketing opportunity. The advantage of basing the decision process on the technology guiding principles is that appropriate, but not unnecessary, time and energy is spent in analysis based on the planned use of the technology.

Keeping this background in mind, the analysis for selection should be driven by the added value provided by the DBMS vendor. Factors contributing to the value proposition are:

- Vendor technical and marketing support.
- The working relationship.
- The availability of application packages using the DBMS.
- The availability of skills and education.

In other words, the current and potential benefits of a long-term relationship can overcome several short-term technical considerations.

The technical criteria for DBMS selection change every three to four years. In the mid-1980s, considerations such as compliance to the relational model, referential integrity, support of views, and on-line utilities were paramount. In the early 1990s, connectivity to other products, end-user query tools, triggers, stored procedures, and row-level locking took the center stage. In the mid to late 1990s, the emphasis has shifted to replication, user-defined data types and functions, and exploitation of parallel processing. One can assume that by the time the twenty-first century arrives, new criteria will have emerged.

Exhibit 2 depicts a framework that graphically summarizes the above discussion.

Looking strictly from the perspective of MPP, the technical evaluation considerations should include the following:

- *How will the DBMS interact with legacy and other transaction-oriented systems with respect to data and metadata?* It is very likely that the use of MPP in an installation will be first introduced for OLAP in an IDF (i.e., data warehouse) environment, which involves large quantities of data that are likely to be sourced from these systems.
- *What tools are available to assist in designing and implementing data bases and data partitioning?* Partitioning tools are of great value in implementing partitioned-data DBMSs. Less obvious is the significance

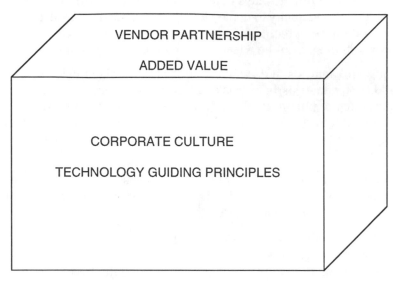

Exhibit 2.   A framework for DBMS selection.

of partitioning for shared-data architectures. Data partitioning offers ease in management from a utilities perspective and is required for either architecture when large data bases are involved.

- *What SQL functions are parallelized?*   Does the DBMS support all appropriate SQL statements or only a subset? Is the optimizer sophisticated enough to choose an appropriate level of parallelism on its own, or does it require user assistance? An SQL programmer should not have to bear the burden of coaxing the optimizer to use parallelism.
- *Does the DBMS support the installed or planned hardware platform?*   The considerations for choosing a hardware configuration are discussed in more detail later in the chapter.

Finally, one needs to consider the parallelization of data base administration utilities, perhaps the most important consideration. Will the DBMS perform the following in parallel?

- New table loading, appending data to existing tables, and purging tables of old rows?
- Redistribution of data if the system load is unbalanced? Can it be accomplished granularly, or must all the redistribution be done *en masse*?
- Can the backup and recovery utilities be executed in parallel against partitions of data? This is important regardless of the software architecture used.

- Are performance and monitoring tools available in the parallel environment? Can the tools help in isolating poor performing queries in a multiuser environment? What tools are available to project capacity requirements?

All these facilities not only must perform with small amounts of data and a limited number of users, but they must also scale up when data size increases. In addition, they must speed up if more resources are added and the work load is maintained constant. These tools should be able to deliver their functionality without adversely affecting user data availability.

This is clearly a tall order for any DBMS to satisfy, but progress is being made. Commercial MPP is possible today, as seen in implementations by such companies as MCI and Sears.

As DBMS evaluation and selection is being made, the next consideration is which hardware configuration to deploy.

Hardware Configuration Selection

As discussed earlier, the choice of hardware configuration is also quite complex. Of the three options discussed — shared everything, shared nothing, and shared disk — there are no clear-cut winners or losers. They all have applicability, depending on the type of work load.

Information Delivery Facility. All these configurations have a place in the computation of the OLAP workload. Attempts to define their positioning has led to identification of data base size and CPU resource consumption by the SQL statement as two significant parameters. Exhibit 3 shows how these can be used to divide the solution domain into four quadrants, using the parameters of required CPU resource and data size.

Required CPU Resources. Assuming that the disk and other costs are the same, the required CPU resources parameter (assigned to the Y-axis from low to high) represents the major differentiating execution time cost variable. One might use SQL complexity as a proxy for this parameter, and that is valid if care is exercised. At times, however, complex and long SQL statements with lots of predicates are inexpensive to run, because they narrow the data selection criteria. On the other hand, very simple-looking SQL statements can be extremely expensive, because they require scanning and joining large tables without any filtering. On the Y-axis, any parameter that represents the differentiating run-time CPU cost is acceptable.

Data Size. Data size, on the X-axis from megabytes to terabytes, represents the total size of the data base. However, this is really a metaphor for the ability of the hardware platform (along with a suitable DBMS with its

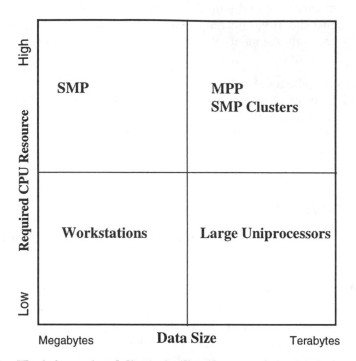

Exhibit 3. The information delivery facility (data warehouse) solution domain.

utilities for loading, backup, recovery, reorganization, and management of data) to support user data bases.

Computational solutions that reside in the lower left quadrant can be addressed by increasingly powerful desktop or desk-side workstations available today.

When the data size grows, the systems management sophistication and I/O bandwidth requirements lead to the solution domain of large uniprocessors in the lower right quadrant. Water-cooled technology-based (known as BIPOLAR technology-based) SMP mainframes are also possible options here. Sophisticated systems management disciplines, learned over decades to manage hundreds of gigabytes of data, position them very well here. This is evidenced by installations that use DB2 for MVS successfully for OLAP in this domain.

The upper-left quadrant is the domain of comparatively small data bases, but with those OLAP workloads that put large demand on the CPU resources. SMPs, including the new air-cooled (CMOS technology-based) mainframes, are solutions in this domain because the CPU resource is available less expensively on these platforms than on alternative configurations.

When the data base is large and the required CPU resources are high, MPP offers the solutions in the upper right quadrant. Such configurations, along with the partitioned data and shared data software, have already proven their capabilities to handle problems in this domain. SMP clusters also have the potential to be players in this arena. However, there are no widely known successful SMP clusters installations that can be used for illustration.

The size of data base that divides the X-axis is an interesting consideration. A wide variation in valuation is possible. Also, as time passes and the industry gains more experience, the value seems to move to the right. A few years ago, 25 to 50GB would have been considered the top end for SMP configurations. Today, 100 to 150GB seems to be the consensus opinion, and the value is likely to go higher in the next few years.

OLTP and Batch Environments. For this workload, the use of SMP configurations is well established. Also, SMP clusters have been successfully employed. Introduction of MVS Parallel Sysplex by IBM is an example of the increasing popularity of this configuration for OLTP and batch work load. What is new here is that MPP configurations are also starting to be deployed as application and data base servers for OLTP and batch. SAP R/3 implementation using Oracle 7 is an example. Interestingly, there is no intra-SQL parallelism exploitation here. After all, OLTP work load, by design, issues SQL statements that perform direct access and update of few rows, which do not gain significant benefit from the intra-SQL parallelism.

The motivation for deployment in such cases is the ease in systems management. The packaging of MPP simplifies the problems associated with the maintenance and distribution of software to the equivalent number of distinct nodes that would be required for the same workload. A few operational considerations also favor MPP. This chapter does not discuss these considerations, because the focus has been parallelism. Whether this deployment is a flash in the pan, or whether it becomes more common, depends on several factors including pricing schemes, marketing considerations, and enhancements made in the systems management arena by the alternative solutions of physically distributed nodes.

APPLICATION ARCHITECTURE AND DESIGN

Currently, the primary use of MPP is for the Information Delivery Facility, and the architecture and design consideration for those kinds of applications should be followed when implementing MPP. From the application-architecture point of view, care should be taken to ensure that the application does not prevent the exploitation of the parallelism features. From an

SQL coding perspective, the use of parallelism is transparent to the application programmer.

Data base design requires careful consideration. In addition to the traditional design issue (e.g., data normalization and denormalization, indexes, and design issues), partitioning and load balancing considerations need special attention. To some extent, these considerations depend on the architecture and features of the selected DBMS and the hardware platform. For this reason, a good understanding of the underlying DBMS architecture and the vendor's implementation of the architecture is essential.

The DBMS architecture section mentioned the use of data parallelism to exploit parallelism. Data partitioning enables data parallelism. How data is partitioned depends on its planned use and the available partitioning features of the selected DBMS. Some popular techniques are:

- *Key Range.* Data is partitioned based on key value ranges. With this scheme, queries that scan a limited range of data, such as those with BETWEEN, LESS THAN, or GREATER THAN predicates, can be isolated to certain partitions.
- *Expression Based.* This is similar to, but more sophisticated than, the key range partitioning scheme. SQL-like logic is used to partition data and to direct some user queries to specific partitions. It is more flexible than the key range partitioning scheme and provides fine-grained control but also incurs a slightly higher cost.
- *Hash Based.* Data is partitioned based on a hashing scheme and permits more uniform distribution of data. It is the most widely used data distribution scheme and permits the SQL query work load to be widely distributed among the nodes. If the values in the distribution key are skewed, hashing does not result in uniform data distribution. It can be the best performing partitioning scheme for row-level retrieval, because the request can be directed to a single partition.
- *Round Robin.* Data is distributed equally among all nodes without any regard to primary or other column values. This results in uniform distribution of data and processing; however, the retrieval can be expensive for key value access, because all the partitions are accessed.
- *Schema Partitioning.* This implies no partitioning at all and generally is used for small tables. The whole table belongs to a single DBMS instance and is located on one node. When needed by other DBMSs at other nodes, the entire table is transmitted.

Not all DBMSs support all of these techniques.

Such products as DB2 Parallel Edition, Informix XPS, and Sybase MPP require that data be partitioned for exploiting parallelism. There is one major exception: Oracle7 does not require data partitioning. During execution, data blocks are directed to the different Oracle7 instances to implement

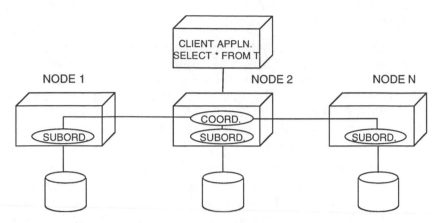

Exhibit 4.   A partitioned data architecture executing on a shared nothing configuration.

the notion of data parallelism. On the one hand, this results in increased MPP interconnect traffic. On the other hand, this helps Oracle7 in balancing load among different nodes of an MPP.

LOAD BALANCING

Load balancing can be viewed from two points of view: physical and logical. The physical involves balancing loads among physical resources, primarily multiple processor nodes. The logical involves with load balancing different tasks accessing a logical resource such as a table.

Physical Load Balancing

A partitioned-data software architecture executing on a shared nothing configuration owns its fragment of the data and executes operations associated with the SQL plan assigned to it by the coordinator task, as shown in Exhibit 4.

A DBMS instance executing on a given node controls its own I/O, performs locking, applies the local predicates, extracts the rows of interest, and transfers them to the next stage of processing, which may reside on the same or some other node. A node may become overloaded if there is too much demand for data managed by the DBMS executing on the particular node. Redistribution of data is the remedy to reducing the load.

Data may be redistributed by selecting another distribution key or by using a different partitioning scheme. This assumes that the use pattern is fairly consistent and does not change frequently. Much more importantly, it requires *a priori* knowledge of usage of data, which can be very difficult to anticipate in an OLAP environment.

A data distribution approach that can balance the node load is known as a "round robin." As discussed, this scheme also avoids the problems associated with skewed data. There are, however, many negatives associated with the round-robin scheme. Any query that otherwise might benefit from data clustering, such as BETWEEN or GREATER THAN, are forced to execute on multiple nodes. A query that might return only two to three rows requires perhaps 100 tasks in a 100 node example.

The shared-data software implementation does not suffer from this node overload problem. Here data is not partitioned but shared among all the nodes. At run time, all rows are visible to all nodes. This point is frequently emphasized by implementers of data bases based on this architecture, such as Oracle. (From a technology perspective, an installation data base and system administrator have to consider these issues in making a DBMS selection.)

Assuming that node-level balancing has been obtained in a partitioned data implementation, a second-level partitioning scheme within a node can lead to minimization of I/O. For example, Informix XPS offers a hybrid partitioning scheme, in which hash partitioning leads to distribution of data to all the nodes, followed by a second level of range partitioning within a node to limit I/O to a few devices.

Logical Load Balancing

This is concerned with attaining a balanced load for a logical resource, like a table. Contrast this with physical load balancing, in which the emphasis is on load balancing of physical resources, such as nodes and devices. Logical load balancing requires execution time algorithms that can spawn tasks based on the work characteristics. An example is shown in Exhibit 5.

Assume a shared nothing configuration, partitioned data DBMS, and a sales table that is partitioned 12 ways, one partition for each month, without realizing that the last three months partitions have more data as compared to others. A query for computing average sales per month results in unbalanced load for the last three months. This can be remedied by using a number of redistribution techniques, discussed earlier. As this discussion suggests, the new partitioning scheme of data to achieve balanced load requires *a priori* knowledge of data usage, which can be a challenge.

Next, let us assume that we want to compute average sales for items sold in the month of May. This again provides a nonuniform load situation, with one partition and the corresponding node being very busy. To

JAN. FEB. MAR. APR. MAY JUN. JUL. AUG. SEP. OCT. NOV. DEC.

☐ ☐ ☐ ☐ ☐ ☐ ☐ ☐ ☐ ☐ ☐ ☐

Assume: More sales data - Oct. to Dec.

Data Assignment	Query	Result
Partition by month	Avg. sales by month	Unbalanced load
More partitions Oct to Dec (a priori knowledge)	" "	Balanced load
" "	Avg. for May	Unbalanced load (SN) Requires multiple tasks
" "	Avg. of Tee-shirt Sales	Unbalanced load. Requires varying number of tasks

Exhibit 5.   Logical load balancing.

---

achieve parallelism, the DBMS must have the sophistication, during execution, to logically partition the data for the month of May into four parts, one for each week. The DBMS must also spawn four tasks or threads to process the parts using shared data and buffer software architecture within the node.

Assuming that this can be achieved, the next query computes average of T-shirt sales. This presents an additional level of challenge in that the number of tasks needed for the summer month partitions, when T-shirts are sold, will need different numbers of tasks.

Current commercial DBMS offerings are attempting to address the challenges encountered in exploiting MPP. The major vendors have selected either the partitioned-data or shared-data as the underlying architecture of their choice. But their implementations are hybrid in nature and use features that make classification difficult. With each new release, one vendor leap frogs over its competitors in several functions. Under these conditions, how one may proceed to choose a DBMS and appropriate hardware configuration is quite complex.

CONCLUSION: IMPLEMENTATION AND MAINTENANCE

Best practices developed over the years for system implementation and maintenance continue to apply. Some of the considerations that one must pay particular attention to include procedures for redistribution of data to account for skew, and system management. The availability of tools to facilitate these operations should be a major consideration in the DBMS and platform selection. Training and support should be made available to permit their use.

Chapter III-5
Building an Information Delivery Facility

Chapter II-5 introduced the Information Delivery Facility (IDF) as a richly functional solution that embraces end-user applications, metadata, a data refinery, and a collection of refining processes (Exhibit 1). In addition, that chapter discussed the concepts behind the architectures and technologies used in building an IDF.

This section provides implementation details behind those concepts, to support the actual analysis, design, and construction of an IDF. This chapter provides that information from two perspectives: the architectures needed to build and operate an IDF, and the techniques needed during the analysis, design, and construction.

The successful uses of data warehouses have inspired many companies to build them, but the real key to success is the use of the information to drive the business.

Wal-Mart provides one of the most brilliant success stories. At the beginning of 1997 its data warehouse was 7.5T bytes of data on NCR parallel processors. The warehouse contains daily updates on every item in every store. Buyers and suppliers share access to the same system, allowing them to collaborate on replenishment. Items are replenished weekly; select items are replenished three times a week. Sixteen million replenishment decisions every day allow Wal-Mart to offer its customers one of the lowest out-of-stock percentages in the business. The key to Wal-Mart's success is the active use of warehouse data to drive replenishment activities.

An HMO uses its warehouse to determine average hospital stays for specific illnesses. Using that information, staff contact physicians who have not discharged patients at the end of an average stay, asking whether continued hospitalization is necessary. The reminders to physicians have triggered a 10 percent reduction in hospital stays, providing significant savings for the HMO.

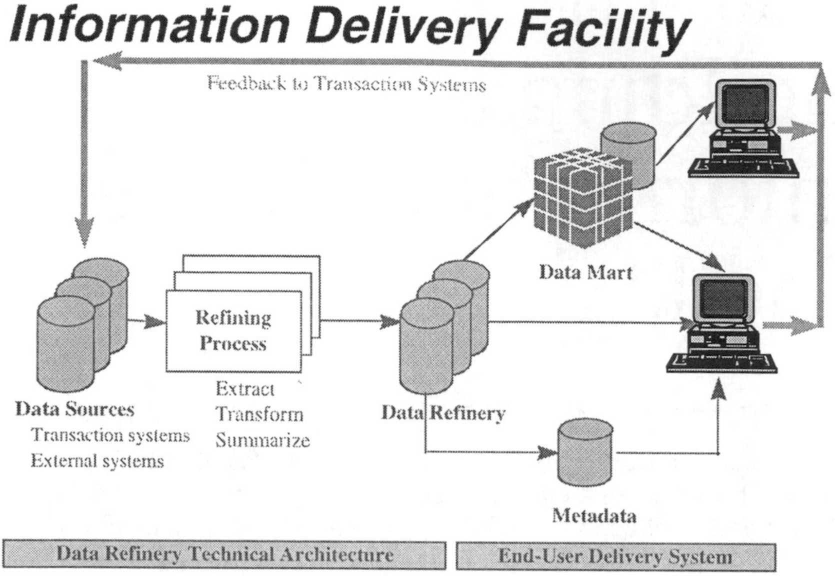

Information Delivery Facility

Exhibit 1. The information delivery facility.

Schieffelin & Somerset is a Scotch whiskey importer. It uses data warehousing to analyze external data on customer demographics, to develop profiles on targeted segments. As a result of targeted marketing, using the profiles it developed, it has become one of only two of the top 10 brands which have been increasing sales despite a declining market.

The critical factor for successful warehousing is the ability to take information from the warehouse and use it to drive business decisions to affect the bottom line of the company.

This chapter is organized in four parts:

1. End-user access and the products and applications needed to support end-users.
2. Metadata.
3. The data refinery and its design and construction.
4. The refining process, regarding implementation issues and product selection.

END-USER ACCESS

This section describes how information is delivered to the end user and how that information is used in the decision-making process. End-user access applications provide windows into the data refinery with intuitive graphical user interfaces (GUIs) and access to enterprisewide data for analyses, report generation, and decision making. There are many different types of end user access, distinguished by their various capabilities. The specific type used depends on the various requirements and knowledge levels of each end user. Because user requirements vary greatly, it is uncommon for one end user application to satisfy all the user and business requirements. So, an organization commonly uses more than one application to meet these requirements.

In the world of convergence, many users are remote users of the information delivery facility. As remote users, they face many unique problems not shared by local IDF users, such as security, data structuring, homogeneity of equipment, and system performance.

The true value of the IDF, however, is evolving to be the ubiquitous access to critical business information for remote users, whether it's the store manager in Wal-Mart, helping a customer determine what other stores have that special Christmas gift item, or a salesperson on the road getting a flash report on the most recent activity against a customer's account, or dealers examining what other successful dealers are doing and improving their own performance through emulation.

There are several categories of tools designed to access and analyze data. They offer different advantages and disadvantages, depending on the needs of the user. These categories are: ad hoc querying, ad hoc aliasing and reporting, decision support systems (DSS), executive information systems (EIS), enterprise intelligence systems, data mining, and data visualization. However, as vendors try to provide tools that serve multiple types of customers, many tools are adding capabilities that place them in more than one of these categories. Exhibit 2 shows the level of analysis each type of tool supports and the typical user level.

Exhibit 2.   Data access and analysis tools.

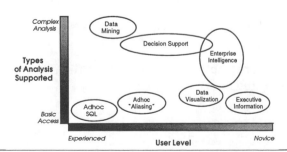

Identifying a tool as a single type is usually not possible. The following table summarizes how each end-user access category employs information and the typical users for each access category.

Access Category	Information Usage	Users
Ad hoc query	Fact finding querying	Power analysts specialists
Ad hoc aliasing and reporting	Fact finding reporting	Analysts
Decision support systems	Issue resolution What-if analysis Multidimensional analysis Exception management	Analysts Planners Specialists
Executive information systems	Status reporting Summarizing data Drilling capabilities Projection Planning Proactive	Executive High-Level Management Executive High-Level Management planners and analysts
Data mining	Rule discovery Pattern identification	Specialists Analysts
Data visualization	Interactive graphics Pattern recognition	Executives Managers

Each category of end-user access is designed for different functional capabilities and user levels. A large organization might have many users with various requirements and abilities. In this situation, it is possibile to have several tools accessing the same data, but performing different functions. It is important to select an end-user access application that closely matches the user's functional requirments and abilities.

However, the focus in today's IDF solutions tends to be oriented to one of two solutions:

- The use of DSS products that support multidimensional analysis.
- The use of Web-enabled query to support ad hoc aliasing.

Therefore, the bulk of the discussion of end-user access issues focuses on these two areas.

The following paragraphs briefly introduce the different categories of end user access listed above.

Ad hoc Query

Ad hoc query capabilities are used to support the retrieval of basic information through Structured Query Language (SQL). The ad hoc query returns a basic list of the requested information to the user. This capability requires users who are knowledgeable in SQL and data base structures. As a general rule, users find SQL difficult and tedious and experience a high frequency of bad data generated by incorrect SQL.

Ad hoc Aliasing

Ad hoc aliasing capabilities are used to support the retrieval of basic information when the SQL is transparent to the users. Ad hoc aliasing techniques are accomplished by using common business terms in menus or objects that can easily by selected by the user. This capability requires not only users who have some knowledge of query languages and data base structures but also users who are familiar with the business functions. The advantage of this class of tools when compared to the ad hoc tools described above is that the level of required SQL knowledge is diminished.

Decision Support Systems

Decision support systems (DSSs) are used to support multidimensional analysis of data and in many cases provide advanced capabilities such as statistical and financial modeling. DSSs are typically used by analysts, planners, midlevel managers, and other knowledge workers to carry out day-to-day operations and decisions. The modeling and manipulation capabilities enable users to create and maintain specific data sets of information from the result set generated by a query accessing the data refinery data base. The analysis and presentation capabilities enable users to view data from different levels and viewpoints and the flexibility to display data through vehicles such as graphs, reports, and charts, among others.

Executive Information Systems

Executive information systems (EISs) provide graphical user interfaces for more intuitive access to data. Many EISs also provide capabilities to summarize data and generate a variety of text, graphical, and/or tabular information for the user. EISs are typically used by high-level executives, such as CEOs, VPs, managers, and directors to do strategic planning and view enterprise-wide data. There tends to be minimal functionality for drill-down, under the assumption that the executives who use such systems delegate investigative work to others, who have access to the greater functionality of DSS.

Enterprise intelligence systems is a term that encompasses features included in both DSS and EIS such as data modeling, manipulation, analysis, and presentation capabilities and includes additional features, such as intelligent agents, proactive alerting, and exception monitoring. These systems provide specific focus on detection of abnormal conditions.

Data Mining

Data mining differs from traditional decision support systems in that these tools attempt to interpret the data by using pattern recognition technology. Discovering relevant patterns in large data stores at atomic levels can be important for more effective decision making. Primitive data mining searches for patterns requested by the end user. More advanced data mining detects patterns in the data that are unknown to the end user. Primitive data mining can be conducted using the ad hoc tools described above. Advanced data mining requires special artificial intelligence products.

Data Visualization

Data visualization enables users to view and understand complex information and gain insight into data patterns by using interactive graphics and imaging to represent and manipulate volume data. Presently, most applications have been scientific in nature. The benefits of data visualization to the business environment are being researched with increasing interest. Data mining vendors have made significant strides in using data visualization techniques to present data mining results.

In today's business world, questions are not limited to one and two dimensions, such as "What are total sales for the business?" or "What are total sales for product X?" Today's executives, managers, and decision makers are asking such questions as, "What were total sales for product X in the Midwest region during the second quarter this year, and how did they compare with sales of the same product in the same region, but in the third quarter of last year?"

To be answered correctly, these questions need to cross-reference multiple dimensions of a business model. When using standard SQL for querying and a normalized data storage format, users find these questions difficult to answer; however, when data is stored in a multidimensional structure, users find these questions are simple to answer.

Multidimensional Data Structures

Presently, the trend for end user access is directed toward on-line analytical processing (OLAP), the term used to indicate that a system's primary focus is on interactive data access, rather than batch reporting or

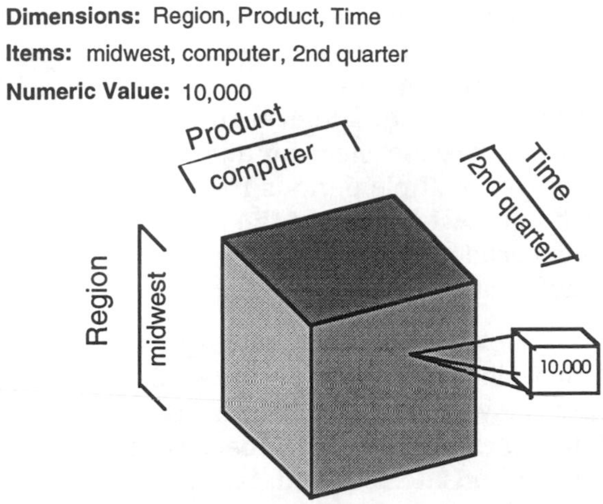

Dimensions: Region, Product, Time

Items: midwest, computer, 2nd quarter

Numeric Value: 10,000

Exhibit 3.   Sample building blocks of a multidimensional data base.

transaction processing. OLAP indicates a type of design or architecture that optimizes the ability to access the data. Many vendors have added OLAP functionality to their products as an OLAP extension or an OLAP engine, which can be purchased separately or as an add-on.

The building blocks of a multidimensional data base lie in the dimensions, the items within the dimensions, and the numeric values associated with the items. Exhibit 3 illustrates the following example. Company ABC's Midwest region sold 10,000 computers during the second quarter of 1997. In this example, region, product and time are the dimensions; Midwest, computers, and second quarter of 1997 are measures of the dimensions, and the numeric value 10,000 measures the association between the dimensions for a business event (in this case, sales).

A multidimensional tool enables the user to perform various forms of multidimensional analyses, which include drilling capabilities, data rotations, data slicing and dicing, and multiple hierarchies. Whereas all these actions are very powerful when performing different types of business analysis, they are also transparent to the user, unlike relational models, in which the data structure is not transparent to the user. With relational models, users are forced to understand flat table structures to perform such tasks as multiple table joins. Multidimensional tools represent data in a business view, giving users the flexibility to easily navigate through the data, by providing multiple views and rotations, for more effective ways to understand business problems.

Multiple user-defined levels on either axis is one type of analysis that is enabled by multidimensional data structures. For example, a product report may have row labels for country, state, city, and office, and column headings for year, quarter, month, and week, with the cells reporting sales for one specified product. The multilevel cross-tab function allows users to easily rotate or pivot the dimensions for different views of the data, such as multiple products for multiple periods for one of the geographic dimensions just described. Restatement of the data may be a simple matter of dragging a column head to the heading or to the row label, causing the data cube to rotate automatically.

Multidimensional data structures are very effective when used in systems (DSS/EIS) in which quick and accurate access to business information is needed across many perspectives. This is because the multidimensional structure facilitates flexible, high performance access, and analysis of large volumes of complex and interrelated data.

Ad hoc aliasing as a category has traditionally been provided by query tools that were more user friendly than were the query tools that require users to construct SQL queries. Some of these traditional tools have added functionality that moves them into the multidimensional category.

Now on the horizon is the reverse phenomenon, in which the multidimensional vendors are extending their tools down into the ad hoc aliasing category. As the multidimensional vendors have delivered Web-enabled query capabilities, they have been constrained by the limitations of HTML, Java, and the Internet. The Web-enabled tools tend to fall into the class of SQL aliasing, rather than multidimensional. The tools deliver tabular responses to simple queries or standard reports stored on the application server. However, the drill-down, what-if capabilities and statistical features that provide so much power to multidimensional tools are generally missing.

This is not to say that the Web-enabled tools do not deliver value. In fact, they tend to deliver simple queries and standard reports at a price point far below that offered by more traditional fat client SQL aliasing tools. Because of the low price point, companies are deploying these tools on a much wider scale than more traditional tools. This wide deployment allows all employees to have access to information to improve their performance in their business function, to the enrichment of overall corporate performance. And deployment need not be constrained to employees. Business partners and customers can now collaborate for their mutual benefit, as in the Wal-Mart case of replenishment.

What is a standard architecture for Web-enabled query? The current Web-enabled products typically provide software that runs on the application server. The Web server and browser are the same software that is used for access to the World Wide Web. The application server accepts a query

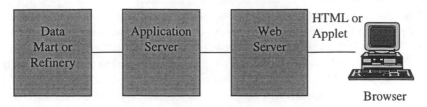

Exhibit 4.   Web-enabled end-user query.

from the browser and responds by delivering the results of a data base query, delivering a stored report, or shipping an applet to the client for execution (Exhibit 4).

Multidimensional Tools

This section provides some example features of multidimensional tools that typically are not available from Web-enabled tools.

Analytical Capabilities. Multidimensional analysis capabilities include comparative analysis, time-series analysis, and what-if analysis.

Ease of Presentation and Navigation. Intuitive data views are natural outputs of multidimensional data bases and include such functions as break rows, comparison capabilities, and sequential operations, which SQL does not provide. Capabilities, such as data surfing, in which the user has the ability to browse or navigate through the data for unique requests and comparisons, are easily achievable in a multidimensional format. Data surfing allows the user to search the data looking for answers without knowing precise questions.

Data Pivoting Capabilities. In a multidimensional structure, alternate data views are immediately available for viewing. Views of various dimensions of the same structure are easily examined without the need to redefine the query or re-read the data base.

Drilling Capabilities. If a user is requesting sales data from an organizational level, the user can then move down to the regional level, and then down to the office level, with a simple mouse click. The reverse process is also possible.

Data-Dicing Capabilities and Drilling Capabilities. A reduced array of selected dimensions can be easily cut-away from the parent structure where computations and rotations can be performed.

315

In today's world of end user access applications, there is a plethora of options to choose from when developing an application to solve business problems. To this point, only packaged tools with ad hoc querying and DSS/EIS capabilities have been discussed. General purpose development tools such as Microsoft's Visual Basic, Sybase's Power Builder, Gupta's SQLWindows and Sun's Java must also be considered when selecting an end-user access application. These development tools have also been used successfully for developing customized end user access applications.

Advantages of Development Tools. Advantages to choosing a general purpose development tool include the following:

- *Leveraging existing skills.* Expertise in such development tools as Visual Basic, Power Builder, SQL Windows, and Java is prevalent in many organizations today. Because of this expertise, many organizations decide that these development tools should be used to develop custom applications for refinery access. By selecting a development tool with which inherent expertise can be exploited, organizations can save valuable development time and training expenses, thereby reducing overall expenses.
- *Flexibility in design.* By developing an application with a general purpose tool, an organization is able to design an application with specific capabilities that precisely meet their needs, such as interfaces, analytical functions, and presentation capabilities. This can be beneficial if an organization requires a simple application, with minimum development time, to produce canned reports or provide simple queries.
- *Less expensive than packaged tools.* General purpose tools are often far cheaper per user than packaged DSS tools. Therefore, some applications can be developed and maintained for less than it would cost to purchase a packaged tool. Ultimately, this is dependent on such factors as complexity of the application, level of expertise of the developers, and number of users.

Disadvantages of Development Tools. Reasons not to use development tools to create an end-user application include the following:

- *Development time.* The cost of establishing a delivery vehicle using a development tool is directly related to the complexity of the desired application and therefore the time it takes to develop that application. The development time is critical, because in many situations capabilities of the desired application expand and development time is underestimated. With packaged tools, an organization has the ability to establish requirements, match as many of these requirements as possible with the capabilities of a packaged tool, and immediately implement their solution. This enables time that would previously have been used for development to now be used for training users on the functionality of the tool. In addition, custom building the applications creates new management problems, as all tools must be integrated together and supported.

- *Consistency of user interface.*   Packaged tools tend to provide a consistency of user interface that general purpose tools cannot match. The general purpose tools could produce the same consistency, if the developer has enough knowledge to build it, but developers are more typically enthralled by the multiple options that can be built into the user interface, creating an eclectic mishmash of presentation formats.
- *APIs as development tools.*   Many packaged tools, both ad hoc and DSS/EIS, provide APIs to developmental tools such as Power Builder and Visual Basic. This gives the flexibility to expand the applications by adding functionality and end-user friendliness.
- *A lack of multidimensional analysis capabilities and therefore less analytical functionality.*   If an organization needs to perform complex business analysis certain packaged tools give the ability to perform multidimensional analysis. These capabilities add significant flexibility when performing business analysis by being able to rotate data views, drill capabilities, data slicing and dicing etc. Multidimensional capabilities can be designed into a custom developed tool, but this would be extremely time consuming and difficult, and these capabilities already exist in off-the-shelf tools.
- *Built-in functions must be created.*   Many packaged tools provide built-in statistical functions to perform analysis such as: what-if analysis, forecasting, goal seeking, risk analysis, time series, etc. To perform this type of analysis with custom developed applications, functions either have to be designed into the application or data has to be exported to another application (spreadsheet, statistical analysis package etc.). This indicates that the custom developed tool has less functionality and would force users to be proficient in another application.
- *Limitations in reporting capabilities because data is accessed through SQL.*   Custom developed applications are limited to the capabilities of SQL. This limits the user's capabilities in performing such common business analysis as comparisons, break rows, and sequential operations such as ranking, listing the top five, etc.

Development tools are very powerful depending on the circumstances in which they are used. They tend to be most effective when an organization is developing a simple data access system, and has significant expertise in using the chosen tool. If an organization requires a more complex system (requiring multidimensional analysis, statistical functions, extensive reporting capabilities etc.) using a development tool as a complement to a DSS/EIS tool can add flexibility for both developers and users.

Application Architectures and Remote Access and Take-Away Use

Throughout this section, a basic architecture has been assumed. However, it is common for several architecture issues to arise. These issues arise for several reasons, including performance and stability claims of tool vendors and the needs of remote users. There are two key issues:

- Two-tier vs. three-tier application architectures.
- Remote access and take-away use.

Two-Tier Vs. Three-Tier Architectures. Many of the DSS/EIS products allow two different configurations:

- *Two-tier configuration.* The data refinery (RDBMS) is on one machine, and the end user access application runs on the PCs. Almost all ad hoc query tools use this architecture.
- *Three-tier configuration.* The data refinery is on one machine, and the end user access application has both a client and a server piece. Most Web-enabled products use this architecture.

With the three-tier configuration, the analytical engine can be on a separate platform or the analytical engine can be on the same platform as the RDBMS. This is an important issue, as both the analytical engine and the RDBMS tend to be resource gluttons. The response times of the IDF in the two configurations should be benchmarked to see if the increase in performance of using separate platforms is worth the cost of purchasing and maintaining the extra machine.

In the two-tier approach, the DSS/EIS client application can access either the RDBMS or a multidimensional store directly. In the three-tier approach the DSS/EIS client must go through the multidimensional engine to access the RDBMS or a multidimensional store. The following list highlights some of the advantages and disadvantages of each configuration.

Two-Tier Configuration

- Heavy client processing. All application logic is on the client.
- More powerful (more costly) client PCs.
- More suitable for takeaway use.
- Heavier network traffic. All the data is brought back to the client for processing.
- Could be slower if the less powerful client is required to do a large amount of processing, such as heavy multidimensional analysis.
- Application distribution problems. Modifications in the end user applications must be updated on every client.

Three-Tier Configuration

- Light client processing. The application is split, with the client only doing presentation plus perhaps limited processing.
- Background processing. Reports and functions such as agents and alerts can run in the background on the server. In some applications, these can be set to run at certain times (e.g., every Sunday).
- Remote use requires a connection to the server. If the laptop cannot communicate with the server, the end user application is unusable.
- Lighter network traffic (between the server and the clients). The more powerful server does most or all the processing, and only sends back the results.
- Could be slower if many clients are competing for the server's resources, or if the server and RDBMS are on the same platform and competing for processing time.
- Updates to the application can usually just be made to the server piece.

Remote Access and Takeaway Use. Remote availability of the end-user application is often important in designing an IDF. In such cases this issue is a major factor in the choice of an end-user application. Two techniques make the data available to remote users:

- *Remote access.* The users dial in to the server for live access (probably Web-enabled).
- *Takeaway use.* The users take the application and part of the data with them.

A three-tier architecture is better suited for remote access. In this setup, a remote user with a laptop dials in to the end user access application server. The server does most or all the data retrieval and number crunching, and just sends the results to the laptop. The client piece of the end user application is primarily concerned with the presentation of these results.

Because only the results are sent back to the client, the network traffic (a major bottleneck) is lower, and the remote laptop does not need to do much (if any) application processing, and can therefore be a less powerful machine. The main disadvantage of this is availability. The remote user (e.g., a traveling salesperson) will be required to dial in to the server, and remain connected for as long as the data is used. If the remote user does not have a connection to the server, the end user application is unusable.

Remote access is important when an organization's remote users need frequent access to a large portion of the data, the updates to the data refinery are frequent (e.g., daily), and the remote users need the most recent data. As an alternative to live remote access, takeaway use is handled by replicating part of the data refinery to the laptop. The end-user application then runs entirely on the laptop, requesting data from its local store.

There are a few ways this can be done:

- *Using a powerful DSS/EIS application with multidimensional data stores.* An organization with a large traveling sales staff may want its salespeople to be able to take a small multidimensional data store with them on their laptops. They could occasionally dial in for updates. The two-tier approach is necessary for this, because all the application logic is on the client.
- *Using a smaller data base on the client.* For applications which must go directly against a data base, the laptops can contain a portion of the data in their own RDBMS. For example, some vendors will run against Microsoft Access on a laptop.
- *Using flat files.* Some ad hoc query applications also allow remote users to take part of the data away. Two-tier products bring the data down to the client for manipulation. The remote user can just take these files away on the laptop.

METADATA

Metadata is a critical component of any IDF. Metadata is defined as data about data. Classically, metadata is stored in data repositories and provides the descriptions of data and systems required by MIS departments to support ongoing maintenance. Metadata takes on significant new meaning in IDFs. Metadata informs users about the information that is available to them in the IDF. User requirements for metadata are quite different than that of MIS. Two quite different repositories of metadata can be distinguished: a business directory and a data repository.

The Business Directory

The business directory, at a minimum, provides a listing of the contents of the IDF and clear business definitions of those contents. When possible, the business directory may also provide information on the transformation rules, the last update of the existing data, and even direct query invocation of the IDF.

The primary success factor for the business directory is the quality of the business definitions of the data. Some of the most successful business directories are simple paper-based pocket guides, containing only the data definitions. A major contributor to the success of these business directories is the effort put into the development of the definitions themselves. Focus groups of users from different organizations who need to share the data serve to elevate the differences in data definitions that exist across every organization and to educate the participants. These efforts sometimes grind to a halt when it becomes clear that there are different definitions, and consensus cannot be achieved on single definitions. These efforts achieve success when the participants recognize the validity of different business definitions and find ways to incorporate multiple definitions into the IDF. Clearly, the definitions of similar but different data items must highlight both the similarities and the differences, to clear away the natural confusion. Oftentimes, companies discover that the IDF delivers, for the first time, a clear analysis of important business data and the subtle variations required to support the business properly.

The natural desire for consensus on single definitions is not the only impediment to success. A second impediment is the MIS desire to standardize terminology and to homogenize the granularity of the data, but the definition must be meaningful to the end-user. The definitions must continue to relate to the information that users know about in the source systems, which are not standardized or homogeneous. Thus, user participation in the development of definitions is absolutely critical. It is often necessary to use aliases extensively, to ensure that communication about the IDF data is clear and understandable to all users.

Rather than paper-based pocket guides, most companies prefer an electronic solution, since maintenance of definitions is so much easier electronically. Whereas electronic business directories certainly make maintenance easier, it is vitally important that the delivery of an electronic solution does not dilute the effort required to develop good business definitions. An exotic electronic delivery vehicle with casual, incomplete definitions of the business data, is likely to fail.

The Data Repository

There often is a desire to use the company data repository as the electronic medium for providing the business directory. Careful thought must be given to whether the licensing arrangements make such a solution cost-effective. Even more careful attention must be given to whether the human interface is suitable for casual, nonMIS users. Like a *Webster's Dictionary*, metadata is used infrequently, and must, therefore, be intuitive and useable by untrained casual users.

Many end-user tools require metadata to function. This metadata is more closely linked by its nature to the MIS data repository than the true business directory we have been describing. Multiple tools are likely to require multiple metadata stores. Because of the redundant nature of this metadata, it is best to think of this as ancillary to the real business directory. It should be considered to be MIS technical data that supports the tool, rather than business data that supports the user. The challenge is to ensure that there are enough linkages between the technical definitions which the users will see and the business definitions in the business directory to allow users to move easily between them.

The MIS data repository is a key resource to help the IDF support organization maintain the IDF. They need the technical definitions of the IDF data, the sources of the data, the transformation rules, the inter-relationships between data items, the relationships between tables and columns, between applications and the data the application presents, and the timing of data refreshes.

The MIS data repository is normally electronic. It may consist of a custom solution, using the native capabilities of relational DBMSs to craft a custom solution. Or it may use one of the commercially available data repository products. But most commonly, it is centered on a commercial product that provides extract-and-transform capabilities for extracting data from the source systems. Such products need metadata to perform those extractions and transformations. If the tool's metadata is not rich enough to incorporate all the requirements of MIS, then the solution can typically be extended using the native capabilities of the RDBMS which underlies the extract tool.

One of the pleasant trends emerging from the extract tool vendors is the ability to export the metadata from those tools to populate the end-user tools and to populate stand-alone corporate data repositories. This is a significant development that should be enthusiastically explored .

THE DATA REFINERY

This section discusses the data refinery, which enables the end-user applications previously discussed. The purpose of this section is to clarify many of the frequently asked questions about IDF data bases and to improve the reader's understanding of data refineries.

This section does not discuss in detail how to perform the process of designing a data refinery or the characteristics of specific data base products. Entire textbooks exist on that subject. Rather, the section presents various guidelines for data refinery design and will suggest to the reader important considerations for choosing a data base product. The goal of this section is to explain designing the data refinery from the perspective of:

- Identifying what data is stored in the data refinery and describing the four major categories of IDF data and why they are important.
- Showing how the refinery data is structured including dimensional modeling.
- Discussing issues of data base size.

What is a Data Refinery?

A data refinery is a system that captures, organizes, and stores data from operational and external systems to provide a pool of integrated, historical, cross-organization data for end-user access.

The data refinery is used to investigate business processes. Managers use the data refinery to plan operations, manage the organization, and evaluate performance. Unlike OLTP systems, the usage is read-only and not updatable. OLTP systems are used to get the data in; IDF systems are used to get the data out.

As the data is evaluated, interrelations among information and a historical perspective are much more important in the data refinery than in OLTP systems. Multidimensional business views of the data are critical to the effective use of a data refinery. The following two sections highlight two important features of IDF systems, multidimensional analysis and hierarchies.

The Multidimensional Business View. Multidimensional analysis is the backbone of decision support. It is easier for the user to visualize multidimensional data because it more closely resembles how users analyze data than do normalized tables. Users analyze data with the questions Who?, What?, Where?, and When? With multidimensionality, users can answer multiple questions simultaneously. Also, it simplifies the analysis process because users do not have to formulate complex queries to obtain the information they desire.

IDF analysis is multidimensional (i.e., sales by product by location by month in an array). The multidimensional views allow users to view numerical totals at different levels and facets of the organization. The following questions are easily answered by multidimensional business views:

- Which individual products have had poor sales and in which months? (Sales by month and product, ranked by ascending sales)
- Why have sales in Product Group A fallen below target levels? (Actual vs. target sales, by month and sub-product groups)
- Are there specific weeks to which the product's slump in sales can be attributed? (Sales by week and product)

Much has been written in recent years regarding the merits of multidimensional data bases (MDBMSs). A multidimensional data base, however, is not required to provide a multidimensional view of the data. Methods of implementing multidimensional data views in relational data bases are discussed in this section.

Hierarchies. Typically considered an integral part of multidimensionality, hierarchies show the parent-child relationships between elements of the dimension. Hierarchies are natural structures within organizations, particularly for how they are analyzed and managed (e.g., an organizational hierarchy is Region > District > City; a product hierarchy is Division > Brand > UPC). Hierarchies are used to logically group and analyze information within one dimension.

Considering the distinct characteristics of OLTP systems and IDF systems, the requirements for each are different. They have different types of users. IDF systems are used by knowledge workers and decision makers to analyze the business activity and determine what future activities should look like. The success of the project depends on supporting these requirements.

Characteristics of the Data Refinery

Four critical characteristics of a data refinery are performance, flexibility of analysis, ease of access and confidence in the data integrity.

1. *Performance.* IDF systems typically process large data volumes, which presents unique performance problems. Although IDF systems do not require the sub-second response time of OLTP systems, even moderate performance can be difficult to attain in an IDF system. Acceptable performance means allowing users to ask all relevant questions and eliminating locked-up keyboards while users wait for an answer.

2. *Flexibile Analysis.* All users must have the ability to analyze the data in a manner that enables them to answer pertinent business questions. If the information is not available using the IDF system or the analysis cannot proceed to the full extent of the user's information needs, users become dissatisfied with the system and return to the traditional means of generating reports.

3. *Access.* Whereas dedicated users, such as data analysts, would adapt to forming complex queries for common business questions, casual executive users cannot be expected to perform complex query analysis. Executive jobs need to be focused on analyzing the information and decision making, rather than spending their time determining how to get the information. Therefore, the value of the IDF system is getting users beyond gathering and massaging data by using the IDF system to perform the gathering and massaging. Although end-user access tools can provide the multidimensional view and query writing facilities necessary to provide easy access, proper data base design is required to provide acceptable performance under these circumstances.

4. *Data Integrity.* Because users make tactical and strategic decisions based on the perceived integrity of the information contained in the data refinery, they must have the same confidence in the results

obtained through the data refinery as they would from manual analysis. Because the data refinery places an intermediate step between the transaction systems and the end user's analysis tools, the results obtained from the cleansed and organized IDF data may disagree with reports generated before the IDF was implemented. This may cause a confidence crisis for the user. It is important to build the user's confidence in the new system by ensuring there is consensus on the data definitions and data transformations.

If the above requirements are not addressed to user satisfaction, the IDF will not be used by the knowledge workers. The data refinery should be designed to meet the requirements of the IDF system and enable the use of IDF data analysis. The logical model of the data provides multidimensional data views, including hierarchies. The physical design of the data base provides data structures that meet the four requirements for an IDF system: performance, flexibility of analysis, ease of access, and confidence in the data integrity.

This section discusses the following data refinery design issues:

- Architecture of the data refinery
- What data is stored
- How the data is structured

The Data Refinery Architecture. The design of the refinery architecture is completed as part of system analysis and design, but it must fit into the conceptual architecture created during the preceding conceptual design phase. For this reason, architecture decisions for the data refinery will become important early in an IDF project.

The data refinery architect has several options from which to choose. The data refinery architecture is interdependent with the architectures of the refining process and the end-user access applications (Exhibit 5).

The data refinery architecture is the basic or centralized architecture. The centralized architecture is applicable for most nonenterprise IDFs. However, when the data refinery is used to store corporatewide data, a distributed refinery may be a more appropriate solution.

A fully distributed architecture distributes the data over multiple data bases or locations without maintaining a complete copy of corporate data in a central warehouse. This configuration is more than the combination of many departmental IDF's, in which data is not shared across nodes but allows corporatewide access to data regardless of location. The design and management of a fully distributed refinery is too complex for most IDF solutions; however, the information presented in this section applies no matter what the architecture of the data refinery.

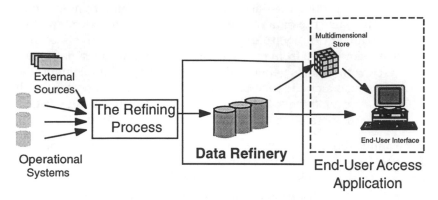

Exhibit 5.   The data refinery architecture.

Often, a partially distributed refinery is an appropriate solution when a distributed data refinery is being considered. Again, a partially distributed refinery only applies when enterprise data is to be supported in the refinery. A partially distributed refinery consists of a central repository of corporatewide data and several departmental data refineries (often called data marts). This architecture is generally implemented for performance reasons.

Finally, some projects may decide to implement an architecture construct separate from the data refinery for operational reporting. Whereas the data refinery is intended for strategic analysis of information, the operational data store (ODS) satisfies operational information needs. The ODS derives primarily from the need to further reduce the workload on legacy systems and to make use of the extract files that were being produced for the data warehouse. The ODS is further discussed later in this section.

A centralized architecture is the most straightforward to implement, because there is one source of data for all applications. A centralized refinery is appropriate when the volume of data and number of users does not degrade the performance on one system. Generally, as the refinery or information requirements grow, either a distributed architecture will be adopted, or multiple IDFs will be established.

The centralized architecture still applies when there are multiple data bases as long as each application accesses only one data base, and there is no duplication of data. This is the case when an organization has multiple IDFs. Each IDF has its own refining process, data refinery, and end-user access applications. Clearly, this is not the most efficient means of delivering information when the systems share common source systems and data. When multiple IDFs are implemented, it is important to have a foundation upon which both architectures are built because this minimizes the cost of maintaining the systems.

Data Marts. In addition to having one central data refinery, an organization can distribute the data in smaller portions within the organization. These partial replications of the data refinery, referred to as data marts, can be either a local distribution (e.g., having a data mart in each department) or wide distribution (e.g., having a data mart in each regional office). These data marts are not necessarily small. One company has a data mart with approximately 600GB of data.

The main concern with data marts is the complexity they add to the design. The data must be logically distributed and maintained yet still retain its consistency and overall completeness. Each data mart will have only the data that is relevant to that department or region, and the data on these servers may overlap. The administrator must keep track of where all the data is located, so that the overall view of the data model is coherent.

Usually the data marts are just replicas of portions of the data refinery; the entire refinery is stored in one central site. However, there are alternatives. If most of the analysis at the central office is on high-level data (e.g., done by executives), only summarized data need be stored in the central refinery. In the regional data marts, however, low-level regional data can still be stored. If the executives in the central office need access to lower level data (e.g., daily sales when the central office has only weekly sales), the requests can pass through to the appropriate region's data mart.

Many situations require all the data to be available from all local servers. This is necessary because end-users may occasionally need to access data which is not in their local data marts. Although most of the requests are handled locally, a key characteristic of an IDF is the unpredictability of the queries. Access to the entire refinery is also useful if there are end users who travel to different offices but still wish to access the same data (e.g., a salesperson or executive).

The location of the data should be transparent to the end user. If an end user needs data that is not on his or her local data mart, the system should know where to get it without user instruction. The system should determine whether to go to another nearby data mart or to the full central server.

With the regional data marts able to access other data marts or the central refinery, security becomes an issue. Should the managers in the western region have access to specific data from the eastern region, or just overall sales figures? With IDF data, access is typically broader than it is in operational systems. Rather than restricting access under the need-to-know principle, data is made available under the empower-the-user principle.

Using data marts requires that updates to the central refinery be propagated to the local offices' data marts, as well. This can be done in many ways, from a live network connection (if updates are frequent) to express-mailing a tape to each local office, although this may cause integrity problems if one location falls behind in loading the updates.

Advantages of distributing the data refinery are:

- It better reflects the structure of the organization. Only the data relevant to each department or region is on its server's data mart.
- It provides improved performance because the data mart is smaller and can be queried more rapidly and is closer to the end users and typically accessed over higher speed networks.
- The availability of the data is improved, because if the server fails at one site the other sites are unaffected.
- It allows for easier growth towards an enterprise-wide IDF. The organization can start with one department, then add others as the process is perfected.
- There is a reduced communication cost, because there is no need to maintain a constant link between every end user of every department and a central server.

Disadvantages of distributing the data refinery are:

- Data integrity is more difficult to maintain, as some of the same data is in multiple sites.
- There is a more complex update process, because the data needs to be divided and distributed to the appropriate data marts. The process must be coordinated so there is no possibility of receiving two different answers from different servers (e.g., a central summary server provides an answer that is inconsistent with the distributed detail server).

The management and organization of the distributed refinery is more complex. This involves issues such as:

- Do all the departmental servers have consistent and complete data (i.e., the most recent update)?
- If a user needs data that is not available on his department's server, is there a way he or she can access another department's server? If so, there needs to be a mechanism for determining which server has the requested data, and some kind of access control to determine if the user has the authority to use it.
- If one department's server fails, can the load be shifted to another?
- Despite the fact that the data is distributed, the uniformity of the data refinery is crucial. The departments should not try to manage their servers differently.

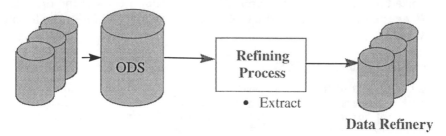

Exhibit 6. Operational data store: Conceptual.

IDF developers often ask whether they should use a relational DBMS or a multidimensional DBMS for the data refinery. As a broad guideline, it is preferable to think of the data refinery as an RDBMS and the data mart as an MDBMS. The major RDMSs offer the advantage of scalability into the hundreds of gigabytes. The MDBMSs offer the advantage of performance for rapid drill-down, surfing and statistical analysis. Not all data marts need the OLAP capabilities of an MDBMS. However, only very small data refineries are able to use an MDBMS.

The Operational Data Store. The operational data store (ODS) is an architecture construct intended for operational reporting. The concept of ODS was created for the following two reasons:

- People found that they could do operational reporting on the extracts taken for the data refinery, and creating an ODS data base to do this reporting was a natural extension of the idea.
- People needed to further reduce the workload on legacy systems; the ODS was created to reduce the legacy workload by performing some operational reporting off-line.

Because of its origins, the ODS shares many characteristics with the data refinery, and fits into the IDF architecture in the middle of the refining process. Exhibit 6 illustrates these concepts. As it is possible for the ODS to contain some summary information, there may be an entire refining process before the ODS, but there will always be additional summarization and possible cleansing before the data is transferred to the data refinery. Also, because they have distinct information requirements, all the data in the data refinery does not originate from ODS and all the data in the ODS does not necessarily transition to the data refinery. The differences between the ODS and data refinery are better understood by the description of the information stored in each.

Both the data refinery and the ODS are integrated (i.e., transformed and made consistent from multiple source systems) and subject oriented (i.e., organized into subjects that match the information needs of the organization). As the table indicates, the ODS and data refinery differ in the following ways:

Operational Data Store (ODS)	Data Refinery (DR)
Current. Data is up to date with operational systems, to enable operational reporting to be performed. No data is stored beyond one accounting cycle.	*Historical.* Data is historical, to enable informational reporting and strategic planning. Every piece of data is associated in some way with a time.
Volatile. Data in the ODS is constantly changing to reflect changes in operational systems.	*Static or Stable.* Data in the DR is static and changes only when updates to historic data are necessary.
Detail Only. The ODS contains detail data only. This is not to imply that there is no summary data, but unlike DR summary data it is very volatile and uncommon.	*Summary Data.* A large percentage of the DR is summary data. The data refinery requires summary data to improve performance and standardize information analysis.

The operational data store is only valid in certain cases. It is intended to relieve the burden of operational reporting from legacy systems and ease the maintenance of those systems by replacing some of their functionality. Generally, an ODS should not be built without a corresponding data warehouse. Also, while the ODS fits into the IDF architecture, a separate project is necessary requiring less effort than the development of an IDF.

The practical implementation of an ODS is different from the conceptual diagram in the previous exhibit. There is no reason to single thread the data flow through the ODS. A more common design is shown in Exhibit 7.

Data Categories. The data in the data refinery is used to plan operations, manage the organization, and evaluate the performance of segments of the organization. Although operational data from transaction systems forms the core of the data, four major categories are stored in a data refinery (Exhibit 8).

Even though the four categories of data can be separated into distinct tables, the development managers should consider the four categories of data as logical divisions or groupings of the data in the refinery that ensure success.

Metadata was addressed earlier in this chapter. The remaining three categories of data play the following roles in the data refinery:

- *Summary Data.* This data provides improved performance over atomic-level data. Summary data is the product of operational data or atomic-level data that has been aggregated according to the model defined in the master data.
- *Atomic-Level Data.* This is the lowest level of operational data. It describes time-based events such as sales, claims, banking transactions,

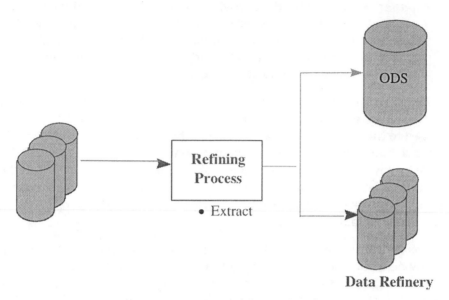

Exhibit 7. Operational data store: Practical.

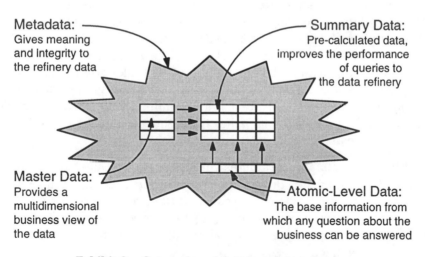

Metadata:
Gives meaning
and Integrity to
the refinery data

Summary Data:
Pre-calculated data,
improves the performance
of queries to
the data refinery

Master Data:
Provides a
multidimensional
business view of
the data

Atomic-Level Data:
The base information from
which any question about the
business can be answered

Exhibit 8. Categories of data in a data refinery.

product utilization, etc. It contains basic numeric information. Depending upon the requirements of the system, this data may represent a summarization of operational data. This data can be aggregated in any way defined in the master data to produce summary data.

- *Master Data.* Master data provides a multidimensional view of the information in the data refinery. It is responsible for maintaining the dimensional structure of the information and the hierarchical structure of the dimensions. This data tends to be static and alphanumeric, such as customers, products, and locations.

Atomic-Level Data. Atomic-level data is operational data that has been cleansed and organized. Of the data in the data refinery, this data is the closest to the operational data, although it may be somewhat summarized. For example, Wal-Mart's atomic data is summarized sales data by item by store by day. In terms of the multidimensional and hierarchical views of the data, this data is the lowest level, or base, of each hierarchy. The term atomic-level data is applied to demonstrate that this is the lowest level of data retained in the refinery.

Summary Data. Summary data can be defined as whatever data is derived from operational and external data that is not atomic-level data. Simply stated, this is data that has been aggregated from atomic-level data. A common misconception is that the summary data is built or calculated within the data refinery. This is not the case. Generally, this data is calculated in the refining process and loaded into the data base. Summary data gives users access to pre-aggregated data. While this data can be calculated from atomic-level data, the performance may not be acceptable for users. Summary data is maintained when it greatly increases the performance of the system. Reading one record for sales of all products for the entire year requires much less time than reading 1,000,000 sales records and adding them together. It is especially critical when users access the data from the top of the hierarchy. Massively parallel computers can solve this performance problem, but few companies have chosen to make the necessary hardware investments.

Although summary data helps the data refinery meet performance requirements, it creates drawbacks for the other three requirements. The analysis becomes less flexible because of the fixed nature of summarizations. Users are restricted to pre-aggregated views of the data or to formulating their own queries against the atomic-level data and must accept slower performance.

Additionally, users may find that ease of access is decreased because they must decide how to formulate the query for the summary data and not the atomic-level data. They must also be aware of how the hierarchies and dimensions are structured as well as the table names where the summary data is located. Ease of use can be restored by using an end user tool or using master data and metadata, as described later in this section.

Finally, the use of pre-calculated data, whether it is summary data or pre-calculated key performance indicators (KPIs) can decrease the user's confidence in the data. The users may become uneasy because they are separated from the atomic data by end-user tools and from the operational data by the data refinery. This uneasiness can be reversed by giving the users access to data about the refinery data, or metadata, as described earlier.

As a final note, there is a group of products that can be termed "aggregate navigators." These products are located between the client machine and the data refinery and automatically adjust the from and where clauses of an SQL query to use the correct summary data. Such a tool eliminates the need to decide the correct summary table, columns, and joins necessary to answer a query from within the end-user application.

While the use of summary data decreases the response time of queries and improves performance, some data warehouse projects do not try to physically store the data in the data refinery. In some part, this is because of the effect summary data has on the access requirements as described above. Other factors that discourage the use of summary data are additional storage space requirements for the summary data and indexes, increased complexity of the refining process and data base administration, and increased time required to load the data. Ultimately, some projects do not implement summary data because the users do not surmount the additional complexity to use it.

Summary data need not be built for every combination of hierarchy levels across all dimensions. This concept is called light aggregation. Only summary levels that are accessed frequently need to be created.This data also tends to be the data that is accessed most often by the most important, or highest level users.

Lightly aggregating the data can increase the complexity of the end user application. The most practical aggregations to build are those that decrease the number of rows that must be searched for the most common queries. For instance, if there are 10,000 UPCs and only 200 brands, 100 cities, and 20 districts, it is more important to build an aggregate of UPCs than of districts; that tactic decreases the number of rows to be searched much more dramatically than for a district aggregation. Also, though users may wish to see a brand's sales across all cities, they are less likely to want to see a city's sales of all UPCs. Although these guidelines can be used to estimate which tables most effectively improve query performance, ultimately, the summary tables needed depend upon the varied access patterns of the end users and therefore fluctuate.

The following two principles help guide the process of building aggregations. The architect should:

- Seek to minimize the size of tables that are frequently subjected to full table scans.
- Seek to minimize the number of joins between tables with the largest number of rows (for instance, in a star schema, the join between the UPC level product dimension table and the atomic-level fact table).

When using light aggregation, metadata and master data become extremely important. Without these two types of data, all the summary levels would need to be stored or the system would be to difficult to use, effectively isolating the performance gains from the end users. Master data and metadata do not have to be difficult to implement if prepackaged metadata management tools are used.

Master Data. Conceptually, master data is the lens that allows the user to see a multidimensional view of an intrinsically two-dimensional data base. For this reason, the master data is referred to as describing the multidimensional business view of the data. This master data contains descriptions of the hierarchies and dimensions that enable the multidimensional business view.

From an operational point of view, master data is used to build summary data from atomic-level data or operational data. Master data is the template or blueprint that describes how the summary data should be built from the atomic-level data pieces. This template can be used by the refining process or the end user access applications to produce summary data from atomic-level data.

The most common master tables are Customer, Product, Location, and Time. A practical example of a type of master data is a dimension table. The following example shows a hierarchy for the location dimension as it could be stored in a relational data base using dimensional modeling.

Market Key	City	State	Region	Country
8410569	Chicago	Illinois	Midwest	U.S.
8410598	Los Angeles	California	West	U.S.
8415926	Miami	Florida	South	U.S.
8419856	Dallas	Texas	South	U.S.
8419989	Montreal	Quebec	East Canada	Canada
8540159	Denver	Colorado	Mountain	U.S.

The purpose of master data is to provide a consistent multidimensional business view to the end user. It alleviates many of the requirements issues generated by the use of summary data.

Using master data helps meet the requirement that the data must be easy to access. It can serve as a template to facilitate the user's queries to the data refinery. For example, the user could request the dimensions of

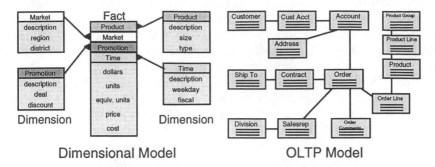

Exhibit 9. Dimensional and OLTP models.

the model to determine how the data can be divided for analysis, or the user could request the hierarchy structure of the dimensions to navigate through the data.

The previous sections discussed issues and described three categories of data in the data refinery. The following sections discuss methods of implementing these categories, to illustrate dimensional modeling and the array of summary tables method. These two items are not mutually exclusive. Dimensional modeling is a method of modeling the data in the data base; the array of summary tables method is a means of partitioning the data for more efficient performance.

Dimensional Modeling and the Array of Summary Tables Method. Dimensional modeling was popularized by Ralph Kimball to address the need for a data model for decision support systems. The models produced by dimensional modeling are sometimes referred to as star schema, because of the common representation of the tables (Exhibit 9).

Dimensional modeling stores data multidimensionally using fact and dimension tables. Foreign keys are used to join tables that describe the dimensions (i.e., dimension tables) to a central table containing the facts or KPIs (i.e., fact table). This produces a data model that contrasts sharply with the traditional normalized OLTP design.

The exhibit shows the dimensional approach benefits from shorter, less complicated join paths than the traditional normalized method. Reasons to use dimensional modeling over standard OLTP modeling include:

- Fewer query joins result in improved query performance.
- Shorter join paths simplify access.
- Single join paths lend consistency to query results.

The easiest way to begin contrasting normalized data models with the star schema is by contrasting master data and event data. Master data includes customer, product, and location. Event data includes sales, claims, telephone calls, and interest charges. A normalized data model concentrates on master data; events act to alter that master data. A star schema rotates the model 90 degrees by concentrating on collecting events ("facts") over time; analysis of trends reflected in those events is supported by the master data ("dimensions"). The following table illustrates examples of subject areas in a normalized and star shema model.

Normalized Model Subjects	Star Schema Subjects
Customer	Sales
Product	Claims
Organization	Utilizations

Fact tables are organized such that the first set of columns contain keys, one for each dimension, that uniquely identify each row of the table. The remainder of the columns in the fact table contain the facts. The attributes of the fact tables are the numeric, additive characteristics of the event specified by the keys in the dimension column.

Dimension tables contain one column with a key and other columns that are attributes of the dimension. As an example, the dimension table for time could contain the following columns: date, holiday flag, overtime flag, day of the week, fiscal quarter, and fiscal year. These attributes can be used to specify desired facts.

Atomic-level data is stored in one or more fact tables and is associated with a specific combination of dimension keys. The product dimension key for a specific transaction may identify that the product in question had a UPC 89754930909, brand Airy Liquid, trademark Airy, manufacturer Soap Corp., size 20 oz., and a scent lemon. This part of the atomic-level data is contained in the dimension tables. This configuration can make it easy to select rows in the fact table by a variety of different attributes such as UPC, brand, size, or scent.

Summary data also can be incorporated in the model. As in any approach, the presence of summary data increases the complexity of the design. The summary data can be stored in the same fact table as the atomic-level; or, many fact tables can be created, each containing a separate aggregation across dimensions.

The issue with storing summary data in the fact table is how to limit a user's query into the fact table to the summary level that the user is requesting. If the user requests the total of all sales for products with the brand Airy Liquid, he or she must specify an extra where clause that eliminates the total for Airy Liquid brand from the answer set. If the data has also been aggregated by month, the user must specify a separate where clause that eliminates the month totals from the answer set.

The issue with having multiple fact tables is that the user must then know from which fact table to pose the query. This makes the data refinery difficult to use. As mentioned earlier, both issues can be resolved with master data and metadata, but the simplicity and power of the dimensional method can be diminished by the use of summary data.

Master data is incorporated into the dimensional model through the dimension tables. Dimension tables describe each dimension in terms of the attributes that can be used to describe elements of that dimension. For example, the columns of the Market dimension may be Country, Region, District, and City. By associating the elements of one column (e.g., Region) with the elements of another column (e.g., District), the structure of the hierarchy can be determined.

Metadata is not directly incorporated in the dimensional model. If the project incorporates metadata into the application, or purchases an end user tool that uses metadata, a separate data model should be developed for the metadata piece of the data refinery.

When the data refinery is implemented in an RDBMS, the star schema defines the tables and columns of the data base design. Indexes are generally defined on the primary key of the fact table and on multiple hierarchy elements within the dimension tables. Additional indexes on the fact and dimension tables may be necessary depending on the access patterns expected.

THE REFINING PROCESS

The organization needs a process to get the data into the data refinery. Numerous factors are involved in building data refinery management applications, which are run initially to load the data refinery, and then periodically to perform updates. There are two ways of creating the applications: through the use of enrichment tools to automatically generate an application, or manually creating custom-coded applications.

This section attempts to:

- Give a detailed discussion of what must be accomplished in the three phases of the refining process (extract, cleanse, and summarize) and describe issues involved in each phase.
- Describe different strategies for loading the data into the refinery and the associated considerations.
- Describe at a high level the issues and considerations involved in customizing the data refinery management applications.
- Give a brief comparison of the two methods: generated enrichment applications vs. custom-coded applications.

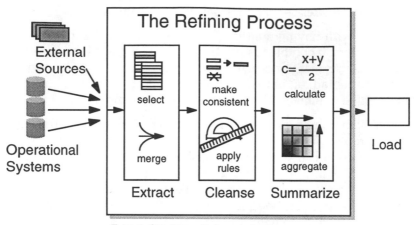

Extract: Get data out of source systems
Cleanse: Organize and insure integrity of data
Summarize: Transform and aggregate data

Exhibit 10. Phases of refining process.

Transporting data from the operational sources to the data refinery involves much more than a simple dump and load. The data must undergo comprehensive purification and reorganization before it can be admitted to the refinery. This is called the refining process. Data refinery or warehouse management software is responsible for extracting the data from the operational systems and external sources and transforming it into the desired form. The goal of the refining process is to generate such applications. This can be accomplished using a suite of third-party enrichment tools or independently.

There are three main phases in the refining process: extract, cleanse, and summarize (Exhibit 10). In the extract phase, the data is physically taken from the source systems. This involves picking and choosing individual pieces of data from operational or other sources. The data is then checked for consistency, consolidated, and organized during the cleanse phase. At this point business rules also can be applied to the data. Any operations, such as calculations of derived fields or aggregations which need to be performed on the data, are completed during the summarize phase. Finally, the data is ready for loading into the data refinery.

The refining process is critical to the success of the IDF. This process is extremely challenging and often is not given as much weight as it should be when organizations are planning their IDF. The data often undergoes a major transformation in form and size on its journey through the data refinery. One medical diagnostics equipment company had an estimated 70GB of production data on its operational systems. After refining, the amount of data finally loaded into the refinery was 20GB. This is not to imply that the size cannot increase; if the data base has many aggregations, the data refinery process can actually expand the amount of data.

The Extract Phase

The purpose of the extract phase is to select the locations in the sources from which the data is to be taken. These sources are primarily operational data bases: The transaction processing systems the organization uses daily for entering information. In addition, the data can come from external sources, such as Nielsen marketing data, Dow Jones News Retrieval service, and Dun & Bradstreet financial information. Because there is typically a variety of sources, the data is likely to be originating from several platforms. Therefore, one consideration is upon which platform the refining process will take place. Possibilities include one of the source platforms, the target platform, or an independent platform. The application may also be distributed across several different platforms. If a third-party tool is used, the choice may be restricted to the platforms upon which the enrichment tool is designed to run.

If a third-party tool is used, the data definitions are first downloaded to the platform on which the refining will take place. The data model may come from an integrated CASE tool, a data dictionary, or COBOL file definitions, or the model may be designed within the tool itself. The developer then graphically selects which data should be extracted from the sources, and maps it to the target data model for the refinery, cleansing and summarizing it along the way.

Choosing which data to extract goes back to the know-the-data axiom, discussed earlier in this chapter.

- *The data should be accurate.* The budget department may keep slightly different versions of the same period's data. The architects should be sure to extract the appropriate version.
- *The data should be the most recent.* For example, if extracting marketing statistics, the architects should get the most current data.
- *The data should be finished.* It is advisable to wait until all the day's sales have been logged in the operational system before starting the day's extraction. With monthly updates, the month should have been been closed before the data is extracted.
- *The data should be the most complete.* For example, one department may have been analyzing data from all accounts; another may have been analyzing data from all major accounts. The unabridged data should be extracted.

- *The data should be nearest to the originating source.* As data spreads throughout an organization, it goes through a limited extraction process each time it passes from one department to another. Each time this happens, the likelihood of discrepancies in the data increases.

The Cleanse Phase

The cleanse phase of the refining process is responsible for resolving any inconsistencies in the data with regard to syntax, definitions, and formats. The issues that might arise during this phase can be divided into three basic categories: syntactic, structural, and semantic.

Syntactic issues are surface differences, usually the result of typing or data-entry. This part of the cleanse phase truly does the "cleansing" of the data; the other two parts deal mainly with coordinating the data as it comes in from different sources.

The extract process is an interface process. As such, it faces that unique interface problem that it may be unaware of changes to the source systems. Such changes can cause the extract process to fail or, worse yet, to unknowingly deliver bad data to the warehouse. Therefore, it is extremely important that the extract process be supported by controls to catch such errors. Oftentimes, simple trending of record counts is sufficient.

Procedural controls should be the IDF's first line of defense. Procedural controls should ensure that the IDF personnel are notified during the design of such changes to source systems. However, because such controls are usually only about 80 percent effective, automated controls are needed, even when effective procedural controls are in place.

Typical cleansing problems include:

- *Spelling errors and other exceptions.* For example, one operational data base has a customer Ted McKendall, and another source data base has a customer Ted McKendal. If the addresses and phone numbers are identical, these probably refer to the same customer.
- *Reference inconsistencies*, such as:
  - Words vs. numbers. One source may use "Forty-Seventh St. Photo" as a customer name, whereas another uses "47th St. Photo"
  - Middle initial. One data base may have "Ted McKendall," whereas another has "Ted R. McKendall."
  - Nicknames. One data base may have "Ted McKendall," whereas another has "Theodore McKendall"
- *Uncleansable data.* This refers to records containing typographical errors or mistakes which cannot be resolved. These are usually sent during processing to an exception file, in which a user can examine and try to correct them.

Just who takes responsibility is an area for considerable negotiation. Managers must not slight the importance or the difficulty of resolving this issue. Data should be fixed at its source, not at the time it enters the warehouse. However, getting agreement from the source systems' administrators can be difficult.

Structural issues refer to the case when internal representation of data is inconsistent between sources. Typical problems include:

- *Definition inconsistencies.* One source may use "m" and "f" to represent male and female, another may use "0" and "1," and a third may use "1" and "0."
- *Different character sets.* One of the sources may use EBCDIC, and another source (or the target system) may use ASCII. One may use European character sets, whereas another uses American character sets.
- *Data disagreement.* This is caused by clarifying rows with nonunique keys. This can happen if, for example, fields like customer ID are reused. Clarifying fields with invalid values also can cause data disagreement.
- *Data type inconsistencies.* One source may use a 4-byte floating point for "unit price" while another uses an eight-byte floating point; or, one source may use the characters 'm' and 'f' while another uses the strings "m" and "f."
- *Significant figures.* Sales data from two regions are being summed. One of the regions uses figures with two decimal places, while the other uses three. The third decimal place of the resulting sum is meaningless; the target field in the data refinery should only have two decimal places.

The final issue is semantic. Semantic problems occur when the user's interpretation of the data may differ or when the disagreement among source records requires a human to resolve. Examples of this type of issue include:

- *Inconsistent definitions.* Sales figures from one system include returns, whereas sales figures from another system exclude returns.
- *Old information.* Two sources may have records with the same customer ID but different addresses and phone numbers. Which record is current?
- *Optional fields.* Optional fields extracted from operational data bases are often difficult to cleanse. There is no way to constrain these fields to apply rules for cleansing, because there is no guarantee that the fields will contain data.
- *Free-form text fields.* A source field contains the customer's full name, but the target field accepts only the customer's last name. For example, an insurance company used the term *claim* to communicate different

meanings, resulting in confusion across the divisions. To rectify this, new terms were created to uniquely identify the uses of this multipurpose term. These consistent definitions benefit internal communications across divisions.

In the corporate data model, three levels of claims were defined: policy claim, coverage claim, and claimant claim.

A policy claim is the demand against a policy for a single loss event, which may result in multiple coverage claims and claimant claims. At the policy claim level, underwriters evaluate their underwriting performance.

A coverage claim refers to the demand against the policy coverages affected by a policy claim. For example, if an insured's car collides with another car, both cars are damaged, and the other driver and a passenger are hurt, there would be one policy claim (a single event) but three coverage claims: property damage for the other car, bodily injury for the other driver and passenger, and collision for the insured's car.

A claimant claim is the demand by a claimant against a policy coverage. In the example above, there would be four claimant claims: property damage for the other driver's car, bodily injury for the other driver, bodily injury for the passenger, and collision for the insured's car. The bodily injury coverage claim was expanded to two claimant claims.

The divisions had stressed the need for viewing and counting claims at all three of these levels. In some cases, by seeing the different levels of claims, the divisions identified new, more useful ways to look at the information.

To realize this, the following business rule was applied to the data as it was being cleansed: If different claims were made against the same policy on the same day, they were for the same loss event (i.e., there was one policy claim). Although this is not true in all cases, it was believed to be correct more than 99 percent of the time. The few exceptions to this rule were deemed insignificant. This is often the case when applying such business rules; there is a trade-off between absolute accuracy and efficiency.

As the example above illustrates, the cleanse phase also can be used for applying business rules to the data. The application of business rules is one means of resolving several of the issues of the cleanse phase.

There are knowledge-based reasoning tools that construct logic- intensive applications. They can be used to apply business rules to the data to help transform it into the desired model.

The cleansing portion of the refining process consumes the bulk of the implementation effort. Insuring the integrity of the data is vital. Major decisions may be made based on the information in the data refinery; it should be irrefutable.

One interesting point concerns marketing information. The data does not need to be irrefutable, because marketing is not an exact science. There will be situations in which two data sources do not agree, but it is not necessarily the case that one is right and one is wrong. For the data refinery, though, the data should at least be consistent. This can be resolved either by choosing the data from the best source or by another method. In such a situation, it may be useful to provide statistics that describe the reliability of the data. One solution would be to store the reliability information with the metadata for the end user.

The Summarize Phase

Any calculations or roll-ups that need to be performed on the data in order to prepare it for entry into the data refinery are completed during the summarize phase. This is an alternative to having the refinery perform such operations, thus saving valuable processing time.

Computing sums among records based on a hierarchy of attributes the data have in common is called aggregating. Aggregating records produces roll-ups or summary data, which can be stored in separate tables in the refinery, or in the same table.

The issue of storing aggregation records in the refinery is not the same as the granularity of the data discussed earlier. The sales data is still stored at the daily level in the refinery, but there are also separate records for monthly, quarterly, and yearly sales figures.

Beyond simple sums, the summarize phase can be used to compute derived data by applying mathematical formulae to fields to create completely new fields (for example, computing margin from net sales, returns, and cost of goods sold).

By performing the calculations shown earlier (where all the data is together), everyone will be using data resulting from the same calculations. Departments can avoid using different methods for calculating values, thereby avoiding contradictory results.

Balancing is important when performing summaries, roll-ups, and other calculations. Be certain that the information is not changed or lost during the summarize phase. Whenever possible, the data computed during the summarize phase should be compared and aligned with existing reports.

Another issue that may arise is how changes in history affect previously loaded summarizations. There are two methods one can use to accomplish these adjustments. If the changes in history are rare, they can be completed from within the data refinery. The lowest level of data is manually updated, then select and insert statements are used to update the roll-ups. This would likely be faster, but the user must remember to perform the update. The most efficient method is to use a mechanism which notes changes in the operational data, either by monitoring the data or by reading a log file, and automatically determines what updates need to be applied to the lowest level data. The changes are extracted, cleansed, and summarized with the new data during the refining process. Thus, the aggregations and other computations are automatically amended. This is a more complicated process, but it will work much better if changes in historical data are common.

Major changes in the data model and its hierarchy can result from an adjustment to the basic structures of the organization. Businesses change over time, and these reorganizations need to be reflected in the data refinery and refining process. Because decision-support systems rely heavily on hierarchies in order to provide drill-down and other analyses, these reorganizations create special problems.

Note that realignments need to be addressed during the refining process only if summaries are stored in the data refinery. If summaries are only applied by a multidimensional end user application, then the data in the refinery is unaffected. In such cases, the data in the refinery is stored only at the lowest level, and reorganizations do not affect it. Because the end user application calculated the aggregations, it must be changed to reflect these changes.

There are three main methods for resolving realignments. The historical data should not be changed. The historical data should be modified to conform to the current organizational structure. Finally, these two approaches can be combined. When an organization changes, the historical data is realigned to reflect the changes, as in the second approach. In addition, historical metadata tables are created and maintained with effective dating of the dimensional structure. This allows the historical data to be retrieved as a snapshot of the past data (e.g., "What were sales by product based on the product hierarchy of 31 December 1994?").

Usually, the records extracted from the source are sorted early in the refining process, as this facilitates the cleanse and summarize phases. However, if this is not the case, a final step before loading the data into the refinery should be to sort the rows of the file to be loaded. If sorted in the way the RDBMS expects (e.g., by date first, then product, then market), the load will go faster. Sorting may be done by the data refinery management software, or using high-performance sorting tools.

Loading the Finished Data

There are three options for loading the finished data into the data refinery:

1. Load by the data refinery management applications.
2. Load by the RDBMS.
3. Load by a third-party utility.

Most enrichment tools provide the option of loading the data directly into the refinery. The specifics of the refining tool will describe if it supports the target RDBMS. If an enrichment tool is not used, the customized applications can be designed to perform the load.

There are two advantages to this approach. The first is that it saves the time that would otherwise have been spent writing and reading the data on an intermediary store, such as an ASCII file. Second, it requires less human interaction, and one less tool.

A second method is to have the data refinery management software or the enrichment tool, if one is used, create a flat file with the finished data, and then use the RDBMS's own load utility. The advantage of this approach is that many RDBMS vendors provide enhanced load utilities which employ fast loading or specialized loading techniques.

As an alternative to having the load performed by the data refinery management software or the data refinery, there are third-party loaders which can be even faster on certain platforms.

When data is first loaded into the refinery, the data base will be empty. When the source data is changed or has new data, there will be periodic updates to the refinery (e.g., daily or weekly). There are two options for performing these updates:

- *Total load.* Reloading the entire set of data into the refinery.
- *Incremental load.* Inserting only the changed or new data to the refinery.

If much of the information has changed, or the information currently in the data refinery is outdated and needs to be disposed of or archived (perhaps for storage space reasons), it may be beneficial to perform a total load into the refinery (completely replacing the previous information). However, a disadvantage is most refineries exist for the purpose of storing historical data, and regular updates are used to add recent information to them. Also, even total loads into modest-sized refineries (50–100 Gbytes) can take a long time.

On the other hand, if the size of the data refinery is in the range of 2 to 5 GB or smaller, a total load could take an hour or two. Nevertheless, it is more desirable to perform incremental loads. An incremental load inserts new data into the refinery without replacing the old (e.g., adding the newest week's sales figures). Also, it can be used to update the old data as well, when changes in the source data impact existing records in the refinery.

In an incremental load, the task is to keep track of what information has been changed in or added to the source data applications. Enrichment tools can offer limited assistance in this area. However, there are performance and integrity issues involved with incremental loads:

While straight inserts (of new data) are fast, updates that require extra processing (changing existing data) can be extremely slow. Most RDBMS load utilities cannot do incremental loads. Most bulk load utilities do not support restart and recovery. If this is a necessary feature, bulk load utilities cannot be used.

CONCLUSION

This chapter dealt with the architectures and techniques needed to build and operate an IDF. Remember that the ultimate success of the IDF is dependent on several factors, including:

- clear understanding of the kinds of access needed by users to find meaningful data.
- clear sense of the use that will be made of the data retrieved.
- clear link between information retrieved and strategic decisions of the company.

Section IV
Future Trends in Netcentric Computing

The future of computing is primarily marked by competing imaginations. Well-known futurist George Gilder, for example, speaks of something called a dataphone, which capitalizes on the full richness of the convergence of computing, communications, and knowledge. This device, about the size of a watch, will have speech-recognition capabilities and will convert speech to text if you want. It will retrieve news of the day, tailored to your preferences, and read it to you if you wish. You will use it to conduct transactions, and it will replenish your credit smart card, which you will use like cash. It will help you communicate, it will entertain you, and it will help you pay your taxes. It will have an Internet address and a Java run-time engine. It will take digital pictures. For more demanding functions, you will dock it into a more powerful machine.

Gilder's vision is certainly one plausible part of the digital future, one toward which the netcentric environment is leading us. In this final section of the book, we look at several technologies and concepts that will shape netcentric computing solutions in the future:

- Componentware and objects.
- Collaboration.
- Data mining.

This section does not presume to present a comprehensive look at the future but rather some critical and practical considerations.

Chapter IV-1
Componentware

The complexity of netcentric technology means that today's information systems have become more difficult and time-consuming to build and maintain. Long custom development cycles imply that a system designed in one business climate may be deployed in a radically changed climate, losing the window of opportunity to take advantage of the competitive benefits embedded in the system. The goal of designers today is to design systems that are quickly built, robustly tested, and easily maintained as market conditions shift.

Componentware promises to enhance an organization's ability to build robust systems quickly through the use of reusable pre-built software components. Componentware is an approach to software development in which expert software engineers encapsulate core business and technical processes and knowledge into black-box segments of code. These prebuilt pieces of code are then assembled together by less experienced developers to rapidly build robust and flexible systems.

Properly leveraged, components can provide the foundation upon which organizations meet and exceed the demands of a global marketplace which increasingly uses technology as a primary competitive advantage.

COMPONENTWARE DRIVERS

Four major drivers are contributing to the trend toward component-based systems development: a crisis in software engineering, the continued evolution of object-oriented technology (OO), entry into the market by major industry players, and a burgeoning components marketplace (Exhibit 1).

Software Engineering Crisis

Over the years, the science of software engineering has been outpaced by technological advances in computing equipment. Whereas computers have gone from giant room-sized boxes to lightweight laptops, and modems have advanced from 300bps to 36.6Kbps and beyond, systems development has remained largely unchanged. Granted, several systems development approaches (including CASE and Information Engineering) have been proposed as solutions for quick and robust systems building. Even though these have had success in specific areas, they typically

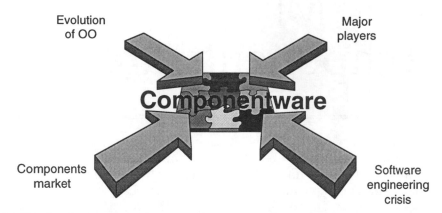

Exhibit 1.   Four major drivers behind component-based systems development.

require significant up-front investment and have not seen widespread acceptance.

Ten years ago, business systems supported the back office by processing accounting data and periodically sharing data with other internal systems. Although necessary for the business, these systems did not provide any significant competitive advantage. It was acceptable to take three years to build a system, and reasonable life spans for software reached to 10 or 15 years. Today, on the other hand, business systems can be a significant factor in a company's competitive advantage. Having the right software at the right time can allow a company to leap past its competitors and gain market share. Early on-line banks are one example. As a result, organizations are beginning to look for systems that can be built very rapidly and that can evolve to meet the changing conditions of the marketplace.

To resolve the software engineering crisis, a development technique is needed that greatly reduces the time required to build a system and increases system quality. Several complementary approaches have been developed to address these needs, as shown in Exhibit 2.

For a development technique to gain widespread acceptance in the marketplace, it must include the following characteristics:

- *Provide for reuse.*   Provide the capability to use a toolbox of pre-built code segments across projects, business units, and corporations.
- *Minimize complexity.*   Break code into smaller pieces and reduce the number of interfaces between units, use encapsulation to hide internals.
- *Provide for tailorable solutions.*   Allow the use of off-the-shelf code which can be glued together to build a variety of products.

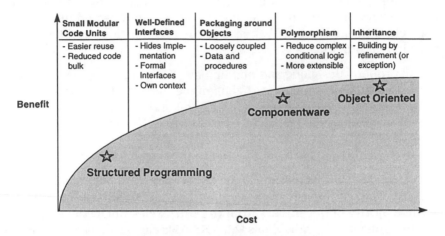

Exhibit 2. Development techniques.

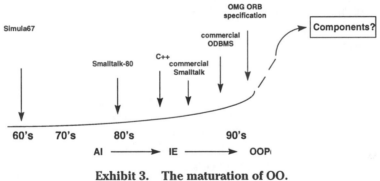

Exhibit 3. The maturation of OO.

- *Lower learning curves.*   Minimize the number and types of specialized skills required from the development team.
- *Increase productivity.*   Allow quicker construction of applications than with other development techniques

The Evolution of OO

Over the past 10 years, object oriented (OO) methodologies and technologies have matured sufficiently to provide the foundation for complex, mission-critical applications (Exhibit 3).

Many organizations have found that a long-term commitment to OO has resulted in significant leaps in productivity as well as more robust applications which are easily modified to react to changes in the marketplace. However, the initial investment in object analysis and design typically delays the visibility of benefits to the organization until late in the development process.

Also, properly designing and building an OO system requires advanced functional and technical skills on behalf of the entire project team. Few people have the breadth of knowledge to design and develop both application-level and infrastructure-level objects. This often results in an intensive effort to retrain existing application developers, as well as locating hard-to-find OO experts to assist with the development process.

For OO to become successful in the mass market, a new paradigm must emerge in which its benefits can be exploited while simultaneously insulating the majority of developers from the intricacies of OO development. With componentware, individuals with OO skills can be focused on the task of designing and building the components themselves. Then, application architects can design applications on top of existing infrastructure frameworks, which less-experienced developers then build by gluing together a set of components. In this manner, OO can be scaled up to massive development efforts when sufficient OO resources are not available.

Major Players

Another of the drivers behind a broad acceptance of componentware is broad availability of the necessary software infrastructure. By building this infrastructure into widely distributed products, vendors such as Microsoft, Sun, and IBM have significantly reduced the amount of work required to build a component-based solution. As a result, software developers can build upon these platforms using standardized frameworks and tools, such as ActiveX (Microsoft), and SOM (IBM).

As these infrastructure pieces have become available, vendors are beginning to build development tools that take advantage of them. These tools provide for rapid application building and deployment based partially or wholly upon component technologies. For example, with the release of Microsoft Visual Basic 4.0, the mass market of over two million VB developers has access to a tool which can be used to build component-based applications.

Components Market

Now that the necessary infrastructure and tools are becoming available, a components market is beginning to appear. Currently, this market is made up mainly of smaller vendors offering components, such as spreadsheet widgets and data base connectors. As the market matures and more developers become familiar with the use of the component technologies in their applications, additional vendors will be providing products, including the major software houses such as Lotus, IBM, and Microsoft. Eventually, components are likely to become a commodity software market. Early examples of this can be seen with the variety of spreadsheet components, and resulting lower prices through competition, available today. However, for componentware to reach widespread acceptance, the market needs to expand past technically-oriented components into business components.

COMPONENTS DEFINED

To best describe componentware, it is necessary to define the concept of a component. Components are packaged pieces of software that exhibit the following characteristics:

- *Marketable.* They provide sufficient and necessary functionality so they are desirable to consumers other than the original developers.
- *Trusted.* They have been tested and proven in a prior implementation and perform as specified without any undocumented side-effects.
- *Well-defined.* They perform one or more specific functions that do not significantly overlap those of another component in the same domain and can be used in ways not necessarily envisioned by the original designer.
- *Plug and play.* They are packaged so that an alternate implementation of a component can be substituted into a system without affecting other code.
- *Encapsulated.* They are made up of public interfaces and hidden internal functions and data structures.
- *Easier to maintain.* They have well-defined interfaces and data and are a lvel of granularity such that maintenance is simplified.
- *Black box.* They are delivered as a closed package; the consumer of a component cannot modify the code of the component.
- *Cross-environment.* They can be used across address spaces, network boundaries and can be hosted in a variety of operating systems; in this manner, components can be built in the language and platform that best suit their developers and then deployed on a different platform.

In addition to these characteristics, components are also defined by their granularity, or the relative size of components when compared to the application as a whole. Granularity can be broken down as follows:

- *Small-grained.* A piece of code containing few internal data structures and comprising minimal functionality, such as an entry field or a collection object.

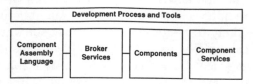

Exhibit 4.   Componentware infrastructure.

- *Medium-grained.*   Code containing several complex internal data structures and providing a number of complex functions, such as an invoice or a mortgage loan form.
- *Large-grained.*   A component providing significant functionality encapsulating a business function (e.g., accounts receivable) or an architectural concept (e.g., distributed transaction processing), although smaller than a complete application.

CRITICAL PIECES

The infrastructure necessary for componentware to become widespread is made up of several smaller pieces. These include a development process and tools, a component assembly language, broker services, components, and component services (Exhibit 4).

Development Process

Assuming a marketplace of widely available off-the-shelf commercial components that match the development effort, the focus of the software development process becomes the location and assembly of pre-existing components. As a result of this shift in emphasis, several new processes need to be performed:

- *Searching.*   Researching the current marketplace for components that match application requirements.
- *Selection.*   Choosing a component and component vendor based upon a variety of criteria such as vendor stability, special component features, and component cost.
- *Integration.*   Reviewing a component's documentation and interfaces to determine the best manner for integrating it into the system; developing an approach for integration.
- *Adaptation.*   Enhancing a component through wrappering (i.e., providing a layer of code which isolates the component from the remainder of the system and variously hides, adds, or modifies the characteristics of the component interfaces) or aggregation (i.e., combining two or more components together so that they appear as one logical unit to the component consumer) to make it work within the

system (it is unlikely that components from different vendors will work together directly, especially while the industry is still immature).
* *Testing.* Conducting thorough testing of the component to ensure that it performs as specified.

Owing to similarities between componentware and object-oriented development, it is possible to leverage many of the existing OO processes and tools for component development. However, there still exists significant opportunity for growth in this market, especially on the side of tools for the component assembler.

Component Assembly Tools

Component assembly tools are not necessarily the same tools as those used for constructing components themselves. Typically, they are less complex third-generation languages, which emphasize rapid application construction over run-time speed or efficiency. The market for component assembly tools currently has a number of entrants, such as ParcPlace/Digitalk PARTs, IBM VisualAge, and Microsoft Visual Basic. These tools provide at least the minimal functionality required for component assembly tools, which is the ability to include pre-built components into applications and glue them together.

However, in order to reach a wider audience, component assembly tools need to move away from extensions to current procedural languages and towards easy-to-use, integrated development environments. A partial listing of the features of an ideal component construction language includes:

* *Component catalog.* Tool used for browsing in-house and third-party brokerages and selecting components.
* *Component inspector.* Tool that allows viewing the various characteristics of a component, such as interfaces, documentation and file size.
* *Component installation.* Interfaces with brokerage services and the operating system to properly register components on the local machine or the appropriate server machines.
* *Component tester.* Tool used to automate the testing of components and their integration
* *Semi-automated wrapping.* Assists with the development of wrappers around off-the-shelf components.
* *Semantic transformation.* Allows components with different application-level semantics to be able to collaborate; e.g., "the customer I am passing to you means the same thing to both of us."

Components

From the consumer perspective, there are two major types of components in the marketplace:

- *Construction components.* Facilitate the construction of the application but do not map to a business entity; can be used in any business domain.
- *Business components.* Components that map to business entities; oftentimes specific to a given business domain.

Both types of components can provide a reasonable cost savings through reduced construction time. However, business components have the potential for dramatically shortening overall cycle time because they also reduce the effort required for system analysis and design. Because of this, business components are considered to be the critical factor in realizing the full potential of the commodity componentware market.

Both types of components, as well as current market conditions are discussed here.

Construction Components. At the most rudimentary form, a construction component can be packaged as a user interface control. Each control has a defined set of events that it responds to, and the developer is responsible for coding the logic in response to each event. Common responses (such as capturing keystrokes into a text box) are abstracted into the control, and event hooks are left for the developer to code additional, business-specific logic (such as the LostFocus event processing in Visual Basic).

Construction components may support complex user interface constructs such as spreadsheet style grids, mapping widgets, conversion controls for multilanguage interfaces, and Web-enabled user interface styles such as HTML-aware controls.

Another common use for construction components is to provide easier data base access to the developer. Simplified, data base-independent APIs are exposed to the developer and internally converted to product-specific data base calls. An extension of this concept is the use of data-aware controls, or user interface controls which can directly manipulate and display data from data base sources without requiring additional coding.

Communications components are also emerging as a growth area. Support for e-mail, fax, communication protocols (LAN, TCP/IP, etc.) and more complex CTI technologies is becoming mainstream. The availability of construction components will likely continue to grow rapidly. Construction components are very marketable, as they can be used across business domains.

The challenge with these components continues to be locating the component in a timely manner. Also, many of these construction components are proprietary in nature and support only specific languages. For example, most data access components are only optimized for a few data bases.

Communications components may require specialized hardware, or specific protocols. And at the far end of the spectrum, some companies claim to support components, but are merely selling existing CASE or development tools with new words. This same trend is paralleled by products claiming to be object oriented.

Business Components. These are standardized business entities, such as customers or insurance discount calculation engines, that can be shared across applications. Specifically, a business component has the following characteristics:

- *Active in the business domain.* An entity that performs a business function or is required for the performance of a business function.
- *Definition.* An entity that has a business name, definition, behavior, relationships, rules, policies, and constraints.
- *Represents a real-world entity.* An electronic equivalent to a person, place, event, or other entity, such as an employee, product, or invoice.

Component Broker Services

Standards are required for collaboration between components that are potentially sold by different vendors, built in different languages, and located on different machines. A "component bus" is the common infrastructure for this interoperability. Minimally, such a bus provides protocols for:

- *Component instantiation.* Creating or asking for a particular component without knowing its location.
- *Component access.* Providing access to a component, even if it is on another machine, which can be used to manipulate it.
- *Service discovery.* Identifying the services that a component provides at run time.
- *Component release.* Telling a component when it is no longer needed, so it can release resources as necessary.

Applications discover and invoke a component's available methods using a common protocol. Methods are specified with an interface definition language (IDL), which is independent of the programming language or tool used to implement the component. Then, the methods on a component can be invoked via one of three techniques:

- In-process, similar to a DLL in Windows.
- Across process boundaries but on the same machine, using a Lightweight RPC (or LRPC) mechanism.
- Across machine boundaries, through RPC, Message-Oriented Middleware (MOM) mechanisms, or Object Request Brokers (ORBs).

Once a component is invoked, the bus infrastructure marshals requests between components. Marshaling bundles the parameters for a request in a format for efficient translation and transmission, potentially across a network. The server component receives the request, unpackages the parameters, and dispatches to the appropriate function. Finally, any return value must be marshaled back to the client. In this manner, standardized marshaling hides the details of another component's location, OS, or implementation language. The service that locates components and manages their communications is an ORB.

Brokers provide additional roles in the component environment, such as management of concurrent requests to a given server, transaction management, and security auditing.

Component Services

Component buses serve as the foundation from which a variety of services can be built. These include:

- *Horizontal.* Transactions, locking, persistence, security, event handling, licensing, compound documents, and printing.
- *Vertical.* Telecommunications, financial services, and health care.

Thus, a bus is essentially the next generation of middleware, for interoperability of distributed components. At this writing, two different specifications, Microsoft COM and OMB CORBA, are currently the leading contenders to become the dominant bus standard.

An example of a horizontal service is that of the smart, or compound, document, which is a collection site for the uniform integration of visual components. Specifically, a compound document framework allows independently created components to coexist in a single document and share visual real estate. These components can negotiate for control of the menu bar, based on which component has been activated. For example, a single compound document could contain stock ticker and spreadsheet components. As the user activated either component with a mouse click, that component could display applicable choices in the menu bar.

Thus, compound documents introduce a higher level of collaboration. Any visual component which follows these rules of engagement can be incorporated into such a document.

DEVELOPMENT MODEL

At a high level, component-based software development involves two parties: the component producer and the component consumer. The producer is responsible for creating components and ensuring that they perform as specified. Producers can be either third-party vendors — mass-market or contractual — or internal component development teams. Components may be developed from the start as components, or they may be harvested from new or existing solutions. For example, a retail company may extract bar-code scanning out of an existing application and repackage it as a construction component for internal or mass-market use.

Component consumers, on the other hand, build applications by assembling components. These components are purchased from a third-party vendor, acquired from internal asset repositories, or contracted out to a component builder. Feedback from the consumers is used to refine existing components and identify additional components to be built.

When using business components, the software development process focuses on the business domain or business model. Instead of dealing with the mechanics of process-to-process communication and calling conventions, developers are able to describe systems in functional terms. By using entities that map to the business model and the information flow within it, development can become less complex and less error-prone, and new code creation is minimized.

By packaging code into cross-application units, business software becomes a collection of reusable assets. Proprietary assets can contain internal intellectual property that can be leveraged from one application to another, for example, a company's policy component or its code for loan approvals can be built into a back-office client/server system, an Internet customer service system, and a multimedia kiosk.

BENEFITS OF COMPONENTWARE

Reuse

The ability to reuse existing prebuilt and pretested components provides a variety of benefits. Through reuse, a single development effort can be leveraged across applications, functional areas within a corporation, or even across corporations. Complex business logic or technical features can be developed once and shared across applications, ensuring uniform application of business rules in the enterprise. By reducing the amount of new code that needs to be developed for each application, code can be more robust and feature-rich. The benefits of component reuse can be seen on a smaller scale by looking at the controls (.VBX and .OCX) available today. By purchasing, and reusing, off-the-shelf ActiveX components, developers are able to add significant functionality to their applications with little additional effort.

Division of Labor

Componentware also allows division of labor among developers. Components are created by more experienced developers (i.e., either third-party companies or an in-house reuse team), applications are designed by experienced architects, and then built by lesser experienced component assemblers. These assemblers are therefore shielded from the intricacies of component development, and instead can focus on the tasks of finding components and integrating them together with higher-level tools. As a result, fewer areas of expertise and a reduced technical skill set are required from developers. For example, a novice developer today can build a custom Web browser out of an HTML control and a few lines of code.

Evolution of Systems

In addition, componentware provides a method for developing applications that can be easily evolved over time. Because most code changes can be performed behind public component interfaces, they are much less likely to affect other parts of the system. Functionality in large and complex systems is isolated into various components that can be individually modified; no longer is it necessary to search through the entire application to find all of the code related to a single business function.

CHALLENGES OF COMPONENTWARE IMPLEMENTATION

Interoperability

Interoperability includes two major facets: the ability for components from a variety of sources to coexist in a single solution and the ability to substitute one vendor's components for those of another. Specific requirements for interoperability include:

- *Common interface across vendors' components.* Similar components from different vendors, such as grid controls and customer objects, must have common interfaces so one can be substituted for another; standards groups have begun work on this field, but it is still unclear if these standards will be widely accepted.
- *Language independence.* The interfaces between components must not be dependent on the languages in which they were written.
- *Platform independence.* Components on differing platforms must be able to communicate with each other, without needing to include custom data type translation code into the components themselves.
- *Communications infrastructure.* Components must be able to communicate across machines without the inclusion of communications-specific code in the components.

- *Location independence.* Services must be available that can be used to provide location-independent component communications.
- *Glue language specifications.* A standard set of interface constructs is required that can be used to "glue together" components from various vendors.

Many of these challenges have been met within the CORBA and COM standards. However, the resulting products have yet to reach maturity, such as distributed computing with OLE, and CORBA under the Windows platform.

Configuration Management

As systems move from single-vendor monolithic applications to multi-vendor component-based solutions, configuration management will become an ever greater challenge. Originally, with single-vendor applications, configuration was straightforward: Systems were installed according to the vendor's specifications and had little interaction with other software on the same machine. Licensing was equally simple, with licenses paid according to a single vendor's terms. However, the component-based model introduces a series of challenges that are only beginning to be addressed in the market:

- *Packaging and delivery.* Traditional shrink-wrapped software packaging for monolithic applications will be replaced by electronic distribution of software; this will also spur the development of new payment and licensing techniques.
- *Licensing.* As solutions become conglomerates made up of many components, traditional licensing techniques will not always apply; the use of one-time unlimited-use payments will increase, as well as new schemes, such as pay-per-use micropayments (i.e., the transfer of a very small amount of money, such as .01 cents, via an infrastructure that efficiently supports such small transactions).
- *Component repositories.* Software developers must have electronic warehouses where components can be stored along with a record of their distinguishing attributes, such as descriptions, interface definitions, and version numbers. These repositories must be extremely easy to navigate, or developers will not use them.
- *Versioning.* When a single component is used by several applications, versioning becomes significantly more complex (as can be seen in the case of DLLs in Microsoft Windows). Advanced versioning software, including system support for versioning, will be required.

Market Segment/Maturity

Although growth is expected in the componentware market, there currently are few commercially available business components. Now that the technical hurdles have been crossed, the following issues need to be addressed by the market before business components will see widespread acceptance:

- *Business case and economic model.* The benefits of components must be that they are more cost-effective than traditional development.
- *Defined business domain.* Specific business domains where components can have the greatest impact need to be identified and well-defined; this is likely to emerge first in strong vertical markets, such as health care.
- *Domain compatibility across vendors.* As different vendors begin to make business components available, the existence of standardized functional domains will allow for plug-and-play component substitution.
- *Market momentum.* The component market needs to gain momentum through the entrance of several larger vendors, as well as high-profile success stories.
- *Strategic assets.* Corporations will need to decide which components are indeed generic, such as customer components, and which are strategic to their business, such as an insurance pricing engine.
- *Intellectual property rights.* As components are embedded in larger components and systems, royalties or other methods of protecting intellectual property will need to be constructed.

Discovery and Acquisition

Real-world experience has shown that a significant problem with component reuse is discovery and acquisition. With today's rudimentary discovery tools, once repositories grow to contain thousands of components, they are no longer navigable, and developers resort to re-coding functionality already implemented in existing components.

As software engineering moves toward component-based solutions, an even larger part of the engineering process will be that of component discovery and acquisition. This will involve searching through electronic components catalogs, both internal and external to the corporation, to identify the components that best fit the requirements of the development project. This can be aided by storing metadata for each component which can then be used for both design- and run-time negotiation.

The increasing popularity of the Internet, specifically the World Wide Web, has made the location task somewhat easier; however, component search technologies are still in their infancy. Current component sales venues include:

- *The World Wide Web.* Various component consortium homepages.
- *Direct from vendors.* Through catalogs or other informational materials.

- *From component brokers.* Potential future services which match component requirements with commercially available components.
- *Catalogs or magazines for component languages.* These *include Visual Basic Programmer's Journal* and the *Programmer's Paradise Catalog.*

Robust Technical Infrastructure

To enable the rapid construction of nontrivial applications using components, the underlying infrastructure must provide features over and above those available in today's tools. These additional features include:

- *Transactional integrity across components.* These are especially important in distributed component environments, where it is necessary to be able to perform a single transaction across multiple components and rollback partial changes in the case of an error.
- *Cross-component trace tools.* These provide for tracing application execution across components regardless of original development language, process boundaries, or location in the network.
- *Scalability and performance.* These allow smaller solutions to be grown into larger environments while still retaining good response times.
- *Load balancing with failover.* These provide the ability to deploy a class of components on multiple servers for high-throughput transaction processing.

TARGET APPLICATIONS FOR COMPONENTWARE

Because the construction of applications using commercially available components is relatively new, there is not yet a lot of experience with these technologies. An exception to this is the recent proliferation of OCXs under Microsoft Windows. However, a few types of applications have been identified as well-suited to the use of component technologies:

- *Highly graphical.* Programmers can use construction components, such as grid controls and specialized drop-down list boxes, to reduce the amount of time required to design graphical, highly interactive interfaces.
- *Rapid development.* These tools are prevalent in fields in which the underlying business model is stable, allowing reuse of well-defined business components, but applications evolve quickly; for example, the banking industry, as new offerings are created.
- *Throwaway.* This type of tool is useful when the business model is stable, but applications are built for single-use or limited-time use, for example, a promotional feature added by the carrier to a cellular line.
- *Multi-mode deployment.* These are applications that are to be deployed across multiple user interfaces, but where the core logic is

the same; for example, a loan approval application which is deployed internally via a Visual Basic client, and externally via a World Wide Web site.

- *Migration of legacy applications.* These are solutions that partition pieces of the solution into components which "wrap" legacy systems; components separate the interface from the implementation, providing for rehosting of the components to a new OS or language.
- *Volatile business applications.* These encapsulate application variability so that changes to the implementation (reflecting variability in the business models) are hidden from other components.

CASE STUDY: ABC SHIPPING COMPANY

ABC Shipping Co. wanted to build a shrink-wrapped application that allows customers to print out custom shipping labels on their premises. A review of their current custom applications showed that these applications:

- Shared a common core of features that made up at least 50 percent of the functionality for each application.
- Shared very little code.
- Were written using a variety of tools.

A 10-person team used object-oriented techniques to create small-grained business objects, such as shipment, receiver, and invoice, as well as construction objects, such as transaction and print handler. These were then built as OLE Automation objects using Visual C++, and assembled into an application using Visual C++ and Visual Basic.

Using OLE allows the company to reuse and extend these components for other systems. The business case here included several example scenarios. For example, the company could re-deploy the application on the Internet, using any Internet tool which supports OLE protocols. Alternatively, the company could extend the components for enterprise-wide reuse. The business case cited the sample work involved to reuse the components in a shipment notification system.

SUMMARY

Companies today must begin by gaining a better understanding of the consumer side of component-based software engineering, and the market surrounding it, including the following steps:

- *Performing an ongoing technology investigation.* Companies should continue investigating the use of OLE as a foundation for desktop integration of construction and business components into working systems.
- *Identifying leading projects for componentware.* Companies should identify key projects that are candidates for building systems using a

producer/consumer model, using technologies such as OLE, ActiveX, or CORBA.

- *Monitoring component marketplace.*   Companies should identify new trends, such as expanded offerings of business components, monitor known component vendors, and watch for new entrants in the component marketplace.

Chapter IV-2
Collaborative Computing Solutions

This chapter builds on the netcentric architecture concepts and framework by discussing the issues and future scenarios associated with collaborative computing solutions.

Collaboration focuses on supporting the nondeterministic, interpersonal, people aspects of complex business processes. Such aspects typically deal with highly unstructured and incomplete information, and the often random, spontaneous nature of people. This is in stark contrast to traditional information technology (IT) systems, which assume that all data and processes are definable and orderly. Because of their training in the structured, linear analysis of building these traditional transactional systems, many IT professionals are ill-equipped to understand the dynamics of collaborative applications development and deployment.

Many people believe that the future belongs to flat, nonhierarchic, marketlike, flexible enterprises that enable autonomous knowledge workers to instantly form flexible teams to conduct business processes, respond to opportunities, and solve problems. Such enterprises have several decisive advantages over the traditional hierarchical command-and-control organizations: efficiency, flexibility, agility, and price.

However, these new organizations have much greater needs for collaborative interactions. When interaction is expensive, it is cheaper to move information through an organization via a hierarchy. When interaction is inexpensive, the hierarchy loses this advantage. Therefore, if information technology can enable interactions to be made inexpensively and flexibly, an organization can operate in a more effective fashion without the overhead of a large hierarchy. Collaborative solutions can enable an organization to reap the benefits of flattening without increasing costs.

AN EXAMPLE FROM THE PHARMACEUTICAL INDUSTRY

One of the strategic imperatives of a pharmaceutical company is to bring new drug products to market quickly and continually. The new-drug development process is highly complex and can take literally dozens of years.

Conversely, reducing a single month from this process and introducing a product to market more quickly can mean millions of dollars in added revenue.

There are several outside entities with which a pharmaceutical company must interact constantly to bring a new drug to market, particularly government agencies. In the US, the Food and Drug Administration (FDA) is responsible for approval of new drugs and is intimately involved with the entire drug-approval process. The FDA review team itself consists of a wide variety of specialists, each with his or her own particular technical expertise: chemists, pharmacologists, physicians, pharmacokineticists, statisticians, and microbiologists. In addition, numerous clinical trial research companies are also heavily involved with the pharmaceutical company and the FDA throughout the process. A pharmaceutical company is thus dependent upon people outside of the organization, as well as on a variety of disciplines inside the organization (i.e., research, production, finance, and sales), to create new drug ideas and streamline the drug-approval process. The effective and efficient sharing of experiences and knowledge among all of these entities is what leads to new products and reduced time to market.

COLLABORATION DEFINITIONS AND FRAMEWORKS

Despite the growing importance of technology-enabled collaboration, the information technology community has paid insufficient attention to it. This is partly because collaborative activities, being primarily unstructured and nondeterministic in nature, are so very different from the classic, precise, if-then-else character of information technology solutions. Now that the need to enable collaborative activities has been more clearly identified, it is still the unstructured nature of collaboration that causes it to be overlooked by the IT community. After all, how can something so unstructured and nondeterministic be a candidate for improved effectiveness?

A collaborative activity has a single focus of attention and produces a well-defined output, even though the activities leading up to the deliverable are not predictable nor well defined. This focus on the deliverable distinguishes collaborative activities from other social and professional interactions, and the focus on unstructured activities distinguishes them from procedural workflow. In workflow, the mutual influence and interactivity of workers on each other is often minimized by the existence of well-defined and compartmentalized tasks. In a "pure" workflow system, the input/output relationship is dominant and, in a sense, the goal is to eliminate mutual influence by perfectly streamlining the process and thus eliminating any need for flexible and thus unpredictable, uncontrollable human interaction. In reality, workflow alone is a poor model for the majority of business processes that involve teams of knowledge workers.

One way to begin to understand how to enable more effective collaboration is to understand the nature of a particular type of collaborative activity. Collaboration covers a very wide area, and it is necessary to further refine different collaborative scenarios if it is to be seen how technology might be applied to improve the overall effectiveness of a given scenario.

Dimensions of Collaboration

Collaborative interactions can be classified based a number of related dimensions:

Size. The size of the group has a significant impact on collaborative processes. What is possible in a small group can be impossible in a large community. Not much can be achieved in a meeting with a thousand people except a speech and a round of voting.

Location. Collaboration has typically been accomplished through in-person meetings in which all participants are located in the same physical location. However, technology is increasingly being used to facilitate collaborative interactions among individuals who are not co-located.

Impression. Media used for collaborative activities have different levels of impression. Video gives the highest level of impression, whereas audio and text have successively lower levels of impression.

Interactivity. Different collaboration scenarios exhibit different levels of interactivity or intensity. For example, a collaborative session to initially engage someone in a subject or discussion requires a lower level of interactivity, whereas a session to persuade or solve a problem requires a very high level of interactivity.

Anonymity. In a typical meeting, when a person speaks, everyone knows who that person is, so all comments are attributed. However, in military organizations and other highly hierarchical rank-conscious structures, this attribution may restrict freedom of response; everyone may line up behind the highest-ranking member of the group. Such situations may call for technologies that allow for anonymous contribution from participants in a collaborative exercise.

Several factors greatly influence collaborative activities. This chapter focuses on collaborative situations that are remote and attributed, supporting a group size between two and ten. This leaves the dimensions of impression and interactivity for segmenting the different types of collaborative support, as depicted in Exhibit 1.

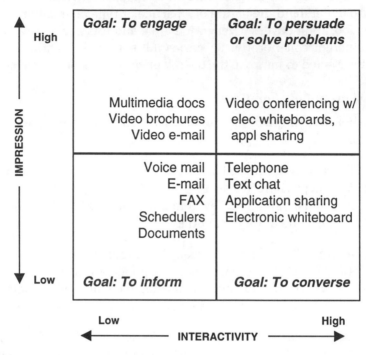

Exhibit 1.   Interactivity and impression matrix for collaborative support.

Collaboration Technologies

Using Exhibit 1, this section describes different types of collaborative tools by starting with the goal of the collaboration.

Quadrant 1: To Inform. Quadrant 1 represents a collaborative situation that is both low impression and low interactivity. Quadrant 1 tools are useful for routine asynchronous collaboration, in which the context of the information being exchanged is well understood. Situations include question and answer, status, and review of work. Technologies include voice mail, E-mail, fax, schedulers, and document repositories.

Quadrant 2: To Converse. Quadrant 2 covers collaborative activities that are low impression and high interactivity. Quadrant 2 tools are effective when the people collaborating are familiar with each other and already have a working relationship or when the purpose and goals of the collaboration are clear to all parties. Situations include revising a process flow, discussing an installation plan or monitoring progress in real time. Technologies include the telephone, text chat, application sharing, and electronic whiteboards.

Quadrant 3: To Engage. This covers collaborations that exhibit high impression and low interactivity. Quadrant 3 tools are useful when a rich communications medium is needed to convey the information, but the information is static or can be shared asynchronously. Situations include annotating documents, explaining a concept or product, giving presentations, or conducting training. Technologies include multimedia documents, video brochures, and video E-mail.

Quadrant 4: To Persuade or Solve Problems. Quadrant 4 covers situations that call for both high interactivity and high presence, those that simulate face-to-face meetings. This is needed when the content of the meeting is dynamic and subject to change during the meeting, forcing people to make quick adjustments. Situations include early stages of a project when people do not know each other, as in design work and project planning. Technologies in this quadrant include video conferencing in conjunction with real-time collaborative tools, such as electronic whiteboards and application sharing.

Collaboration Approach

A generalized approach for collaborative activities can be used regardless of the type of collaborative scenario outlined above. This approach starts with a simple observation that many collaborative activities consist of three steps:

- Generating ideas for what to do.
- Reaching consensus on what to do by identifying and resolving potential issues.
- Planning and executing coordinated actions.

One example is the process of requirements definition for a system development project. There are many approaches to this process, JAD (joint applications development) being one of the most popular. The first step in JAD is to make sure that nothing relevant is forgotten, that all ideas for requirements are considered. To achieve this, all constituencies potentially affected by the contemplated system are asked to send a representative to the JAD session. In a brainstorming session, the participants generate, discuss, and rank the initial set of requirements according to priority. Representatives of various constituencies raise potential issues with the proposed requirements. These may include dependencies, constraints, and outright contradictions. The group negotiates and resolves the issues. Once the synergy is achieved, the group divides the work of creating the requirements document. Because different parts of the document depend on each other, the group decides how the work should be coordinated. This may include status meetings, draft reviews, etc. Finally, the group executes the plan and produces the requirements document.

In reality, the above process is rarely linear. Teams may go through several rounds of brainstorming and raising issues before converging on a plan of action. Even after the requirements document is created, groups may go back to the issues step to make sure that nothing was overlooked.

These steps are not limited to requirements definition but are common to many team activities. In addition, when these steps are not all made explicit — when teams skip some of the steps — breakdowns, mis-coordination, and floundering begin. For example, when the group skips issue raising, it may fail to achieve synergy and leave hidden contradictions unresolved, only to discover them too late during the execution stage.

IDEAS, ISSUES, AND COORDINATED ACTIONS

This section presents a formal model of collaboration called IICA (ideas, issues, coordinated actions), which follows the belief that collaborative team activities in business can be modeled as a combination of a few elementary actions. Understanding the elements and how they combine to form collaborative activities helps in the understanding of support and the improvement of current forms of collaborative work, and possibly to devise new forms.

The three steps of the IICA model are depicted in Exhibit 2 as large circles. The following sections examine each of these elements in greater detail.

Exhibit 2.   The ICAA model.

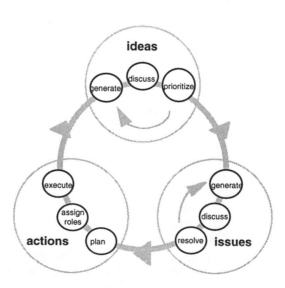

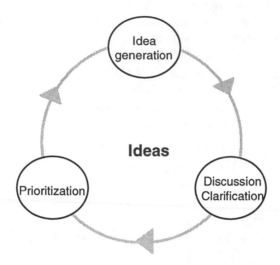

Exhibit 3.   The three steps of idea processing.

Ideas

When a team is facing a task such as design of a system or developing of a business plan, the first step is usually to establish a shared understanding of what needs to be done. Without such an understanding, individual members may misinterpret the task or, worse, they may pull in different directions or work at cross-purposes. Valuable approaches may remain unexplored. To build a shared understanding, meeting facilitators in a wide variety of situations often use a three-step process, as shown in Exhibit 3.

Step 1: Idea Generation. Traditionally, the idea-generation process has been conducted in face-to-face brainstorming meetings (i.e., co-located, same time, attributed). The participants take their turns proposing one idea at a time (i.e, sequentially). The facilitator often goes around the table asking for a contribution (i.e., mandatory participation). Depending on the size of the meeting, usually, there is time for two or three rounds of contributions. This approach to idea generation is beginning to change. Increasingly groups are taking advantage of electronic support systems, such as Ventana's Group System 5, to make their meetings more productive. Busy groups are using the online discussion facilities of products such as Lotus Notes to conduct brainstorming without bringing everyone into the same room. These new forms of collaboration use different modalities which have a significant effect on mutual influence and, ultimately, on collaboration results.

With the electronic support, the sequential mode of contributions can be replaced with the parallel mode. All participants can type their contributions into the electronic brainstorming system at the same time. This leads to an order of magnitude increase in the quantity of contributions. This is the good news. The bad news is that a great deal of mutual influence is lost in the process: In a sequential mode, participants tend to react to each other contributions, while in parallel mode, each participant is focusing on his or her contributions paying little attention to the others.

The result of parallel brainstorming, anonymous or otherwise, is very "dirty." In a traditional setting, when a participant makes an unclear contribution, the person taking notes would usually ask for clarification. In a parallel mode, this "instant" clarification does not take place. In addition, the parallel mode results in many similar ideas that need to be consolidated. This necessitates a much more extensive second step of the process: discussion and clarification.

Mutual influence is a powerful factor in idea generation. By limiting mutual influence during brainstorming, we tend to get a greater diversity of ideas. By increasing mutual influence, we tend to get a "denser" and deeper coverage of a narrower area. Experienced facilitators select from a variety of modes to achieve both diversity and density of ideas.

Step 2: Discussion. The second step of the idea process is important, even if the first step is skipped. For example, there are many situations when what needs to be done is well-known in advance. Even in these cases, the discussion may reveal critical misunderstandings that can affect the process later.

Step 3: Ranking According to Priority. The goal of the third step is to reach joint understanding and consensus on what is important. When a group skips this step, each member may rank the ideas differently. This can lead to a serious breakdown of the teamwork later. Although small groups can rank their ideas informally, larger groups need a more formal approach. There are several techniques for achieving this goal. Here are some of the most common:

- *Everyone orders all the items.* For each item we compute the sum of all positions assigned by each participant and divide it by the total number of participants. The list is then ordered according to the resulting weights.
- *Everyone selects five most important items.* Each item gets the number of points equal to the number of participants who selected this item.

- *Everyone is given 10 votes that they can distribute among the items.* For each item, the sum of all votes assigned by each participant is computed and the list is ordered accordingly.

Delphi is a well-known variation of the first technique in which the ranking is conducted in several rounds. After each round, participants can compare their ordering with the group ordering. In this way, the emerging group opinion influences individual participants and leads the group to a consensus if a consensus exists. This technique was developed at RAND Corporation during World War II and was considered so powerful as to be classified as a military secret.

Shared Knowledge. Mutual influence without shared knowledge is dangerous. It often leads to a battle of unsubstantiated opinions, guesswork, or the "follow the leader" syndrome. When a team member proposes an idea, it usually comes from one of the two sources:

- Packaged knowledge (e.g., text books and methodologies).
- Previous experience (e.g., cases).

Even very novel ideas usually have some relationship to prior experiences (e.g., modification or synthesis of prior cases). To help teams ground their discussion and stimulate their creativity, easy access must be made to the company's knowledge capital relevant to the present discussion. Electronic knowledge management systems can be of great help in this task. They can augment the individual experience of team members with the collective experience of the whole enterprise.

Issues

Once a team has determined what needs to be done, the process of synergism or consensus building is not finished. The team needs to examine the list for possible omissions, pitfalls, contradictions, incorrect assumptions, etc. This is done through the process called *issue resolution*. This process contains three steps, as illustrated in Exhibit 4.

Although small groups can go through this process informally, larger groups need a more systematic approach. The pitfalls of an inadequate approach to issue processing include missing an issue, endless discussion without a resolution, and a lack of "buy-in" by the team members. This section proposes a fairly formal approach to issue processing that contrasts sharply with some existing approaches.

Step 1: Issue Identification. During the first step, the participants are asked to raise issues with the proposed list of ideas. There is a fundamental difference between an issue at this step of the process and clarification

Exhibit 4. The three steps of issues processing.

requests during the idea discussion. The person who raises an issue has to specify three things:

- A problem statement.
- A set of alternatives for issue resolution.
- A procedure by which the resolution will be reached.

A prototypical example of an issue (as defined here) is the instructions a judge gives to a jury: "You have heard the arguments and now you must decide whether the accused is guilty of a first-degree murder, second-degree murder, manslaughter, or is not guilty. You will reach a decision by unanimous vote." These instructions refer to a problem statement, give a set of alternatives, and specify the resolution procedure, namely unanimous vote. In a business situation, an issue may be the choice of an operating system — the alternatives being Windows NT, OS/2, or UNIX — and a resolution procedure a majority vote.

Although this definition of an issue may seem a bit too formal, it has considerable advantages:

- The person who proposes an issue has to think it through so as to define a complete set of distinct positions that one might reasonably take on the proposed issue.
- The amount of "flaming" is reduced and the discussion focuses on the differences between the proposed positions.
- Team members spend less time talking to people with whom they are in agreement and more time talking to people with whom they disagree.

- The clearly specified resolution procedure encourages negotiations and compromise and discourages posturing.

This formal definition of an issue contrasts sharply with the treatment of issues in the Issue-Based Information Systems (IBIS) framework. In IBIS, issues are arbitrary statements on which people can take positions, which are also defined as free-form statements. Positions can be either supported or refuted by arguments. In this free-form definition, positions are not forced to be distinct and represent a set of alternatives, and resolution procedures are not specified. In lieu of a more formal definition of issues and positions, the IBIS framework can still be useful in documenting issues, their discussion, and resolution. The best-known implementation of IBIS is MCC's gIBIS system and its commercial successor CM/1 from Corporate Memory Systems.

Step 2: Discussion & Negotiations. During the position-taking and discussion phase, participants take positions on the issues and try to influence participants who take different positions. There may be several reasons why two people take different positions on an issue. Different types of disagreements require different approaches to their resolution. Inappropriate approaches to disagreement resolution can lead teams to conflict and loss of trust and productivity. This section proposes a procedure for the analysis and resolution of several common disagreements.

When two people take different positions on an issue, the first thing that needs to be established is whether there is a disagreement at all. People may simply interpret the issue differently or assign different meanings to the terminology, or they may use different value scales. For example, when the suitability of a particular manager to lead a project is considered and assessed on a 1-to-5 scale, some people may give that manager 3 points and some 4 points (5 being the best). The problem may be the use of different standards. Standards are set either by rules or by prior cases. Teams need to have easy access to the relevant rules in order to establish standards for position taking.

Sometimes the normalization of standards is not sufficient to resolve an issue; there may be a genuine disagreement. What often helps in these cases is to try to isolate specific areas of disagreement. To continue the above example, the team may list the qualifying criteria for the job and then treat them as separate sub-issues. Everyone may agree that the manager in question has good technical skills but disagree on the extent of his supervisory experience. This process of issue decomposition should continue until the parties have a clear and precise understanding of their disagreement. Here again, access to precedents and specific cases can greatly facilitate issue resolution.

Finally, an apparent disagreement may mask other problems, such as insufficient information to resolve the issue. Some members may consider themselves unqualified, or the team may lack interest in the issue itself and treat it as unimportant. It is important to identify these problems during the discussion phase. An issue resolution system developed at Andersen Consulting's Center for Strategic Technology Research (CSTaR), called "OMNI," addressed this problem by asking the participants to indicate the importance they attributed to the issue (low, medium, high), and the degree of their confidence in the position they were taking (low, medium, high). Low confidence for highly important issues usually indicated the need for further investigation. The confidence and importance indicators help team members identify good candidates for persuasion and make the consensus building process more efficient.

Step 3: Resolution. A number of different resolution procedures are possible. Unanimous vote is one of them. Simple majority vote is another. Alternatively, a team leader may allocate a specified time limit for the discussion and then make a unilateral decision. Many other resolution procedures are possible. What is important is to have one.

Shared Knowledge. Previous cases and packaged knowledge are reliable sources of potential issues. For , internal investment, for example, many issues that need to be examined in this context are known in advance: return on investment, alternatives, and available resources may be a problem. In fact, the whole process of due diligence is designed to uncover all the important issues of a proposed investment. Teams can use these knowledge sources to ensure efficiency and completeness in issue-raising.

As previously discussed, it is critical that people support their positions by pointing to specific prior cases, policies, or best practices rather than engage in battles of opinions. Here again, electronic support can provide instant access to the relevant knowledge capital.

The two key results of the issue processing step are:

- A common understanding of the task and team consensus on what needs to be done.
- A list of dependencies between various parts of the task.

Both the consensus and the dependencies are critical during the next step: the action part of teamwork. The first of the above items is fairly obvious: When teams lose the common understanding of their task, the risk of failure is high. The second item is more subtle. Issue identification, discussion, and resolution help teams identify various dependencies among the proposed tasks which will generate the need for coordination. After all, if there is no dependency between tasks, there is no need for coordination during their execution. Many projects fail because some dependencies were not identified and provisions for the appropriate coordination were not made.

Actions

Once all important issues have been successfully resolved, it is time to act. This is done in three steps. First, it is necessary to plan the team's actions taking into considerations the dependencies discovered at the previous step. Second, specific actions need to be assigned to specific individuals and, third, these individuals need to carry them out in a coordinated fashion.

The key to successful team work at this stage is coordination, which this section defines as a relationship among actors, tasks, and objects. This relationship reflects dependencies among planned actions and represents a commitment by actors with respect to these dependencies.

The following are the five dependencies: goals and deliverables, sequencing and flow, constraints, shared resources, and synergy. The existing planning and project management techniques focus primarily on the first two types of dependencies. The other three dependencies often remain implicit in the work plans. These dependencies are coordinated primarily through mutual influence among the team members and need explicit representation in the team's plans, and teams need explicit mechanisms for dealing with them (Exhibit 5).

Exhibit 5. Coordinated action steps.

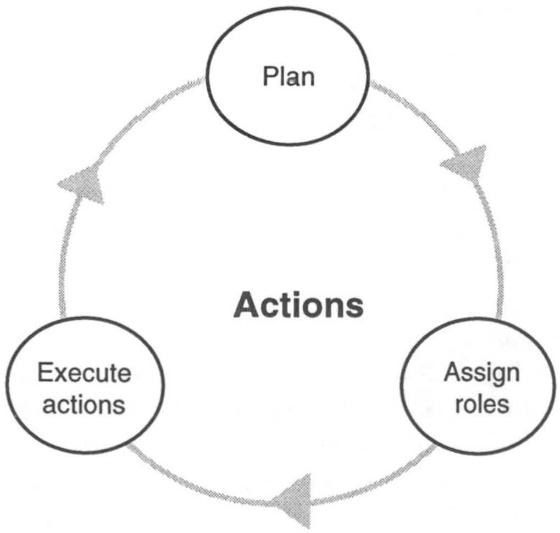

379

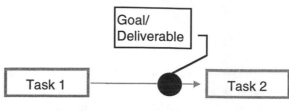

Exhibit 6. Goals and work flows.

Goals/Deliverables. One actor can commit to deliver to another actor a deliverable with certain characteristics. Usually, there is some form of handshake, during which Actor 1 announces the delivery of the product and Actor 2 acknowledges that the product is satisfactory and that it has been delivered. This dependency is illustrated in Exhibit 6.

Sequencing/Flow. This is the traditional work flow. Task 2 cannot start until Task 1 is completed. For example, a company may not want to initiate the shipment of goods until the payment is received.

The traditional treatment of workflow and project management is usually limited to goals and sequencing of tasks. The following three types of dependencies are just as critical.

Constraints. Constraints on money, time, space, and form create the need for coordination. For example, there may be only a limited amount of money and time allocated to a combination of tasks. Team members may also be constrained to a certain form of deliverables (Exhibit 7).

Resource Sharing. Several actors may be sharing the same piece of equipment or access to the same knowledge source. The shared resources need to be scheduled and may be subject to various constraints.

Synergy. This is the most important factor, as well as the least appreciated form of coordination. When team members begin to execute their assignments and confront real world problems they may develop divergent ideas about the problem and its solution. This is a frequent cause of failure of team work. It is extremely important for the whole team to maintain shared understanding of the problem. To achieve this, teams have to set up explicit mechanisms to keep the team members informed about their actions, the information they gain during these actions, and of any changes in their understanding of the task. Synergy is usually maintained through status meetings (Exhibit 8).

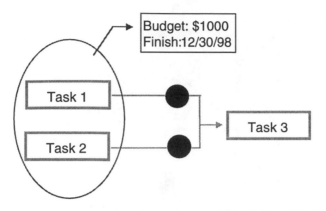

Exhibit 7. Constraints.

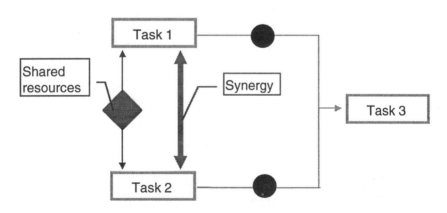

Exhibit 8.   Shared resource and synergy maintenance.

For example, a team consisting of a manager, Sue, and two assistants, Jim and Bob, is doing a study. The study is for a client located out of town, and requires frequent interaction with client personnel. The plan is to send Jim and Bob to the client's location, while Sue continues her usual hectic travel schedule supervising several projects.

Jim's first task is to get additional client information, while Bob is getting information from the relevant vendors. It is critical that Jim and Bob keep each other informed while pursuing their separate tasks, because many of the questions Bob ask vendors depend on what Jim learns, and vice versa. In addition, during the first phase, Jim and Bob msut share one car and

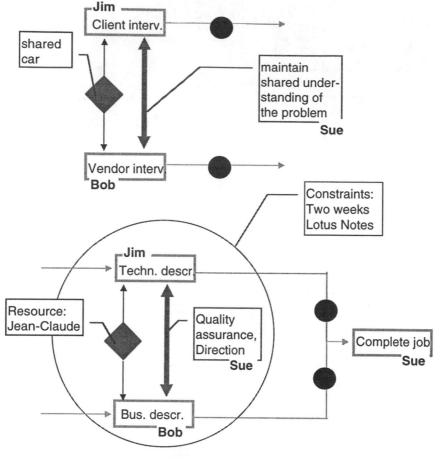

Exhibit 9.   Dependency/coordination links.

arrange their schedules accordingly. At the end of the first phase, both Jim and Bob are expected to produce reports on their findings (Exhibit 9).

During the second phase of the plan, Jim writes the technical part of the study, while Bob writes the business part. To enable and encourage information sharing, they use some specific groupware forms for their work in progress. Sue accesses these forms from the road and conducts status meetings. Jim and Bob communicate with Jean-Claude, who is a very busy technical specialist. They batch their questions together, so as not to bother this resource too often. Finally, in two weeks, Sue is supposed to receive the technical and business sections of the study from Jim and Bob and synthesize them for the final report. The notation makes a first step toward concisely and explicitly depicting the many complicated dependencies involved in coordinating the team's actions.

SUMMARY

The IICA approach for team collaboration attempts to provide an integrating approach to guide the analysis and design of team processes. It focuses on mutual influence, knowledge management, and coordination, and it proposes an explicit mechanism for their implementation. The approach bridges the two ends of collaboration: reaching consensus on what needs to be done and executing the agreed-upon actions in a coordinated manner. The missing link between the two ends is the systematic identification, discussion, and resolution of issues. This process reveals the hidden dependencies among the proposed actions; coordination manages these dependencies. The IICA model consists of nine steps:

- Ideas
  - Idea generation
  - Idea discussion and clarification
  - Idea ranking according to priority
- Issues
  - Issue identification and generation
  - Issue discussion
  - Issue resolution and dependencies identification
- Actions
  - Action planning
  - Role assignment
  - Coordinated execution of actions

This approach can be useful for different collaborative processes, and can help set the stage and define requirements for the increasingly large numbers of collaborative tools and technologies that are emerging in the industry.

Chapter IV-3
Data Mining

Organizations have been accumulating large amounts of data through their transaction systems for the last two decades. Although this data has a great deal of potential value, organizations have lacked the resources and the ability to process it to recover that value. Most of the time, the data has simply languished in dusty archives until lawyers or regulators pronounced the data safe to purge.

New tools and techniques, called data mining, are allowing organizations to sift through their data archives to find previously undiscovered "golden nuggets." In fact, the ultimate goal is to find more than just nuggets: It is to tap into a mother-lode of knowledge that can help an organization understand its customers, markets, and business better. One of the key distinguishing features of data mining is the high degree of automation involved in discovering hidden relationships and patterns existing in data.

Although enterprises from any industry sector can take advantage of advanced techniques in data mining, many early adopters have been organizations in the retail, finance, and health care industries. A few success stories also can be found in insurance, chemical, petroleum, manufacturing, security, aerospace, transportation, and the environmental industry sectors.

Data mining is becoming attractive to business organizations because it can provide a competitive edge. It is now gaining more momentum because of the availability of tools such as neural networks and massively parallel processors, which provide large computing power at relatively lower cost.

This chapter describes data mining concepts, discusses a framework for understanding data mining, and explores specific tools and techniques.

WHAT IS DATA MINING?

Data mining is the process of extracting valid and understandable, but previously unknown, information from large data stores in a format that supports making useful business decisions. Mining makes sense out of huge data stores by unveiling implicit relationships, trends, patterns, exceptions, and anomalies that were previously transparent to human analysts. Data mining begins by organizing and storing data in an appropriate fashion.

It then sifts through this large data volume using pattern recognition algorithms, as well as statistical and mathematical techniques.

The process is data-driven, an extraction and presentation of data and information to a knowledgeable user for review and examination. Even though the process is data driven, users play an important and essential role. Ultimately, only they can decide if the information is interesting, relevant to the business, and useful to the organization. So data mining requires substantial human effort and interaction throughout the process.

BENEFITS OF DATA MINING

Data mining enables organizations to leverage data stores for strategic advantage. For decades, corporations have been storing enormous amounts of data about customers, sales, finances, inventories, and operations. These data stores are primarily designed to streamline and facilitate day-to-day operations. During the last 15 to 20 years, these data stores have reached varying levels of maturity; in some cases, they are quite robust and stable. A number of organizations are in the process of transforming this data, ensuring its accuracy, and making it available to the business analyst for strategic information processing by implementing an information delivery facility (i.e., a data warehouse).

When organizations reach the level of sophistication at which they view data as an asset and make it available for business analysis purposes, they have yet another opportunity to leverage it for additional strategic advantages. From this realization, the leading-edge technology exploiters are putting data to a secondary use, over and above the traditional information delivery facility, for untapped knowledge.

With data mining tools, organizations can comb through their data looking for patterns and relationships that predict customers' buying behaviors, that identify consumers likely to default on loans or perpetrate fraud, or that anticipate unusual demands on inventory. Business analysts can use this information to develop strategies to increase return on investment, minimize risks, and adjust inventory levels.

EXAMPLES OF DATA MINING

Data mining techniques find applications in almost all industries, including insurance, finance, manufacturing, health, and environmental science. There are many examples where data mining can yield useful patterns that can be applied beneficially for business.

It could be argued that these applications could be implemented with traditional methods without the use of data mining tools. Perhaps, but it is unlikely. Data mining brings to bear new techniques of analysis. An analyst following hypothesis-driven methods are unlikely to find the patterns turned up by data mining, as shown in the following examples.

The Supermarket and Retailing Industries

The ability to know customers as individuals, rather than as members of a faceless mass, allows organizations to alter their business practices to serve customers better and increase profits. With adequate knowledge about customers, stores can redesign layout, pricing, and promotions to increase margins and at the same time make the shopper's trip more enjoyable and efficient. By building the customer's loyalty, a company can avoid competing on price alone.

Knowledge about the shopper and about the shopper's purchases — the market basket makeup — affects strategy and operations at various levels. At one end of the spectrum, it permits serving the customer as an individual; at the other end, it allows for development of marketing strategies for a group of stores in a region. In between, it helps in designing efficient store layouts and making profitable operational decisions.

Thousands of market baskets are checked out each day at a supermarket or retail store. Almost all stores collect point-of-sale information, and they generally summarize and use that information for inventory planning and accounting purposes. However, the use of data mining techniques such as neural networks or inductive reasoning on the market baskets can discover some surprising information.

Such tools may categorize baskets into 20 to 25 types, such as staple stock-up, vegetable and fruits, Mexican food, bread and milk, snacks and soda. Each basket type represents the needs and wants of a shopper and the profitability of the basket. Knowing this information, store layout can be improved to make the shopping experience more efficient, pleasant, and profitable. The mix and profitability of the individual items in a market basket type can lead to some very creative and profitable promotions and price adjustments.

For example, at one chain, analysis revealed that the market baskets characterized as "cosmetic" also contained greeting cards 28 percent of the time. The retail chain is redesigning the stores to capitalize on this knowledge. In the example cited earlier, potato chip purchases were accompanied by a soda purchase in half the cases. That figure increases to 75 percent when accompanied by a marketing promotion. This association can be used to adjust promotion or pricing.

If the store has a customer name or identification associated with the individual market basket, opportunities exist for a higher level of targeting or customizing. Now, the store operator can see what a specific customer or perhaps household is like. What is the pattern of the purchase behavior and its impact on profitability? With an answer to this question comes an opportunity for cross selling and target marketing.

Another example is the customer who buys a sleeping bag and a backpack; he or she will also buy a camping tent in the following two months in 65 percent of the cases. This information can be used to target a customer either for an earlier purchase or to ensure that the purchase is made at the same store.

Finally, by combining the market baskets, groups of stores can be supplied with an optimal mix of goods for maximizing profitability as compared to the intuitive stocking of the shelves based on zip code demographics and unproved hypotheses.

The Airline Industry

In the highly competitive airline market, data mining tools can be used on data from reservations, travel, ticketing, and operations to discover patterns, relationships, or associations to improve a number of important factors ranging from customer satisfaction to flight yield management.

Fliers can be grouped and classified into categories, and appropriate frequent flier program features can be developed for the various groups to maintain the fliers' loyalty and improve the margins. New marketing channels can be developed to increase the market share. Target marketing to a highly profitable segment — for example, the business traveler — can be performed. In addition, hospitality and other travel linkages can be developed based on the various grouping of the travelers.

Product value can be enhanced or differentiated by understanding the behavior of a group of fliers. The number of business class seats or flight departure times may be adjusted. Finally, based on the passenger boarding patterns and the distribution patterns at hubs, flight yield management can be positively affected.

One might argue that the benefits described above can be achieved without performing data mining. The argument is valid to some extent. However, data mining contributes by offering a more precise and automatic grouping of the fliers which might not otherwise be possible. Manual grouping may mask the behavior of important fliers who are few in number but contribute significantly to the profitability of the airline. The data mining techniques can identify such small groups which can be easily missed with manual or intuitive groupings.

The Banking Industry

Data mining can benefit several areas in the banking and financial services markets with applications varying from one-to-one marketing to branch profitability to predicting stock and bond prices based on the rules determined from the historical trading patterns. Such patterns may not be intuitively obvious because of the massive amount of data. Of all the applications, those associated with credit card operations have received most attention.

Grouping credit card holders into different categories based on their spending and payment histories is the basis for several business strategies. Predicting future behaviors of the existing and new card holders using pattern-based groupings can significantly help in this business where the customer base is essentially flat and the gain of a new card holder is at the cost of another company. Classifying a card holder according to one of the following categories can lead to some precise and cost-effective target marketing:

- *Attriters.* These are customers who are likely to be lost to competitors because of their marketing programs. In the US, where the credit card business is now a zero-sum game, companies typically lose 1 percent to 10 percent of their customers to competitors.
- *Revolvers.* These are typically the best customers who do not default on payment, yet keep high revolving balances and are not constantly shopping for the lowest interest rates.
- *Transactors.* These customers neither keep balances nor pay interests. They pay their monthly balance on time but generate fees through transactions.

Finding and acquiring the lucrative customers from hundreds of millions of potential consumers is expensive. Keeping the existing customers is relatively less expensive. Data mining techniques have been particularly effective in target marketing to both existing and potential customers.

Exhibit 1 illustrates how an effective target marketing program can cut down on the cost of mailing, while generating almost the same response (i.e., revenue) from the customers.

Bourgoin discusses how such techniques have been used by a company to increase their ROI by effective target marketing (Mario O. Bourgoin and Stephen J. Smith, "Big Data — Better Returns," in *Artificial Intelligence in the Capital Markets*, Probus Publishing, 1995). Their experience indicates that because of "attriters," the company had to acquire at least 7 percent more clients each year just to maintain status quo.

The available data on customers in this case was large both in the number of customer records (in the millions of records) and in the number of

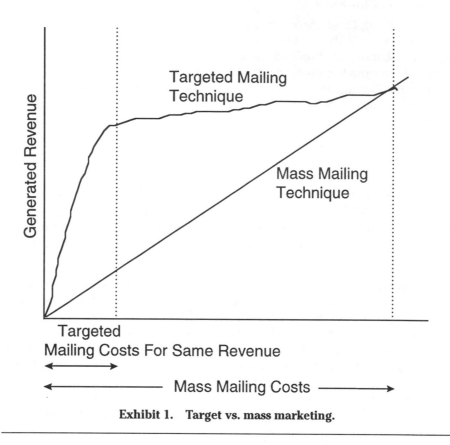

Exhibit 1. Target vs. mass marketing.

fields maintained for each customer (approximately 500). Much of the data was hidden and could not be used by older technologies such as queries, statistical analysis, and expensive computers. The data was hidden not because the company was unaware of their existence, but because the older technologies could not build models that were complex enough to draw information from hundreds of fields, and process the same for millions of customers. So only a small fraction of fields were used. Even if all the fields could have been used, processing all the records in a reasonable amount of time would have been impossible. This unused and hidden information is often what is required to effectively decipher fact from artifact: what traits and patterns really matter and can be used to predict customer behavior and which ones are the idiosyncrasies of the data used for analysis.

The company issuing the credit cards was able to use the new data mining techniques to identify those customers that it could keep most cost effectively. Data analysts were able to find associations they never before realized existed in their customer data because many important fields had previously been ignored. These new patterns pointed out relationships that they could depend on for more precise target marketing.

FRAUD DETECTION USING DATA MINING

Fraud detection via data mining techniques has found applicability across several industries. An example from an automobile manufacturing and distribution company illustrates the concept.

One large company has a network of dealers throughout the U.S. and overseas. Claims for the warranty work performed by the dealers is submitted to the company, which reimburses them promptly. The company has a small team of auditors who manually ensure, after the payment, that the claims are justified. The auditing process is very time consuming; therefore, less than 10 percent of the claims are actually audited. Because only a small number of claims are audited, a real understanding of the extent and type of unjustified claims is not possible. Claims are unjustified if they are invalid (e.g., if too many parts are used or if there is excessive labor time) or if the claim is fraudulent (e.g., identical warranty claims are made for the same vehicle identification number).

In this area, the company's business objectives included:

- A reduction in payment for warranty claims.
- A reduction in time for selecting claims for review.
- An increase in the probability of identifying dealers/claims in need of auditing/investigating.
- A change in dealer behavior.

Several data mining techniques were considered, and a tool based on inductive reasoning was selected and used to discover patterns in the warranty claim records. This technique not only classifies records based on patterns, but also indicates the reasons for their classification into a category.

The company expects to meet most of its objectives. An annual savings of about $3 million is expected. Additionally, the auditors have discovered some relationships between a dealer makeup and warranty claims that were previously unknown. For example, dealerships that possess a large number of used cars tend to submit more claims. The company was unable to find this relationship without using data mining techniques. The correlation is easily understood once the pattern has been identified. The dealers repair used cars under warranty, increase the value of the car, and sell it to the public at a higher price. Knowing this, the company can alter the behavior by offering limited warranty on used cars. Another intangible benefit is uncovering the relationship between car usage and defects, which is being passed to the car designers.

INCREASING INTEREST IN DATA MINING

Why is data mining gaining more visibility now? One can take two perspectives on this question: business driving the technology, and technology enabling a new way of doing business.

Business is becoming more and more competitive every day, and the leading companies are looking for every tool that provides an extra edge. Data assets, when mined for new knowledge, provide that edge. The cases discussed in the previous section show the driving forces in the business world that require technology to step up and enable the solutions.

At the same time, data mining algorithms, such as inductive reasoning and artificial neural networks, are reaching a level of sophistication and maturity, where they can now be applied to discover data patterns for commercial applications, some of which can require large computational resources.

Coincidentally, after years of promising potential, parallel processing hardware technology has now reached a stage on the technology take-up curve in which is it commercially viable to deploy it with the new data mining software algorithms. (Parallel processing is not required in all data mining solutions.) This combination of parallel processing hardware technology and data mining software algorithms is now poised to enable businesses to uncover the hidden value in their data.

At the same time, the emphasis on the information delivery facility (i.e., data warehousing) applications have helped data mining in two ways:

- Information delivery facilities have raised the awareness of the value of the data asset. Businesses want to deploy data assets as a competitive advantage.
- Some of the implementation steps required for information delivery facilities and data mining are common. Gathering of the data for mining requires understanding its sources, currency, accuracy, cleansing, extraction, and reformatting. These steps are also part of the processes involved in the information delivery facility, which has been a catalyst in the development of tools and skills for data preparation. An information delivery facility is not a prerequisite for data mining, but it can facilitate it by making reliable data available more quickly for mining purposes.

DATA MINING AND THE STRATEGIC INFORMATION PROCESSING MATRIX

Data mining is part of an organization's overall strategic analytical information processing, in which data-driven discovery of patterns is paramount.

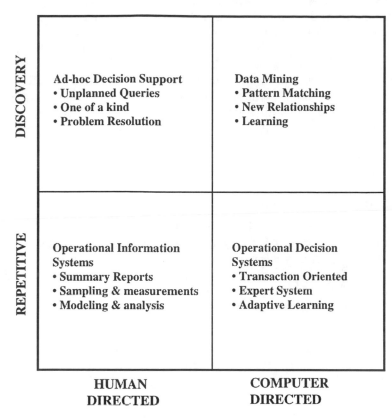

Exhibit 2. Strategic information processing matrix.

It can be distinguished from other strategic analytical processes by the type and the extent of automation and human interaction involved.

Exhibit 2 shows the strategic information processing matrix, which organizes types of systems and processes according to a number of criteria.

This chapter uses this matrix as a framework to organize the discussion of alternatives when attempting to use corporate data resource for strategic information processing. Alternatives along the y axis of the matrix are whether the process used is repetitive or discovery oriented. Repetitive processes are prescriptive in nature, and are generally parameters driven for execution on a regular basis to provide timely information. Discovery-oriented processes, on the other hand, are not repetitive. Here the data is examined by humans and computers to discover or reveal new information.

The x axis represents the level and style of automation — the manner in which humans and computers interact during the information processing. Of course, there is always both human and computer involvement. It is the style of involvement that is different. On the left side, in the human-directed arena, the user raises specific queries to solve a problem or to gather information. On the right side, in the computer-directed arena, the human involvement is that of observation and participation to ensure that the problem is relevant, the data is accurate, the tools are appropriate, and the solution is actionable.

The four quadrants discussed in the following sections are formed by the two-by-two matrix.

Quadrant 1: Operational Informational Systems

This represents work that is prescriptive in nature and that requires coding of queries or programs by a user with a specific report or solution in mind. Examples of such work include summary or detail reports produced on a regular basis for business measurement, analysis, modeling, and management. These reports are generated on a repetitive basis and are generally parameter driven. One obtains the information that has been pre-planned.

Canned queries are generally the basis for quadrant one work, including "What are the sales in New York?" and "Are the new products better received in urban or suburban markets?" Sophisticated multidimensional programs and tools may be used to generate queries and output displayed in attractive graphical reports. In such cases, these programs or tools become the proxy for humans for developing the actual query, but the paradigm remains the same.

Quadrant 2: Ad hoc Decision Support

This represents work that is discovery oriented. The queries are not repetitive or prescriptive in nature. A user codes these queries to find information in order to solve a specific problem. The queries are one-of-a-kind and not pre-planned. Although the work in quadrant two is very different from that in quadrant one, in one respect the work is very similar. In both cases, user-initiated queries are the basis for information processing. The computer is a facilitator, responding to the questions that the user already knows to ask.

In this quadrant, ad hoc queries are generally created to analyze a problem. For example, an organization's sales in a specific region during the last quarter did not meet the forecast. Queries may be developed to examine the sales by cities, comparing actual vs. forecast, revealing one particular city as the culprit. Additional queries may indicate that sales were very low in certain localities during one month. Further investigation may reveal that the cause was an aggressive sales campaign by a competitor. Strictly speaking, this style of processing, although discovery oriented and facilitated by automation, is not data mining.

Queries such as those issued within quadrant two return an answer set that satisfies the query predicates. Whatever new information is discovered either supports or nullifies the hypothesis that the analyst started with. The successive iterations of queries and the examination of the retrieved data is driven by the analyst based on his or her hypothesis. The iterations of the queries end when the hypothesis is either proven or rejected in the analyst's judgment. This is the essence of the user-created-hypothesis verification model.

From the analyst's viewpoint, new data facts are being discovered. The queries may be either user-generated or formulated by some query tool, which may have a point-and-click graphical user interface. Multidimensional products are examples of such tools that make it easier for the user to drill down into the data. However, these are still manifestations of the verification model.

Many vendors offer products to facilitate such analysis. They often call these verification model "data mining tools" to garner a share of this emerging new market and to benefit commercially from the increasing expenditure for data mining.

Quadrant 3: Data Mining

With data mining, computer algorithms, rather than the analyst, examine data to discover patterns. Unlike quadrant 2, where the analyst started with a hypothesis, computer algorithms create hypotheses based on data patterns. This is the discovery model, as opposed to the verification model discussed above.

This is significantly different from traditional computational work, in which the computer is used merely to respond to predefined queries, or crunch the numbers to arrive at answers rapidly. Here the data is being examined by a computer to generate new hypotheses.

It may be argued that an analyst using the same data and collective experience may generate the same or a very similar hypothesis to the one that a data mining tool may discover. However, for data with many variables and a large number of records the possibility is low that the analyst will determine the pattern, for several reasons. It is impractical to run repeated *ad hoc* queries against large data stores due to the required elapsed time and computer resources. In addition, the analyst's time is expensive. Finally, and most important, an analyst may not be able to conceive a hypothesis because of prior biases or the large number of variables involved. Traditional queries provide responses to the questions that a person thinks of and decides to ask; they do not, however, seek for patterns in data that can lead someone to discover hypotheses that exist, but have not been thought of or that even contradict the analyst's views and judgments.

Patterns can be associations, sequences, and classifications. Classifications are sometimes also called "clustering" or "segmenting." Associations occur when occurrences are linked. For example, a study of supermarket baskets may reveal that 50 percent of potato chip purchases are accompanied by a soda purchase. When there is an associated marketing promotion, soda is purchased 75 percent of the time. This association can be used to adjust promotions or pricing.

In sequences, events are linked over a time period. For example, data mining might determine that when a customer buys a sleeping bag and a backpack, in 65 percent of cases the same person also buys a camping tent in the following two months. For this sequencing pattern to be identified, the customer identification must be maintained along with the record of purchase. Many supermarkets have initiated a frequent buyers reward program, in which the buyer is offered an incentive to provide a linkage between their purchases over a period of time.

Classification is probably the most commonly-used data mining process today. It identifies patterns that can be used to classify items into segments with similar characteristics. For example, the financial industry uses classification to determine whether or not a particular customer is a good credit risk.

Data mining techniques currently being used with some frequency can be classified into several categories, including:

- Inductive reasoning.
- Neural networks.
- Data visualization.
- Memory-based reasoning.

Some methodologies and tools for data mining are based on a combination of these methods including statistics-based algorithms, which have been widely used in the business in the past. Some of these data mining techniques are discussed in more detail later in this chapter, with the exception of data visualization.

Quadrant 4: Operational Decision Systems

These systems are repetitive, rather than discovery oriented. They are prescriptive in nature and may apply the patterns and knowledge discovered by data mining to business use. (Of course, such applications can be implemented using other knowledge, which has nothing to do with data mining). An example is the automated underwriting of an insurance policy to a new applicant classified into a segment based on a pattern discovered by data mining. Another example is granting a mortgage loan to a prospective home buyer based on the classification of the applicant.

Such applications also can assist in real time. For example, a particular cellular phone number, usually used to make only domestic calls, is suddenly used for making a series of overseas calls. This may indicate fraud and necessitate corrective action.

DATA MINING TECHNOLOGY COMPONENTS

The next few sections discuss the significant technology components of data mining. The discussion is organized as follows:

- Common types of information.
- Supervised and unsupervised mining.
- Data mining tools.
- Data mining techniques.

The first section discusses the types of relationships and patterns that can be discovered, namely: associations, sequences, and clusters. This provides the basic understanding of important data mining concepts . Before discussing the actual data mining tools and techniques, the second section introduces the notion of supervised and unsupervised mining. This is necessary because the tools (i.e., algorithms based on data mining techniques) must first be trained to work with the available historical data. This training is generally classified as "supervised" or "unsupervised." The third section, techniques and tools for data mining, discusses the actual techniques, such as induction trees and artificial neural networks. It begins with a short discussion of the preparation process that a tool typically goes through before use for prediction in the actual use environment. Finally, the actual techniques are discussed.

Common Types of Information

There are three common types of information that can be discovered by data mining:

1. Associations.
2. Sequences.
3. Clusters.

Some other terms are frequently encountered in discussions of information types. Classification is sometimes considered another type of information discovery. However, classification is really just another aspect of clustering; it determines the cluster to which a new item belongs. Forecasting, yet another concept related to data mining, is about predicting the value of an unknown field or variable. Both classification and forecasting indicate something about an unknown: classification indicates a cluster to which a new item or record belongs, while forecasting estimates a value of the unknown field or variable in a new record.

There are no clear-cut and agreed-upon definitions to many of these terms, and vendors and their product literature often use these terms interchangeably.

Associations. Associations are occurrences that are linked in a single event. Recall the examples of the supermarket baskets. In the first example, basket analysis indicated an association between cosmetics and greeting cards. In the second example, there was an association between potato chips and soda. Such associations can be used for store layout design and promotions.

Sequences. In sequences, events are linked over time. Recall the example of the link between the purchase of a backpack and the purchase of tent. This link is discovered through analysis of a sequence of sales records.

The concept of similar sequences is somewhat related to sequential patterns. Given a series of events, similar sequences discover patterns similar to a given one. Typical examples include finding stocks with similar price movements, products with similar sales patterns, or stores or departments with similar revenue streams.

Clusters. Clustering discovers patterns that recognize the grouping within data. This is perhaps the most common activity in the data mining field today. An example is the clustering of credit card customers (i.e., an attriter, revolver, or transactor) discussed earlier in this chapter.

The clustering process forms the groups. The algorithm, or tool, discovers different groupings within the data, such that each group is made up of similar objects but is distinctly different from other groups.

The matching of the profile of a new item with that of an appropriate cluster group is known as classification, which presupposes the existence of such clusters.

Forecasting is a concept similar to classification. It estimates the future value of a variable, such as revenue. Both forecasting and classification are about predicting something about a new item. Classification identifies the cluster to which a new item belongs, whereas forecasting estimates a value of a variable for a new item.

Supervised and Unsupervised Mining

The concept of supervised and unsupervised mining relates to whether a set of historical records can be used for focused learning or training of a tool. For example, if a set of records containing existing customer profiles with indicators for good or bad credit risk exists, a tool can be trained to discover patterns for predicting credit-worthiness of future new applicants. In this case, the process of discovering the pattern and tool training is called supervised learning or mining.

On the other hand, if there is no identified target field of interest and the data mining process results in segmentation of data, the process is known as unsupervised learning or mining. For example, a set of auto accidents and related repair records can be mined for patterns, which may result in two segments, one containing 98 percent and the other containing the remaining 2 percent of records. Further manual auditing may reveal interesting facts about the segments, such as excessive charges or fraudulent behavior for the smaller set. This is unsupervised mining, because there was no interesting (or target) field in the record on which the tool could focus initially.

Data Mining Tools

Commercially available data mining tools use stand-alone data mining techniques, such as induction reasoning or artificial neural networks, or combine several of them to provide a useable product. New phrases, or jargon, depending on the perspective, are being coined and introduced at a rapid rate as new tools and techniques, or variations of old ones, are being introduced.

Before a tool can be put in production for actual use, however, it needs to be prepared. Preparation includes training, evaluating, and assessing the likely accuracy of the prediction results. Put differently, during the preparation process, tools figure out the answer or the pattern by examining a subset of the data where the outcome or result is already known from the historical data. Then, during production, they apply the pattern knowledge to other data records to predict the answer or response for the unknown field or records. Tool vendors use different names and steps for the preparation process. For ease in understanding this process, Exhibit 3 illustrates a scenario that uses three steps or phases.

1. Training
2. Testing
3. Evaluation

Tool users designate some field of interest in the historical data base as the response or answer field. This is the field that the user desires to predict (i.e., supervised mining). Sometimes it is also called the target or

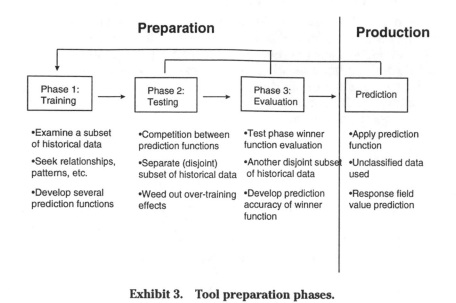

Exhibit 3.   Tool preparation phases.

dependent field. The other fields in the record are known as independent or variable fields.

The Training Phase. In the training phase, tool modules examine a subset of historical data, seeking patterns and relationships between the values of variables and response fields to establish functions that would enable the tool to predict the value of the dependent field based on the values of the independent fields. The output of the training phase is a family of prediction functions, which are candidates for further investigation in the subsequent phase for the selection of the best one.

The Testing Phase. In the testing phase, the candidate prediction functions are applied to a test subset of the historical data. This subset consists of records which are distinct from the ones used previously for training purposes. Candidate-prediction functions use the new variables to predict the related response. The winner is the function that statistically best approximates the answer. This approach also minimizes the effects of over-training of the function. It is likely that in the training phase, functions may have adopted, or over-trained, themselves to the unrepresentative idiosyncrasies of the training subset of the historical data.

The Evaluation Phase. The winner from the testing phase will be used for the actual prediction during the production process. However, it first goes through the evaluation phase, where it is applied to yet another set of historical records to estimate the accuracy of the prediction function. Because the answer or the outcome in the historical data is already known, the ratio of prediction function answer to the actual outcome gives a degree of confidence in the predictability of the selected function.

The actual steps and preparation process varies with vendors. Also, the degree of automation, process control, and amount of manual intervention required are some of the distinguishing features of the tools.

Finally, during production the prediction function is applied to unclassified data, for which the value of the response or dependent field is not known.

It might become necessary to go back and start from the training phase again for several reasons, such as the use of a different technique or tool, changes to the parameters, changes to the historical data, or changes to the business environment. A prediction function that works well in a 3 percent inflation environment, for example, may not be equally applicable in a 9 percent environment.

Data Mining Techniques

There is no commonly agreed-upon classification scheme for data mining techniques. This is not surprising, because this is a new and emerging computational arena in commercial processing. For discussion purposes, the more popular techniques are classified into the following types:

- Inductive reasoning.
- Artificial neural networks.
- Data visualization.
- Memory-based reasoning.

Although this section discusses these techniques individually, typically commercial products combine these techniques along with statistical analysis and other advanced techniques such as fuzzy logic and genetic algorithms to produce hybrid tools.

Inductive Reasoning. Induction is the process of starting with individual facts and then using reasoning to reach a hypothesis or a general conclusion. By contrast, deduction is to start with a hypothesis and trying to prove or disprove it by specific facts. In data mining inductive reasoning, the facts are the data base records, and the hypothesis formulation usually takes the form of a decision tree that attempts to divide or organize the data in a meaningful way. The tree can then be used to create rules, generalities, or hypotheses, with the nodes serving as decision points.

Decision trees divide the data into groups using the values in the fields or variables. It resembles the game of "20 questions." The tree is a hierarchy of if-then statements that group the data. These tests are applied at

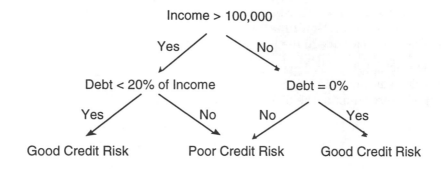

[Confidence Factor: 0.97]

Exhibit 4.   Sample decision tree.

each node to a record (for example, is income greater than 100,000, is debt less than 20 percent of income, and so forth). The result of each test indicates the choice of which test to perform next. The tests are designed to extract a set of characteristics that reliably predict the value of the response (i.e., answer) field. Exhibit 4 shows a simple decision tree for classification of individuals as sound or poor credit risks. To keep the example simple, the response at each node is assumed to be binary valued. In actual cases, multivalued responses are encountered.

One of the key advantages of tools based on decision trees is that in addition to using a decision tree to make a prediction, the user may examine the tree itself. Looking at the tree allows one to observe the prediction criteria or rules that the tool has induced for a particular set of records in order to discover the pattern. There has been a surge in decision tree-based products because of this visibility to the induction rules and because such tools tend to be faster than those based on neural networks.

A variety of parameters are used to control induction functions or rules, including the rule length, an importance factor, the maximum or minimum number of rules to generate, rule confidence factor, error margins, and training and validation data set size. Tools provide default values for these parameters. However, user analyst's input based on the type of problem and business knowledge is critical.

Decision trees are not suitable for all kinds of problems and may not work with some types of data. Some decision tree-based tools have problems dealing with continuous sets of values, like revenue or age, and may require that these values be grouped into ranges. In addition, the way the ranges are specified may inadvertently hide patterns. For example, grouping customers aged 16 to 23 together may hide a significant break that might occur at age 20. Tools like Darwin from Thinking Machine avoid this problem by using techniques to best cluster the data first. Information Harvester from Information Harvesting Corporation solves this problem by assigning values to groups based on fuzzy logic: Each instance of the same value is assigned to a different group.

Also, there is a limitation that the questions must generate discrete responses such that a record can traverse only along a single branch at each node. More important, a significant segmentation opportunity could be missed if analysis is based on the sequencing of the earlier questions. For example, if questions are based on sex, age, and education level, the segmentation may not be as revealing if the sequence were to be reversed. Tools use a variety of techniques to overcome this limitation.

Another problem is that a set of if-then statements can get very difficult to understand, particularly if the condition list is long and complex. In many cases, the tree created through induction may not be hierarchical and may have overlaps. Different tools resolve such issues differently. Tree pruning and partial tree generation are some of the remedies.

Neural Networks. Neural networks simulate the way the human brain works, and apply the research done in the field of artificial intelligence to business problems. A neural network is a computer implementation to simulate the biological process of the millions of neurons, which comprise the brain.

These networks can be better understood by considering the makeup of a neuron and how pulses are emitted and propagated along the neural paths (i.e., nerves) in the brain (Exhibit 5).

- The soma (1)is the center of the nerve cell where the collection of inputs from dendrites are combined and processed.
- Dendrites (2) receive input from other neurons.
- Axons (3) are the parts of the nerve cell that produce the pulses emitted by the neuron.
- The synapse (4) is the location where electrical pulses are transmitted.

In neural networks, the idea is to map computation jobs to each of the parts of a neuron. The basic unit of a neural network is called a node (see Exhibit 6). The node has a series of N inputs. Associated with each input is a corresponding weight, which are applied to each input, and the result is summed. This is the weighted sum that serves as input to the node and corresponds to the synoptic weighted sum of the human neuron.

Exhibit 5. A neuron.

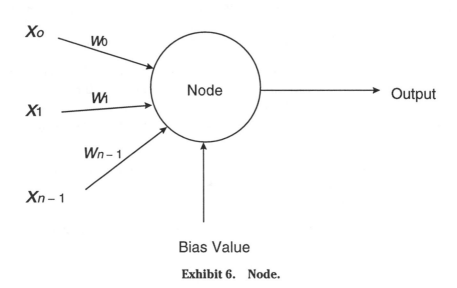

Exhibit 6. Node.

A function is then applied to the weighted sum, adjusted using a bias value. The resulting output value is then released and passed as input to other nodes. This can be represented by the following equation for the output:

$$y = F(h)\left\{ \sum_{i=0}^{i=n-1} W_i * X_i + \beta \right\}$$

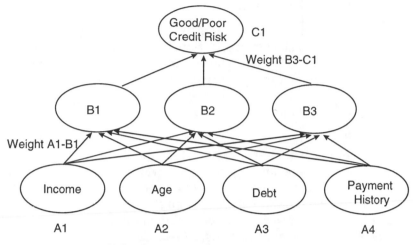

Exhibit 7. Sample neural network.

How, then, are neural networks applied to solving business problems? Neural networks are multilayered networks that learn how to solve a problem by examining and processing data values. They are essentially a collection of nodes with inputs, outputs, and simple processing at each node. Between the visible input and output layers, there may be several hidden intermediate layers.

In general, neural networks provide a method of predicting output values from input values. In the data mining context, the input values are the values of the independent (i.e., known) fields, and the output value is the predicted value of the response (i.e., unknown) field. Exhibit 7 is an example of a simple neural network created for identifying good and poor credit ratings. This neural network of nodes learns by taking the input fields (A1 to A4) and processing their values such that the output field (C1) indicates the answer (Good or Poor Credit Risk). Layer B is known as the hidden layer, and there can be multiple hidden layers, though normally one to two suffice.

Each node processes the input from the nodes from the previous layer and outputs a value, which becomes input for the nodes in the next layer. Values are modified by the weight factors, which are unique between any two nodes. Each record in the training set is processed and the outcome compared with the known value of the response field. If it disagrees, a correction to the weighting factors is calculated and applied such that the output agrees with the known value in the response field. The process is repeated until the output agrees and corrections become less than a given amount. After the neural network has been trained, it can be used to predict values for the unknown set.

Neural networks are an opaque tool, which means that the model produced does not have a clear interpretation. It is usually applied to the business problems without the user fully understanding the reasoning behind its results. This is one of the key reasons why induction-based tools are often preferred for those applications where legal or business needs require clear interpretation.

Some algorithms attempt to translate a neural network model into a set of rules that the business analyst can understand. However, it is generally very difficult, because the function applied at the various nodes can be nonlinear and the bias introduced to achieve a solution can be quite significant. Many applications for neural networks are beyond the typical commercial arena. For example, neural networks may be applied to interpret electrocardiograms, voice recognition and synthesis, and handwriting recognition.

Data Visualization. Data visualization refers both to the creation of visual images of things that are unseen and to a way of displaying qualitative and quantitative data at a glance. Visual images convey quantitative information with greater understanding than a list of numbers. The objective of data visualization is to enable perception of data, and sometimes the vast amount of gathered data can be understood best only when transformed into a visual representation.

Even a well-produced tabulated data or set of rules may reveal more information when visualized with color or texture in two or three dimensions. Addition of the dimension of time may reveal information that was hidden in year-to-year comparisons displayed in tabular fashion. However, data visualization relies heavily on the business analyst for the analysis and pattern recognition.

Visualization techniques are often used with other data mining techniques and are particularly useful during the initial stages for high-level clustering function. They may also be used with decision tree-based tools to show the number of rules generated and the parameter settings. One obvious problem with visualization techniques is the difficulty of depicting relationships among more than three or four variables. Time is often the fourth dimension portrayed, resulting in animated date/time series of displays.

Memory-Based Reasoning. Memory-based reasoning is another artificial intelligence technique used for classification in a fashion similar to what people may do to classify objects by comparing attributes with those of other objects recalled from memory.

Tools that use memory-based reasoning classify records in a data base by comparing them with similar records that have already been clustered or classified. Also called "k nearest-neighbor" (kNN) technique, the following algorithm is used:

1. Find k cases nearest to the examined case.
2. Use a weighted average vote to select a classification or cluster.

When an examined record falls within a group of neighbors that have the same classification, the new record is directed to that class. Otherwise, it is classified with its "closest" neighbors. Closeness is measured by weighted relative importance of the different attributes of the records. For example, StarMatch from Thinking Machine Corporation uses weighted n-dimensional Euclidean distance of the normalized values of the attributes, where each attribute is assigned an axis. Weights for each attribute can be either prespecified by the analyst, or derived by the tool as a part of the training process.

A consideration here is that a single record can influence the classification of the examined record. This can be an advantage or disadvantage, depending on the problem. This consideration does not apply with other techniques like Neural Networks.

This chapter examines in subsequent sections some of the criteria that can be used to narrow the list of available tools for any particular organization.

Statistics and Data Mining. Statistics have been used over the years to analyze business data to derive value and to perform many functions, such as factor analysis, linear regression, and prediction. Frequently used in combination with other techniques, statistics have often been the tool of choice. Statistics-based algorithms will probably continue to play an important role in the future, even as the new data mining algorithms become more popular. Hybrid tools judiciously combining the power of new data mining algorithms with statistical analysis will find increasing demand. Standalone statistics-based tools are at times difficult to apply; they bog down when a large number of variables and nonlinear functions are involved. Most important, statistics-based tools require up-front assumptions and can mask the subtleties of data. It is said that "In statistical analysis, you will never find what you are not looking for."

Exhibit 8 shows an example. Traditional statistical tools (at the top of the diagram) attempt to fit the data to an expected function or pattern (in this case, a sine curve) and do not account for data points that lie outside of the function. These unusual data points outside the pattern, often referred to as "outliers," are typically discarded from the analysis. Nevertheless, given a function and the data points, these tools are very good at finding the best fitting function.

407

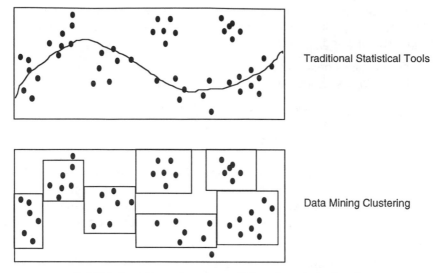

Traditional Statistical Tools

Data Mining Clustering

Exhibit 8.   Clustering vs. traditional statistical tools.

The new data mining tools are likely to begin by clustering the data points and finding the best fitting functions for each cluster without requiring the analyst to provide a function. In the traditional statistical techniques, these functions may be difficult to estimate or, worse, may be missed completely because of one's preconceived notions and biases.

In summary, it is likely that the new data mining tools will include not only the techniques such as induction trees and artificial neural networks, but also the traditional statistics-based algorithms to address business needs.

CRITICAL SUCCESS FACTORS IN DATA MINING

The key to successful data mining is to focus on the business processes, data, and technology. A good understanding of the business problem domain is essential; without it, the misuse of the data and technology is possible. Emphasis on the technology or the tool by itself is likely to lead to failure.

Quality of Data

The quality of data used for data mining is paramount. The old adage of GIGO (garbage in, garbage out) certainly applies here, because the raw material that is being mined is data. If the data is incorrect, inconsistent, or missing, the results are going to be unreliable. The impact of incorrect and inconsistent data is easy to see. Missing data or records can have an equally significant impact. If some records either have never been collected or were discarded during the editing phases in the operational systems, the patterns and relationships developed based on the partial data by the mining tools can be significantly flawed. The problem becomes compounded if the business analyst, who is trying to apply the knowledge gained for effective solutions, is not even aware of the missing records. People responsible for "sourcing" the data and using the data must communicate to avoid this problem.

Another aspect of the missing or incorrect data can manifest itself when some variables in the existing records being mined are defaulted to some values (e.g., zeros, blanks, or high values) or computed to reflect values of some other fields. The impact on the discovered patterns because of the computed field may be very well disguised. In some cases, it may result in the discovery and development of patterns so perfect that it may just reflect what has already been coded in the data in the first place.

The problems and solutions for "sourcing" well defined and consistent data from operational systems is similar to those discussed in Chapter II-5, The Information Delivery Facility: Beyond Data Warehousing. It makes sense to use the data that has already been cleansed and stored in the warehouse. In this sense, having implemented an information delivery facility eases implementation of data mining success. However, it is not necessary to implement the information delivery facility first to use data mining.

Technology and Tools

From a technology and tools perspective, several tools available in the marketplace as of this writing are unable to process large amounts of data and require the user to provide a representative subset. The subset may be horizontal (i.e., a number of rows that represent the entire set), or the subset may be vertical (i.e., including only columns of interest). It may be possible to do this effectively, provided that one fully understands the problem and the data. Several other tools sample the data on their own without user involvement. In any case, the user must understand the implication of sampling and deal with the results cautiously because the results may be tainted by the selected sample.

Furthermore, not every data mining technique is appropriate for every business problem. It is necessary to understand the algorithm used by the tool, and its limitations and to understand the data sampling technique, prior to applying the results to the business situation. If the model developed is very sensitive to a particular variable, one must ensure that minor errors in data values or missing values for that variable haven't resulted in skewed results.

Business Processes

The social issues concerning the use of data is another key consideration. Concerns regarding privacy and use of data for purposes other than what it was initially gathered for should be considered. In the European Common Community, issues regarding the use of data are particularly sensitive.

Successful application of data mining techniques and other computer-based algorithms demand that appropriate processes be put in place to avoid embarrassing business publicity and to meet legal obligations. Recently, a major bank that issues credit cards for a famous toy company denied a card to an individual with apparently excellent credentials: The individual is 41 years old, earns $123,000 a year, has excellent job security, pays his mortgage on time, and has a clean credit history ("A Man Who Governs Credit Is Denied a Toys R Us Card," *The Wall Street Journal*, Dec. 14, 1995, p. B1). The process that rejected the individual uses a computerized scoring system to rate applicants. The bank process ensures that a human checks every application before it is approved, but not every one that is rejected. Examples such as this have legal and social ramifications. However, from a pure business perspective, it is indicated that, if practical, procedures be put in place to review computer-generated recommendations to avoid such incidents.

The rejected candidate said in a speech to the Boston Bar Association, "I would expect credit-scoring type procedures to be overwhelmingly dominant by the end of the decade. We will obtain the fairness of the machine, but lose the judgment, talents, and sense of justice that only humans can bring to decision making."

Besides being instructive, the case is interesting because the rejected individual happens to be a governor of the Federal Reserve Board in Washington, the agency that sets interest rates and regulates banks. As it turned out, the application was rejected because eight other companies had requested copies of his credit history recently. A proliferation of inquiries by potential lenders is a sign that people are really looking for a lot of credit and is not considered a good thing by financial institutions. However, in the case of the governor of the Federal Reserve Board, five of the eight requests appear to have been prompted by the fact that he refinanced his mortgage and shifted his home-equity line to another bank.

Another key success factor is to remain cautious in using the data mining output. An interesting recent story in this regard deals with how a super-regional bank applies this concept and the business and technology implications of "predictive computer modeling" ("To Make More Loans,

Banks Use Computers to Identify Candidates," *The Wall Street Journal*, March 15, 1996, p. A1). Part of this bank's strategy is to increase its share of the consumer loan. For the banking industry, facing all the outside competition that it does, "a couple of years and it's too late to regain market share," the chairman says. The bank's strategy includes taking on lower-quality accounts. As long as there is automotive or real estate collateral to tap, the bank books auto and other loans of less than A-quality credit in its finance-company unit.

The main reason these bankers are not lying awake nights is that they are using powerful computers to analyze large amounts of information about potential borrowers. This helps them spot both the good customers who can afford to take more debt and the marginal consumers who actually are better risks than they seem at first glance.

Using computers for data base marketing by mail, the bank aimed one promotion at new auto-loan customers. Armed with research showing that car-loan customers are more likely to respond to a pre-approved credit-card offer if they are approached right after buying the car, the bank sent 7,000 pre-approved credit offers to such prospects. It got 1,000 acceptances, which it says is a rate six times the normal response rate to mail solicitations of its customer base.

One of its analysts says, "Point and click. That is all there is to it," as he starts tapping away at his terminal. By the time he is finished, he has constructed a diagram that looks like a family tree. On it are boxes representing 30 variables weighted to reveal the six most common characteristics of existing home-equity credit line customers. Those characteristics — the ones most predictive of loan acceptance — include a high number of existing bank relationships, such as a gold credit card, at least 12-year relationship, and a home value of less than $350,000.

Another interesting observation related to risks associated with loan applicants was that at some locations, customers who had held a job less than two years were more likely to pay back loans than some others who had longer tenures on the job. The speculation is that this is because many new fast-growing companies had started up in that particular locale, while downsizing was going on among older, established companies.

To reduce the risks on predictive computer models, the bank measures every single mailing to see if it will meet a financial rate of return. Further, the bank says it is taking a cautious approach. "We do not drop one-million-piece mailings," says its analyst. "If one of those monthly mailings goes bad, it is not going to ruin our balance sheet." A monthly monitoring program tracks the progress of each mailing to see if refinements in the selection process are needed for subsequent solicitations.

In summary, critical success factors require one to keep focused on the business procedures, data, and technology to ensure success and to minimize exposure due to errors in predictive data mining.

TOOLS SELECTION CRITERIA

Data mining is an emerging commercial arena. Thus, there is limited practical experience, and classification schemes for tools have yet to be defined adequately. Below are some criteria that can be considered when selecting a tool and when evaluating it as to how well it solves the problem and integrates within the environment.

- What kind of problems does it solve? Is the tool relevant to the problem at hand?
- What type of user interface does it use? Does it explain the induced rules? Is it easy to use? How does one provide input parameters?
- Can it handle the number of records and variables that need to be processed to solve the problem? Generally, the larger the number of records and variables the tool can handle, the better.
- Can the tool extract the data from the existing store or must customized programs be written to meet its requirement?
- Does the tool guide the user through the multiple steps of data mining and keep track of his progress? Or is the user required to figure it out for himself or herself?
- How is the performance of the tool? Will it take too long to be useful for the problem at hand? Does it exploit parallel processing to provide adequate performance? If direct mailing must be completed within a few days, will the tool be able to process the input in time?

Data mining is an ideal application for parallel computation. In many cases, it is an "embarrassingly parallel" problem, lending itself to parallel execution. Generally, there are two separate challenges in exploiting parallelism: the parallel processing of the set of records and the parallel execution of other remaining processing.

In data mining, if the tool uses SQL queries, the first challenge may easily be met by the use of the relational data base management system. The second challenge, in general, requires more work. However, in the case of data mining, the solution is comparatively easy. The pattern recognition engine usually has several hypotheses and possibilities to consider, and it needs to evaluate many options. Many of these tasks are quite independent, and can be processed in parallel without needing too much synchronization and communication, the two difficult problems associated with exploiting parallelism. The performance of search engines can be significantly enhanced by use of such computational techniques. Some of the questions that need to be answered are:

- How much resources does it require? Are resources available in house? What hardware and software requirements are imposed by the tool?
- What techniques does the tool use for pattern recognition: induction rules, neural networks, memory-based reasoning, data visualization, or traditional statistical analysis?
- What are the training requirements to use the tool effectively ? Does the vendor provide good technical and marketing support to help train the users and provide help if needed? Does the vendor have a good reputation for quality and technology?
- How does the tool deal with variable continuous data, like age and alphabetical data?
- Is the tool very sensitive to data "noise"? How does it deal with it?

However, the emphasis must remain on the business problem and not on tools or the technology, because the benefits that can accrue from discovering the hidden information about customers can be so significant that it may dwarf other considerations.

SUMMARY

Data mining techniques are allowing organizations to uncover significant value in their own data stores. Techniques and tools will become increasingly sophisticated over the next few years, permitting an organization to understand its customers, markets, and business better. However, one must be cautious in applying the newly discovered knowledge. As powerful and sophisticated as the technology is, common business sense must prevail.

Index

NETCENTRIC COMPUTING

I